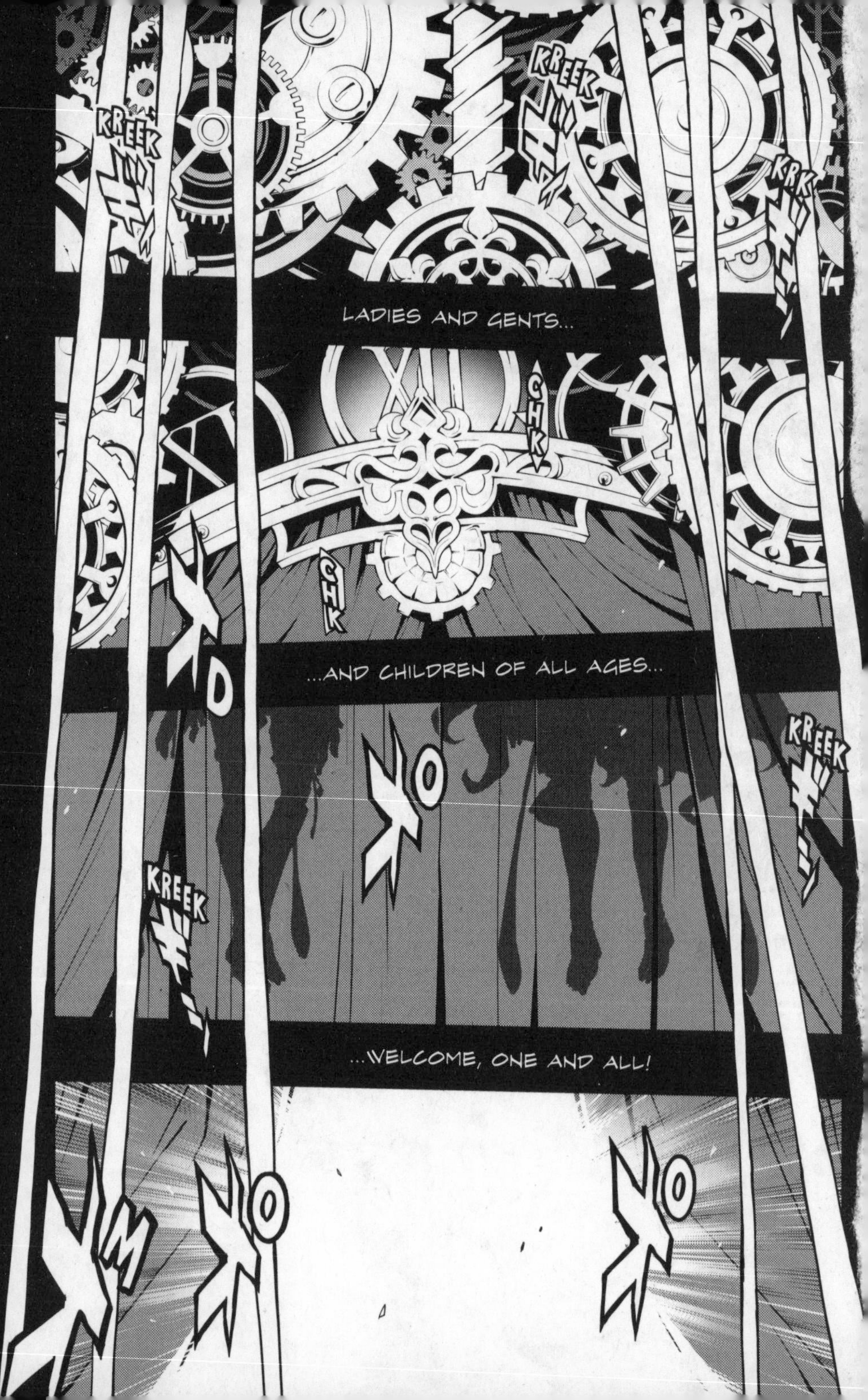
KREEK
KRK
KREEK
LADIES AND GENTS...
CHK
CHK
...AND CHILDREN OF ALL AGES...
KREEK
KREEK
...WELCOME, ONE AND ALL!

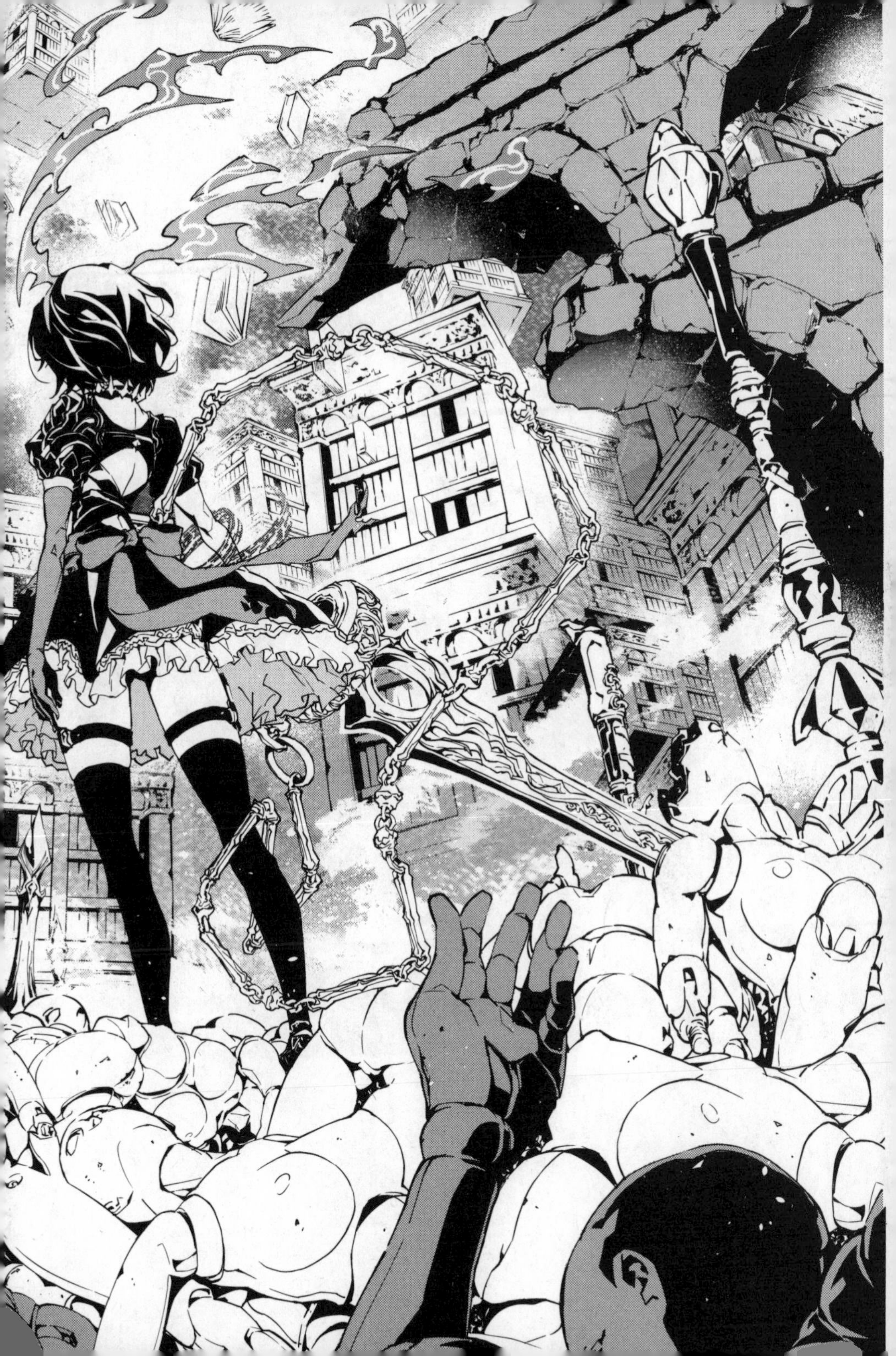

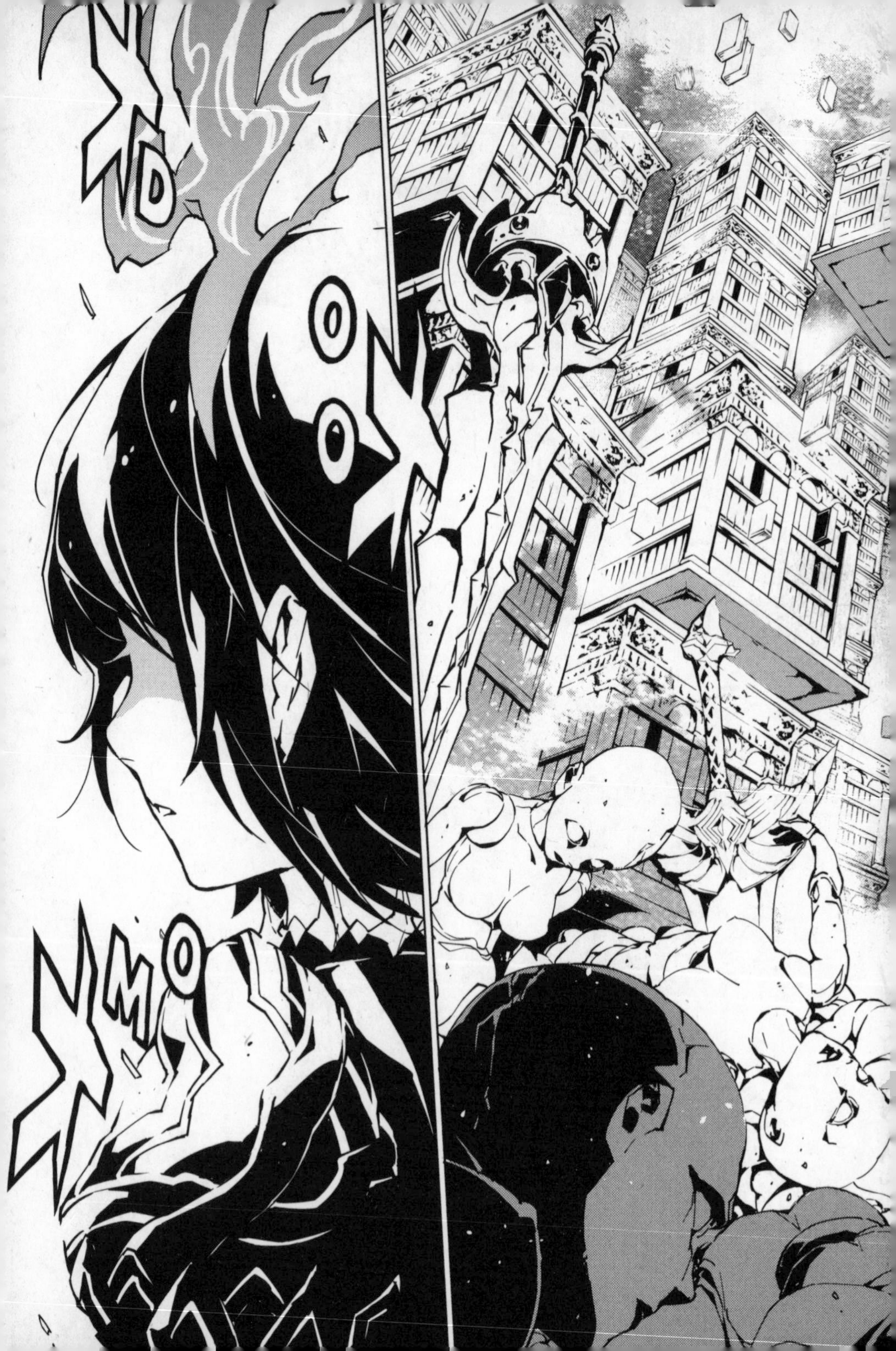

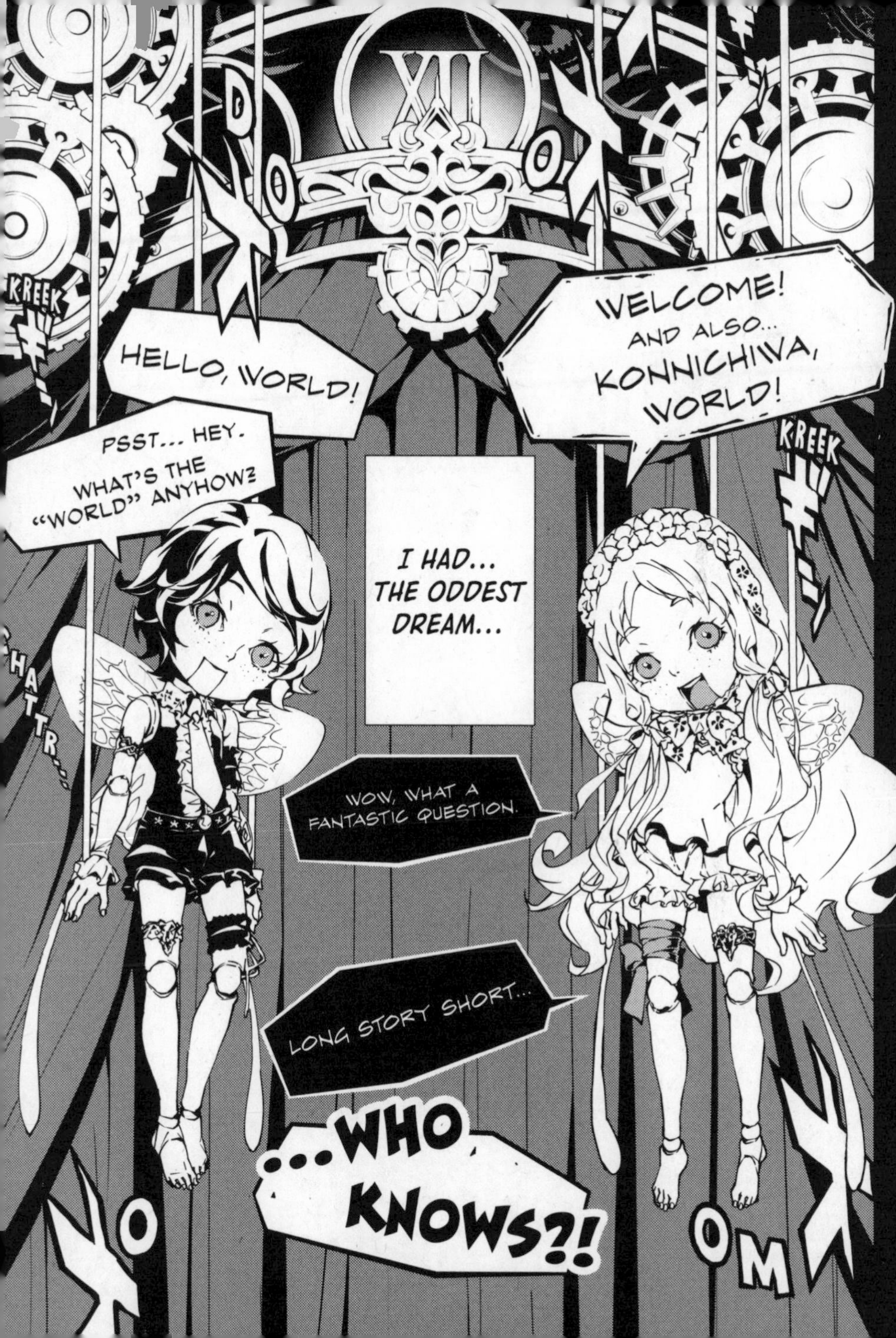
XII
K-REEK
WELCOME! AND ALSO... KONNICHIWA, WORLD!
HELLO, WORLD!
K-REEK
PSST... HEY. WHAT'S THE "WORLD" ANYHOW?
I HAD... THE ODDEST DREAM...
HATTR...
WOW, WHAT A FANTASTIC QUESTION.
LONG STORY SHORT...
...WHO KNOWS?!

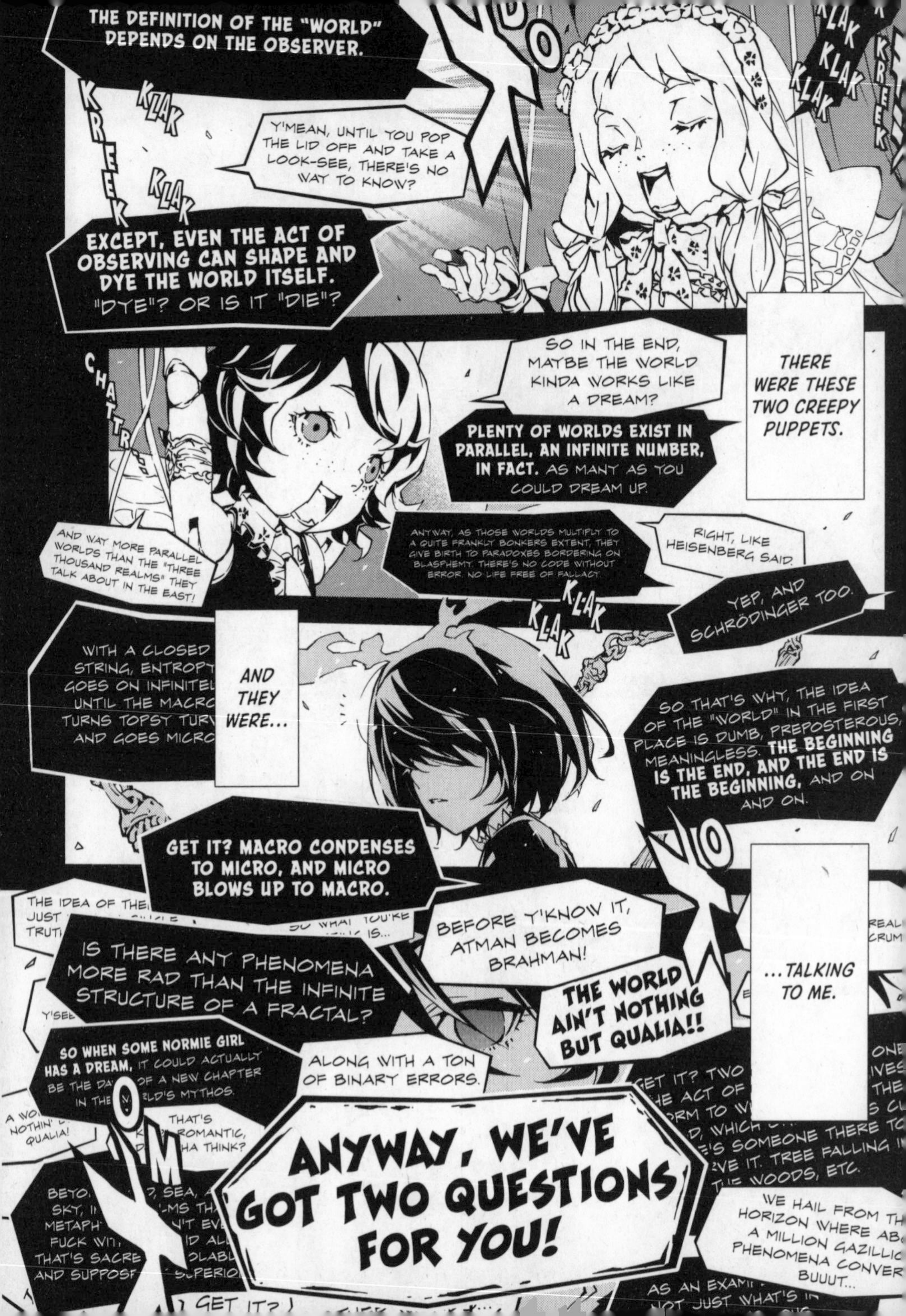

THE DEFINITION OF THE "WORLD" DEPENDS ON THE OBSERVER.
KLAK KLAK KLAK KREEK
KREEK KLAK KLAK
Y'MEAN, UNTIL YOU POP THE LID OFF AND TAKE A LOOK-SEE, THERE'S NO WAY TO KNOW?
EXCEPT, EVEN THE ACT OF OBSERVING CAN SHAPE AND DYE THE WORLD ITSELF. "DYE"? OR IS IT "DIE"?
THERE WERE THESE TWO CREEPY PUPPETS.
SO IN THE END, MAYBE THE WORLD KINDA WORKS LIKE A DREAM?
PLENTY OF WORLDS EXIST IN PARALLEL, AN INFINITE NUMBER, IN FACT. AS MANY AS YOU COULD DREAM UP.
CHATTR
RIGHT, LIKE HEISENBERG SAID.
ANYWAY, AS THOSE WORLDS MULTIPLY TO A QUITE FRANKLY BONKERS EXTENT, THEY GIVE BIRTH TO PARADOXES BORDERING ON BLASPHEMY. THERE'S NO CODE WITHOUT ERROR. NO LIFE FREE OF FALLACY.
AND WAY MORE PARALLEL WORLDS THAN THE "THREE THOUSAND REALMS" THEY TALK ABOUT IN THE EAST!
YEP, AND SCHRÖDINGER TOO.
KLAK KLAK
SO THAT'S WHY, THE IDEA OF THE "WORLD" IN THE FIRST PLACE IS DUMB, PREPOSTEROUS, MEANINGLESS. THE BEGINNING IS THE END, AND THE END IS THE BEGINNING, AND ON AND ON.
AND THEY WERE...
GET IT? MACRO CONDENSES TO MICRO, AND MICRO BLOWS UP TO MACRO.
...TALKING TO ME.
BEFORE Y'KNOW IT, ATMAN BECOMES BRAHMAN!
THE WORLD AIN'T NOTHING BUT QUALIA!!
IS THERE ANY PHENOMENA MORE RAD THAN THE INFINITE STRUCTURE OF A FRACTAL?
ALONG WITH A TON OF BINARY ERRORS.
ANYWAY, WE'VE GOT TWO QUESTIONS FOR YOU!

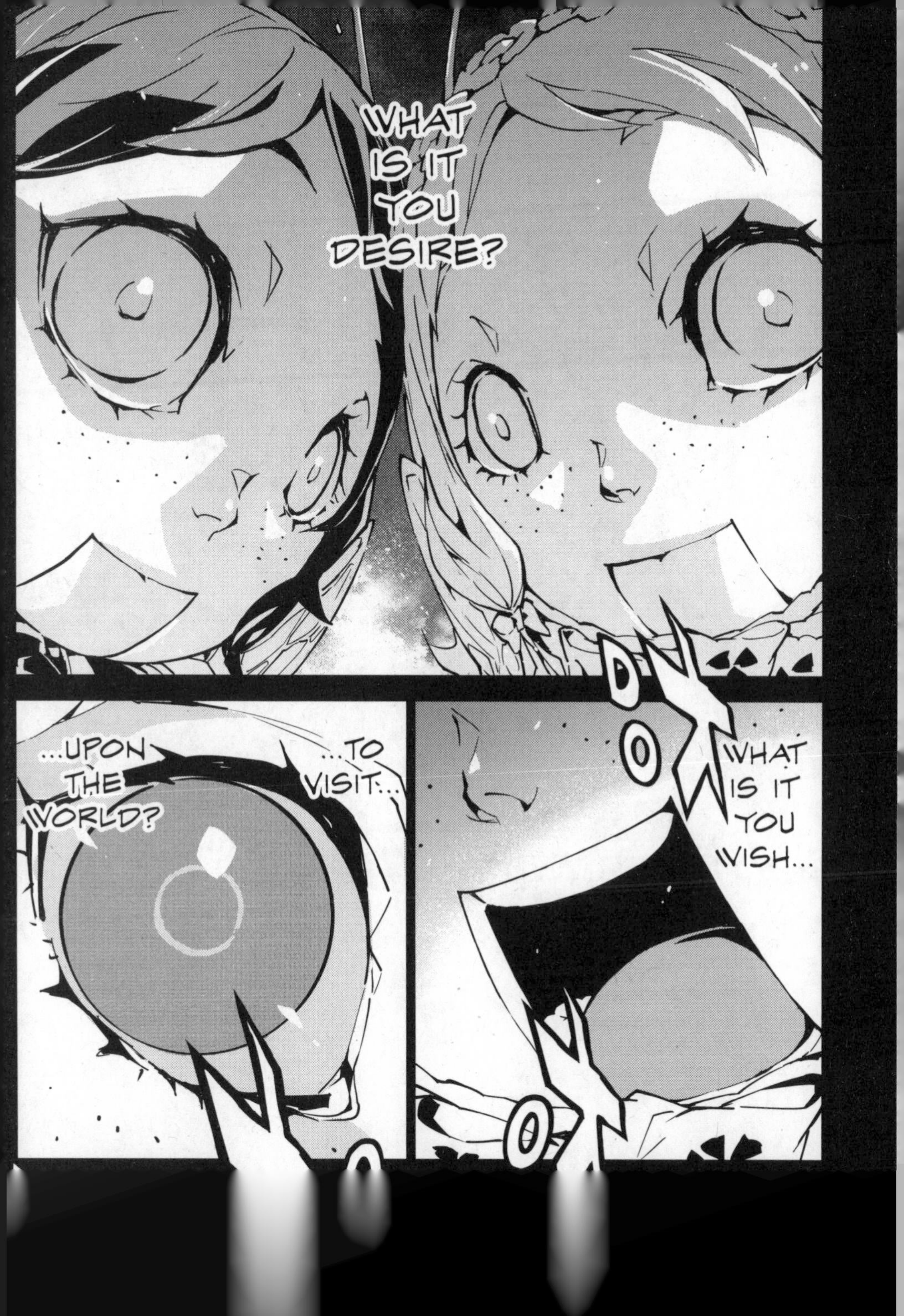
WHAT IS IT YOU DESIRE?
WHAT IS IT YOU WISH...
...TO VISIT...
...UPON THE WORLD?

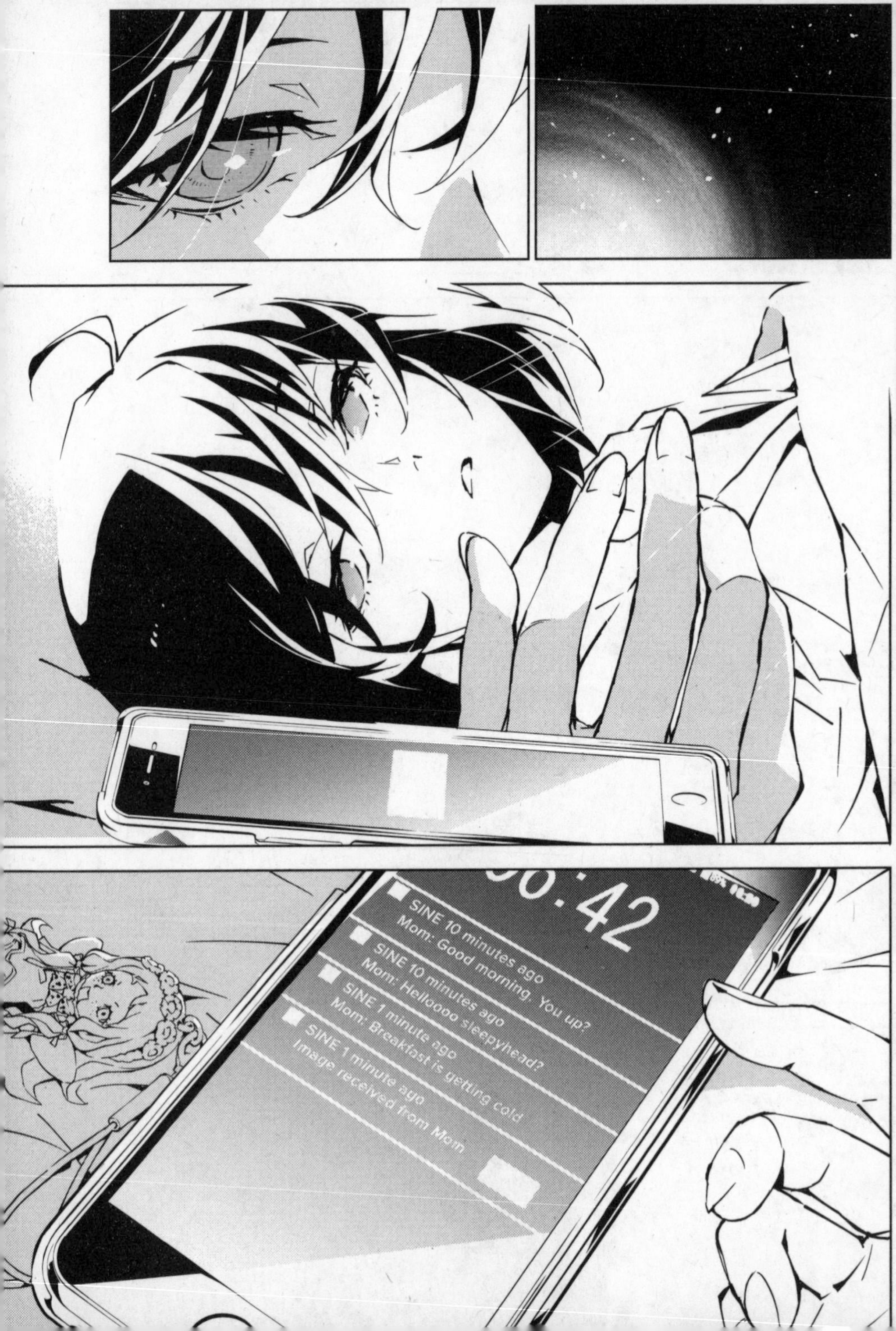
SINE 10 minutes ago
Mom: Good morning. You up?
SINE 10 minutes ago
Mom: Helloooo sleepyhead?
SINE 1 minute ago
Mom: Breakfast is getting cold
SINE 1 minute ago
Image received from Mom

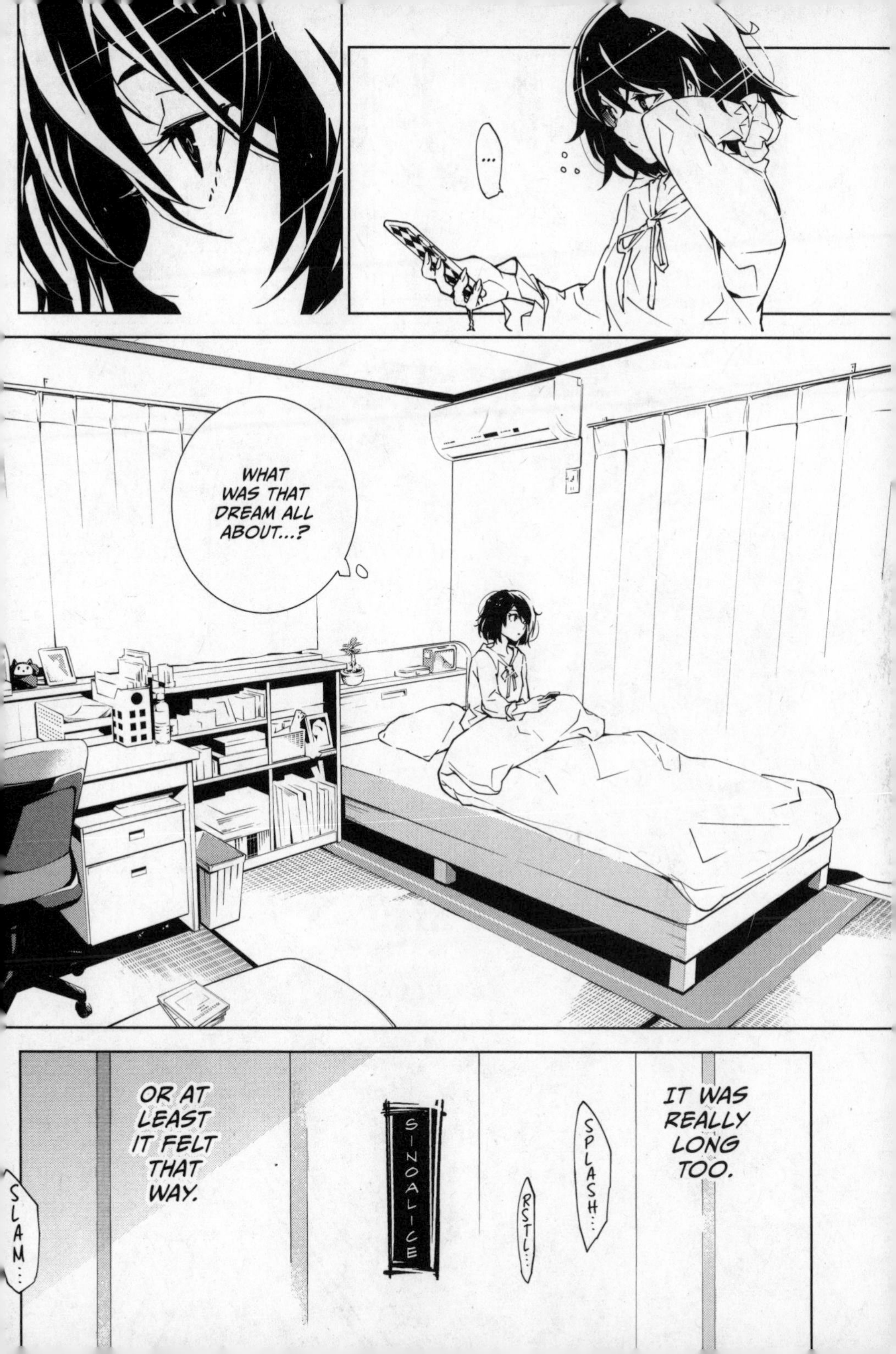
...
WHAT WAS THAT DREAM ALL ABOUT...?
IT WAS REALLY LONG TOO.
SPLASH...
RSTL...
SINOALICE
OR AT LEAST IT FELT THAT WAY.
SLAM...

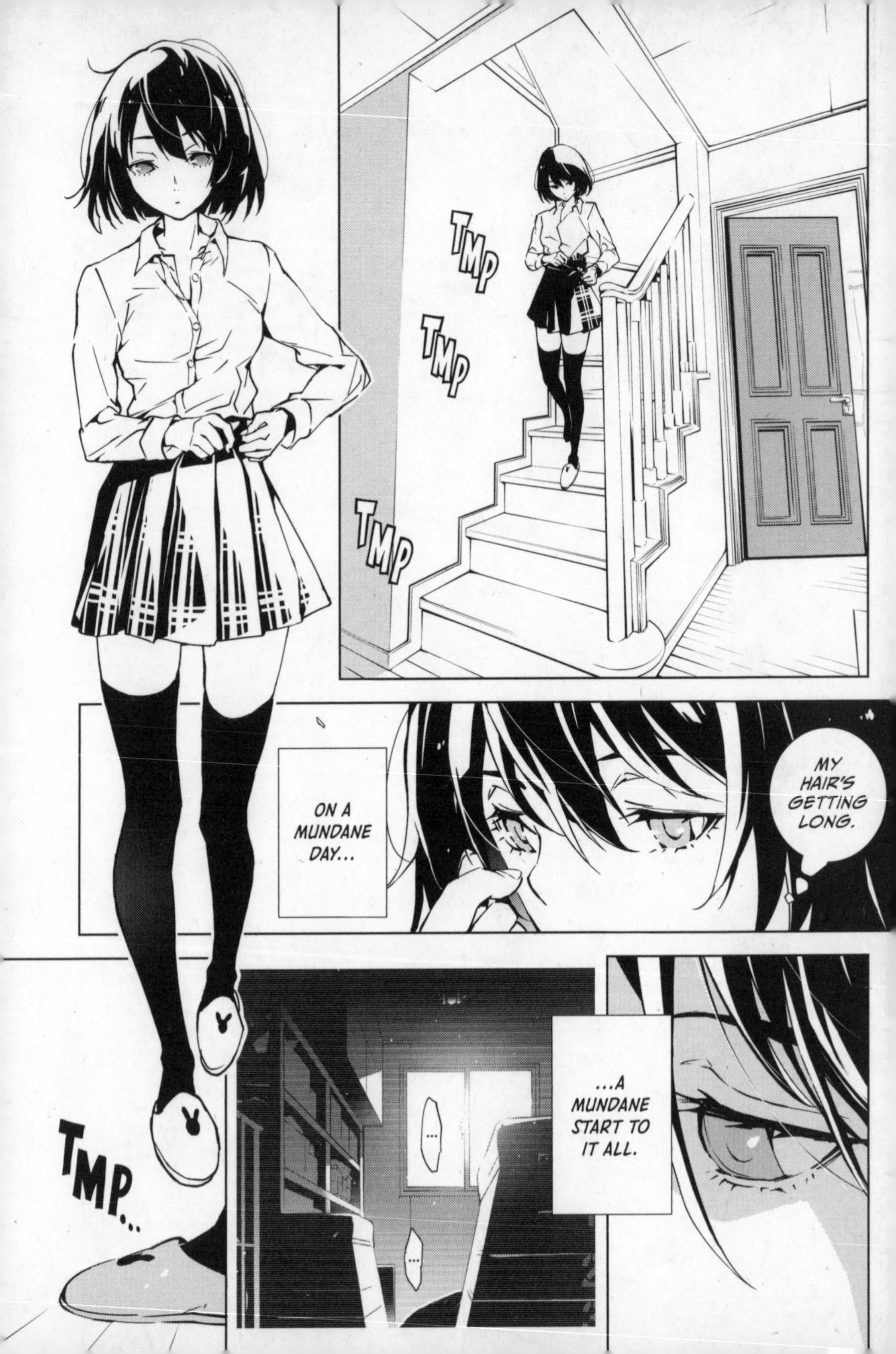
TMP
TMP
TMP
MY HAIR'S GETTING LONG.
ON A MUNDANE DAY...
...A MUNDANE START TO IT ALL.
...
...
TMP...

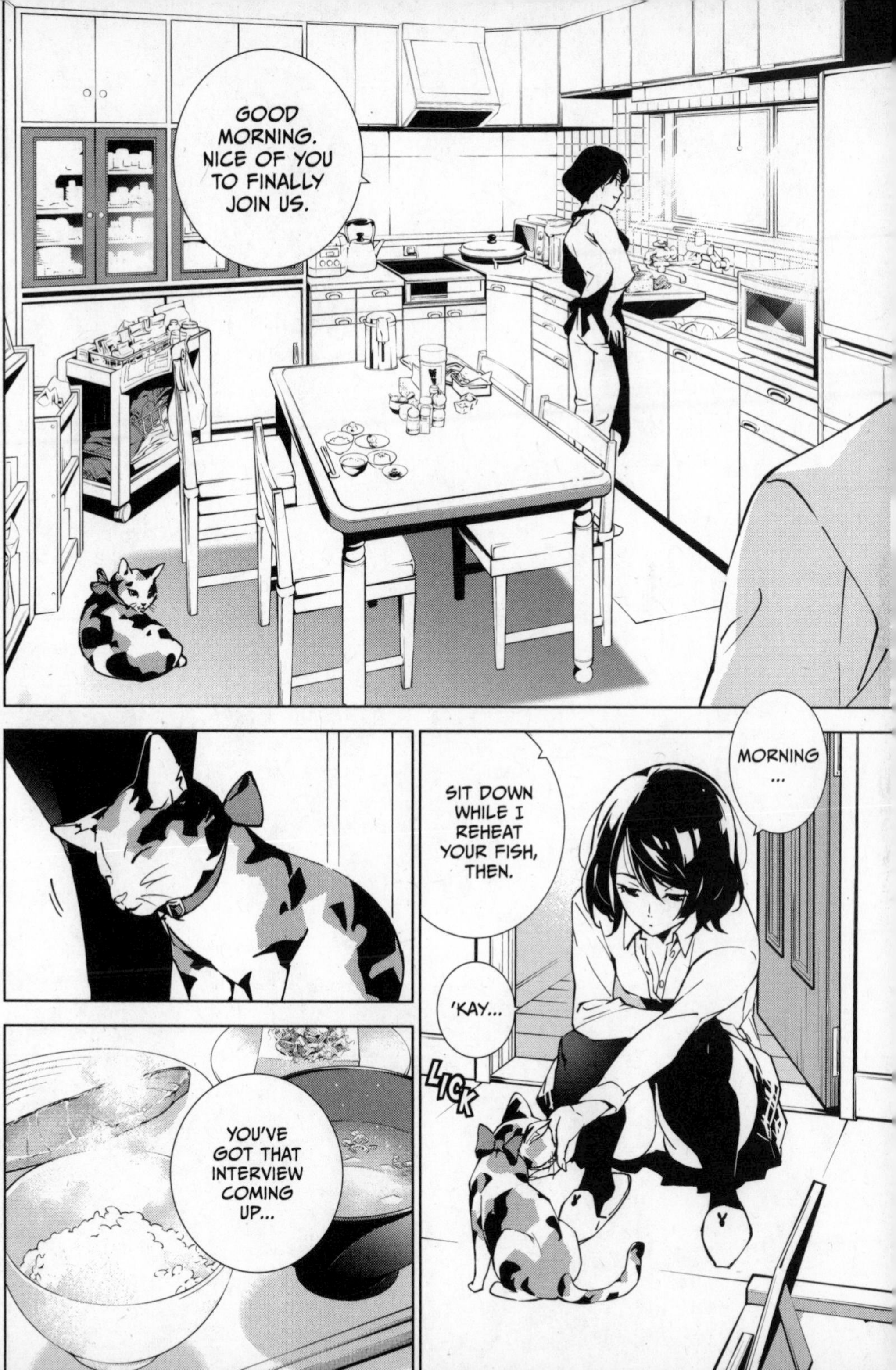
GOOD MORNING. NICE OF YOU TO FINALLY JOIN US.
MORNING ...
SIT DOWN WHILE I REHEAT YOUR FISH, THEN.
'KAY...
LICK
YOU'VE GOT THAT INTERVIEW COMING UP...

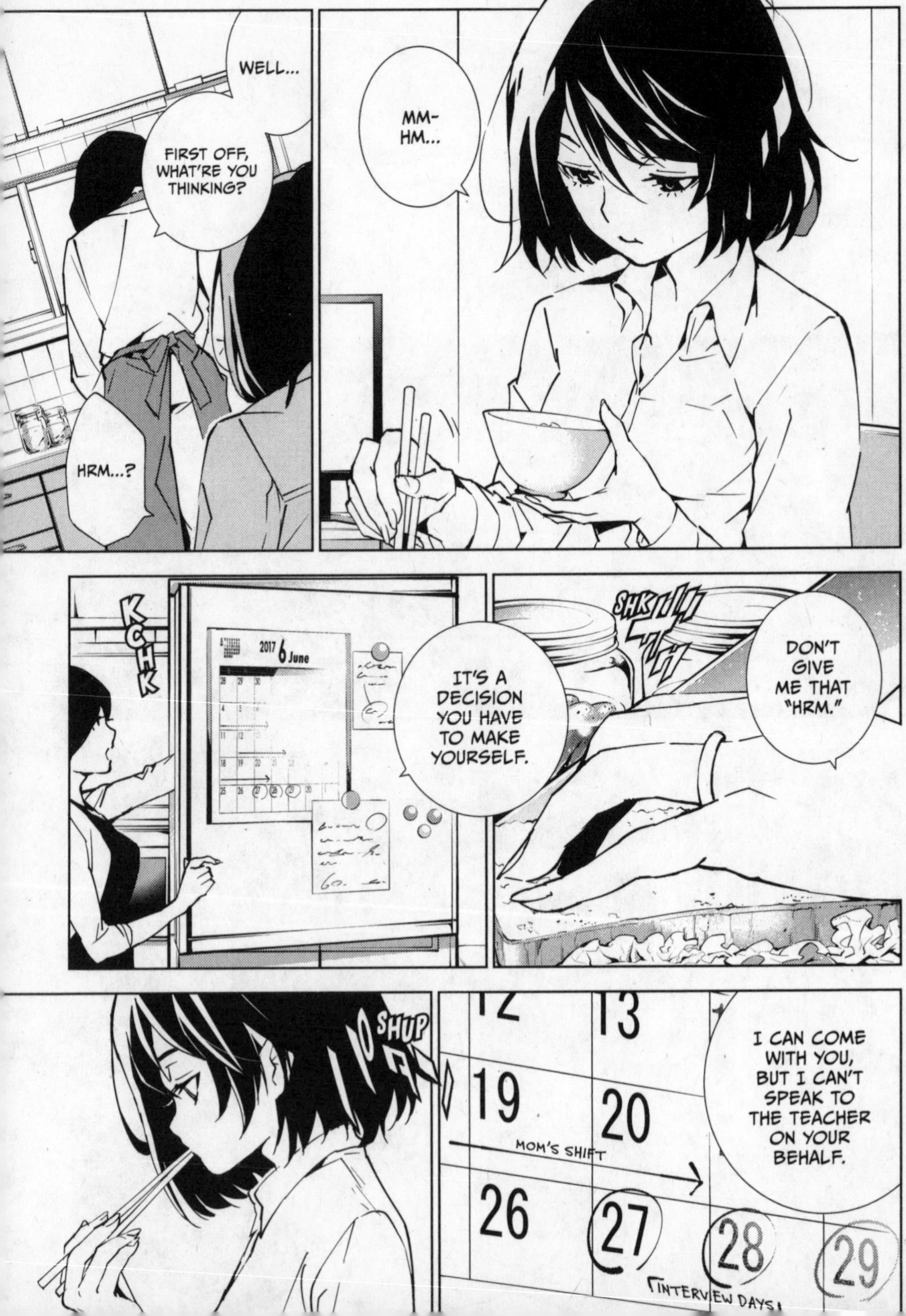
MM-HM...
WELL...
FIRST OFF, WHAT'RE YOU THINKING?
HRM...?
SHK
DON'T GIVE ME THAT "HRM."
IT'S A DECISION YOU HAVE TO MAKE YOURSELF.
KCHK
2017 6 June
I CAN COME WITH YOU, BUT I CAN'T SPEAK TO THE TEACHER ON YOUR BEHALF.
MOM'S SHIFT
「INTERVIEW DAYS」
SHUP

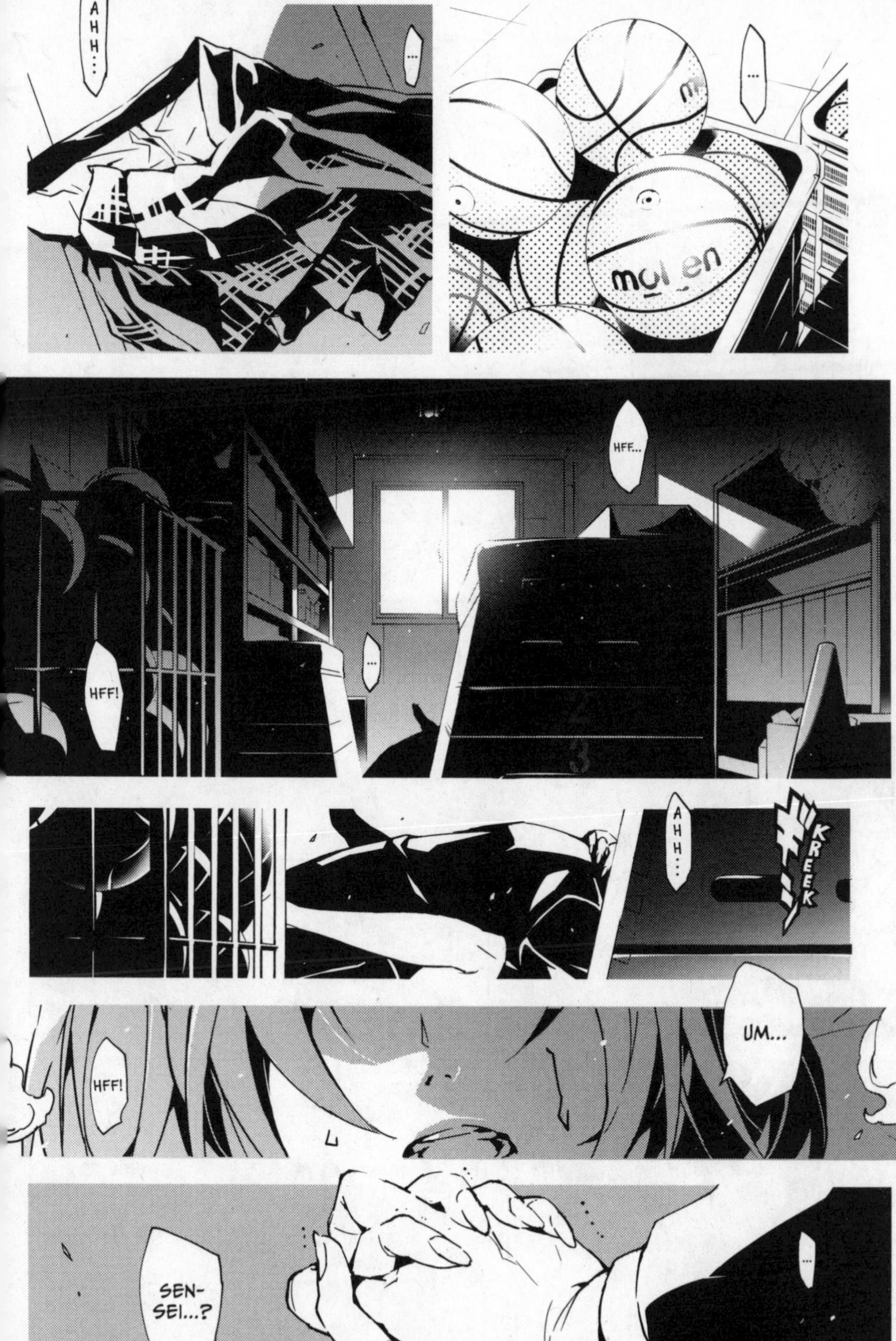
...
AHH...
...
HFF...
...
HFF!
KREEK
AHH...
UM...
HFF!
...
SEN-
SEI...?

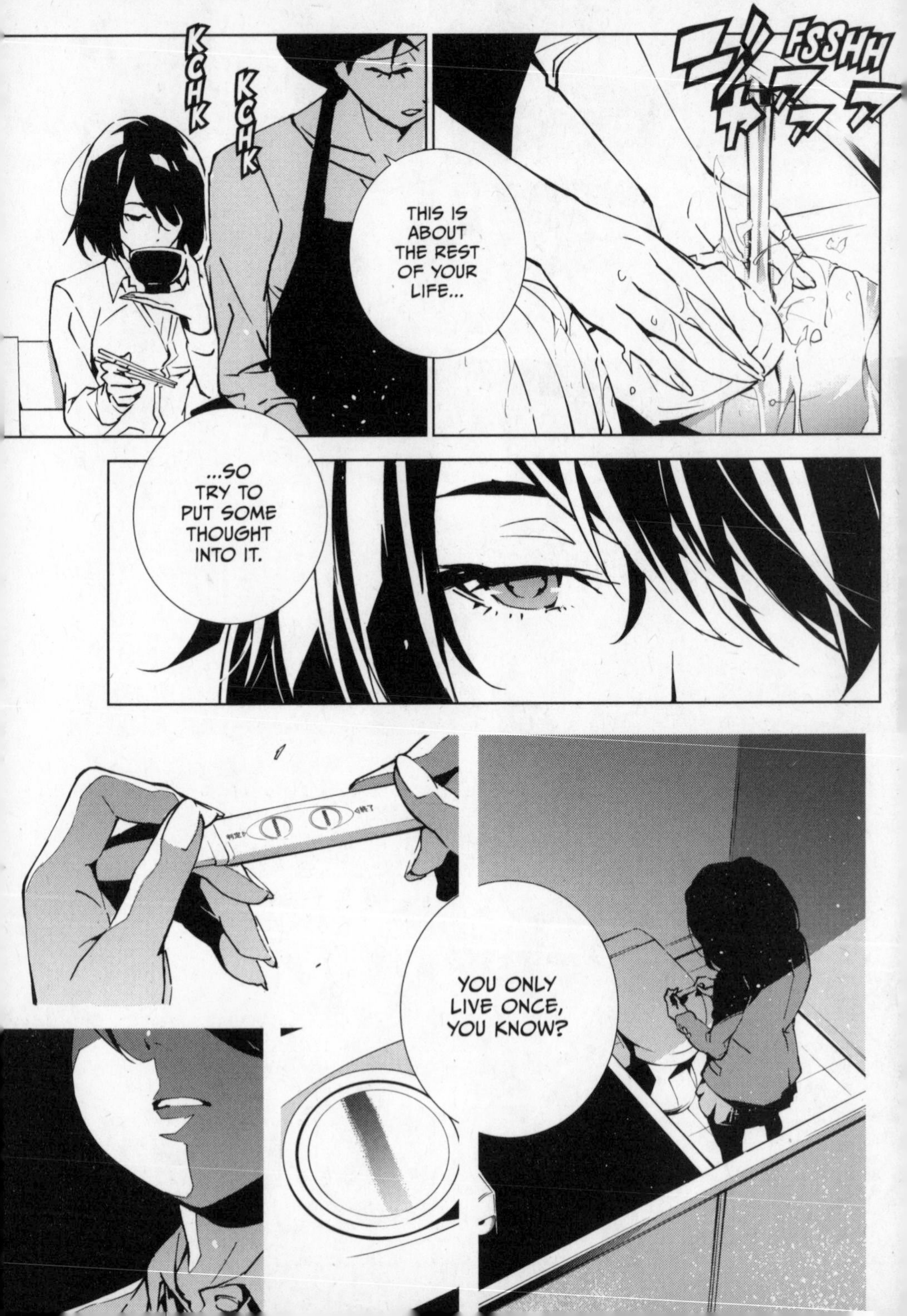
FSSHH
KCHK
KCHK
THIS IS ABOUT THE REST OF YOUR LIFE...
...SO TRY TO PUT SOME THOUGHT INTO IT.
YOU ONLY LIVE ONCE, YOU KNOW?

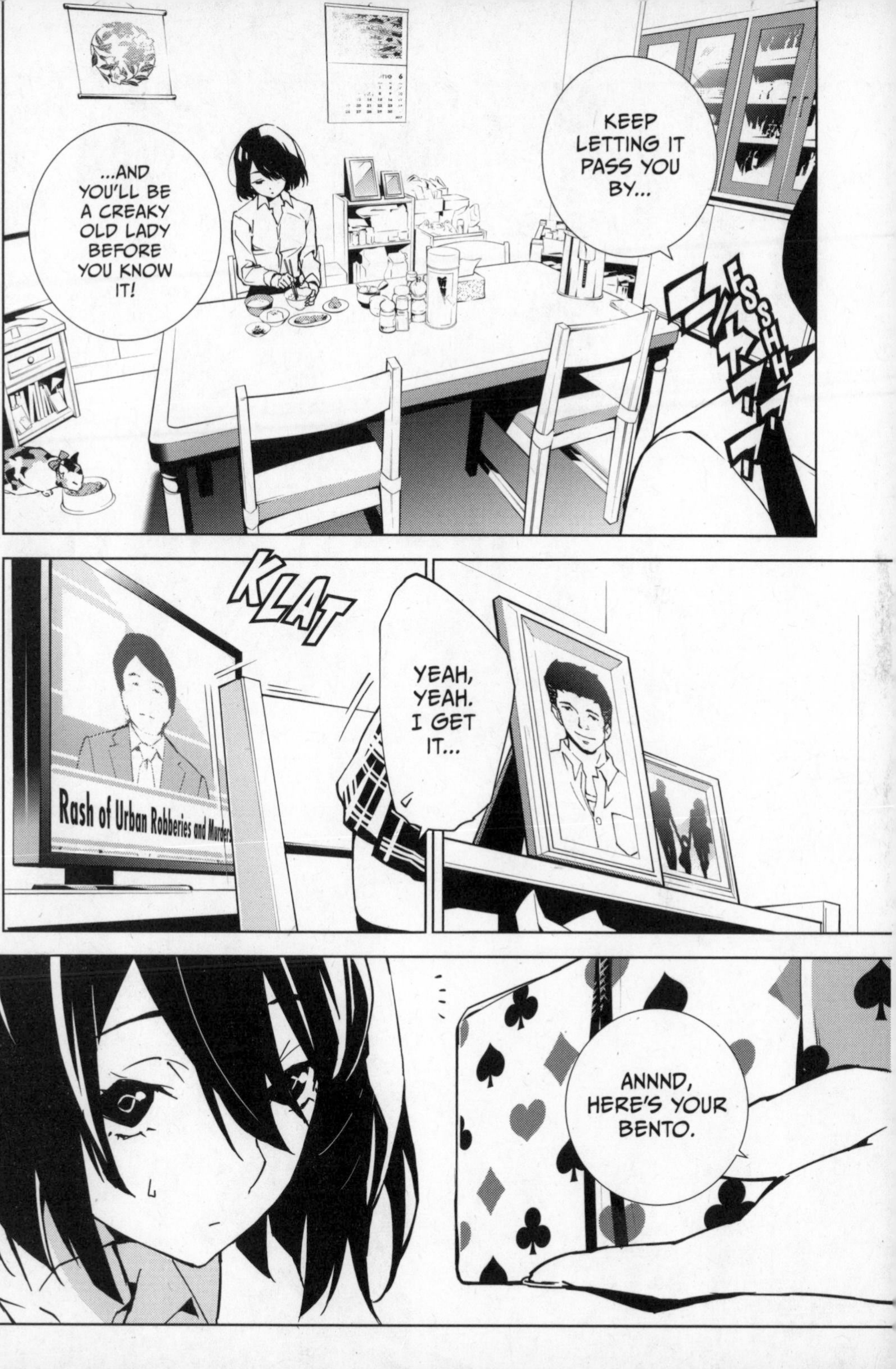
KEEP LETTING IT PASS YOU BY...
FSSHH
...AND YOU'LL BE A CREAKY OLD LADY BEFORE YOU KNOW IT!
YEAH, YEAH. I GET IT...
KLAT
Rash of Urban Robberies and Murders
ANNND, HERE'S YOUR BENTO.

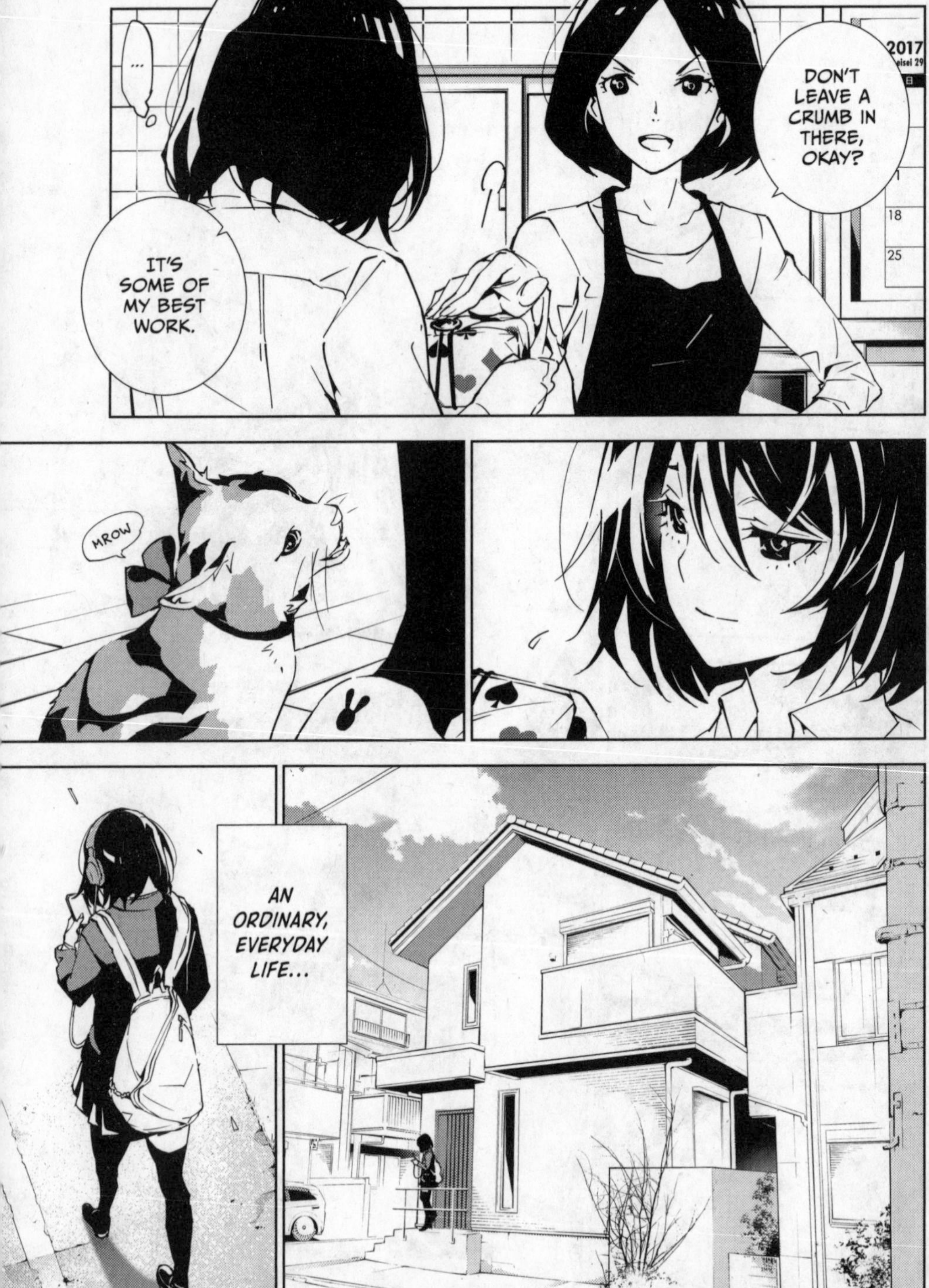
2017
DON'T LEAVE A CRUMB IN THERE, OKAY?
...
IT'S SOME OF MY BEST WORK.
MROW
AN ORDINARY, EVERYDAY LIFE...

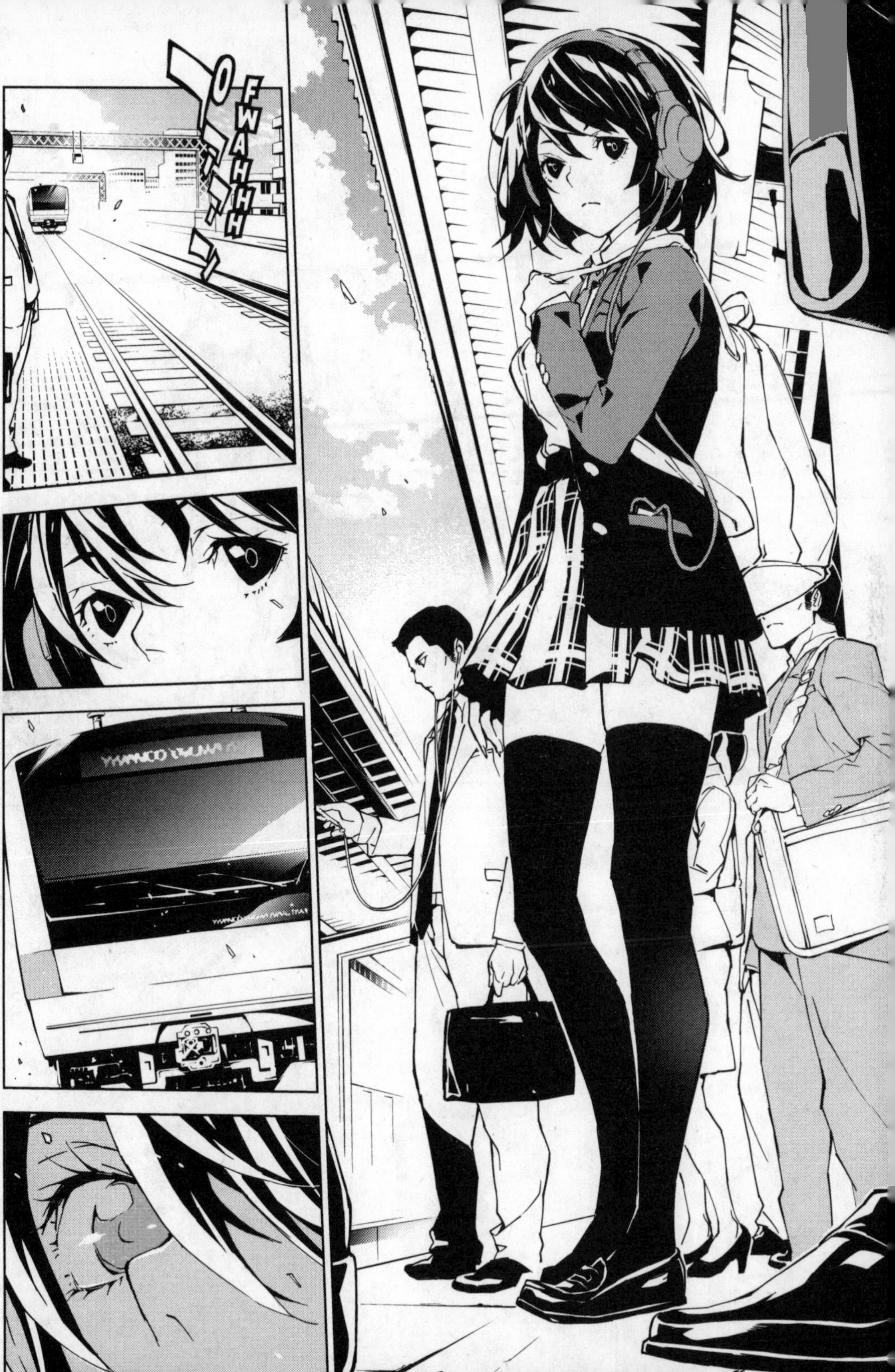
FWAHHH

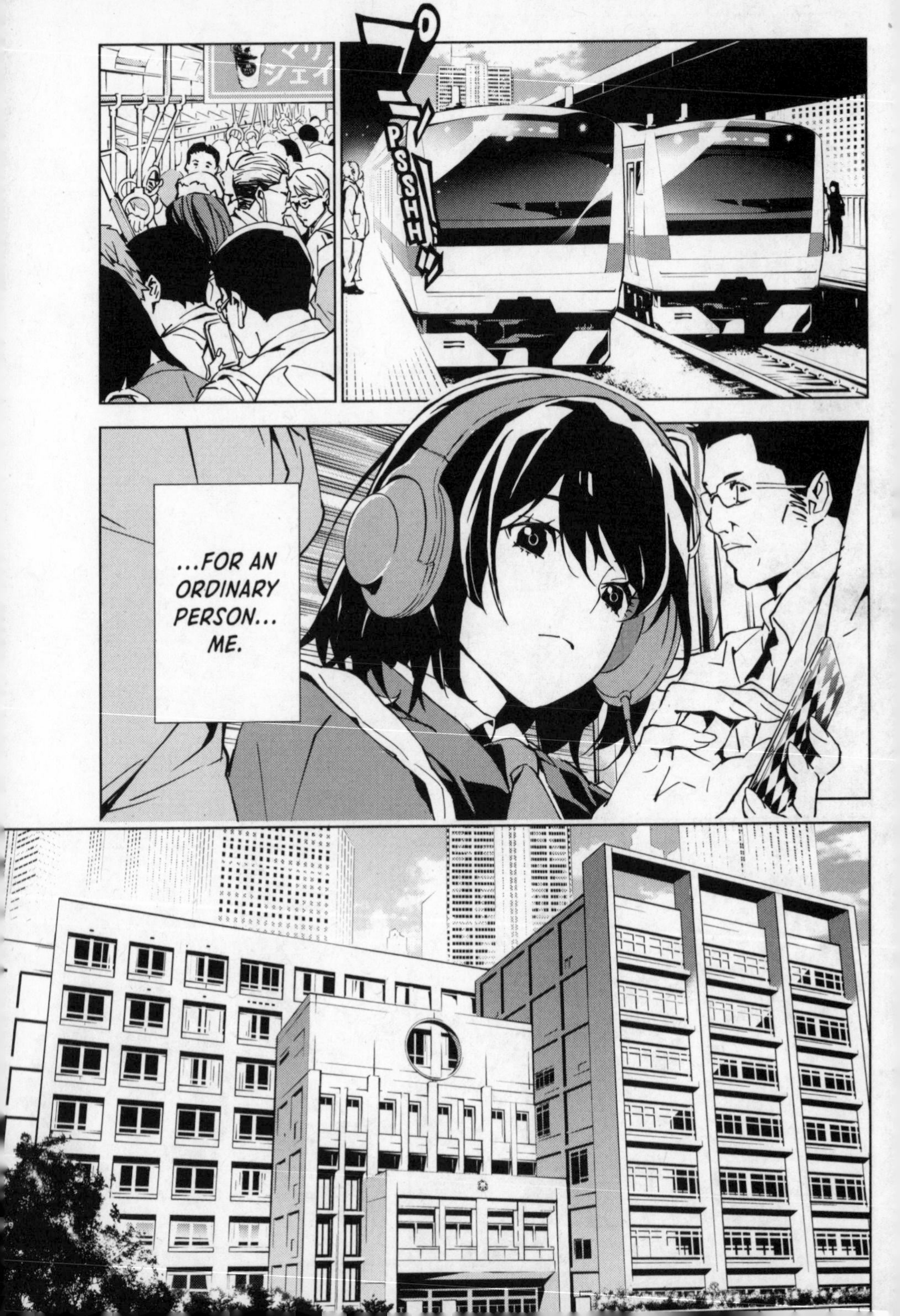
PSSHH
...FOR AN ORDINARY PERSON... ME.

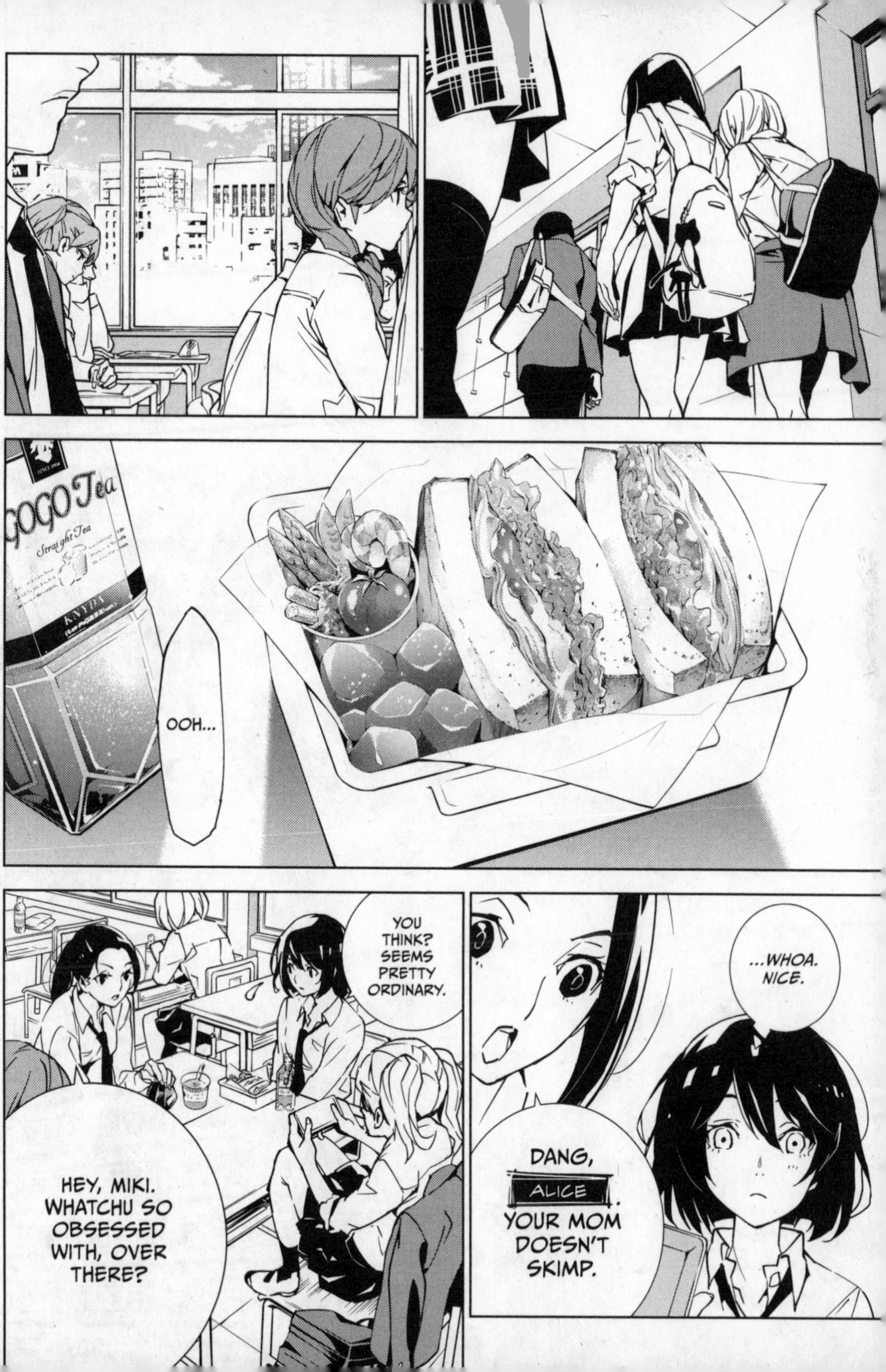
GOGO Tea
Straight Tea
OOH...
...WHOA. NICE.
DANG, ALICE YOUR MOM DOESN'T SKIMP.
YOU THINK? SEEMS PRETTY ORDINARY.
HEY, MIKI. WHATCHU SO OBSESSED WITH, OVER THERE?

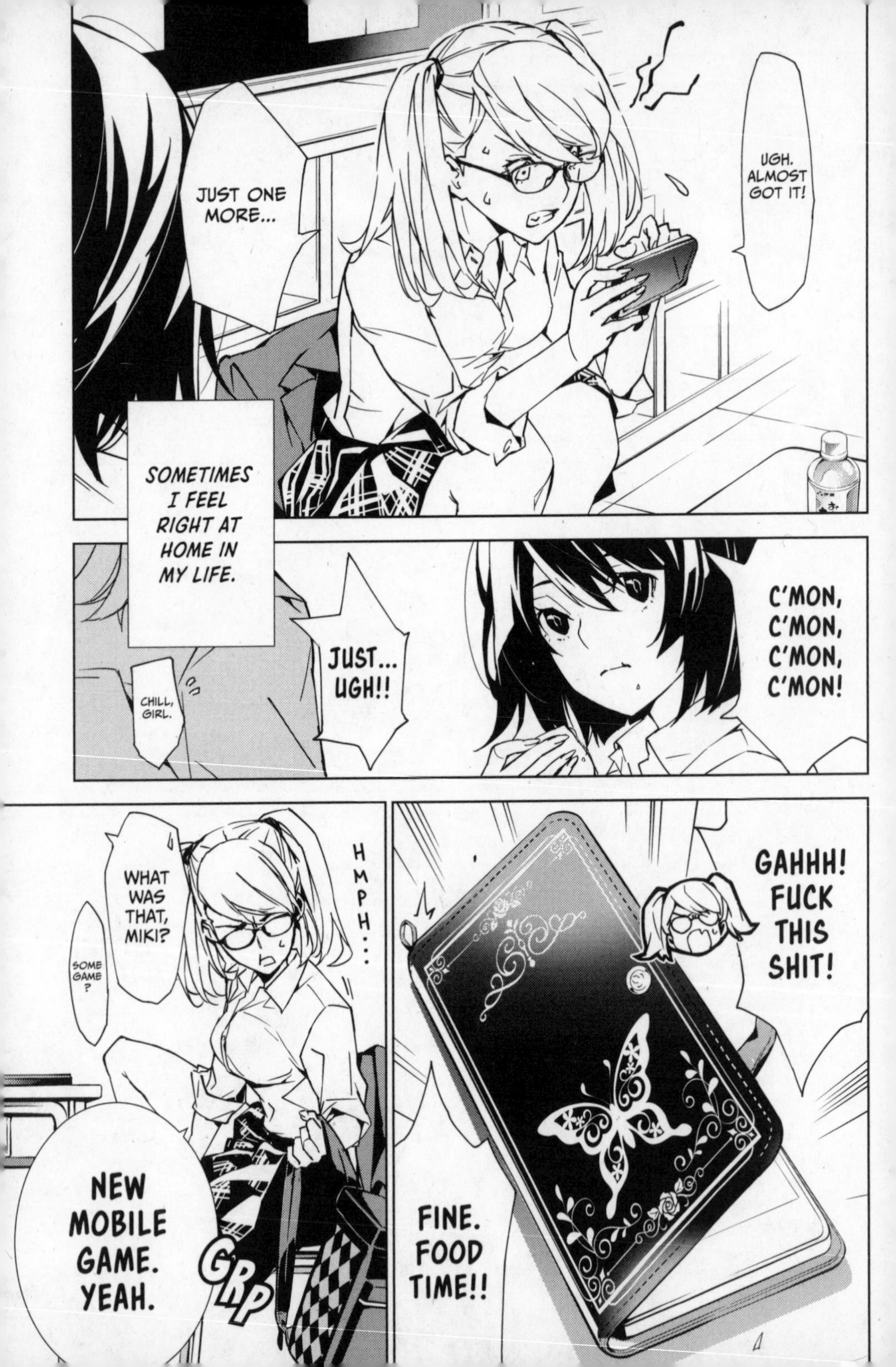
UGH. ALMOST GOT IT!
JUST ONE MORE...
SOMETIMES I FEEL RIGHT AT HOME IN MY LIFE.
C'MON, C'MON, C'MON, C'MON!
JUST... UGH!!
CHILL, GIRL.
GAHHH! FUCK THIS SHIT!
FINE. FOOD TIME!!
HMPH...
WHAT WAS THAT, MIKI?
SOME GAME?
NEW MOBILE GAME. YEAH.
GRP

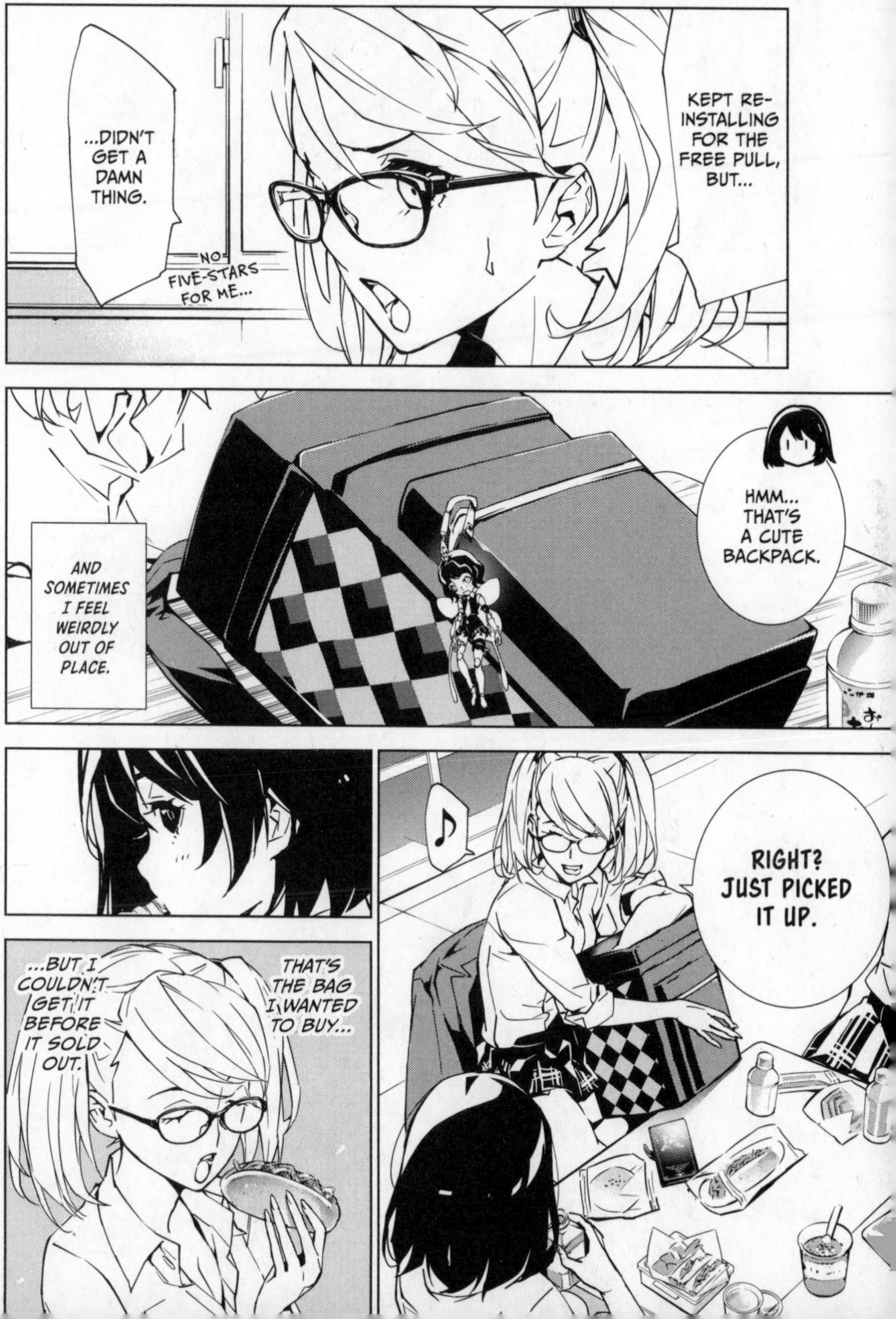
KEPT RE-INSTALLING FOR THE FREE PULL, BUT...
...DIDN'T GET A DAMN THING.
NO FIVE-STARS FOR ME...
HMM... THAT'S A CUTE BACKPACK.
AND SOMETIMES I FEEL WEIRDLY OUT OF PLACE.
♪
RIGHT? JUST PICKED IT UP.
THAT'S THE BAG I WANTED TO BUY...
...BUT I COULDN'T GET IT BEFORE IT SOLD OUT.

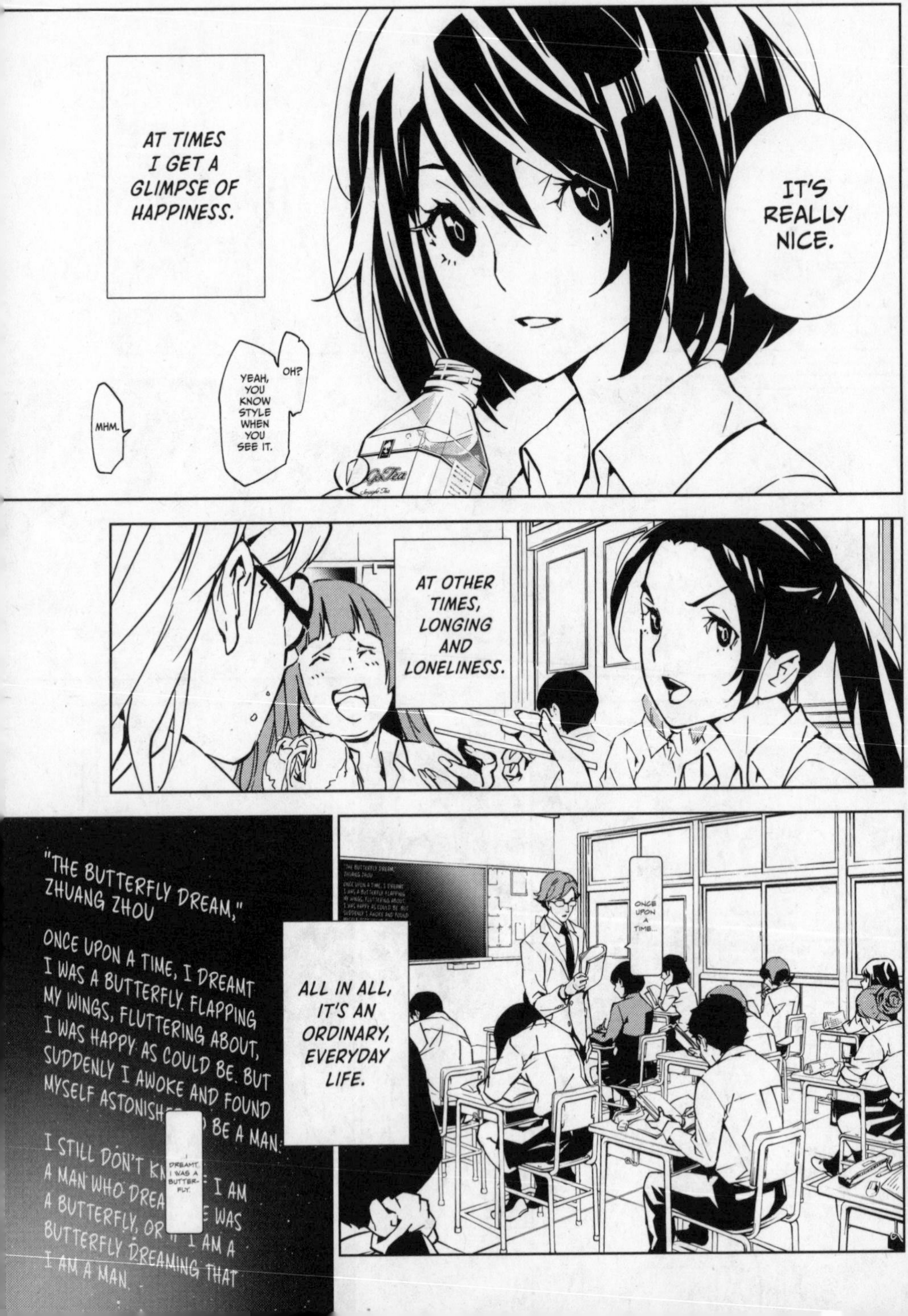
IT'S REALLY NICE.
AT TIMES I GET A GLIMPSE OF HAPPINESS.
OH?
YEAH, YOU KNOW STYLE WHEN YOU SEE IT.
MHM.
AT OTHER TIMES, LONGING AND LONELINESS.
ONCE UPON A TIME...
ALL IN ALL, IT'S AN ORDINARY, EVERYDAY LIFE.
"THE BUTTERFLY DREAM," ZHUANG ZHOU
ONCE UPON A TIME, I DREAMT I WAS A BUTTERFLY. FLAPPING MY WINGS, FLUTTERING ABOUT, I WAS HAPPY AS COULD BE. BUT SUDDENLY I AWOKE AND FOUND MYSELF ASTONISHE BE A MAN.
I STILL DON'T KN I AM A MAN WHO DREA WAS A BUTTERFLY, OR I AM A BUTTERFLY DREAMING THAT I AM A MAN.
I DREAMT I WAS A BUTTER-FLY.

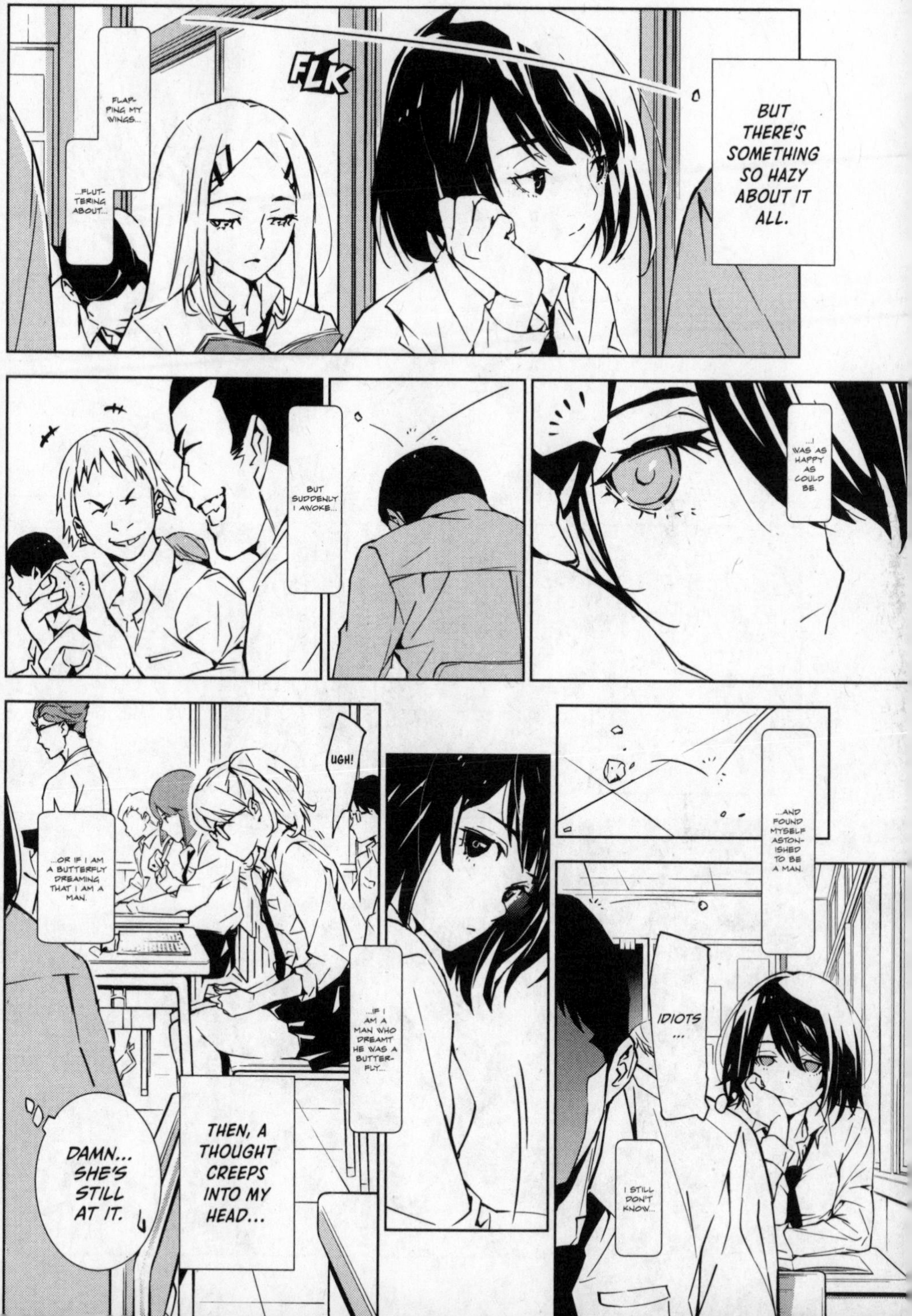
BUT THERE'S SOMETHING SO HAZY ABOUT IT ALL.
FLK
FLAPPING MY WINGS...
...FLUTTERING ABOUT...
...I WAS AS HAPPY AS COULD BE.
BUT SUDDENLY I AWOKE...
...AND FOUND MYSELF ASTONISHED TO BE A MAN.
IDIOTS...
I STILL DON'T KNOW...
...IF I AM A MAN WHO DREAMT HE WAS A BUTTERFLY...
UGH!
...OR IF I AM A BUTTERFLY DREAMING THAT I AM A MAN.
THEN, A THOUGHT CREEPS INTO MY HEAD...
DAMN... SHE'S STILL AT IT.

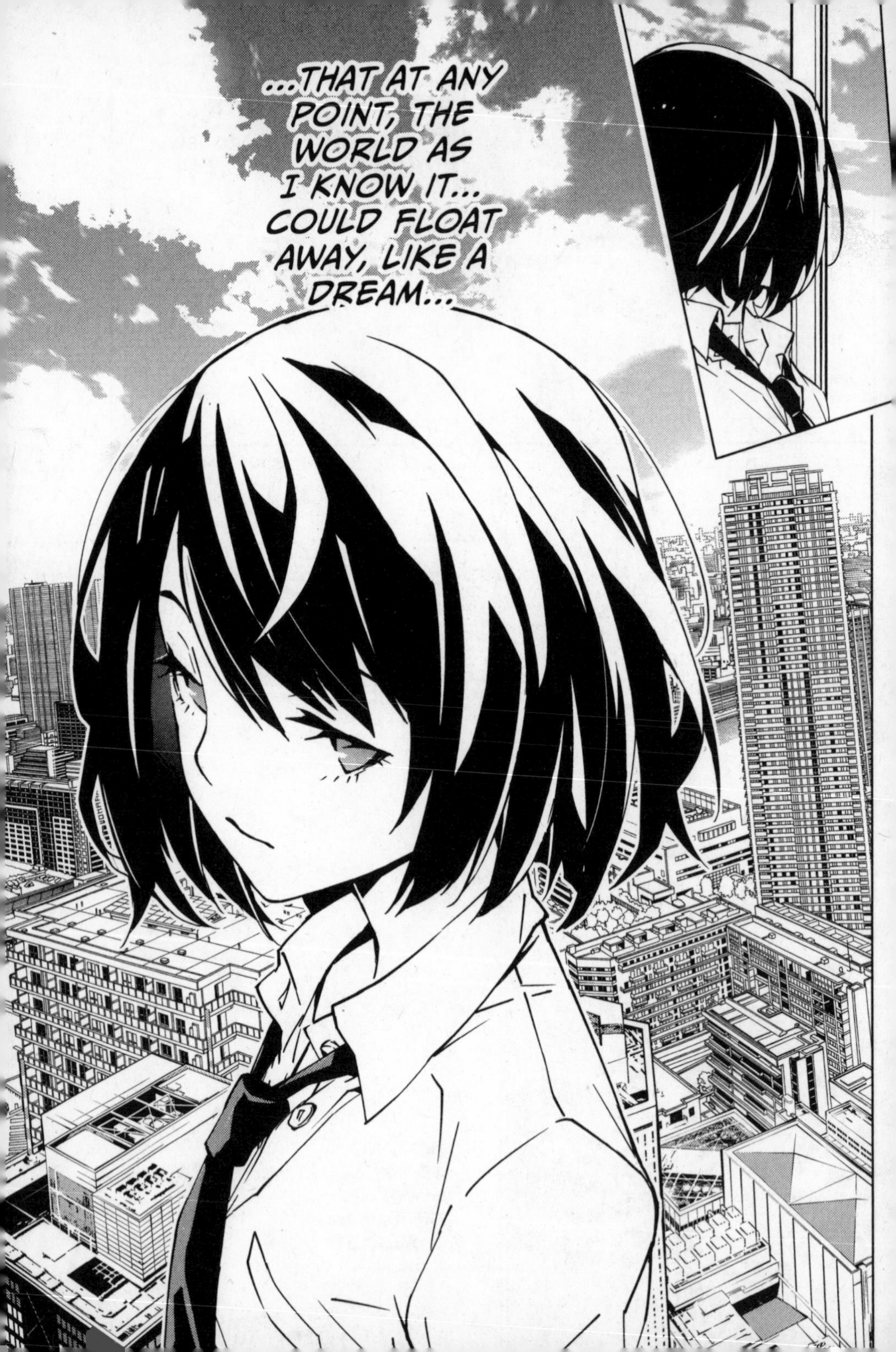
...THAT AT ANY POINT, THE WORLD AS I KNOW IT... COULD FLOAT AWAY, LIKE A DREAM...

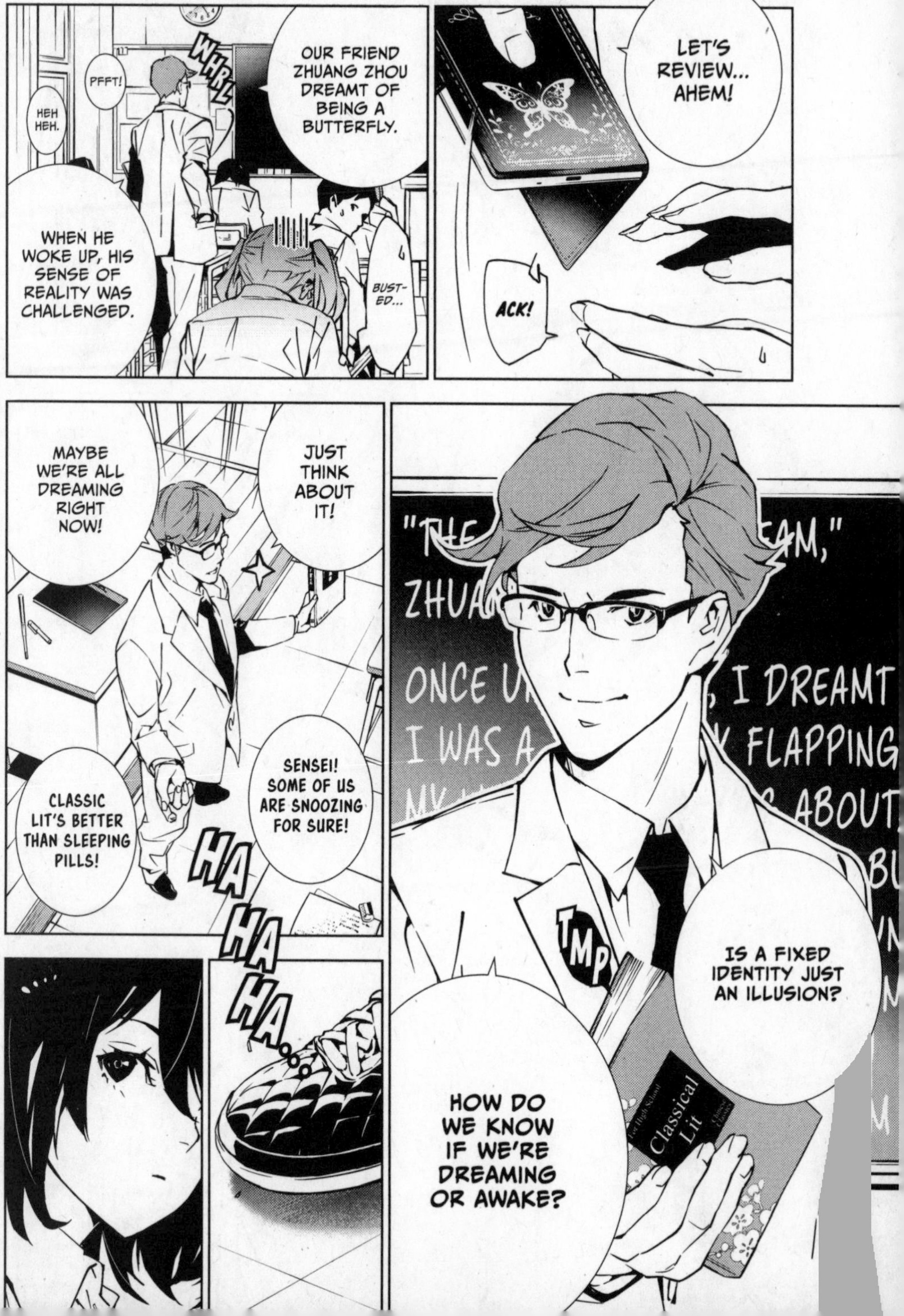
LET'S REVIEW... AHEM!
ACK!
OUR FRIEND ZHUANG ZHOU DREAMT OF BEING A BUTTERFLY.
WHRL
PFFT!
HEH HEH.
WHEN HE WOKE UP, HIS SENSE OF REALITY WAS CHALLENGED.
BUST-ED...
TMP
IS A FIXED IDENTITY JUST AN ILLUSION?
HOW DO WE KNOW IF WE'RE DREAMING OR AWAKE?
Classical Lit
JUST THINK ABOUT IT!
MAYBE WE'RE ALL DREAMING RIGHT NOW!
SENSEI! SOME OF US ARE SNOOZING FOR SURE!
CLASSIC LIT'S BETTER THAN SLEEPING PILLS!
HA HA HA...

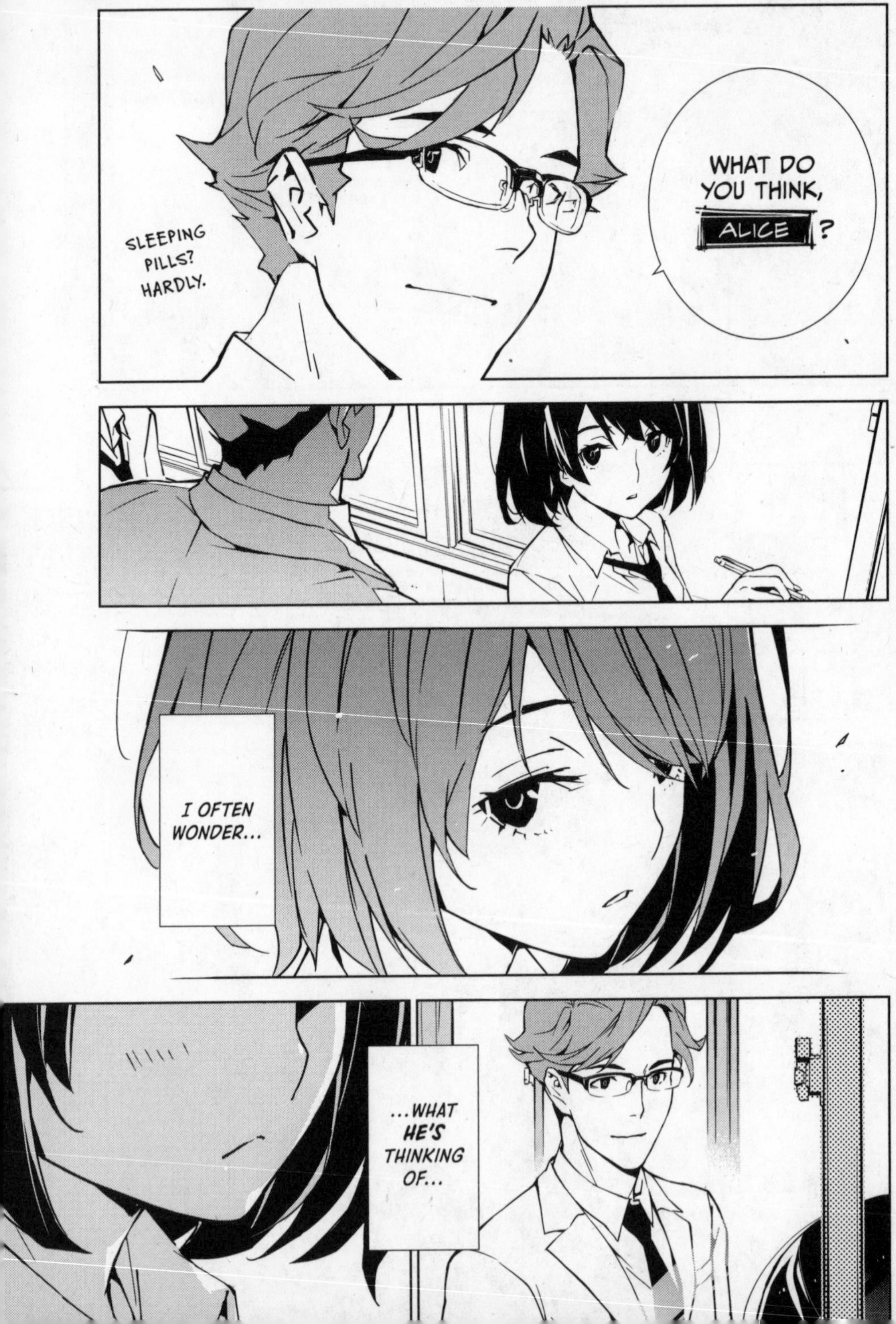
WHAT DO YOU THINK, ALICE?
SLEEPING PILLS? HARDLY.
I OFTEN WONDER...
...WHAT HE'S THINKING OF...

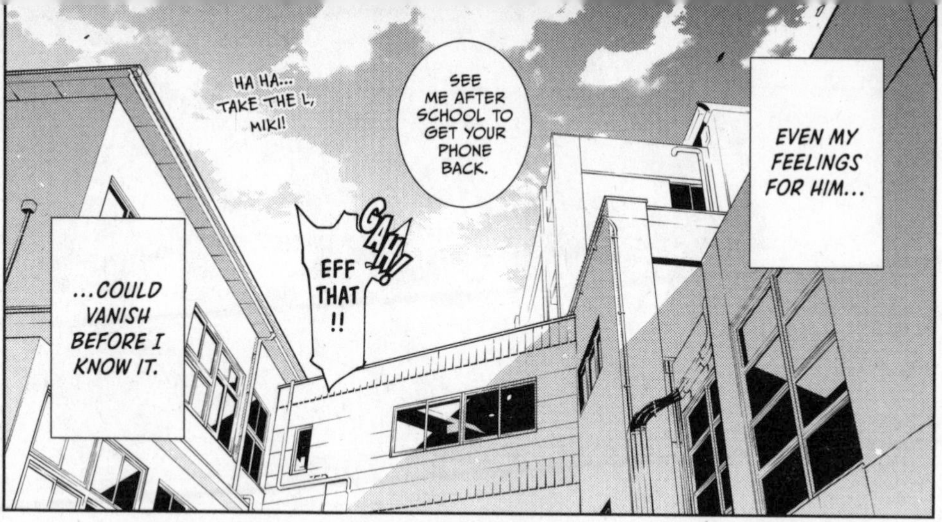
EVEN MY FEELINGS FOR HIM...
SEE ME AFTER SCHOOL TO GET YOUR PHONE BACK.
GAH!
EFF THAT!!
HA HA... TAKE THE L, MIKI!
...COULD VANISH BEFORE I KNOW IT.
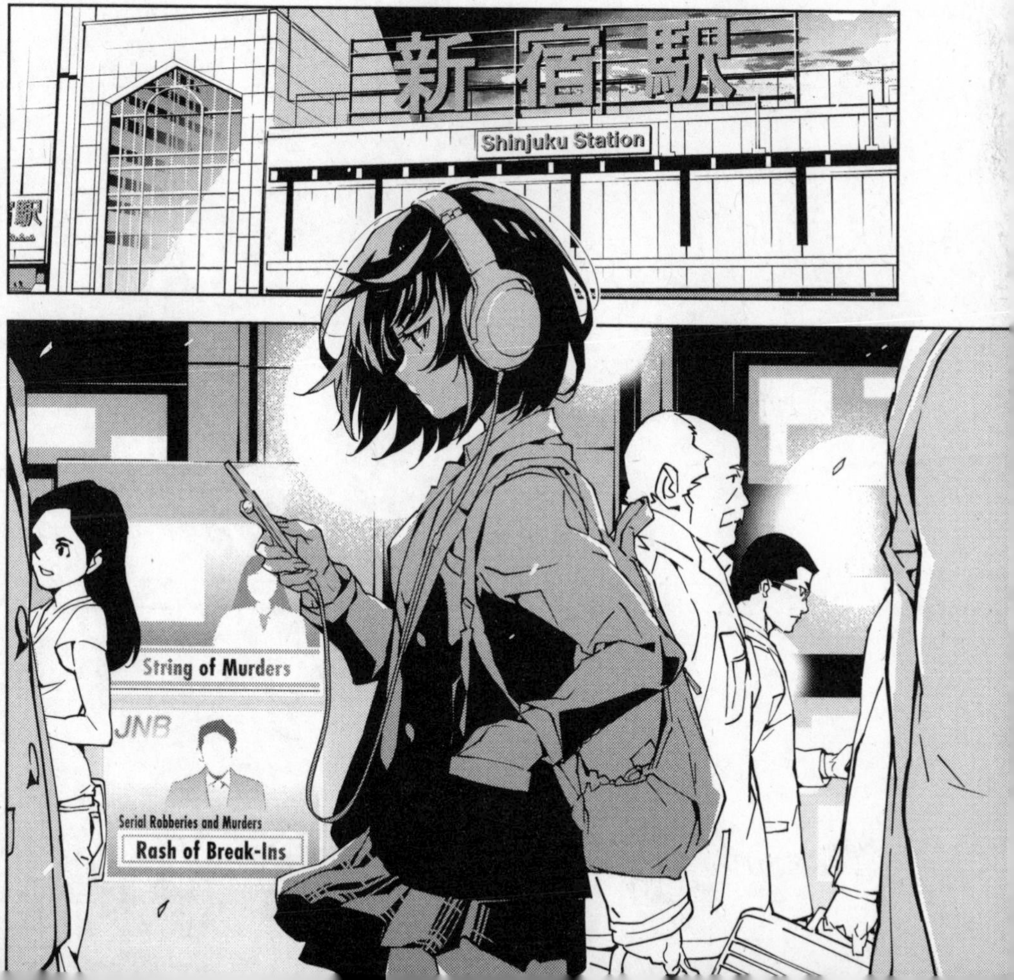
新宿駅
Shinjuku Station
String of Murders
JNB
Serial Robberies and Murders
Rash of Break-Ins

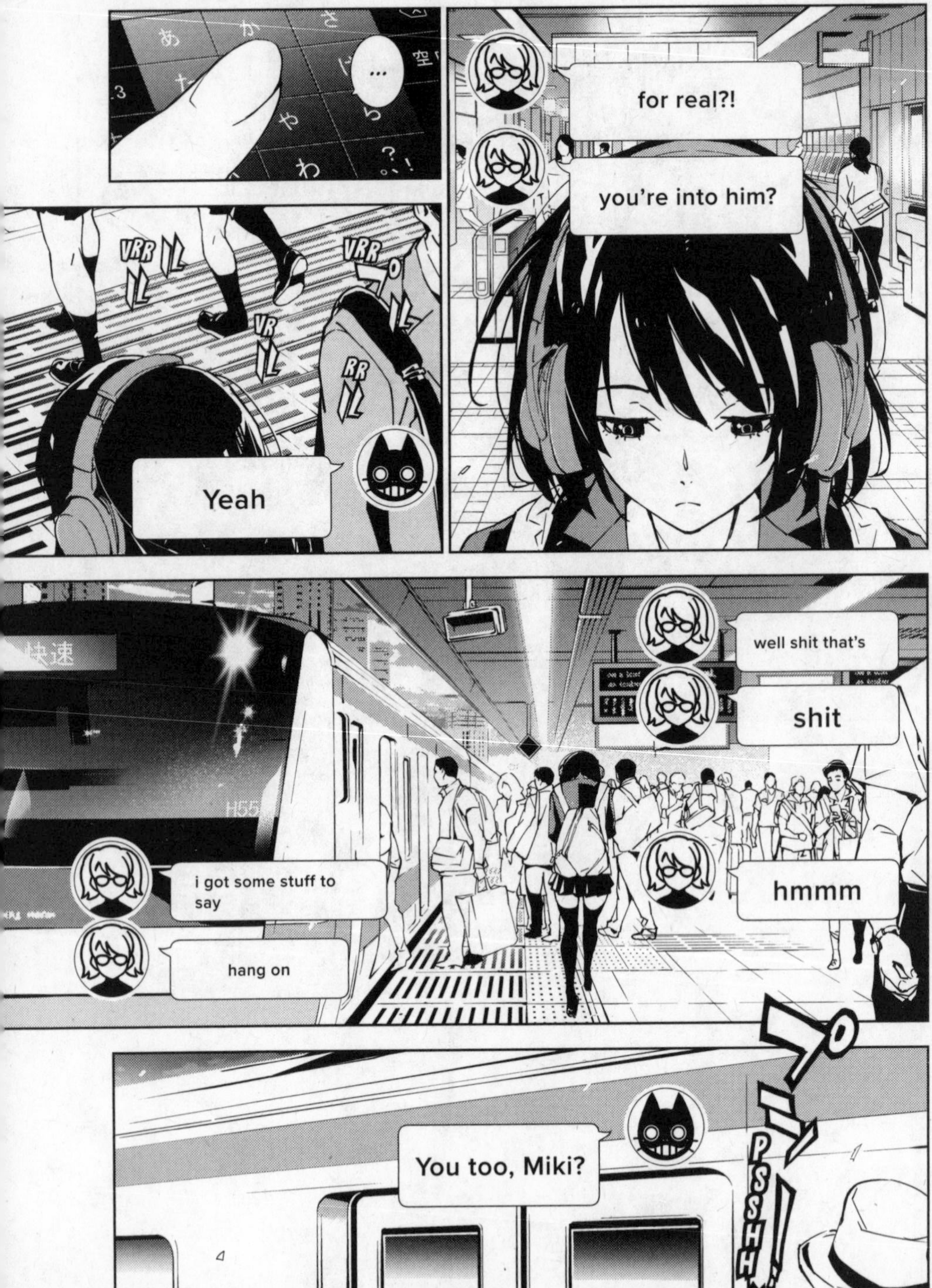
for real?!
you're into him?
...
Yeah
well shit that's
shit
hmmm
快速
i got some stuff to say
hang on
PSSHH!!
You too, Miki?

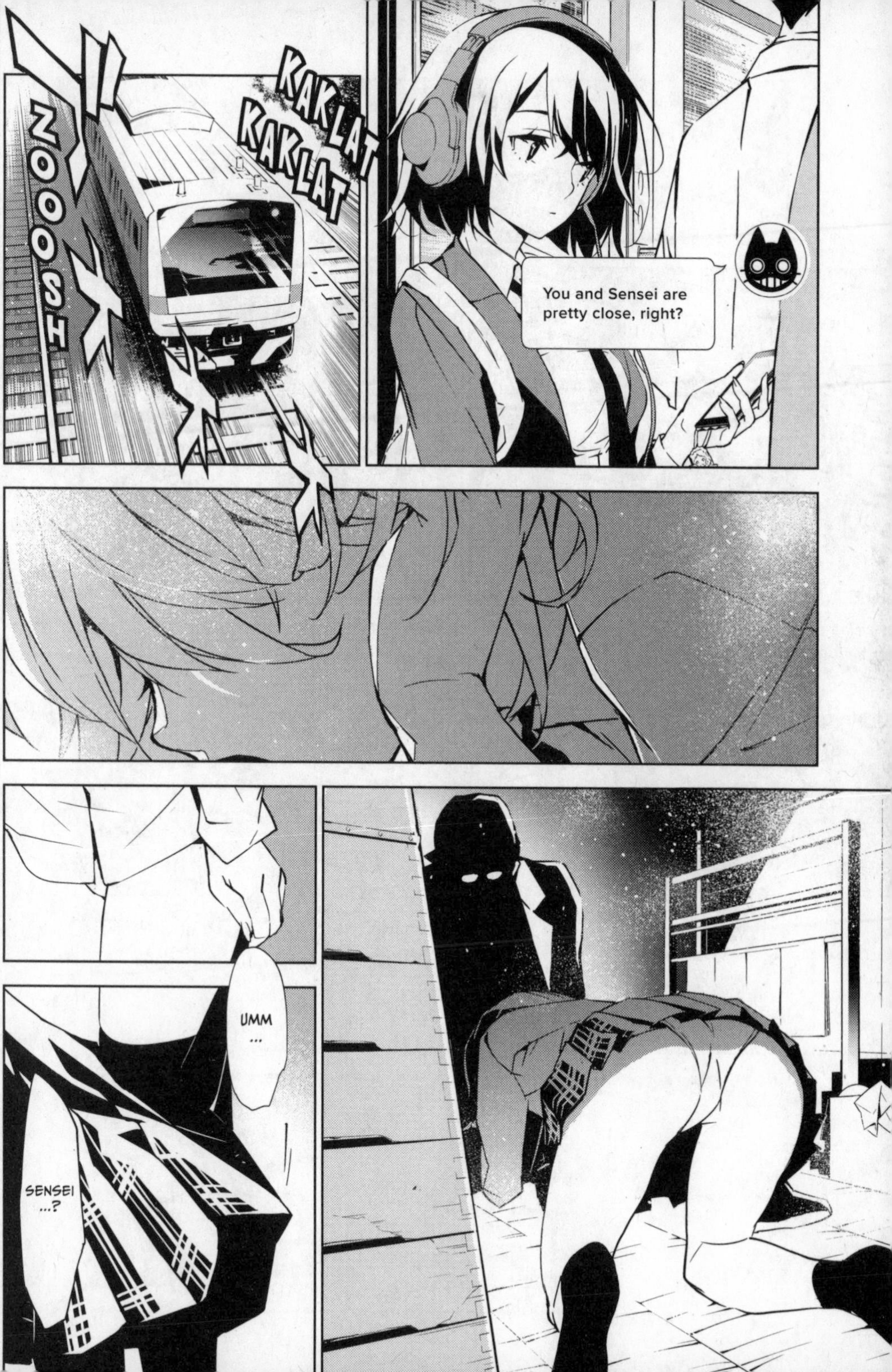
You and Sensei are pretty close, right?
KAKLAT KAKLAT
ZOOOSH
UMM ...
SENSEI ...?

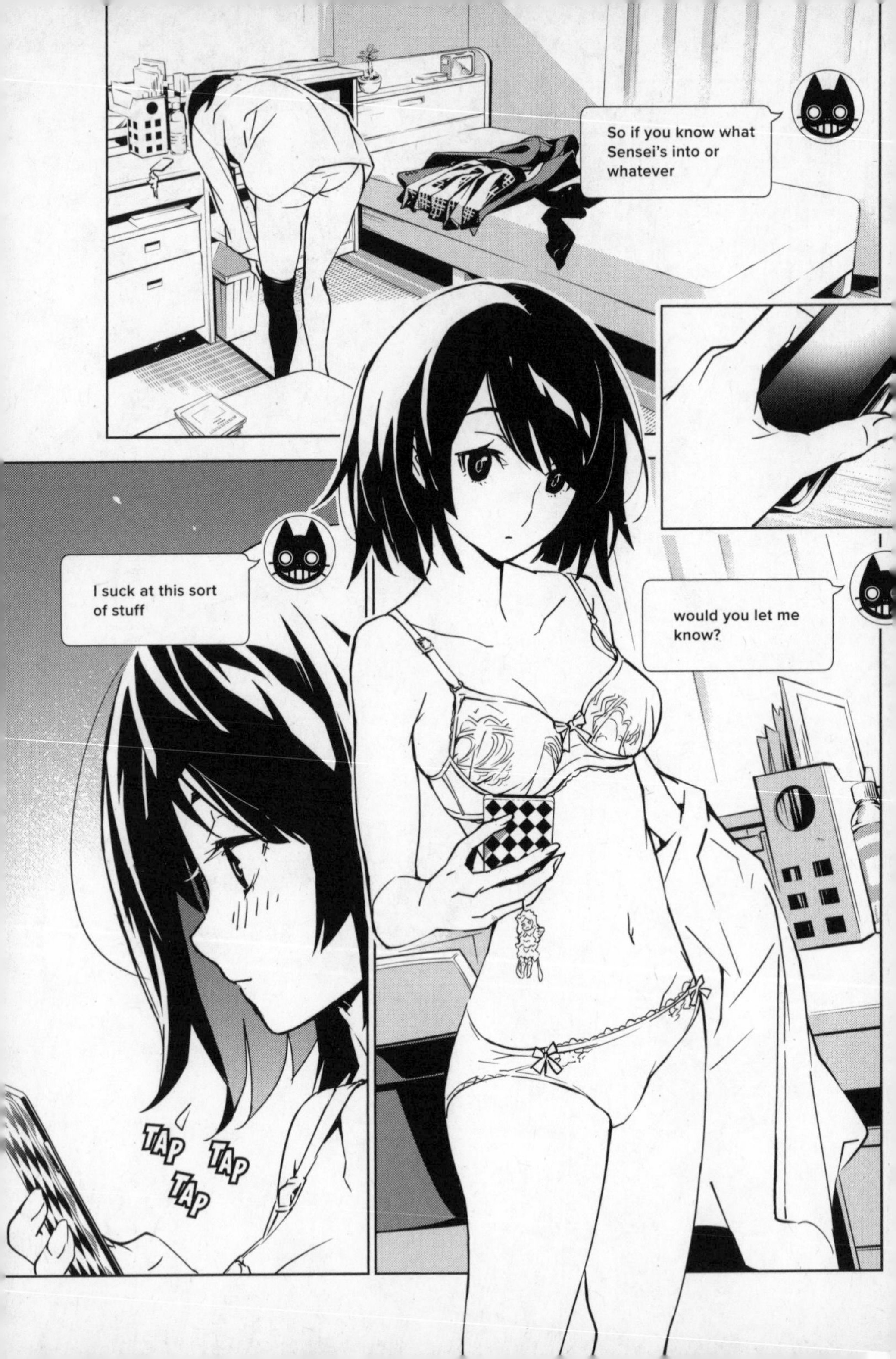

So if you know what Sensei's into or whatever
would you let me know?
I suck at this sort of stuff
TAP TAP TAP

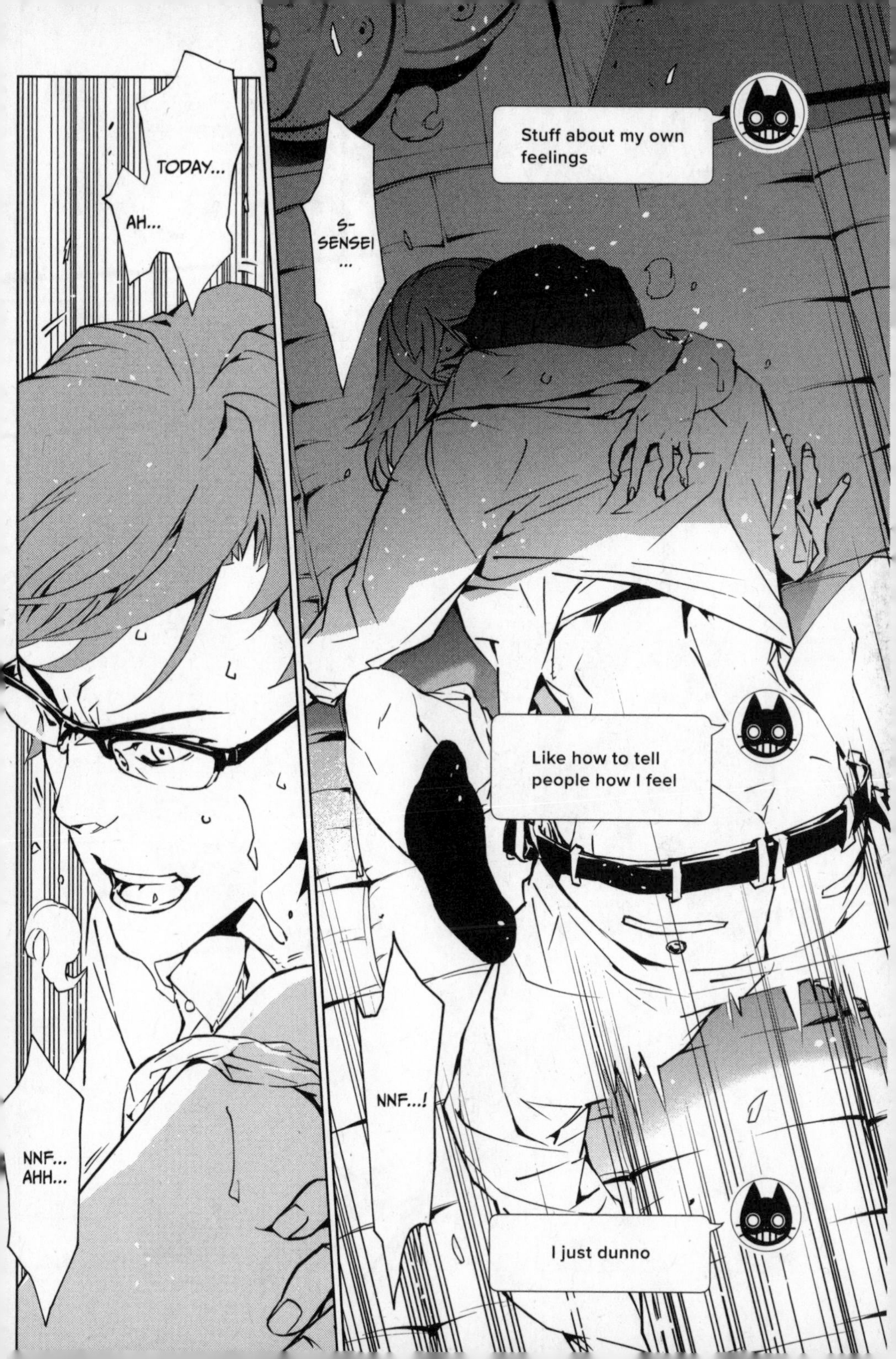
Stuff about my own feelings
S-SENSEI...
Like how to tell people how I feel
NNF...!
I just dunno
TODAY...
AH...
NNF... AHH...

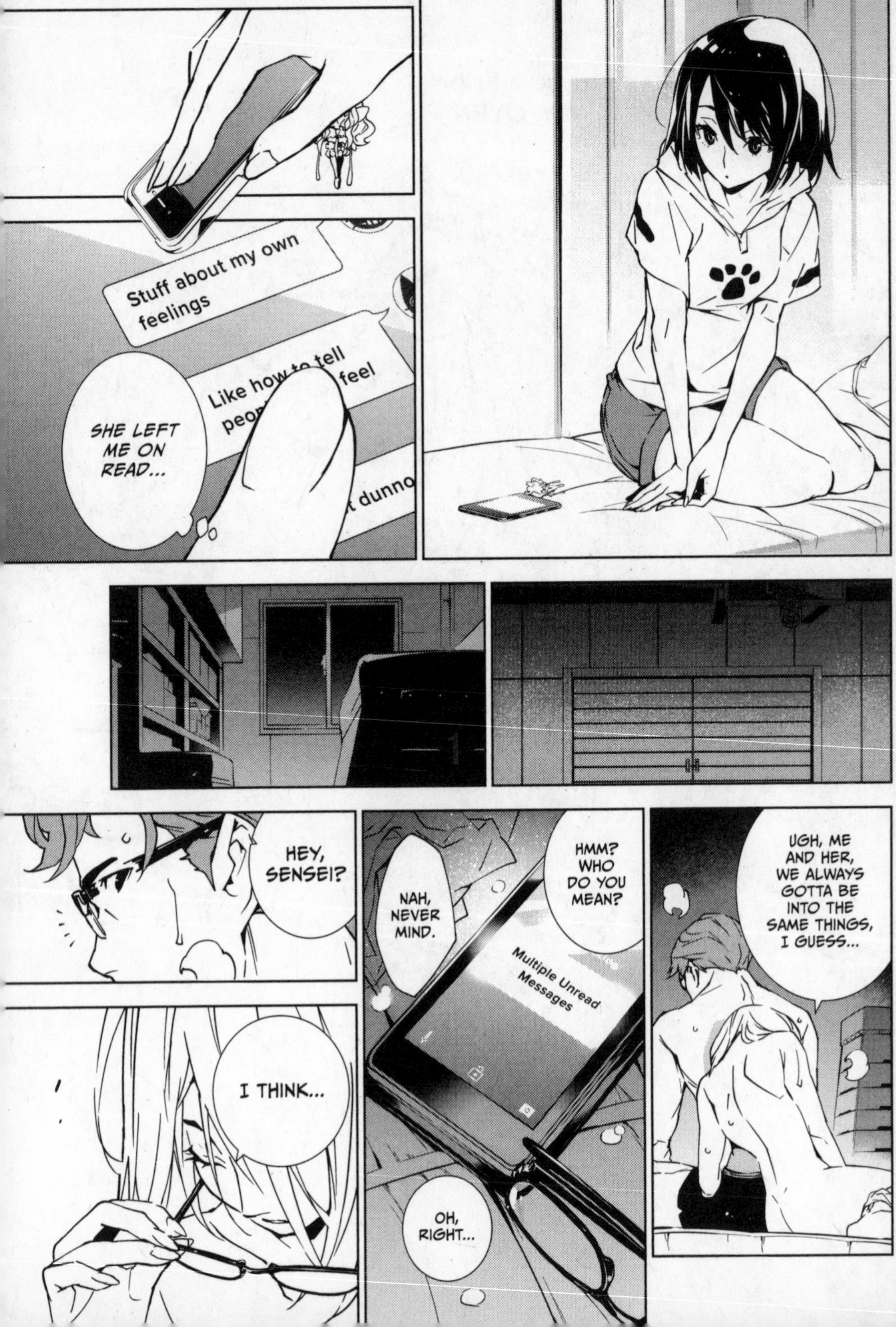
Stuff about my own feelings
Like how to tell peo feel
t dunno
SHE LEFT ME ON READ...
UGH, ME AND HER, WE ALWAYS GOTTA BE INTO THE SAME THINGS, I GUESS...
HMM? WHO DO YOU MEAN?
NAH, NEVER MIND.
Multiple Unread Messages
OH, RIGHT...
HEY, SENSEI?
I THINK...

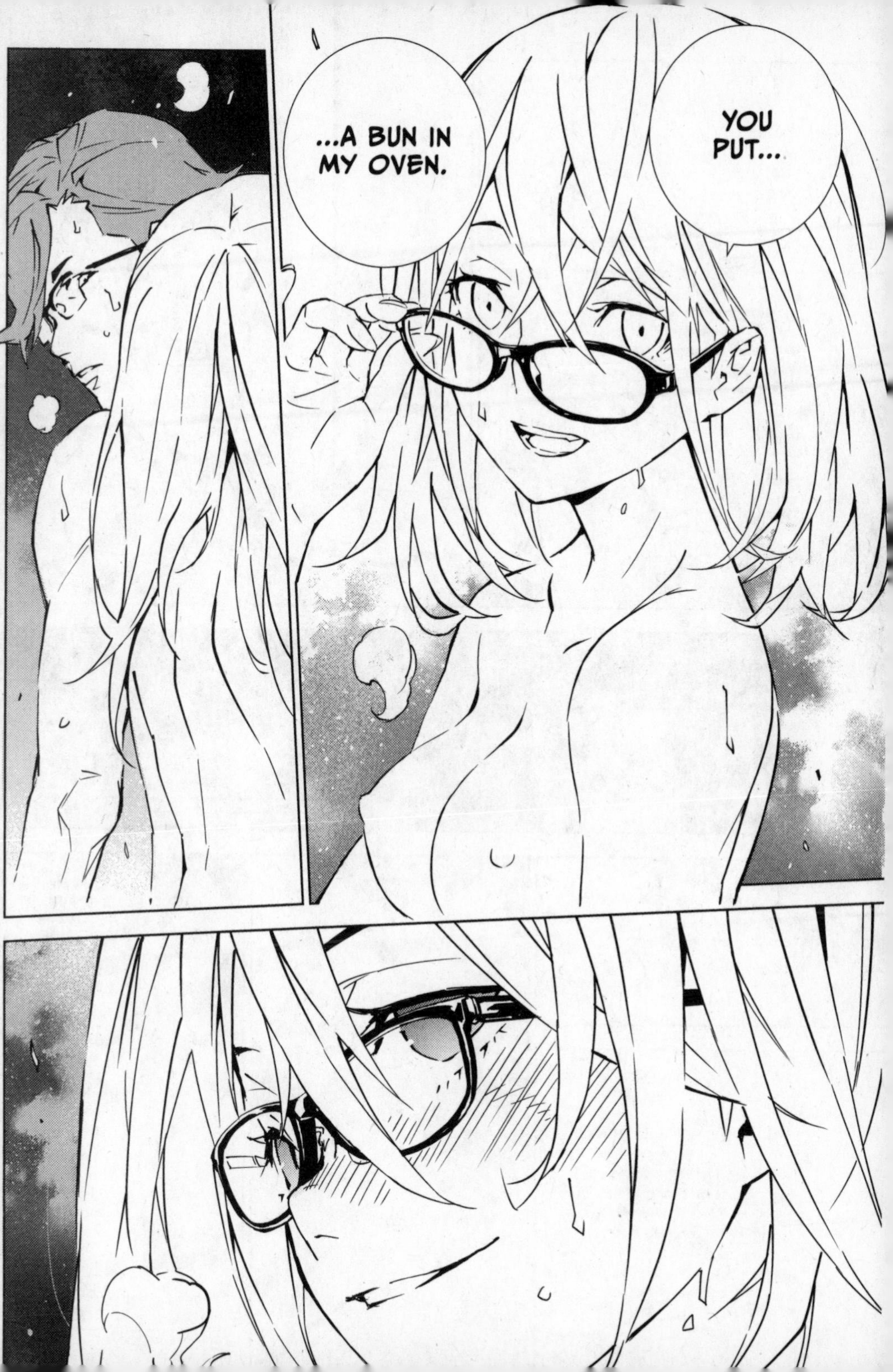
YOU PUT...
...A BUN IN MY OVEN.

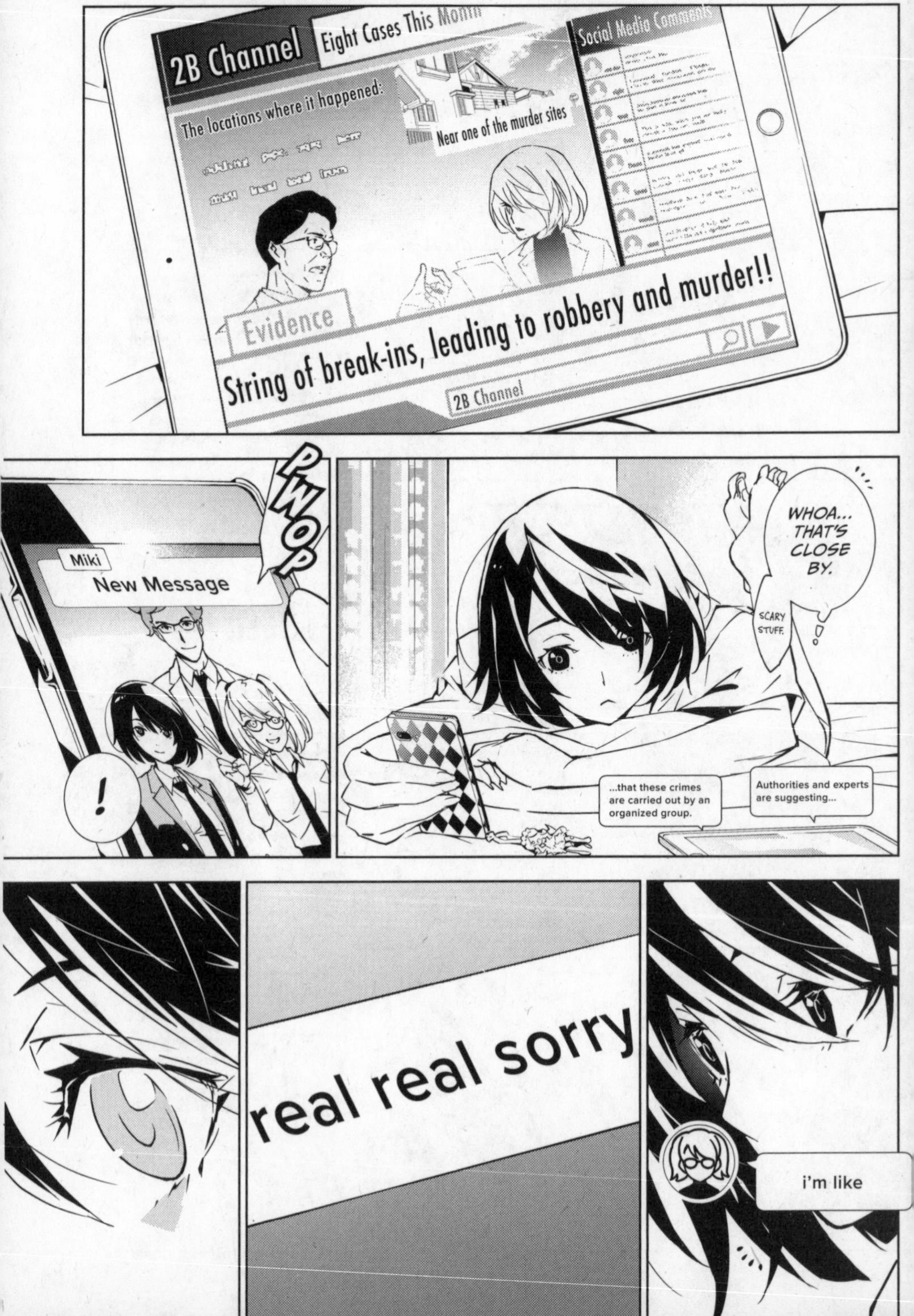
2B Channel
Eight Cases This
Social Media Comments
The locations where it happened:
Near one of the murder sites
Evidence
String of break-ins, leading to robbery and murder!!
2B Channel
WHOA... THAT'S CLOSE BY.
SCARY STUFF.
Authorities and experts are suggesting...
...that these crimes are carried out by an organized group.
PWOP
Miki
New Message
!
i'm like
real real sorry

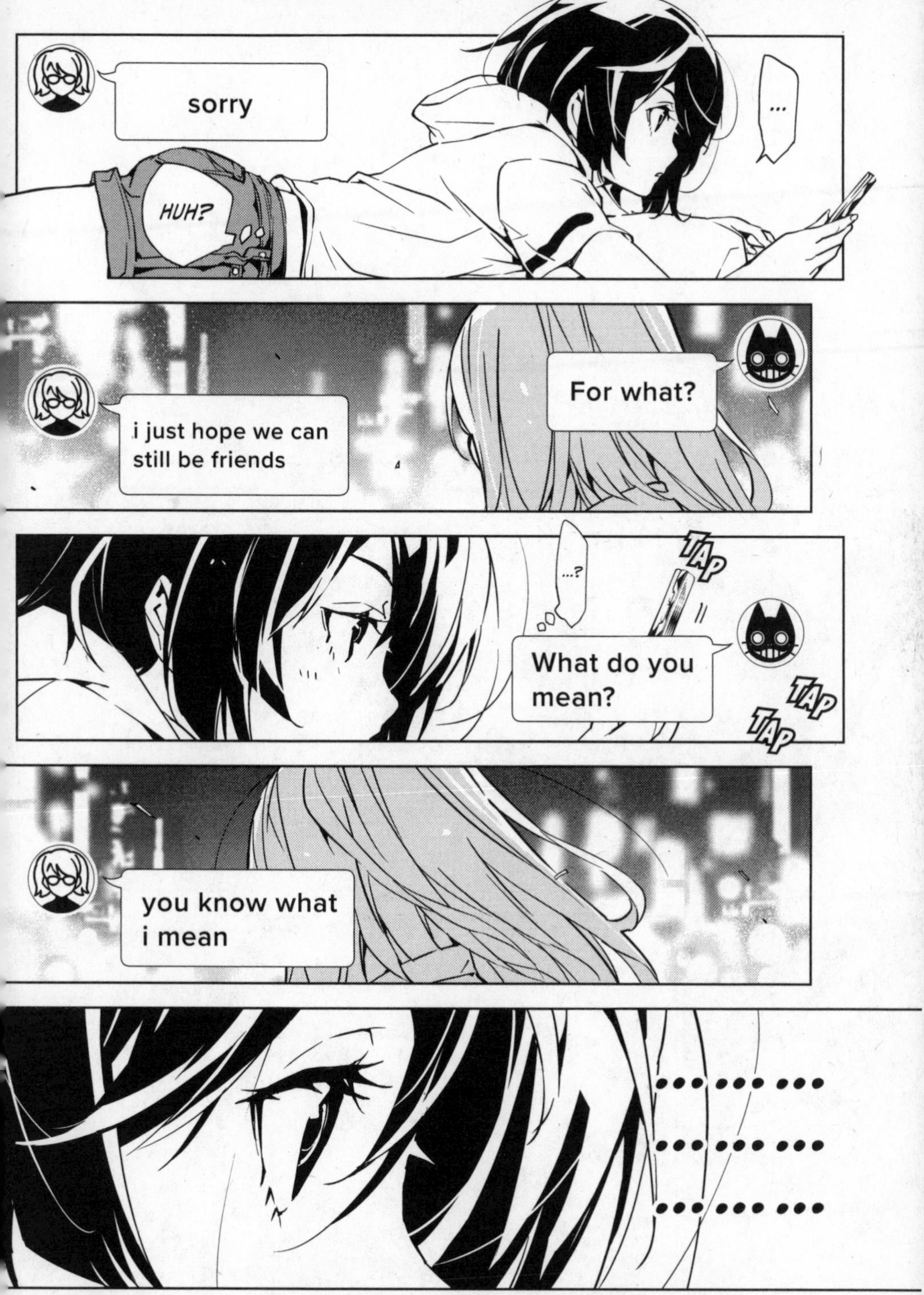
...
sorry
HUH?
For what?
i just hope we can still be friends
TAP
...?
What do you mean?
TAP
TAP
you know what i mean
•••••••••
•••••••••
•••••••••

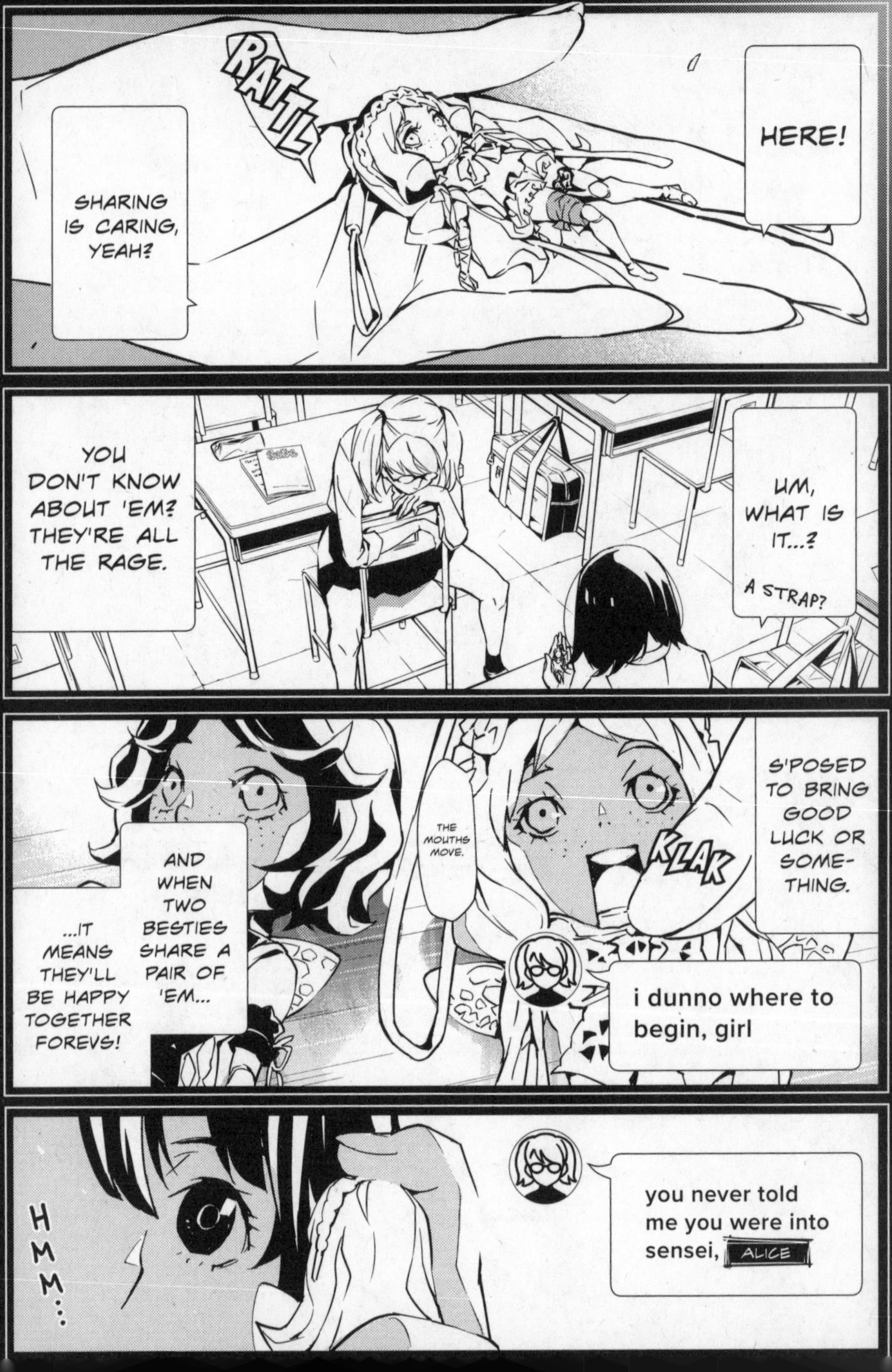
HERE!
RATTL
SHARING IS CARING, YEAH?
UM, WHAT IS IT...? A STRAP?
YOU DON'T KNOW ABOUT 'EM? THEY'RE ALL THE RAGE.
S'POSED TO BRING GOOD LUCK OR SOME-THING.
KLAK
THE MOUTHS MOVE.
i dunno where to begin, girl
AND WHEN TWO BESTIES SHARE A PAIR OF 'EM...
...IT MEANS THEY'LL BE HAPPY TOGETHER FOREVS!
you never told me you were into sensei, ALICE
HMM..

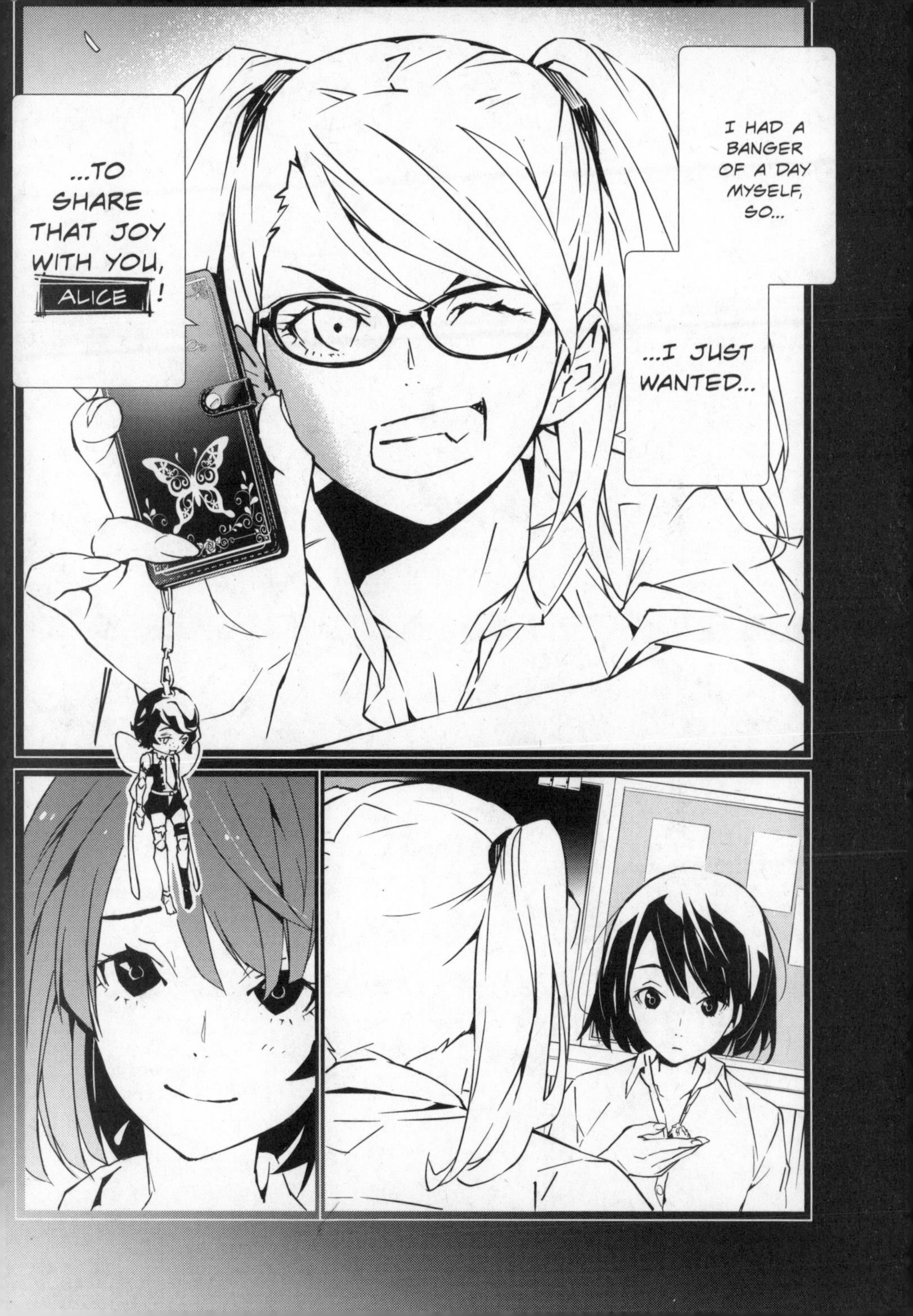
I HAD A BANGER OF A DAY MYSELF, SO...
...I JUST WANTED...
...TO SHARE THAT JOY WITH YOU, ALICE!

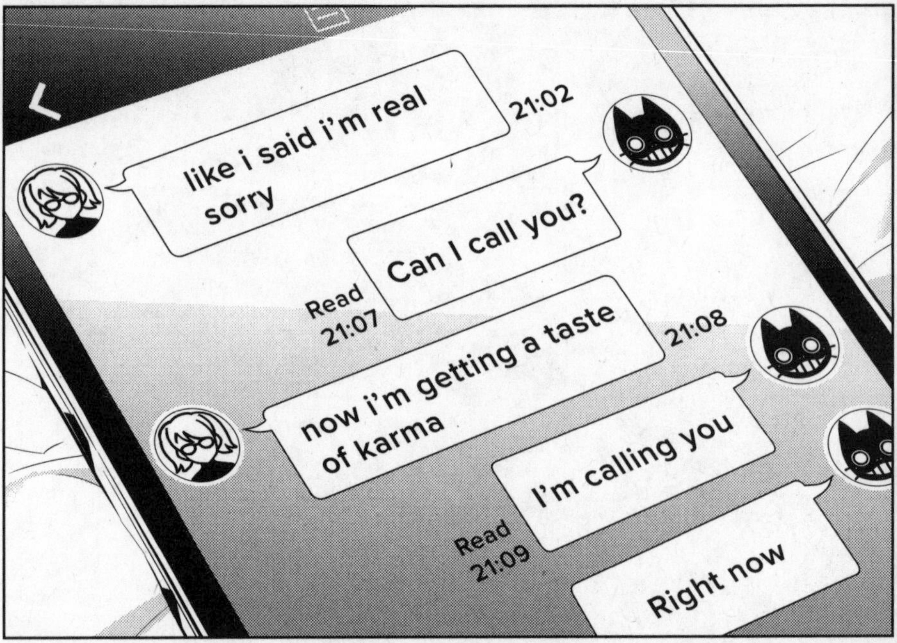
like i said i'm real sorry
21:02
Can I call you?
Read 21:07
now i'm getting a taste of karma
21:08
I'm calling you
Read 21:09
Right now

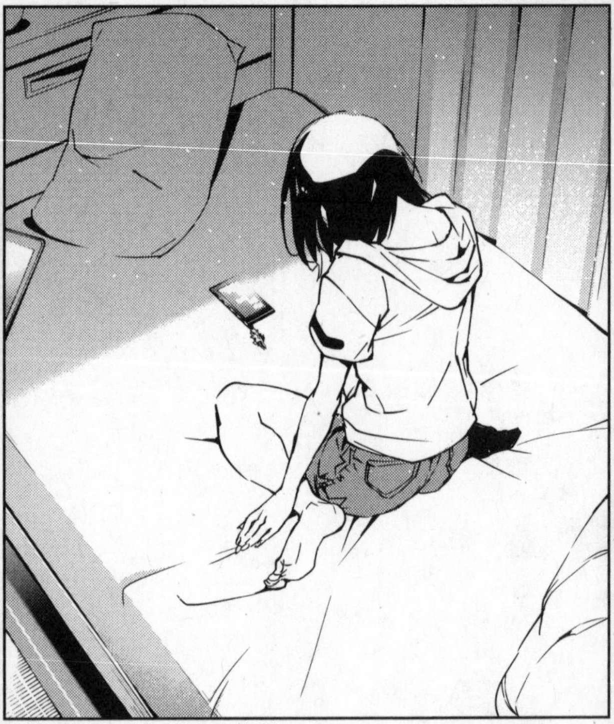

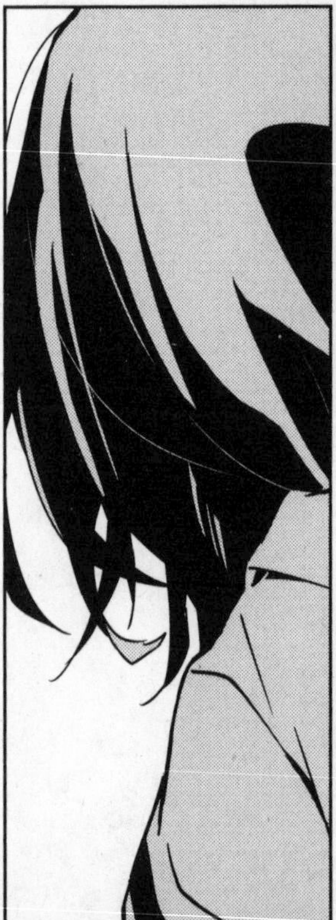

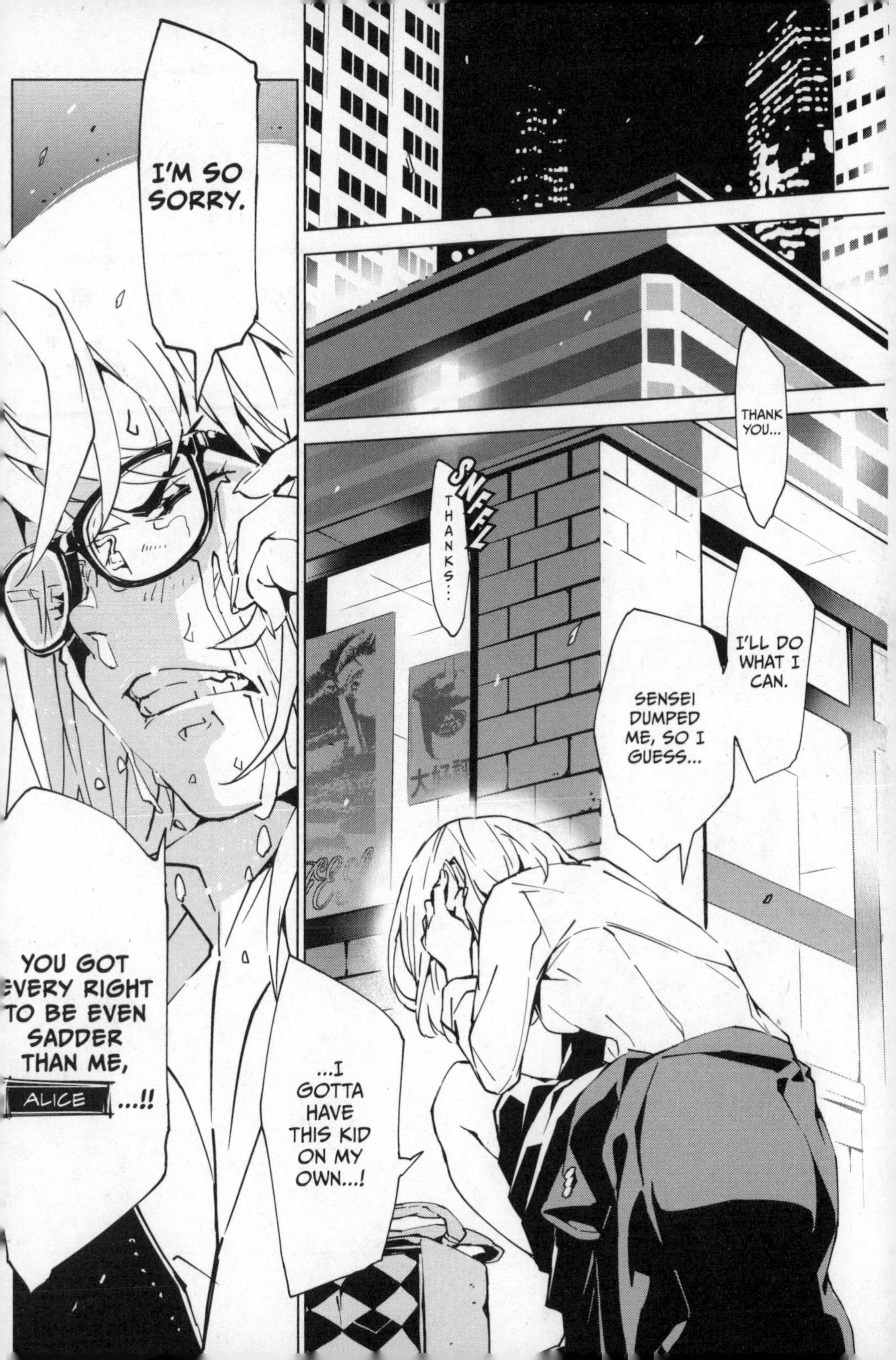
THANK YOU...
SNFFL
THANKS...
I'LL DO WHAT I CAN.
SENSEI DUMPED ME, SO I GUESS...
I'M SO SORRY.
YOU GOT EVERY RIGHT TO BE EVEN SADDER THAN ME, ALICE...!!
...I GOTTA HAVE THIS KID ON MY OWN...!

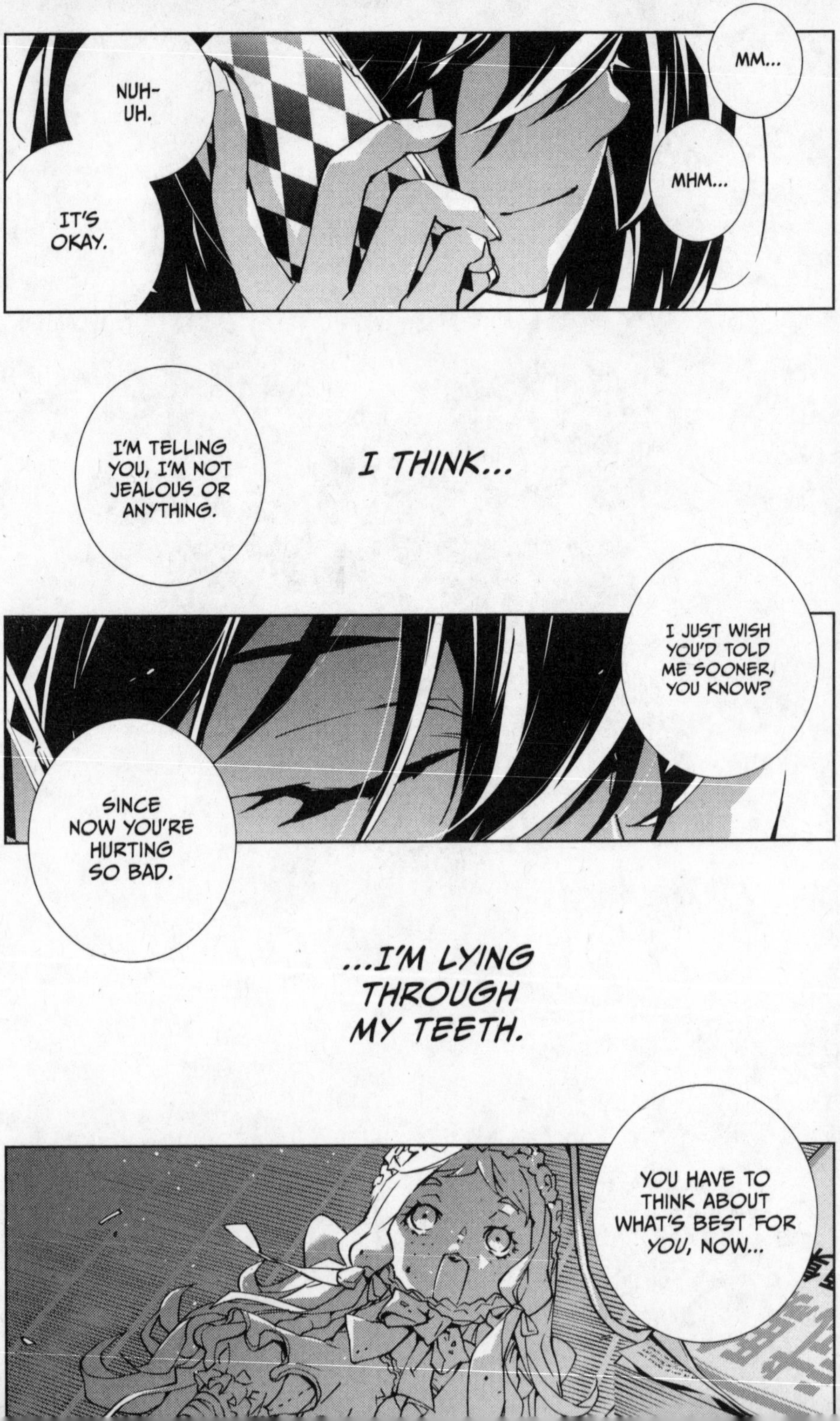
MM...
MHM...
NUH-UH.
IT'S OKAY.
I THINK...
I'M TELLING YOU, I'M NOT JEALOUS OR ANYTHING.
I JUST WISH YOU'D TOLD ME SOONER, YOU KNOW?
SINCE NOW YOU'RE HURTING SO BAD.
...I'M LYING THROUGH MY TEETH.
YOU HAVE TO THINK ABOUT WHAT'S BEST FOR *YOU*, NOW...

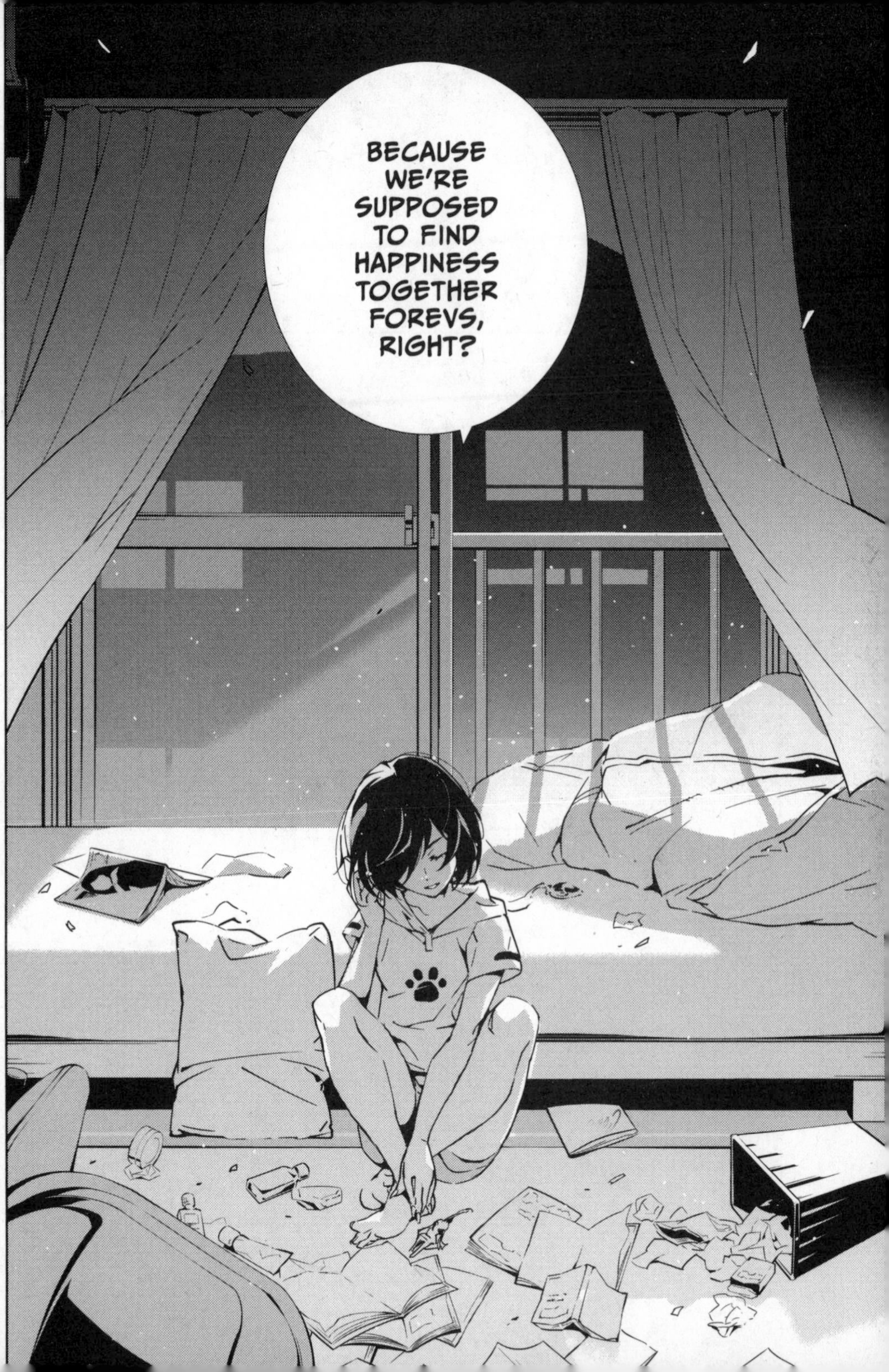
BECAUSE WE'RE SUPPOSED TO FIND HAPPINESS TOGETHER FOREVS, RIGHT?

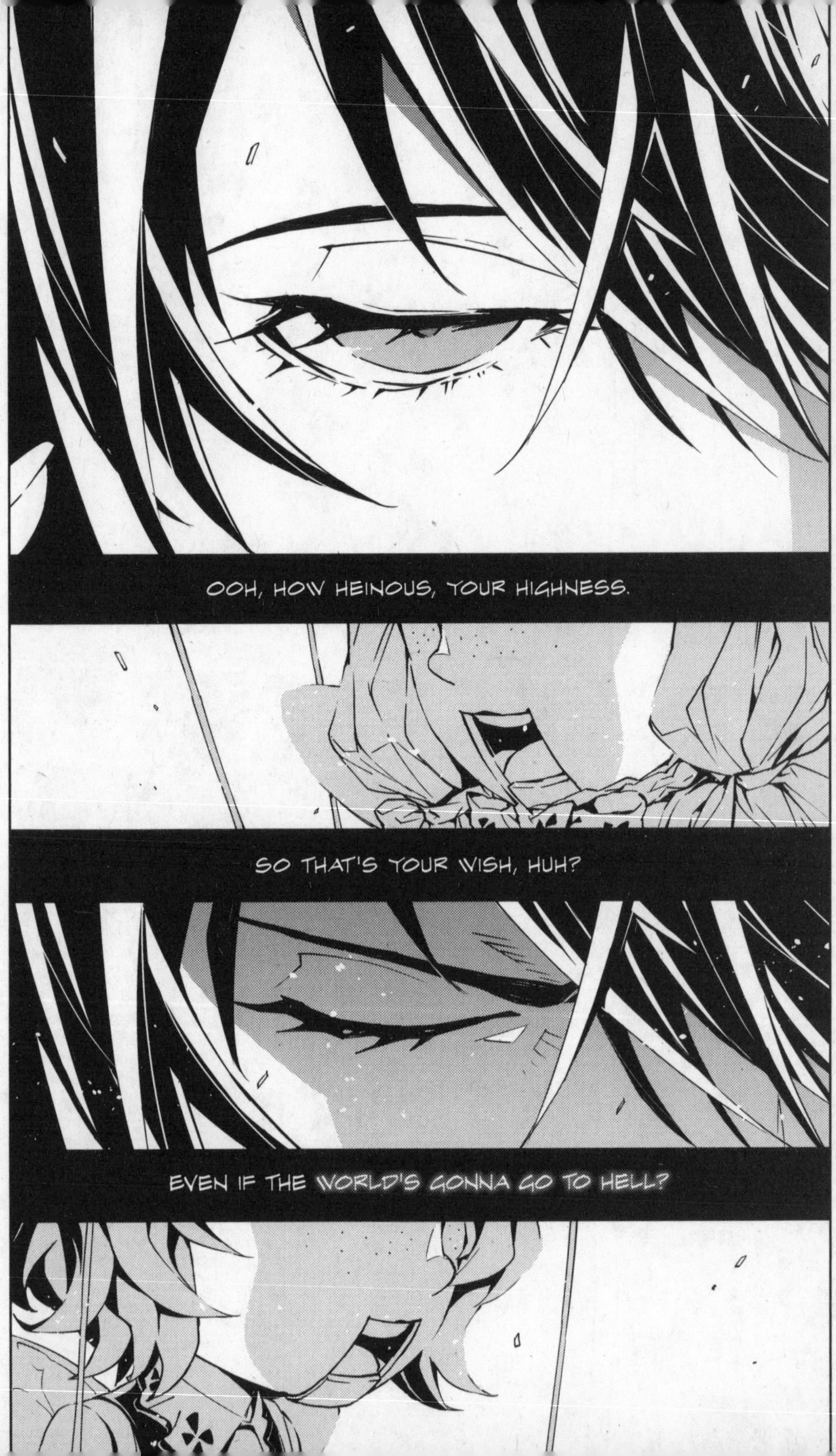
OOH, HOW HEINOUS, YOUR HIGHNESS.
SO THAT'S YOUR WISH, HUH?
EVEN IF THE WORLD'S GONNA GO TO HELL?

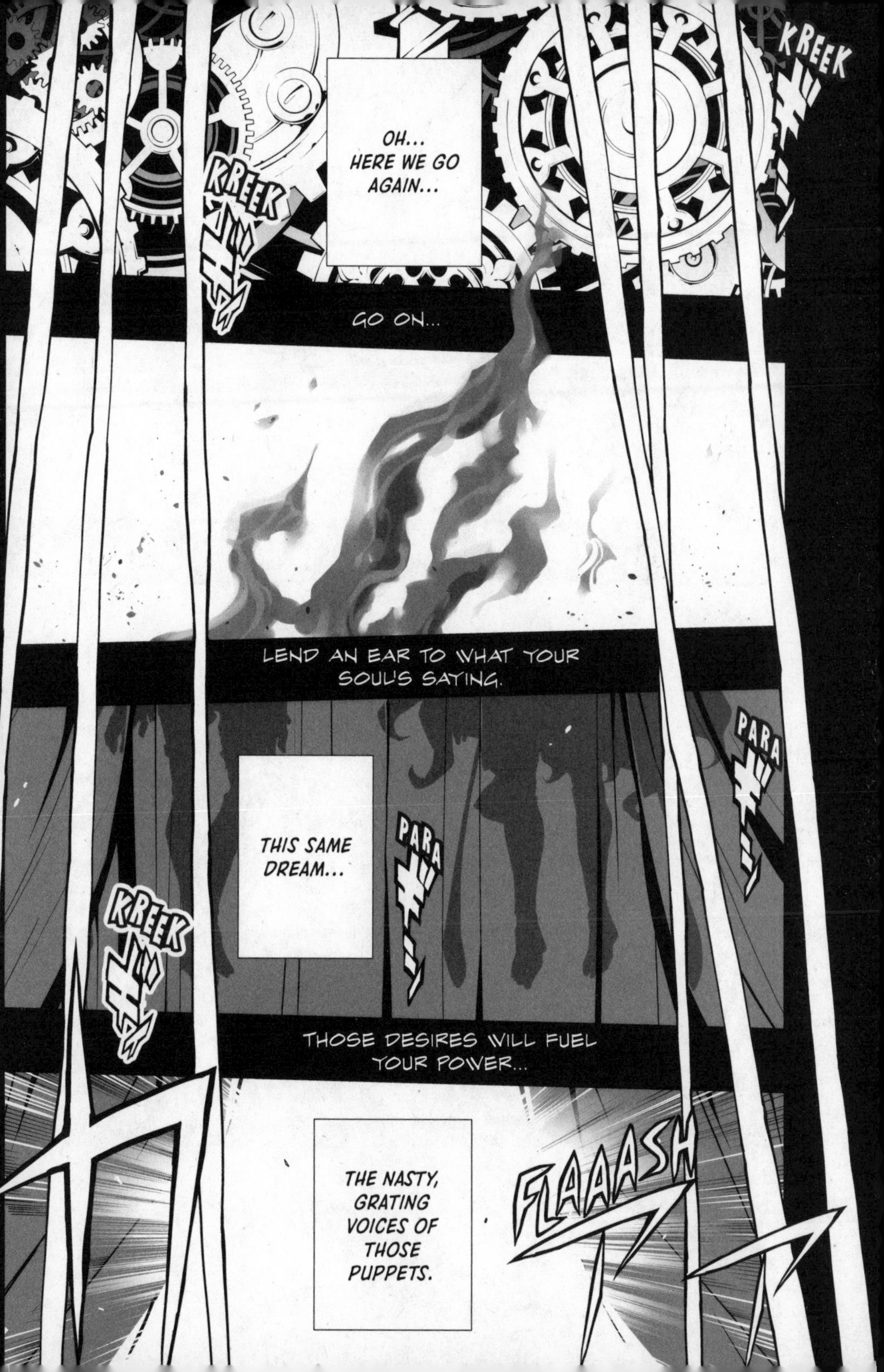
KREEK
OH... HERE WE GO AGAIN...
KREEK
GO ON...
LEND AN EAR TO WHAT YOUR SOUL'S SAYING.
PARA
PARA
THIS SAME DREAM...
KREEK
THOSE DESIRES WILL FUEL YOUR POWER...
FLAAASH
THE NASTY, GRATING VOICES OF THOSE PUPPETS.

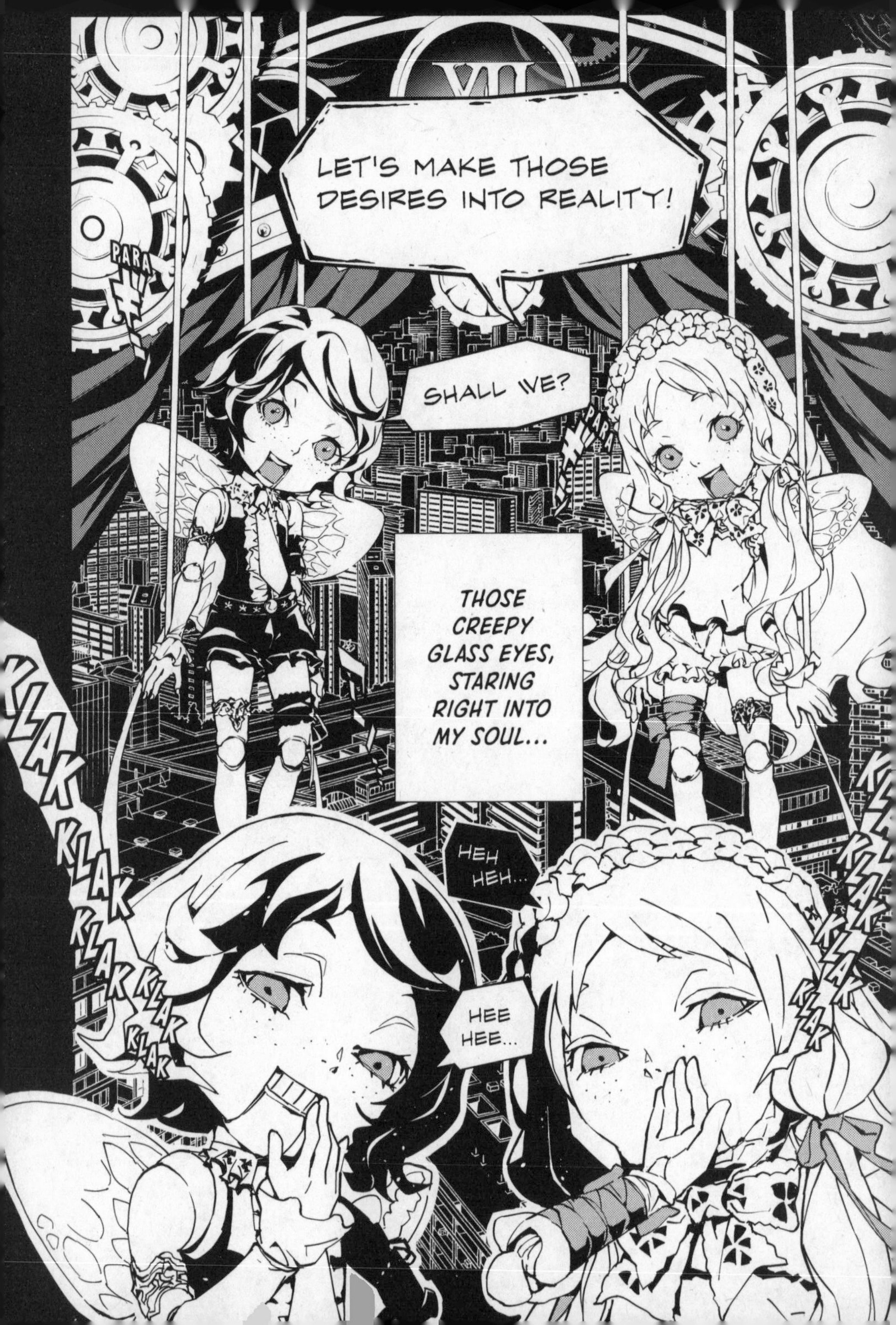
LET'S MAKE THOSE DESIRES INTO REALITY!
PARA
PARA
SHALL WE?
THOSE CREEPY GLASS EYES, STARING RIGHT INTO MY SOUL...
KLAK KLAK KLAK
HEH HEH...
HEE HEE...
KLAK KLAK KLAK KLAK

I HATE
THEM SO
MUCH...

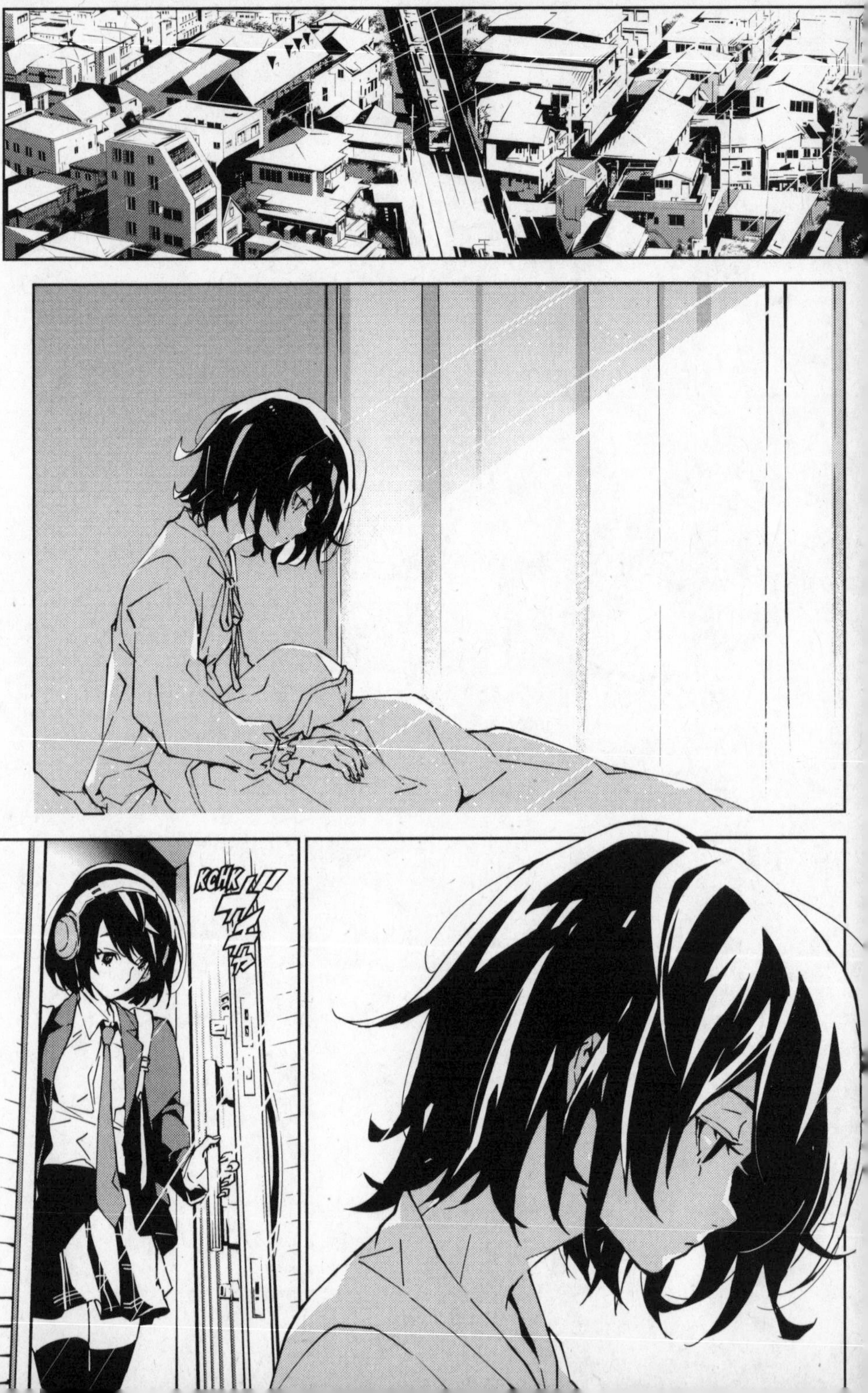
KCHK

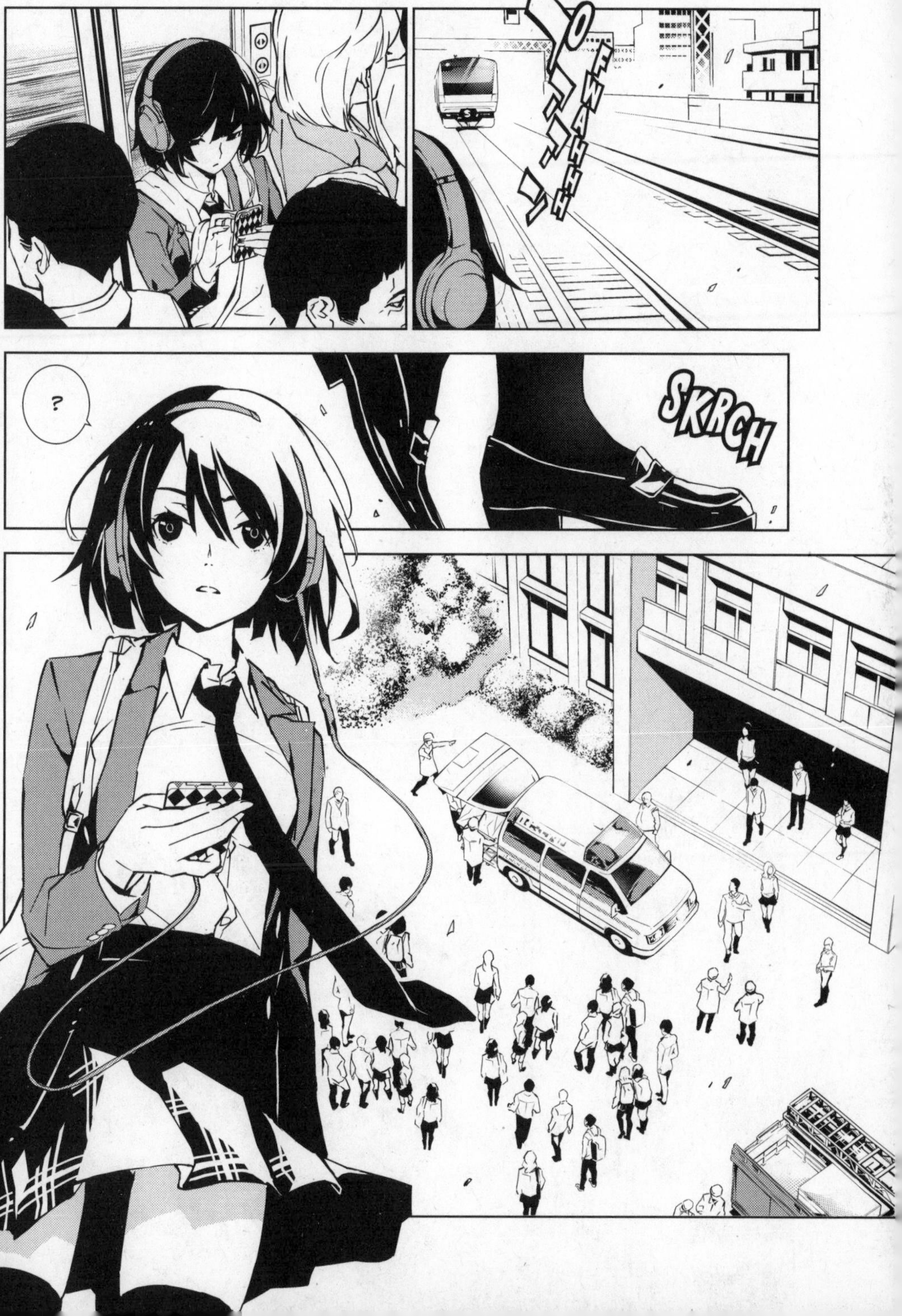
FWAHHH
SKRCH
?

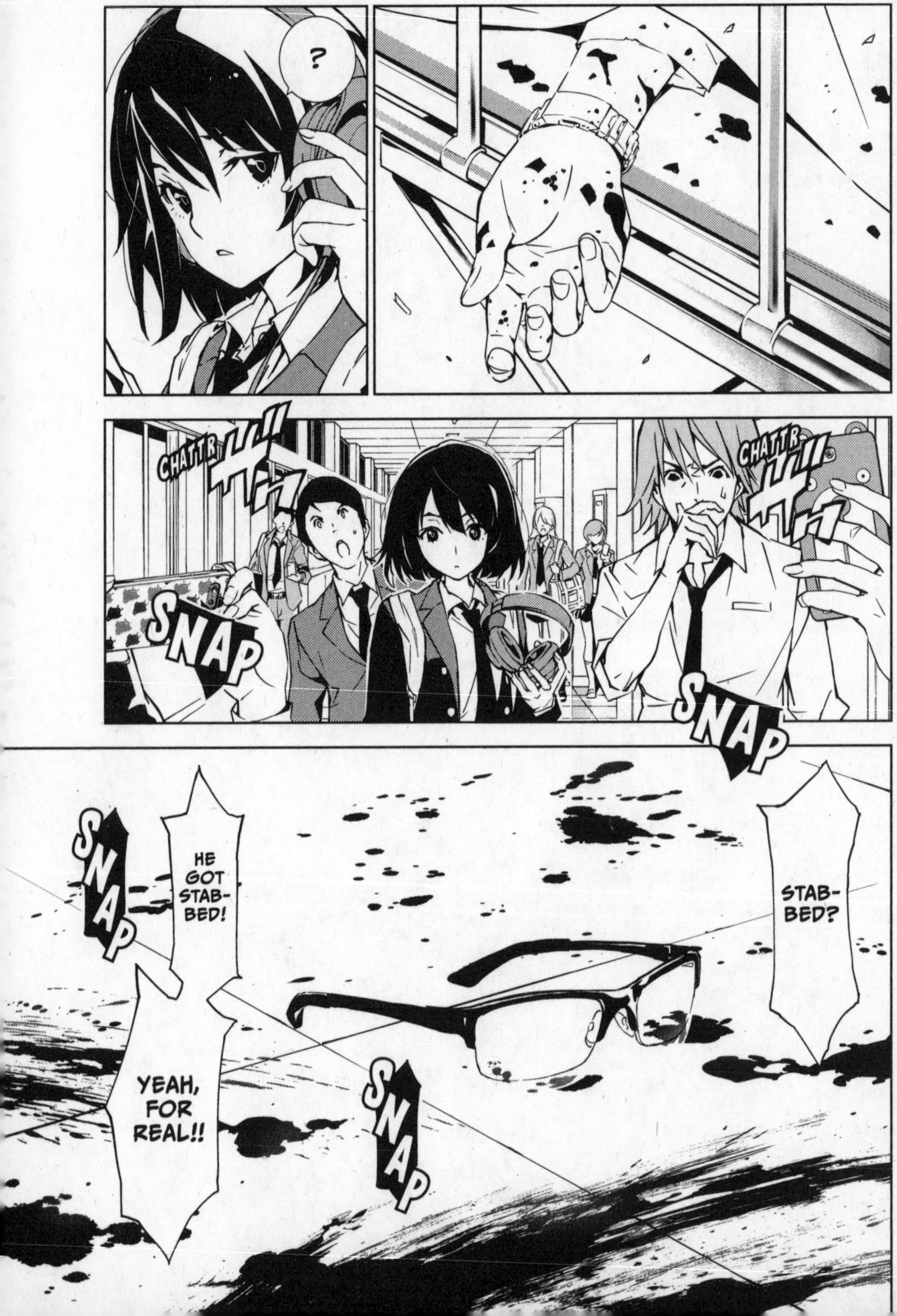

?
CHATTR
CHATTR
SNAP
SNAP
STAB-BED?
HE GOT STAB-BED!
SNAP
YEAH, FOR REAL!!
SNAP

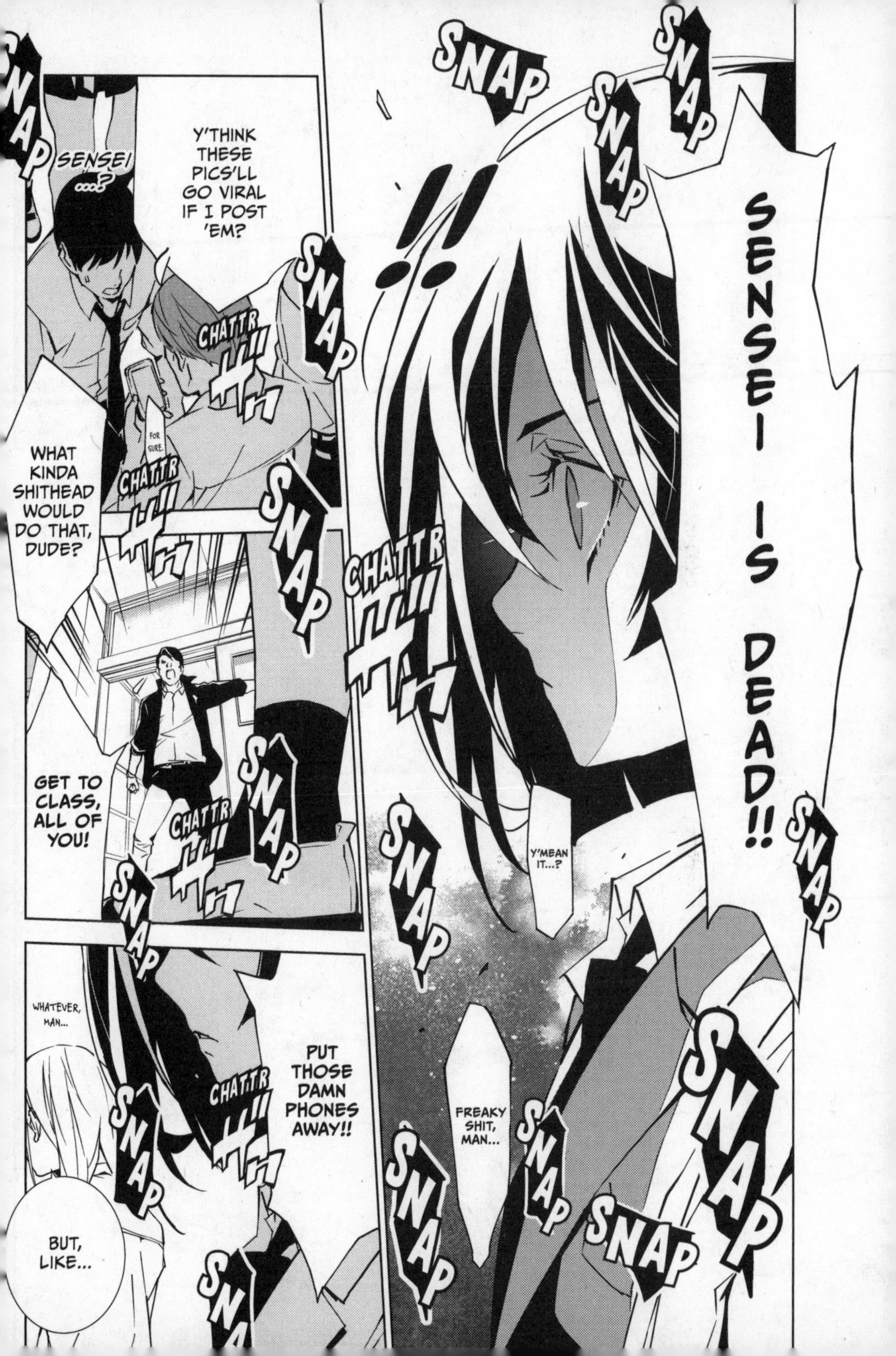
SNAP
SNAP SNAP
!!
SENSEI IS DEAD!!
Y'MEAN IT...?
CHATTR
FREAKY SHIT, MAN...
SNAP SNAP SNAP
Y'THINK THESE PICS'LL GO VIRAL IF I POST 'EM?
SENSEI ...?
CHATTR
FOR SURE.
WHAT KINDA SHITHEAD WOULD DO THAT, DUDE?
CHATTR
SNAP
GET TO CLASS, ALL OF YOU!
CHATTR
SNAP
PUT THOSE DAMN PHONES AWAY!!
WHATEVER, MAN...
CHATTR
BUT, LIKE...
SNAP

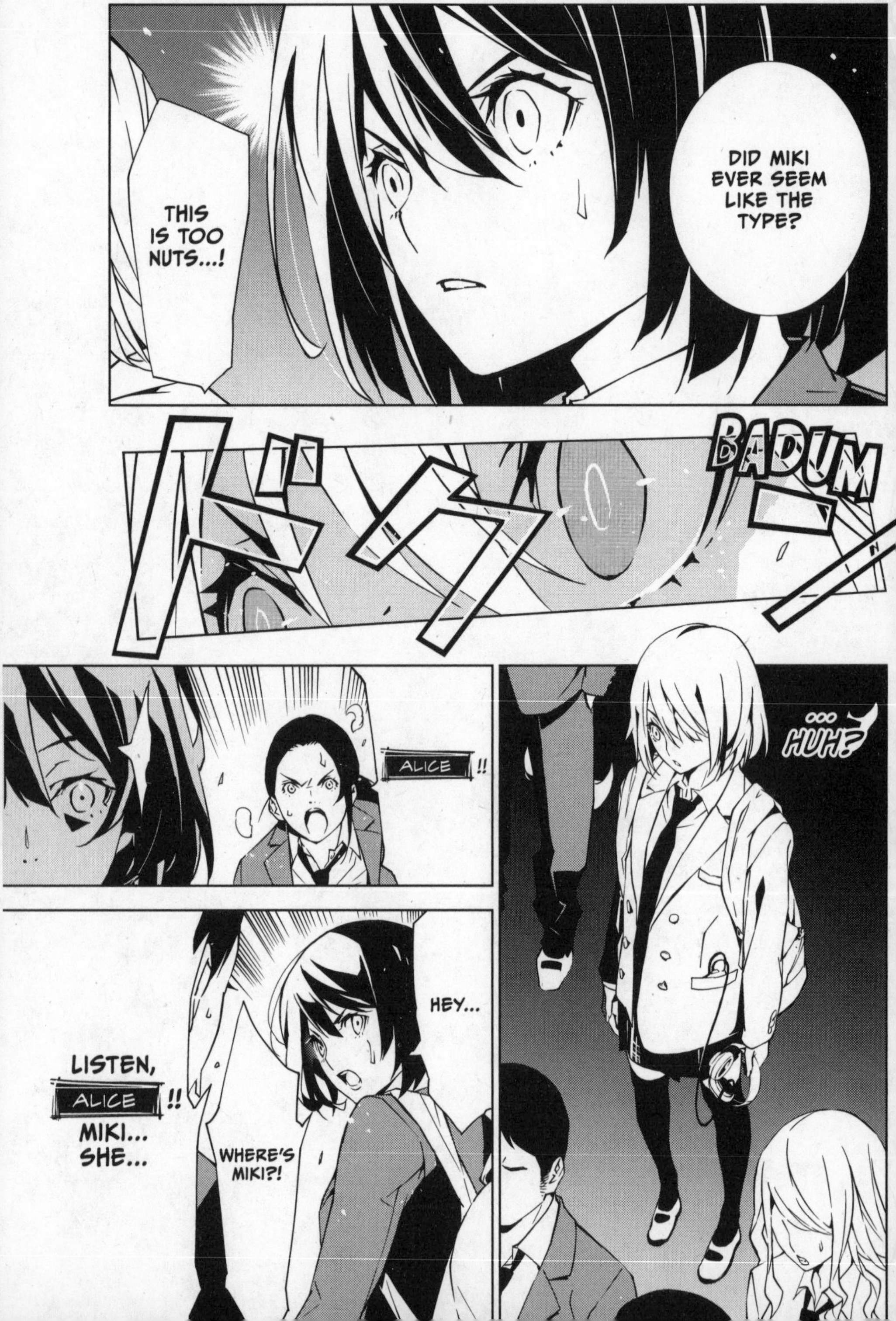
DID MIKI EVER SEEM LIKE THE TYPE?
THIS IS TOO NUTS...!
BADUM
... HUH?
ALICE!!
HEY...
WHERE'S MIKI?!
LISTEN, ALICE!!
MIKI... SHE...

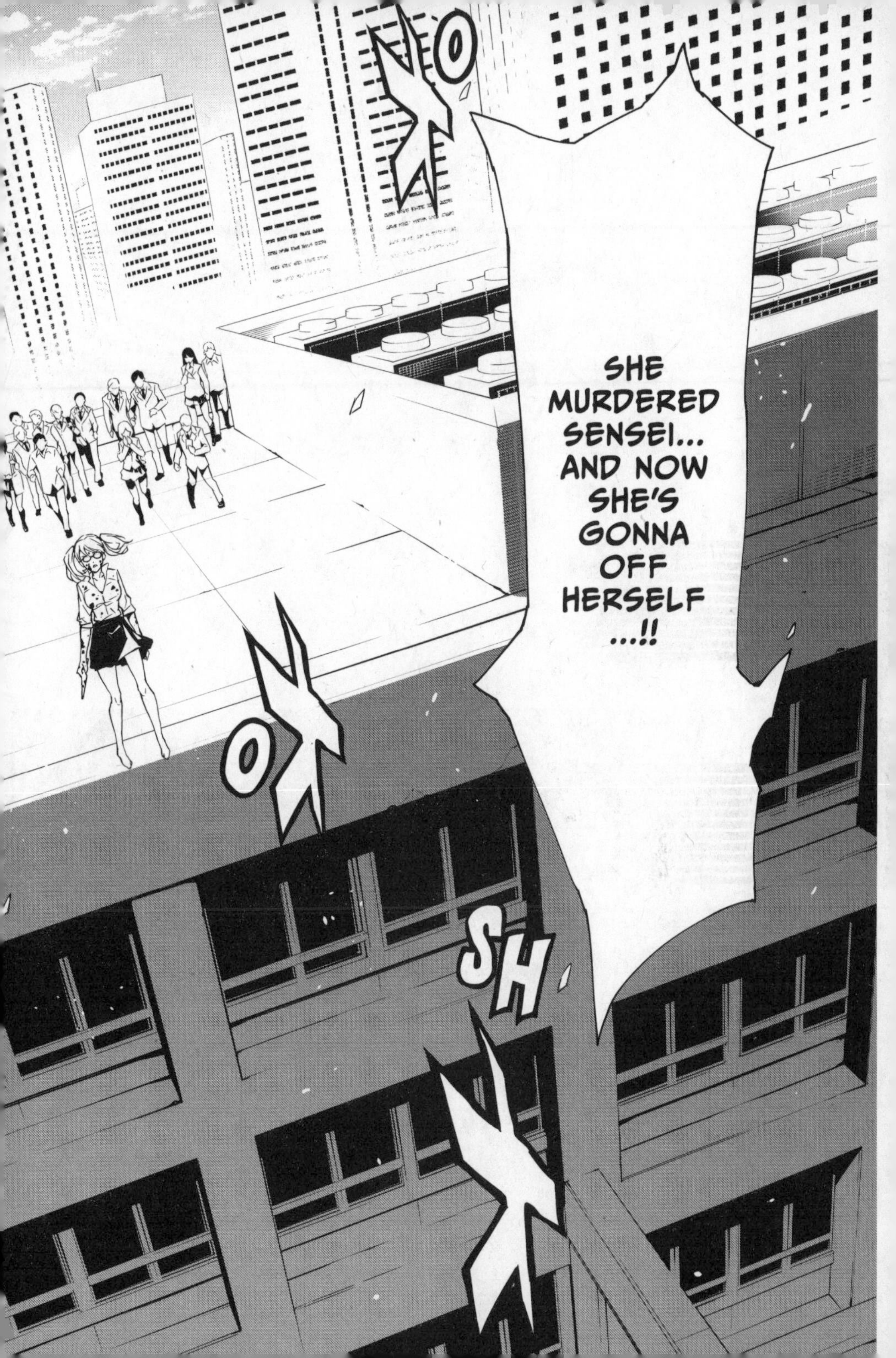
SHE MURDERED SENSEI... AND NOW SHE'S GONNA OFF HERSELF ...!!
SH

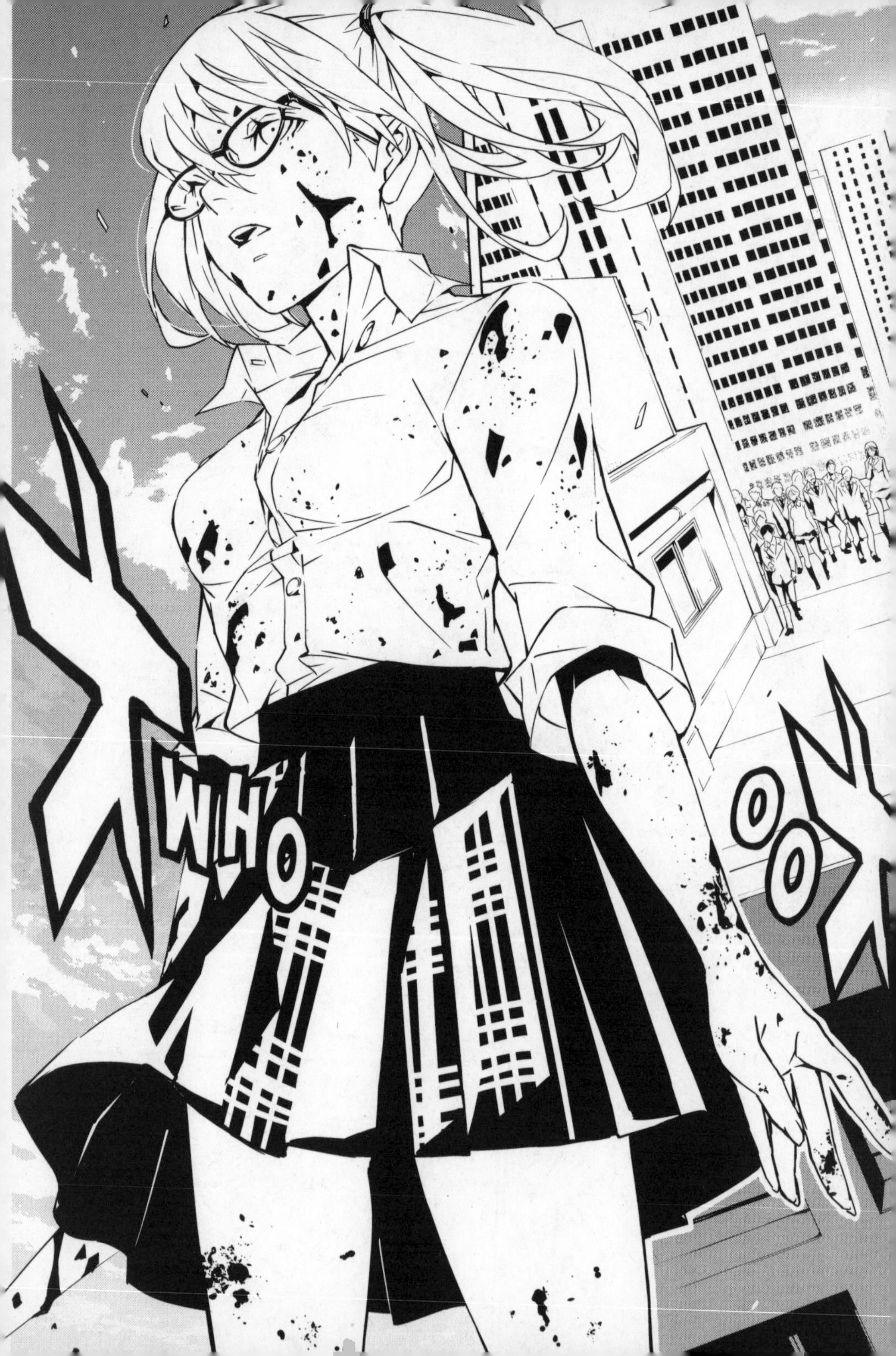
WHOOO

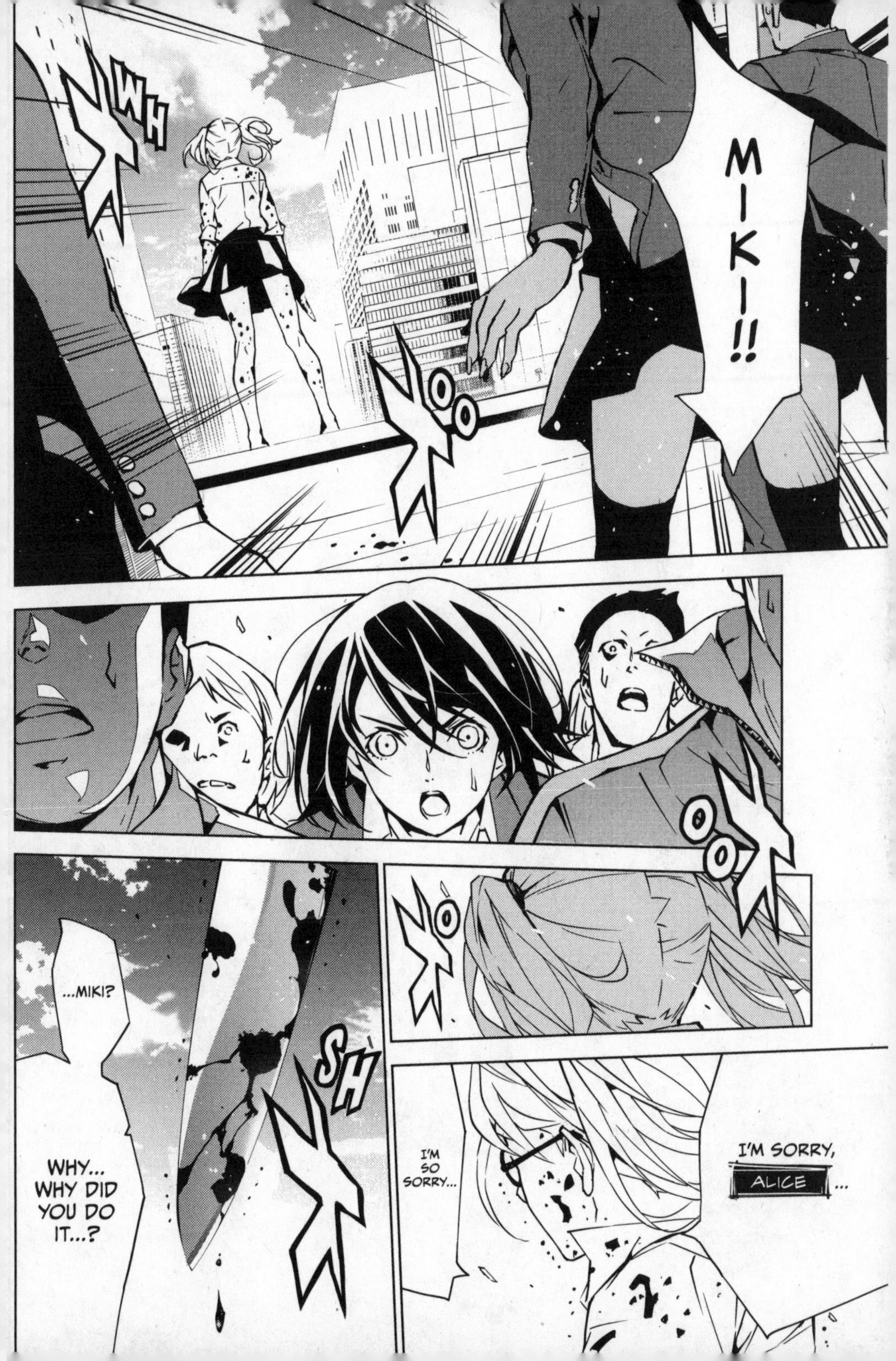
MIKI!!
OO
WH
OO
I'M SORRY, ALICE...
I'M SO SORRY...
...MIKI?
SH
WHY... WHY DID YOU DO IT...?

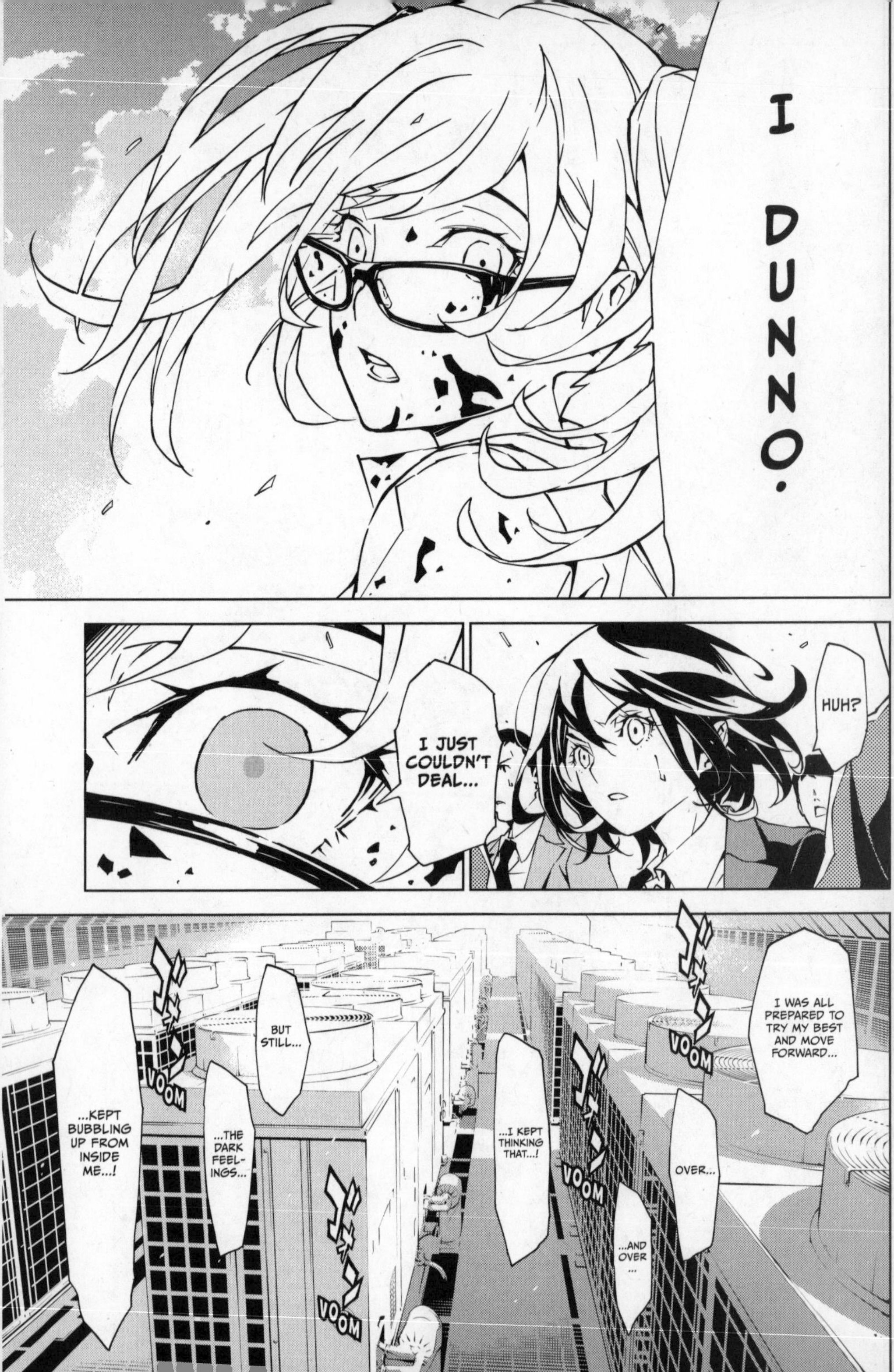
I DUNNO.
HUH?
I JUST COULDN'T DEAL...
I WAS ALL PREPARED TO TRY MY BEST AND MOVE FORWARD...
VOOM
OVER...
...AND OVER ...
VOOM
...I KEPT THINKING THAT...!
BUT STILL...
VOOM
...THE DARK FEEL- INGS...
...KEPT BUBBLING UP FROM INSIDE ME...!
VOOM

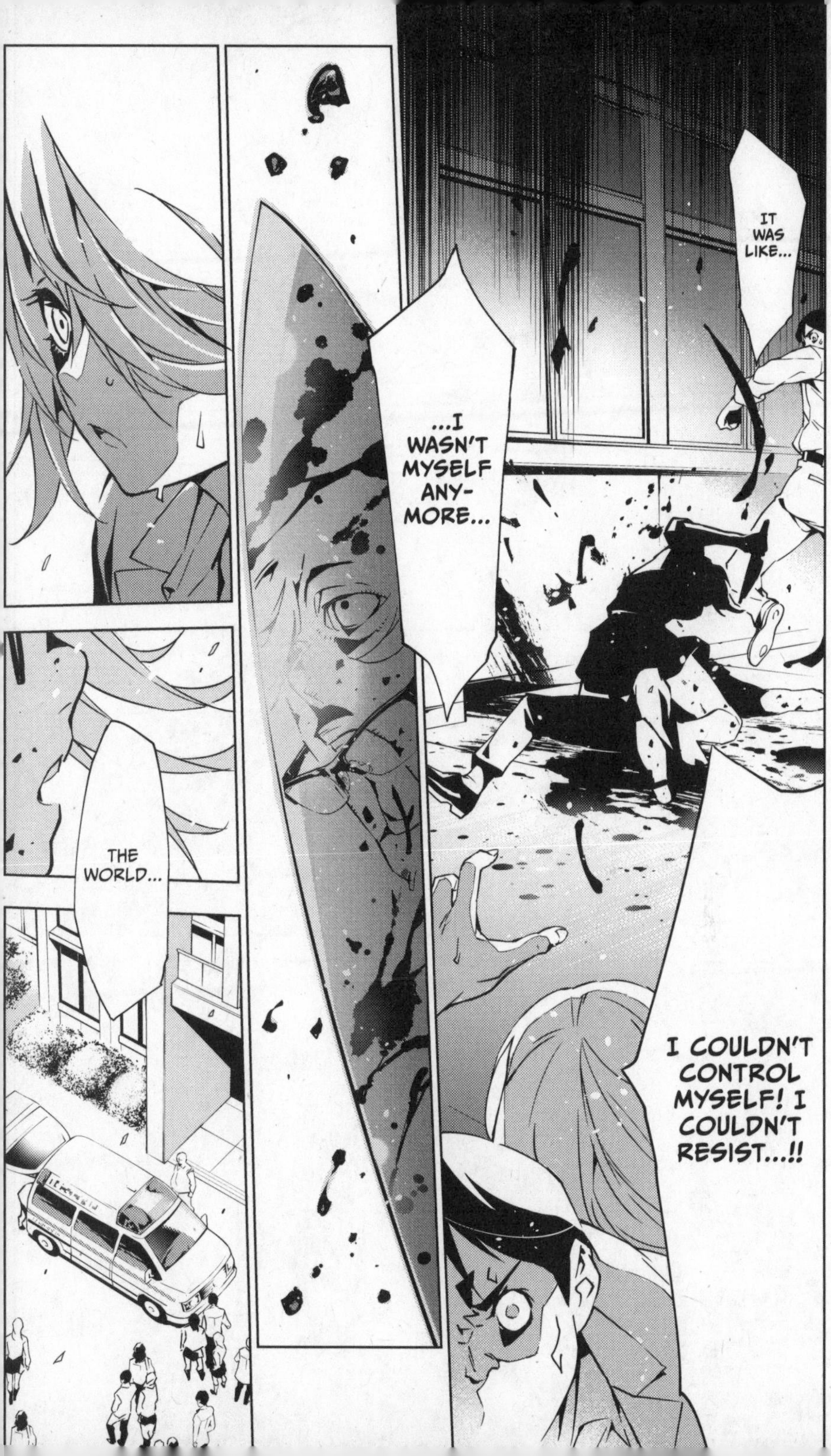
IT WAS LIKE...
...I WASN'T MYSELF ANYMORE...
I COULDN'T CONTROL MYSELF! I COULDN'T RESIST...!!
THE WORLD...

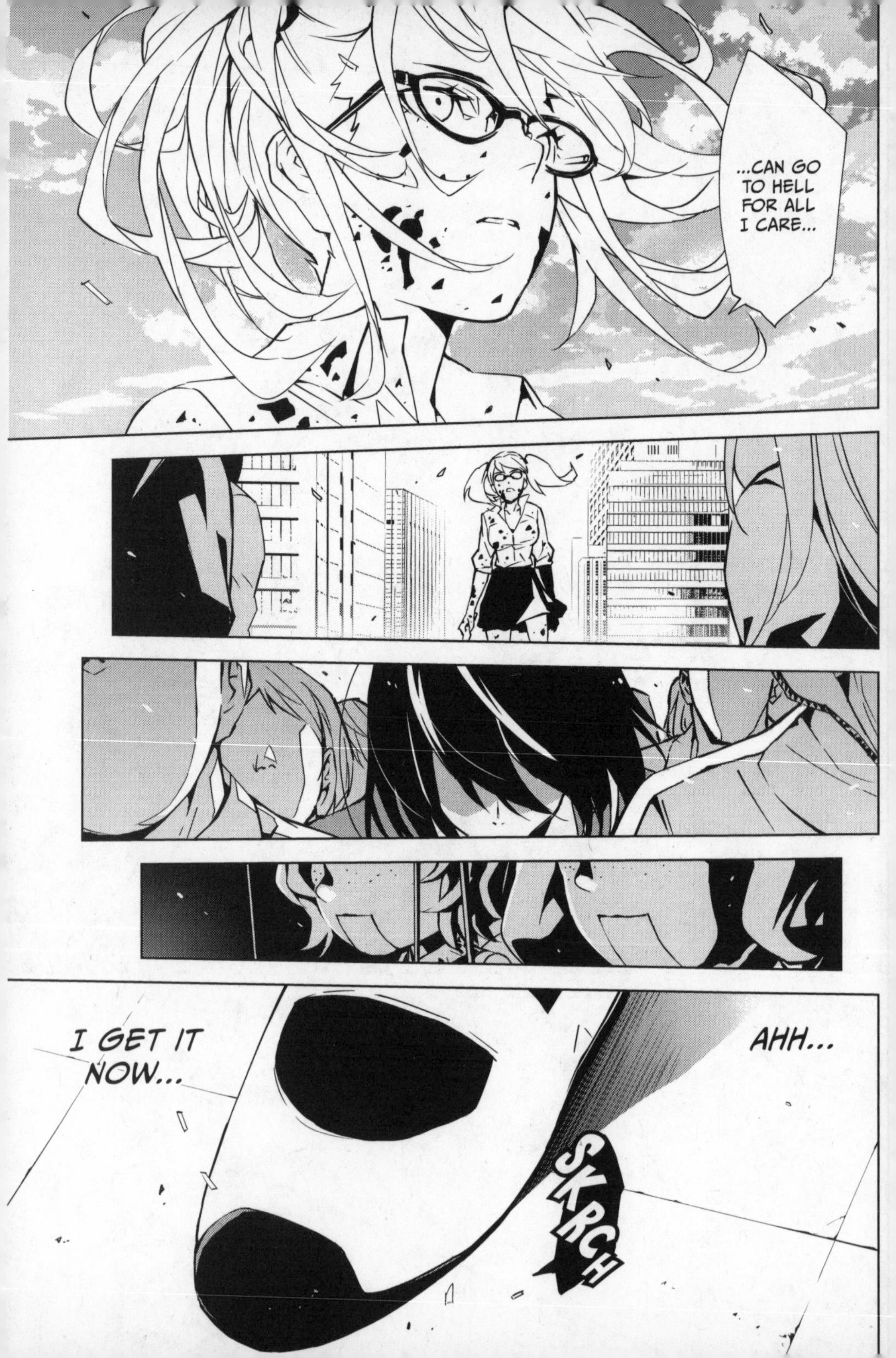
...CAN GO TO HELL FOR ALL I CARE...
AHH...
I GET IT NOW...
SKRCH

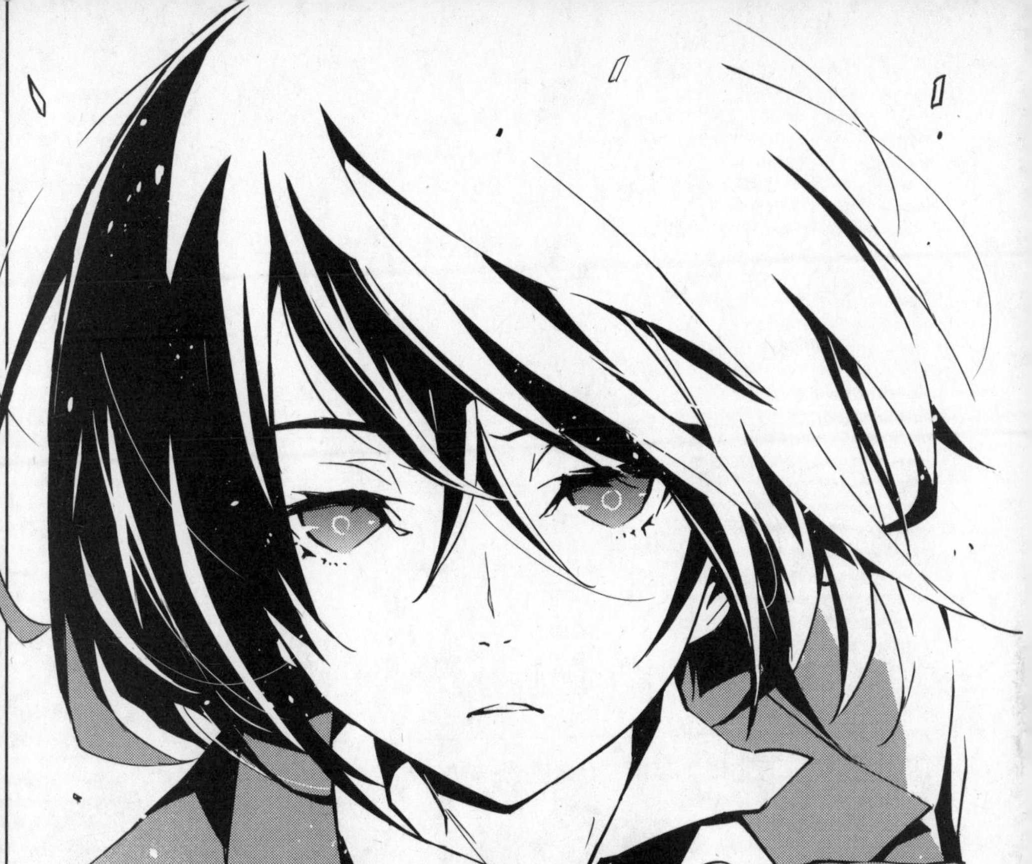

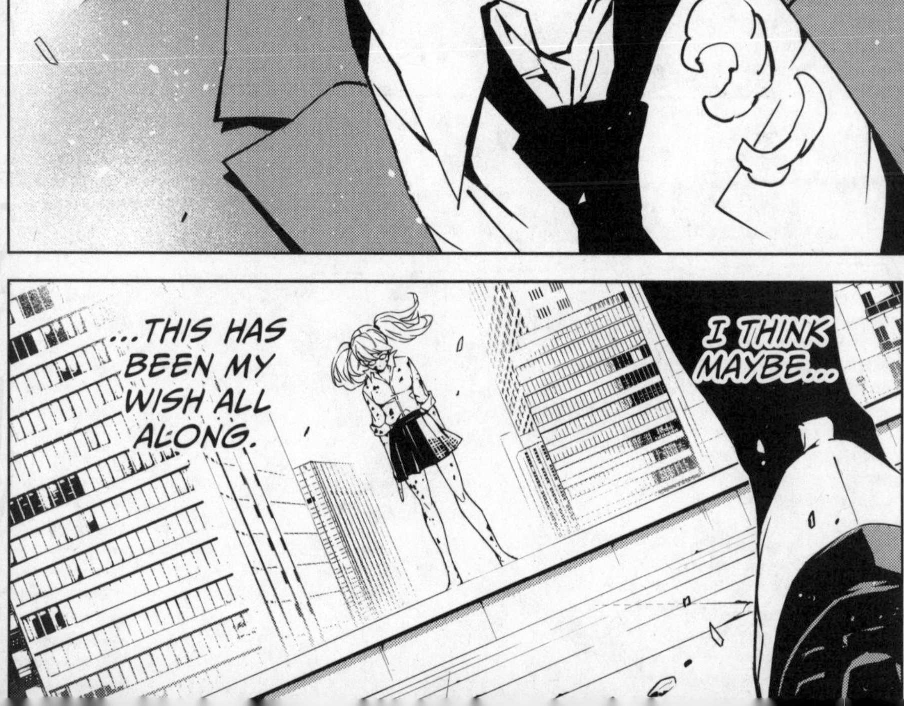
I THINK MAYBE...
...THIS HAS BEEN MY WISH ALL ALONG.

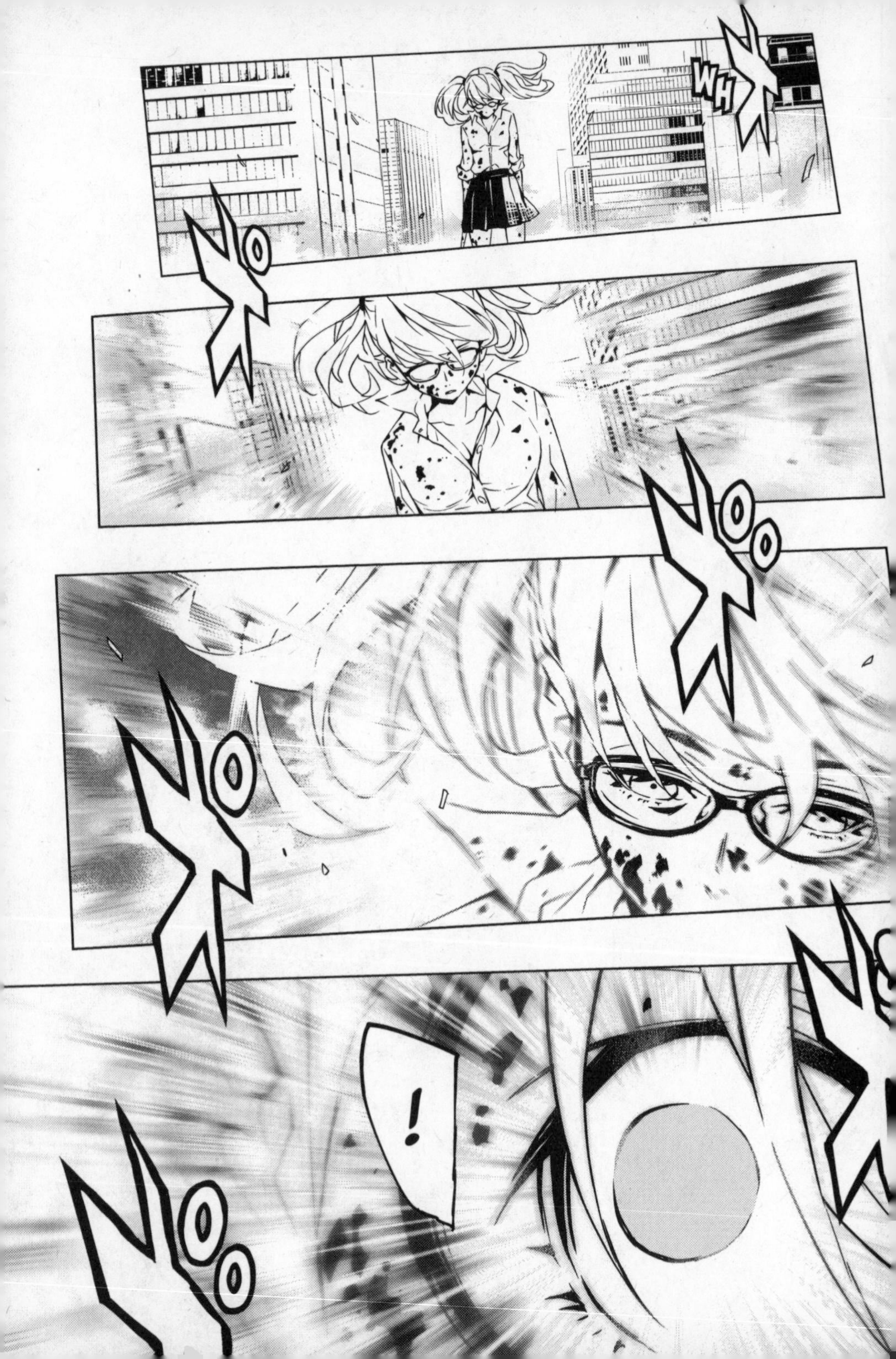
WH
!

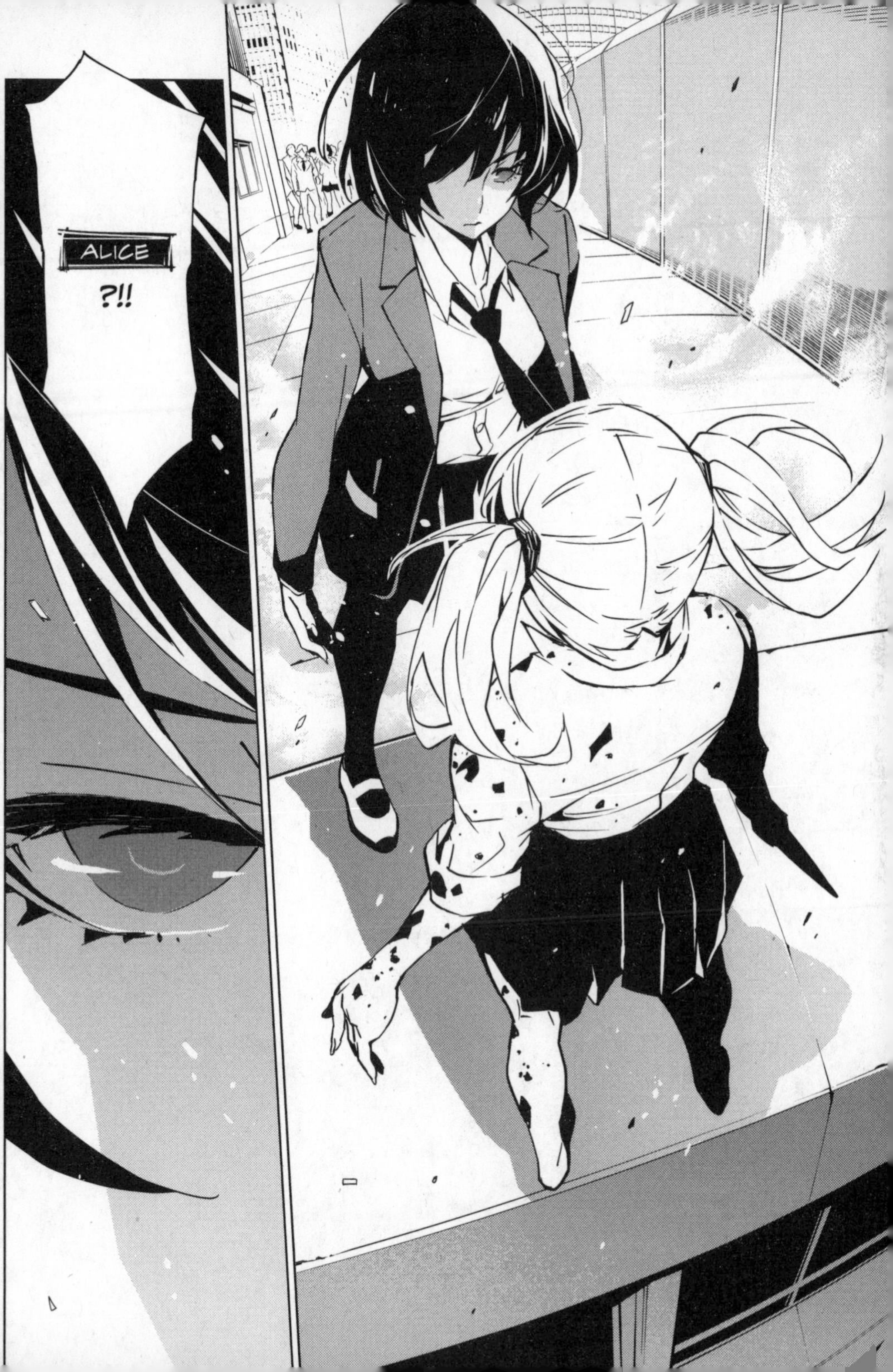
ALICE
?!!

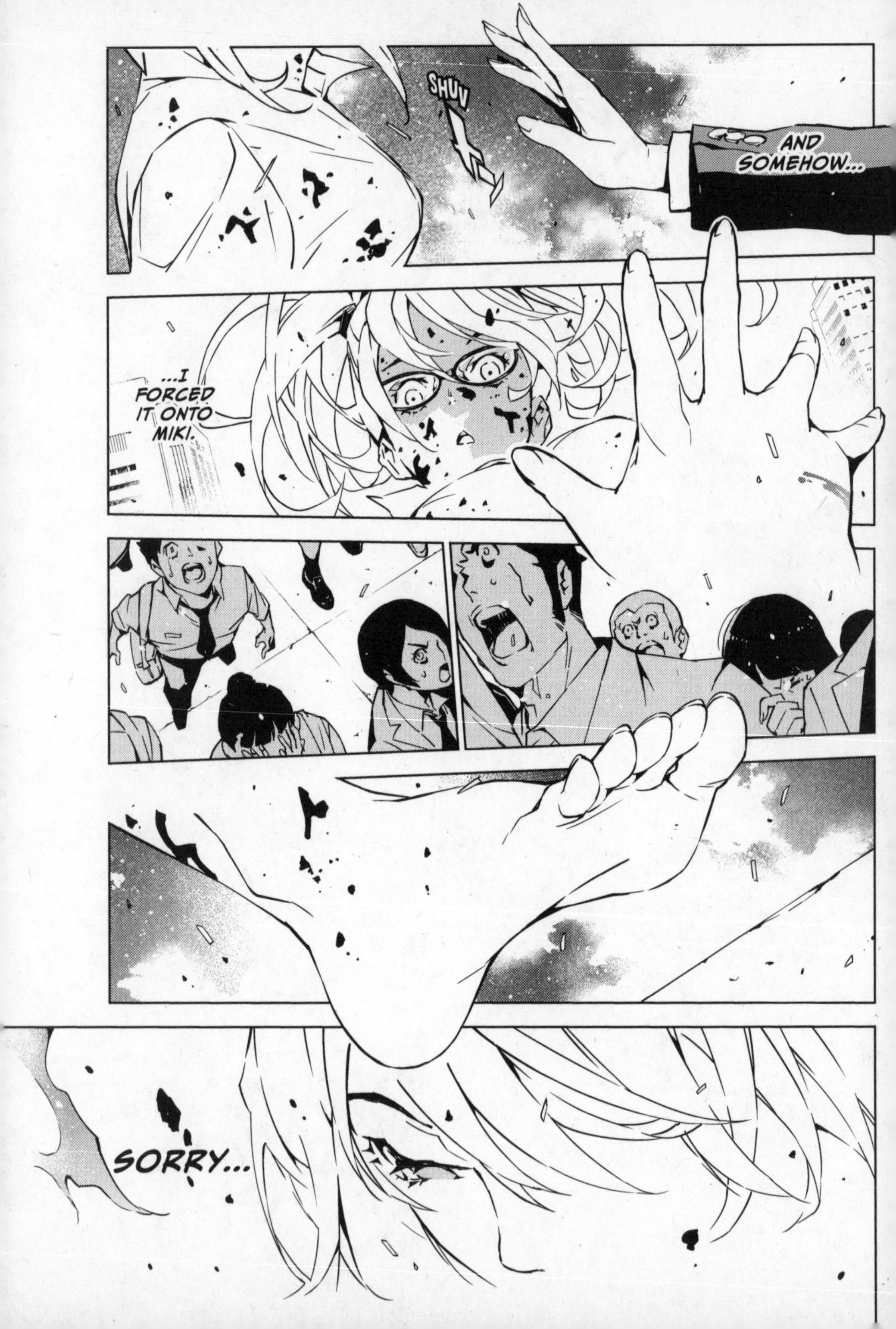
SHUV
AND SOMEHOW...
...I FORCED IT ONTO MIKI.
SORRY...

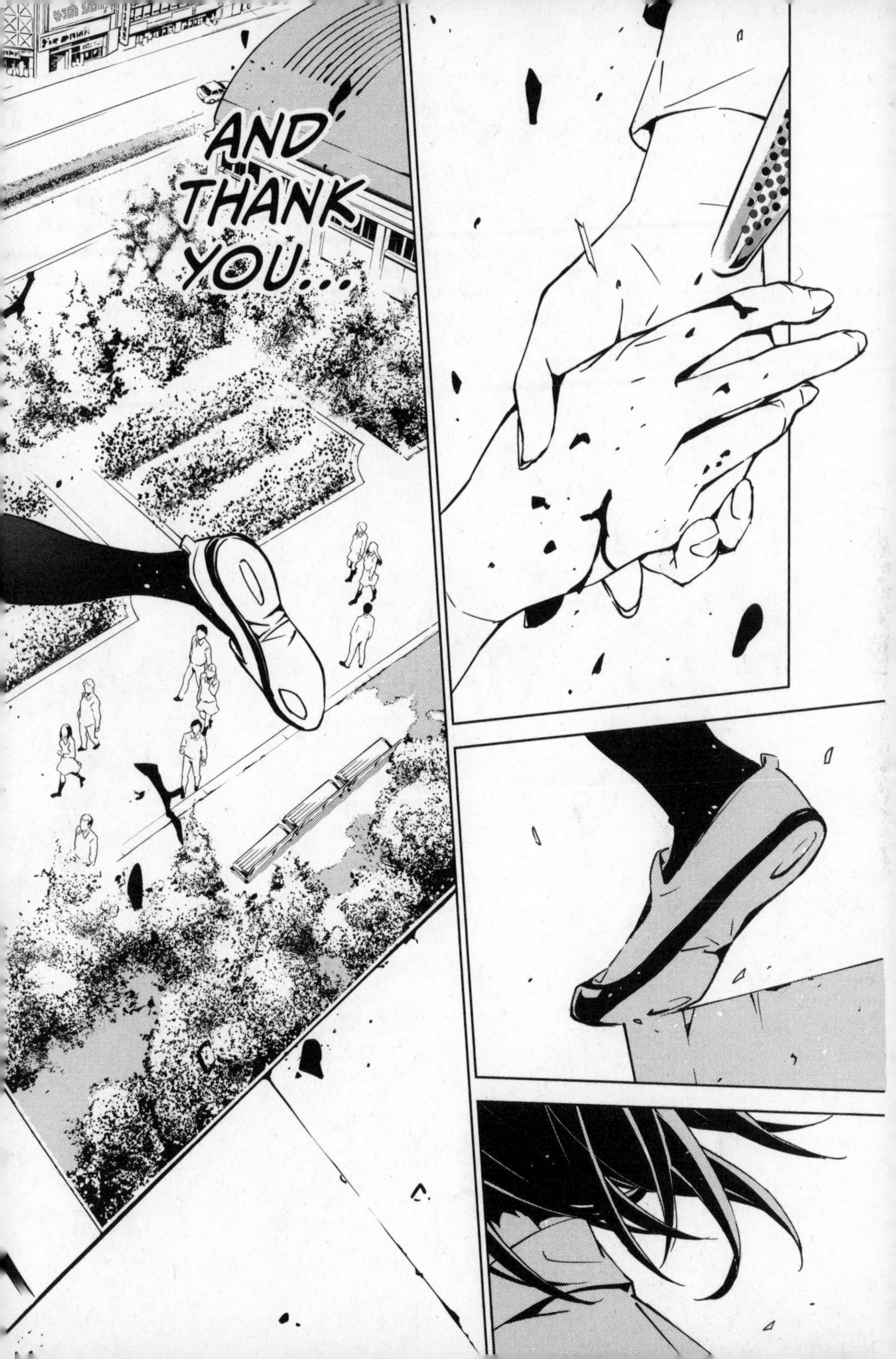
AND THANK YOU...

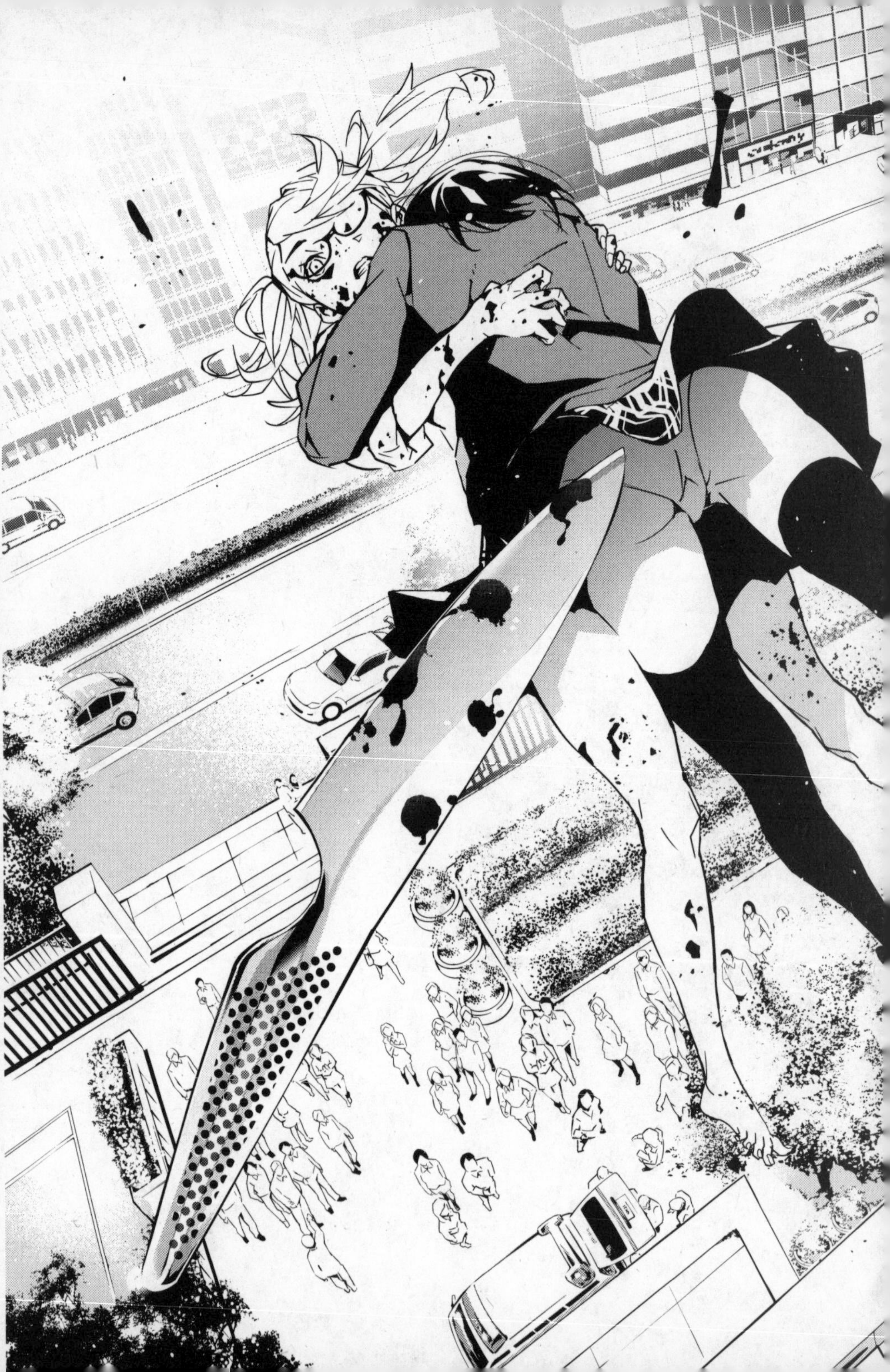

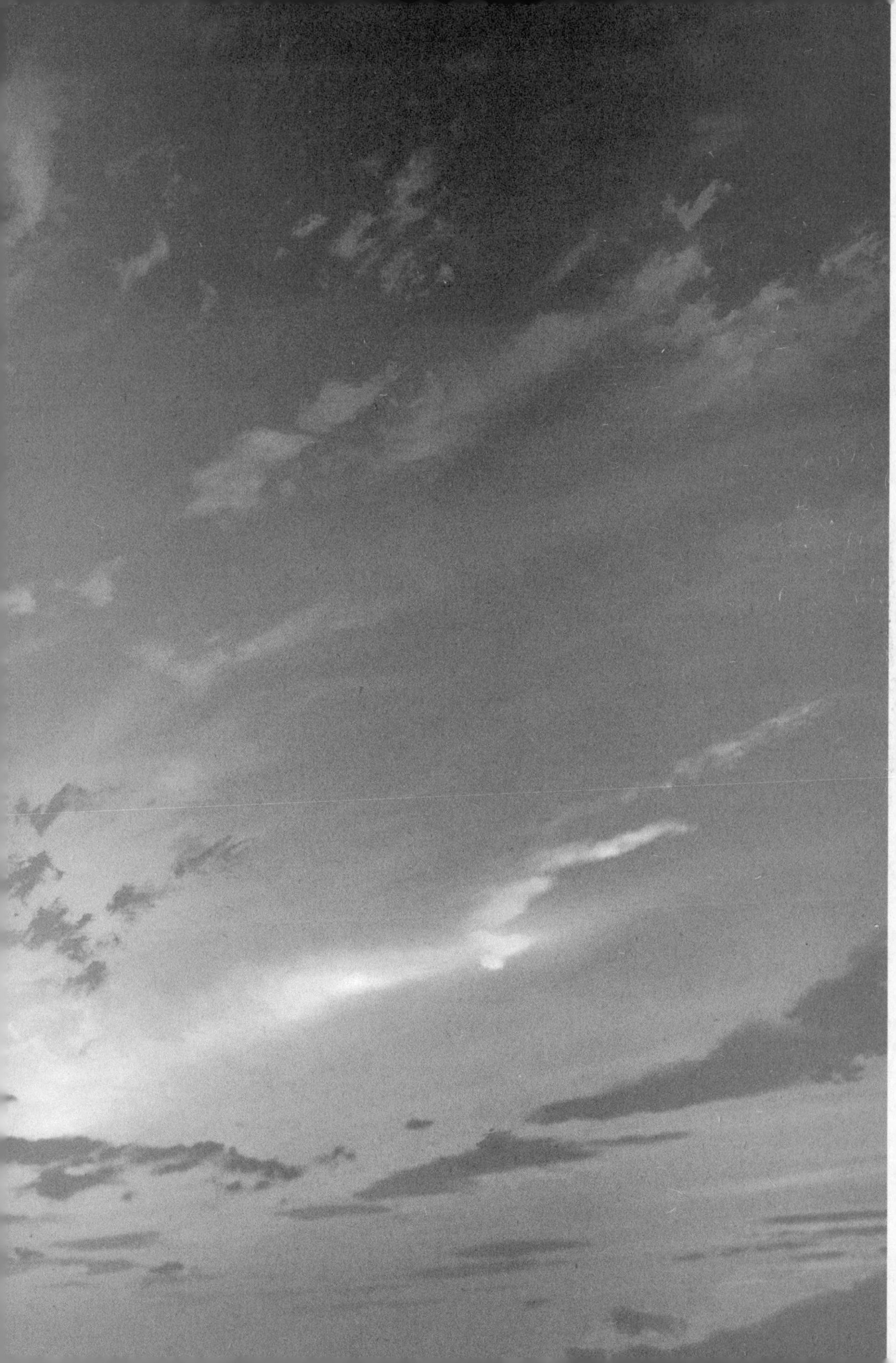

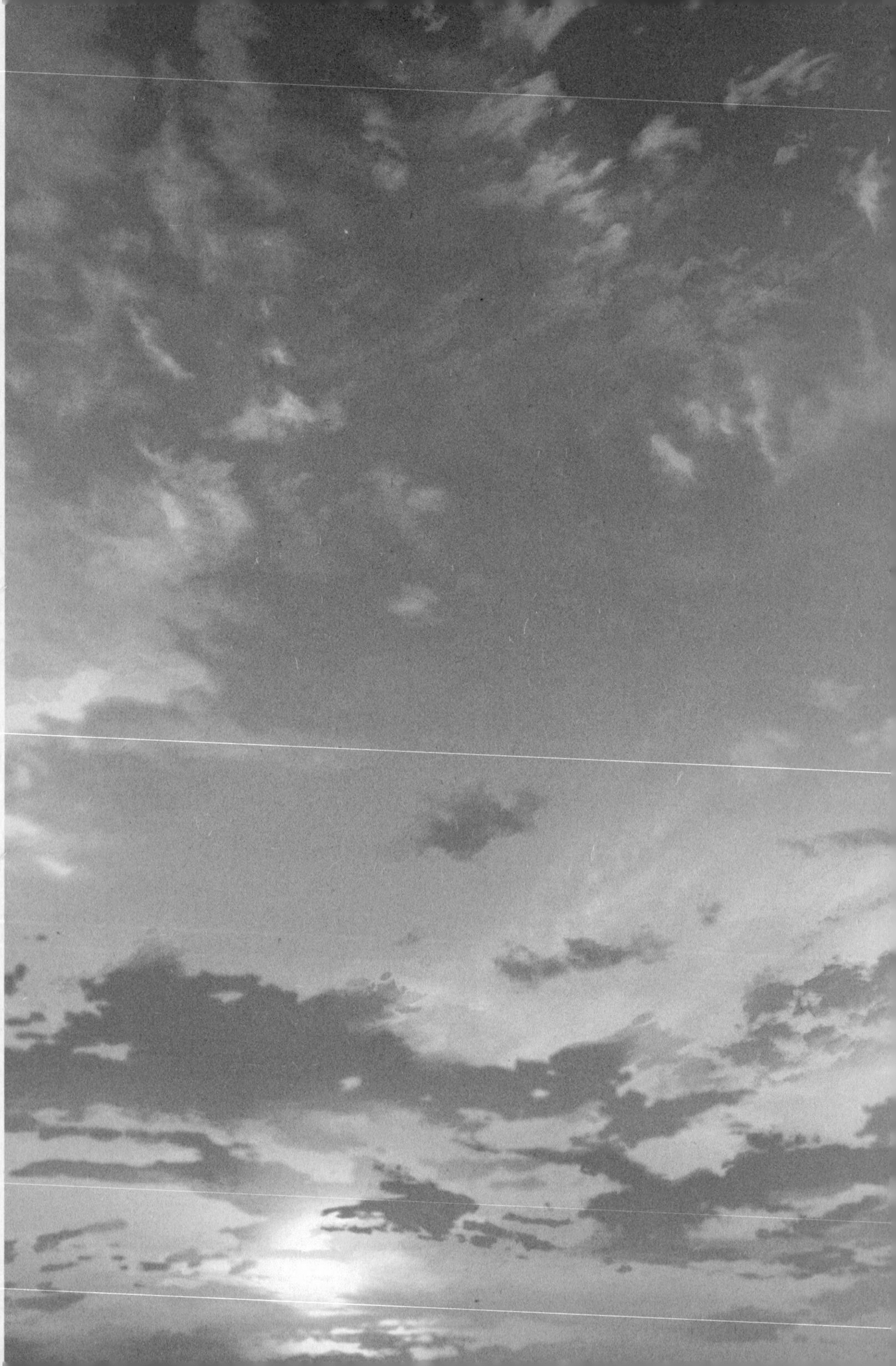

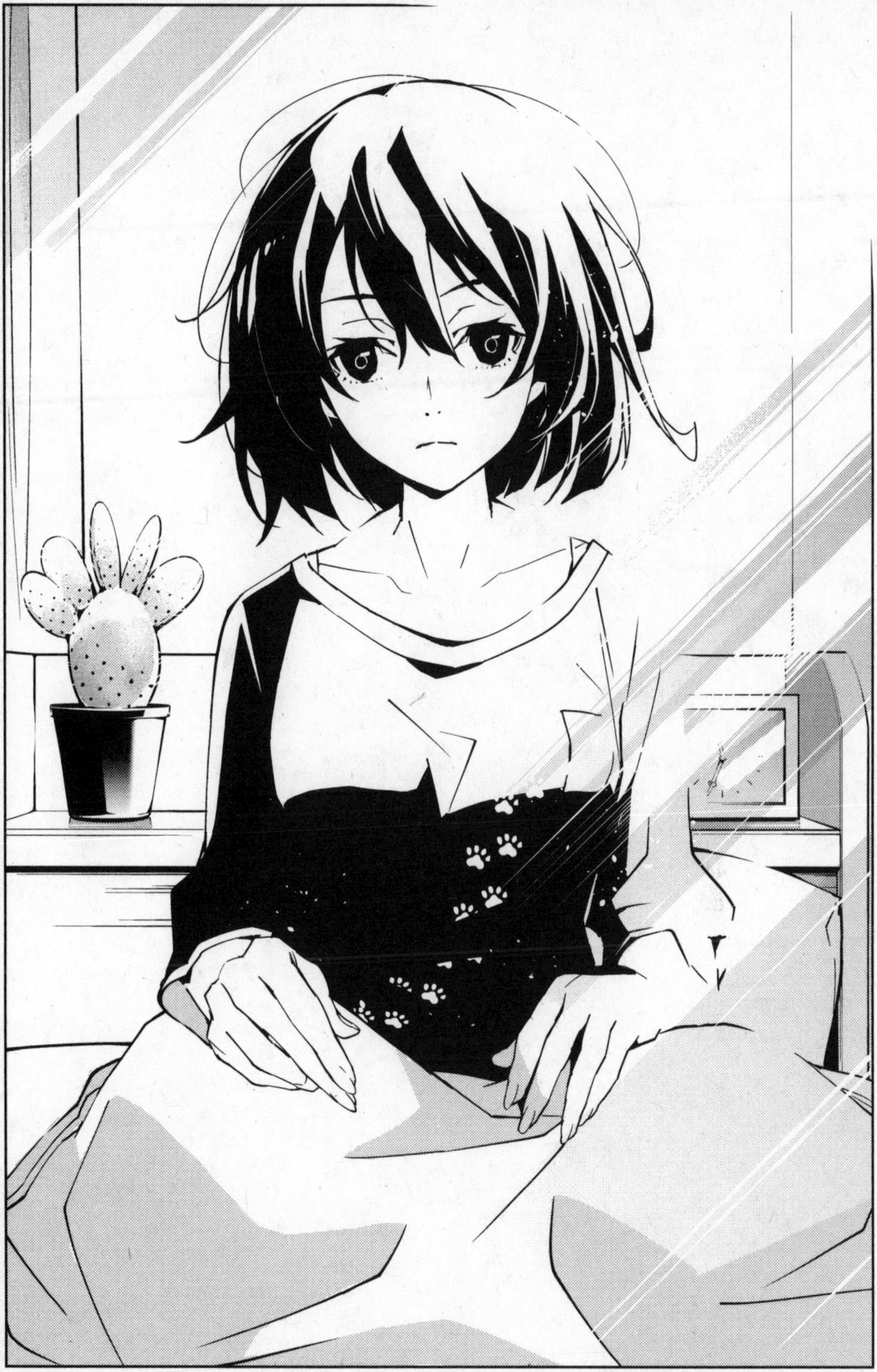

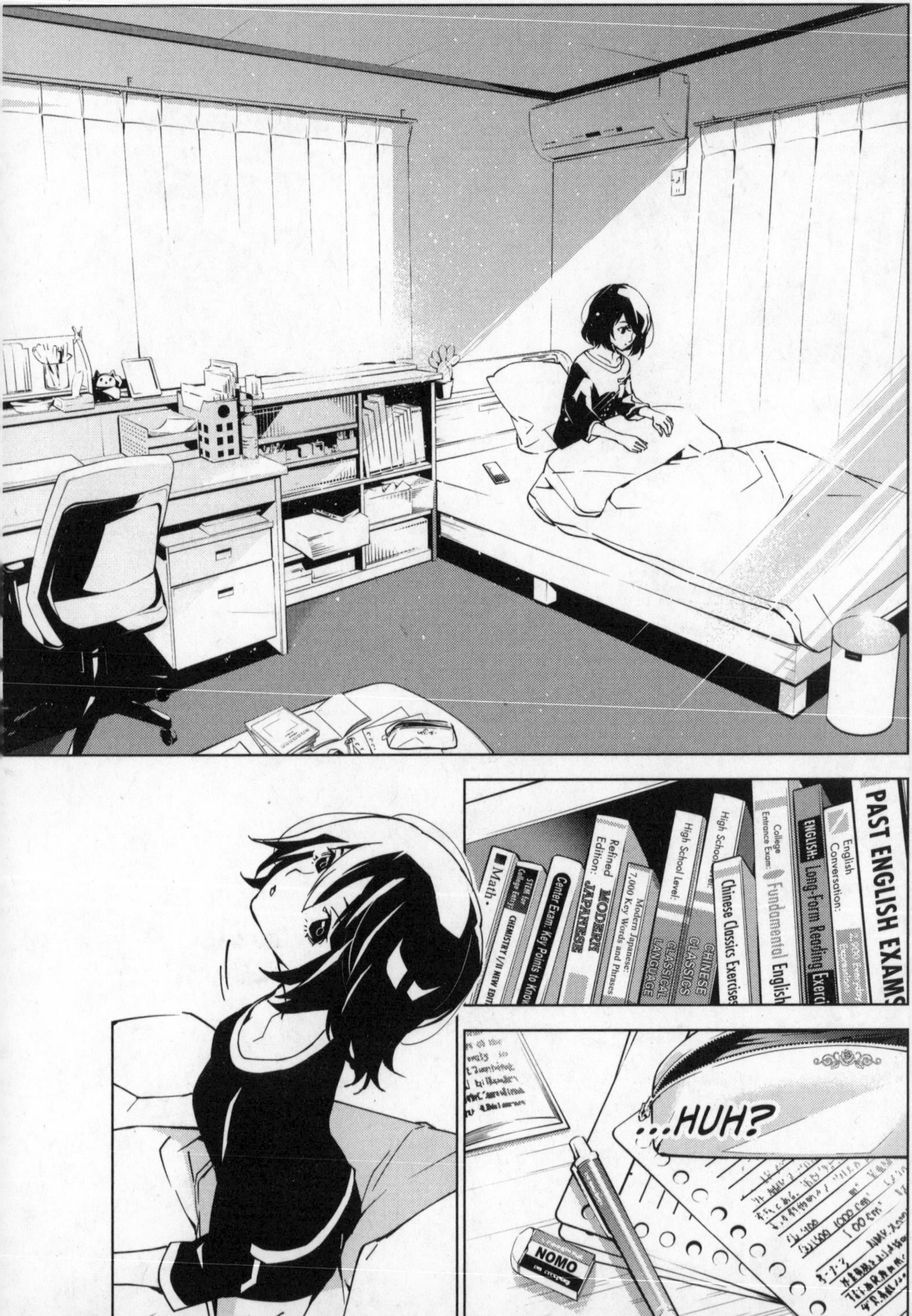
PAST ENGLISH EXAMS
English Conversation:
ENGLISH: Long-Form Reading
College Entrance Exam: Fundamental English
Chinese Classics Exercises
High School Level: CHINESE CLASSICS
High School Level: CLASSICAL LANGUAGE
Modern Japanese: 7,000 Key Words and Phrases
Refined Edition: MODERN JAPANESE
Center Exam: Key Points to
CHEMISTRY I/II
Math
...HUH?
NOMO

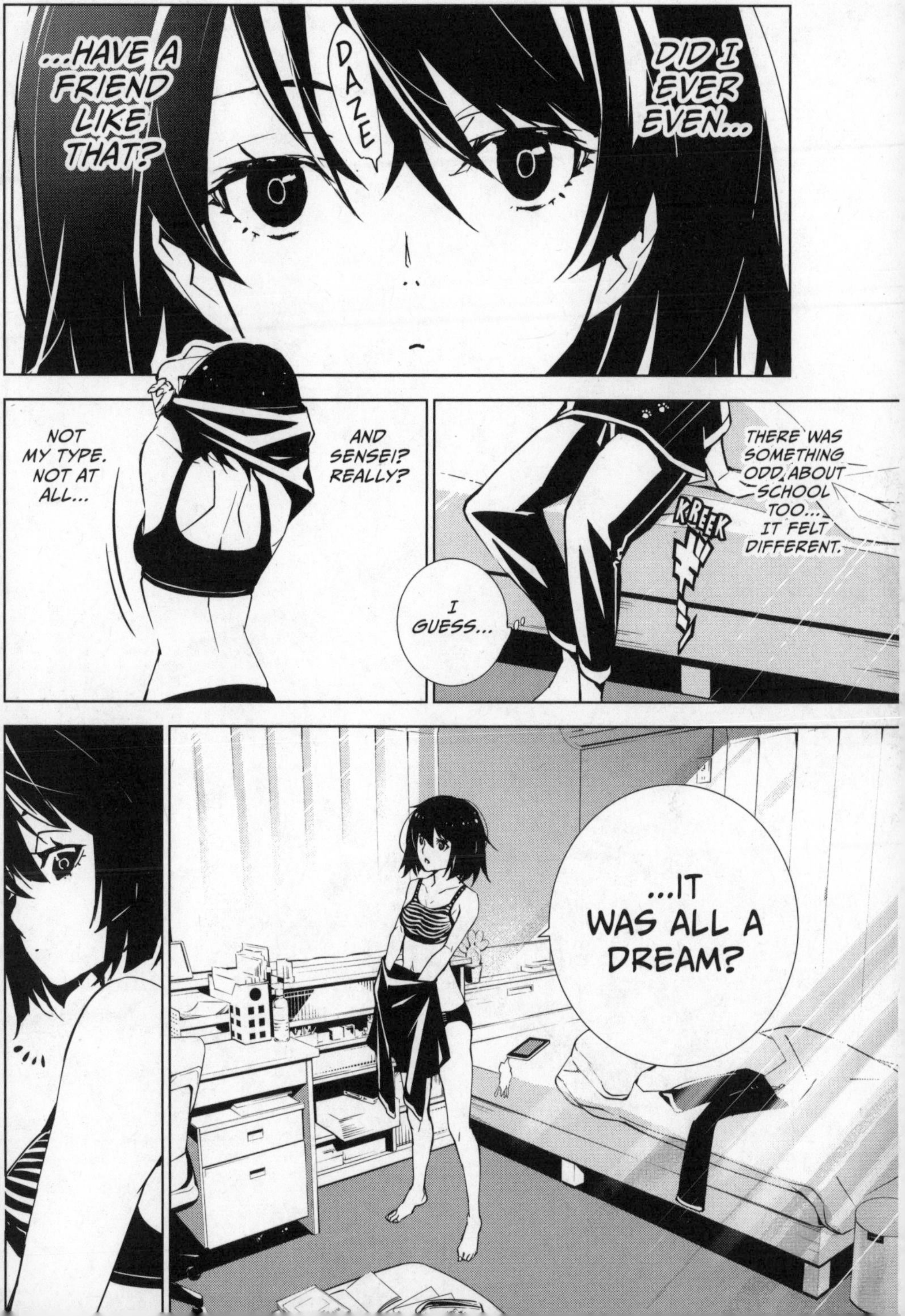
DID I EVER EVEN...
DAZE
...HAVE A FRIEND LIKE THAT?
THERE WAS SOMETHING ODD ABOUT SCHOOL TOO... IT FELT DIFFERENT.
KREEK
I GUESS...
AND SENSEI? REALLY?
NOT MY TYPE. NOT AT ALL...
...IT WAS ALL A DREAM?

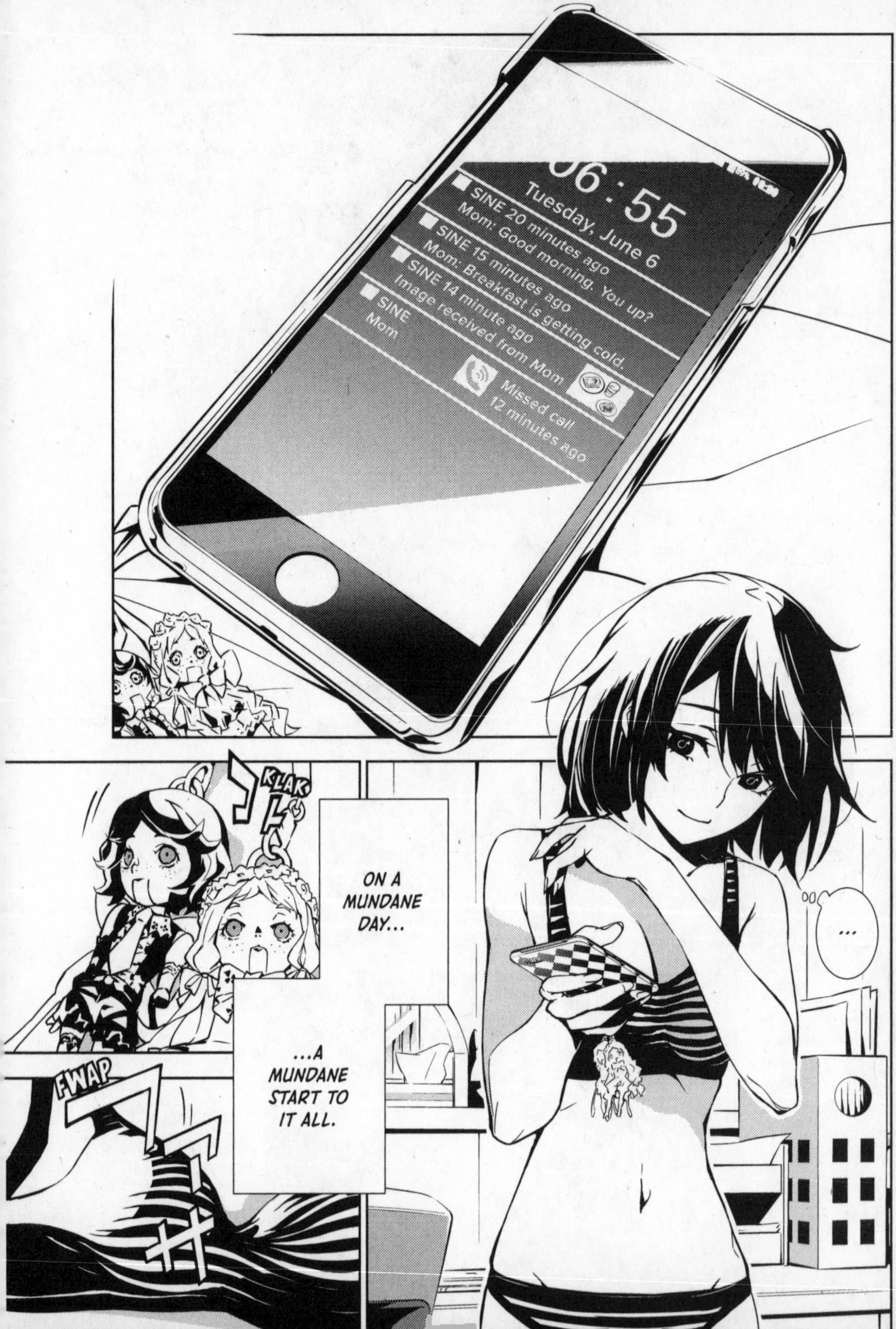
06:55
Tuesday, June 6
SINE 20 minutes ago
Mom: Good morning. You up?
SINE 15 minutes ago
Mom: Breakfast is getting cold.
SINE 14 minute ago
Image received from Mom
SINE
Mom
Missed call
12 minutes ago
...
ON A MUNDANE DAY...
...A MUNDANE START TO IT ALL.
KLAK
FWAP

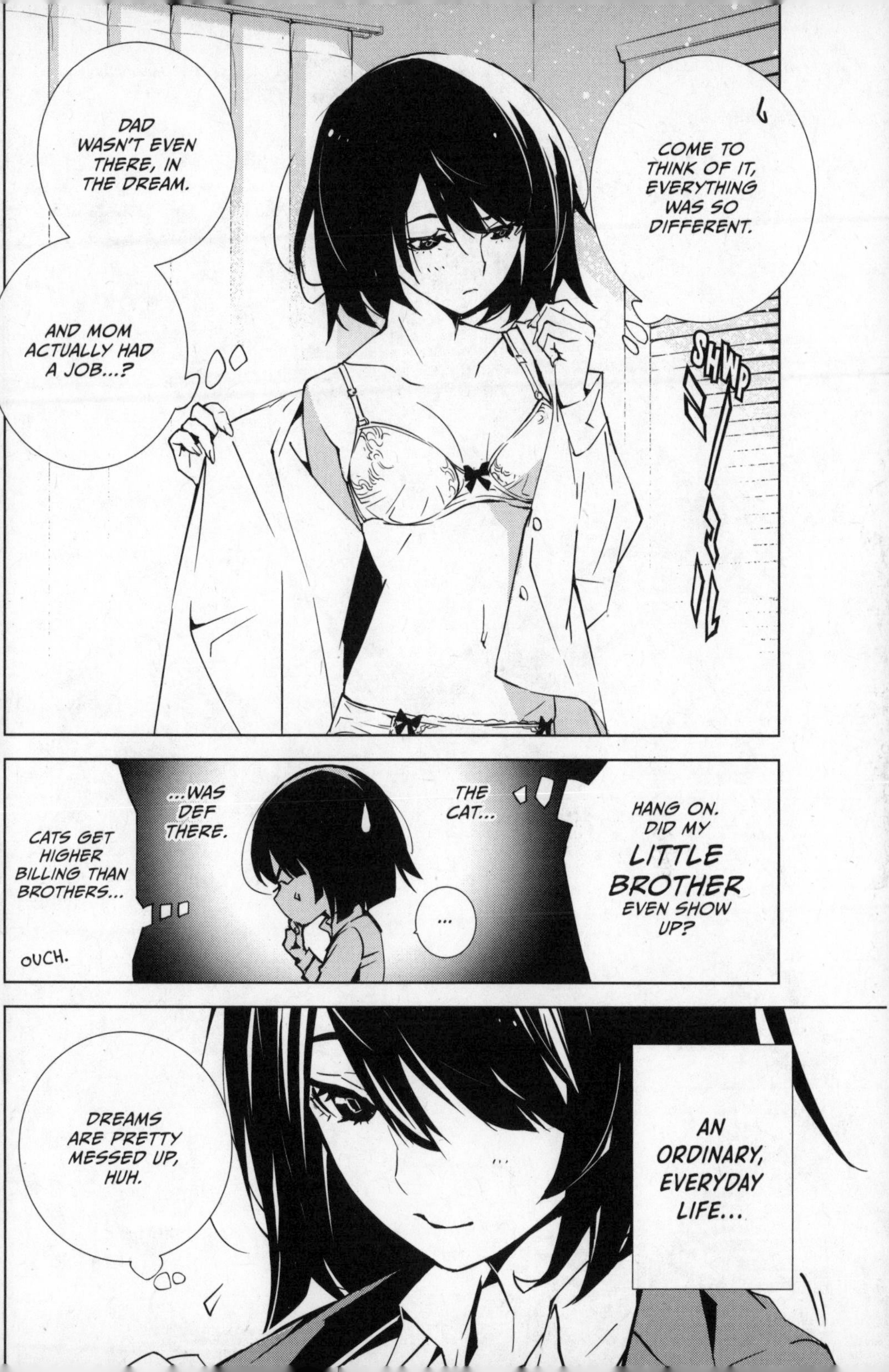
COME TO THINK OF IT, EVERYTHING WAS SO DIFFERENT.
SHWP
DAD WASN'T EVEN THERE, IN THE DREAM.
AND MOM ACTUALLY HAD A JOB...?
HANG ON. DID MY LITTLE BROTHER EVEN SHOW UP?
...
THE CAT...
...WAS DEF THERE.
CATS GET HIGHER BILLING THAN BROTHERS...
OUCH.
AN ORDINARY, EVERYDAY LIFE...
DREAMS ARE PRETTY MESSED UP, HUH.

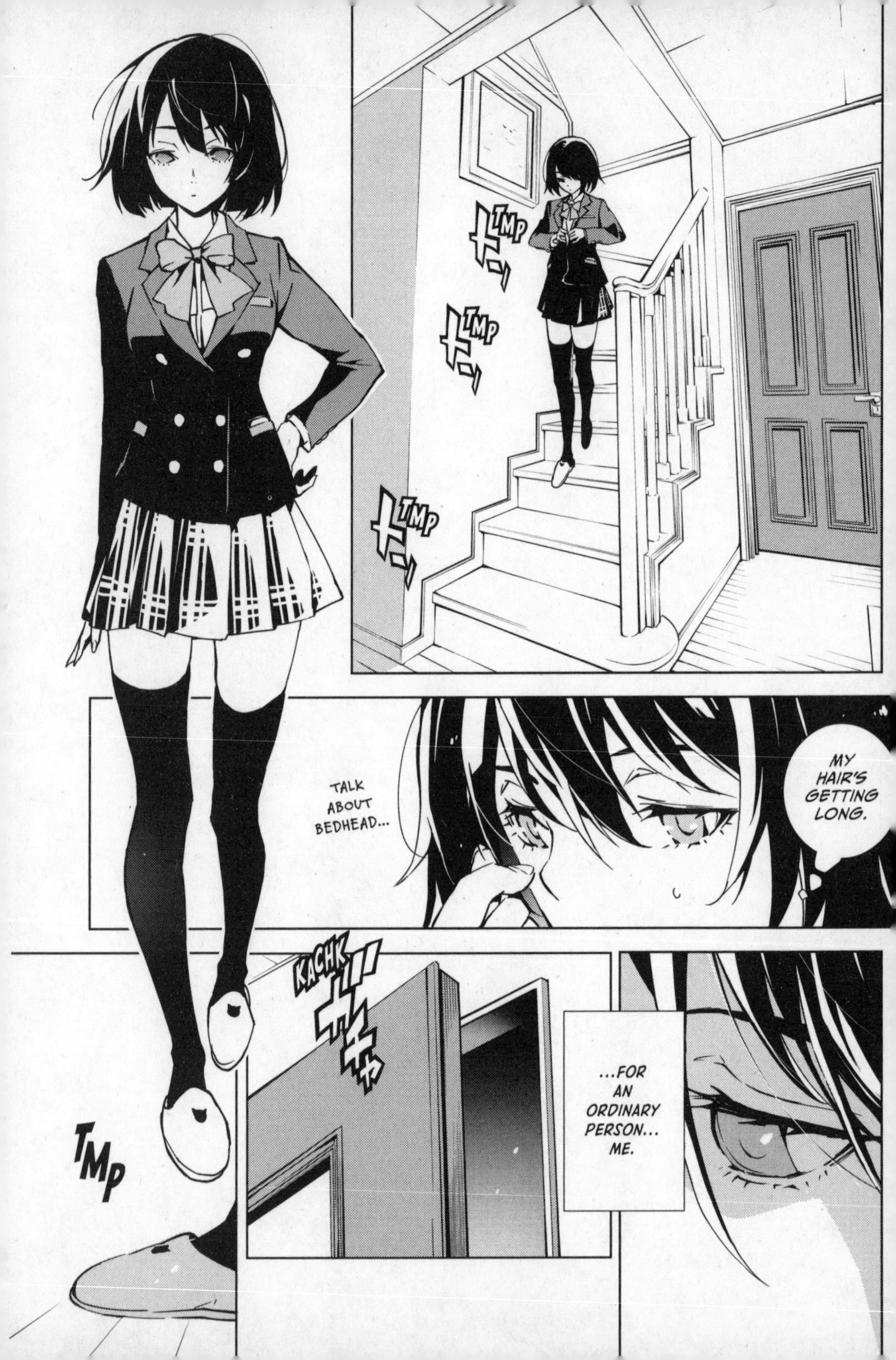
TMP
TMP
TMP
MY HAIR'S GETTING LONG.
TALK ABOUT BEDHEAD...
...FOR AN ORDINARY PERSON... ME.
KACHK
TMP

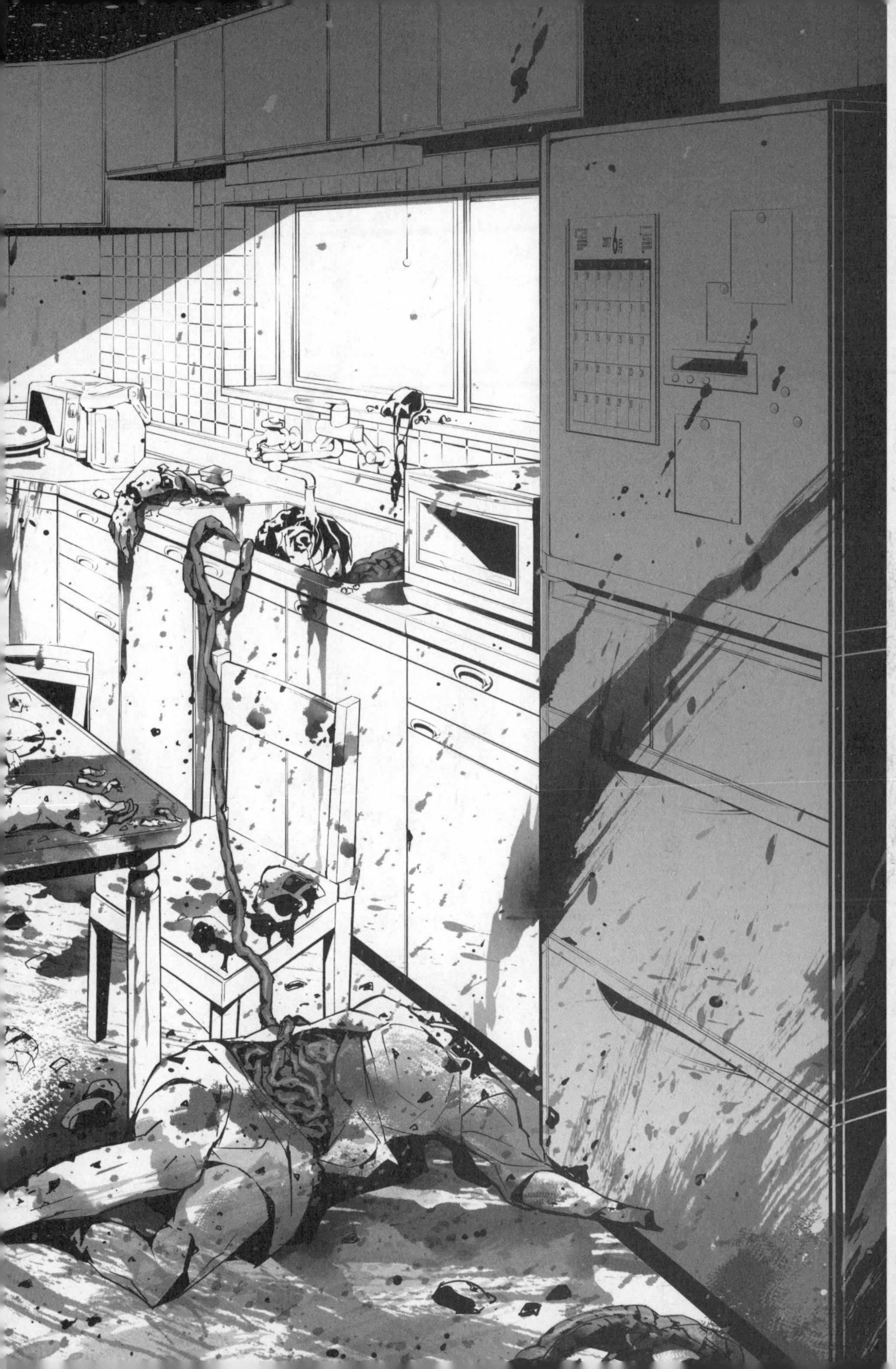
2007 6月

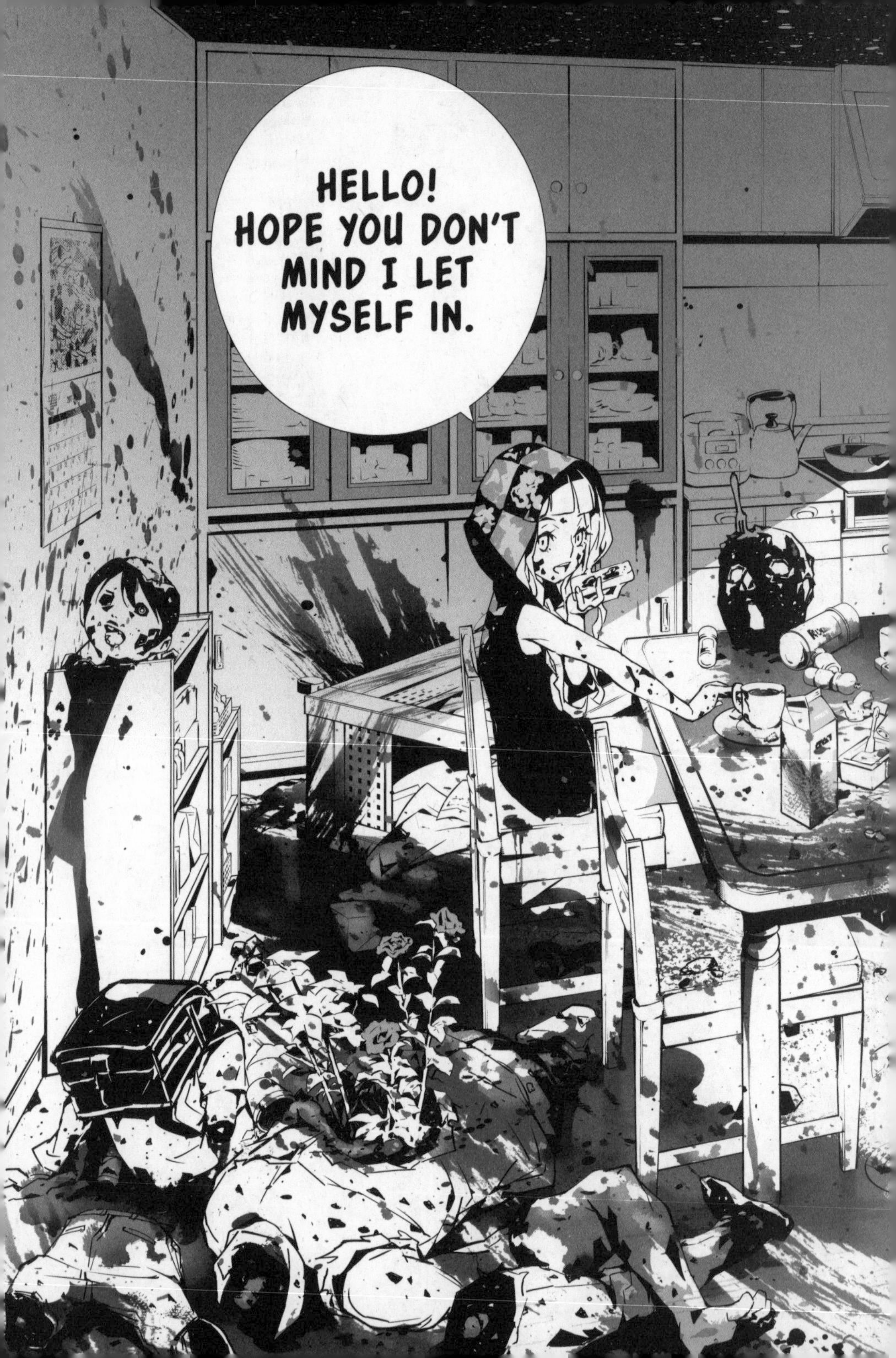
HELLO! HOPE YOU DON'T MIND I LET MYSELF IN.

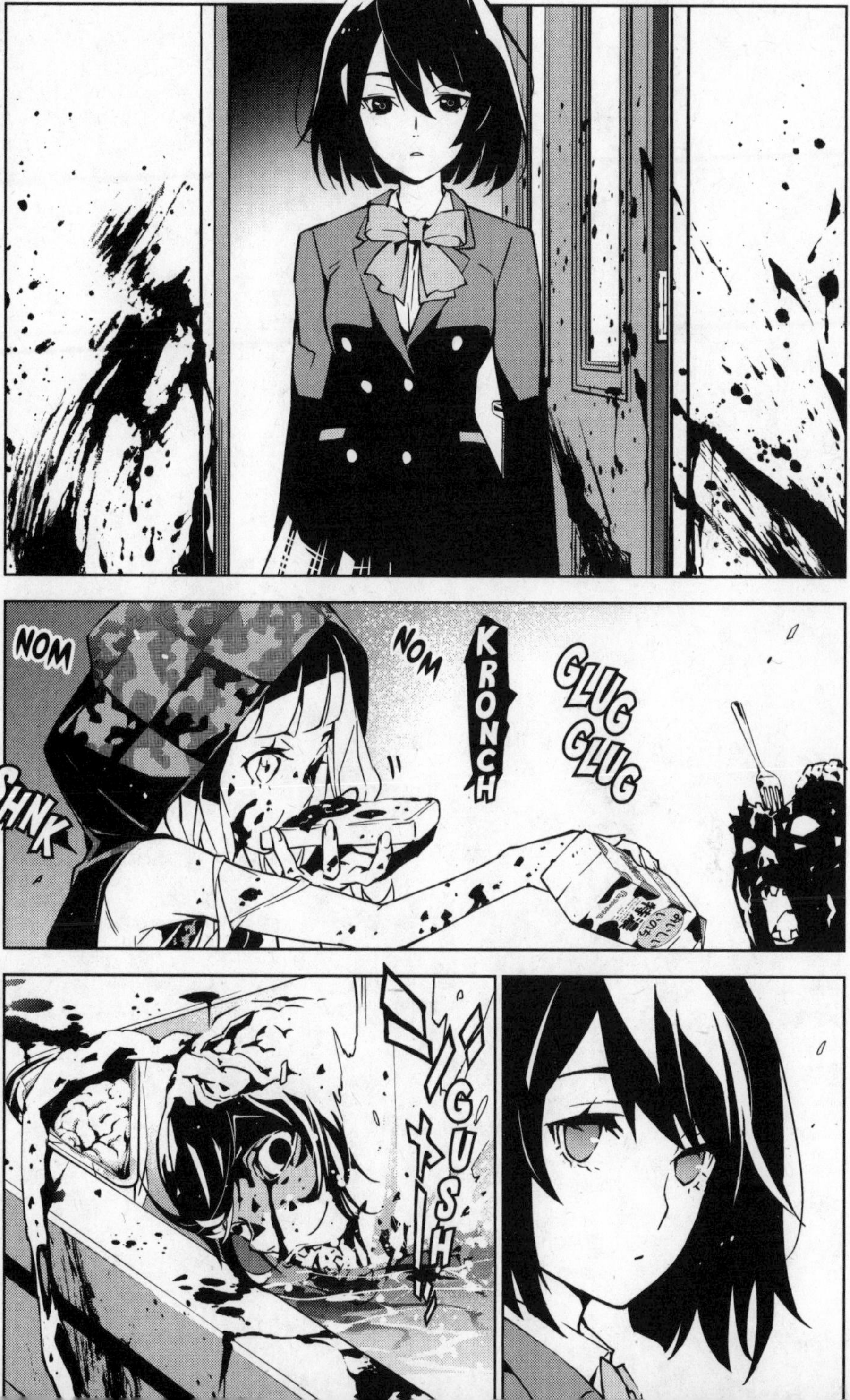
GLUG GLUG
KRONCH
NOM
NOM
SHNK
GUSH

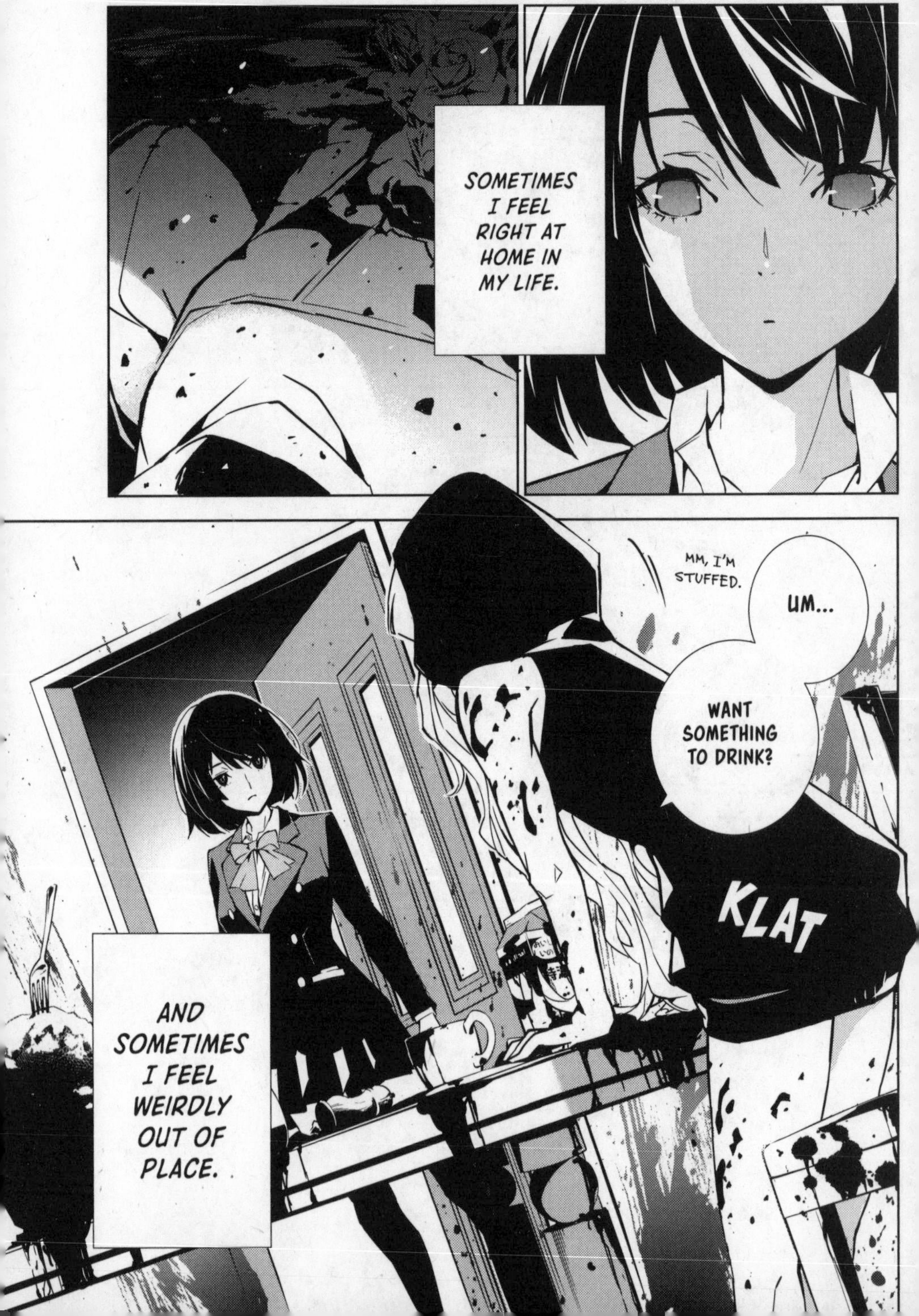
SOMETIMES I FEEL RIGHT AT HOME IN MY LIFE.
MM, I'M STUFFED.
UM...
WANT SOMETHING TO DRINK?
KLAT
AND SOMETIMES I FEEL WEIRDLY OUT OF PLACE.

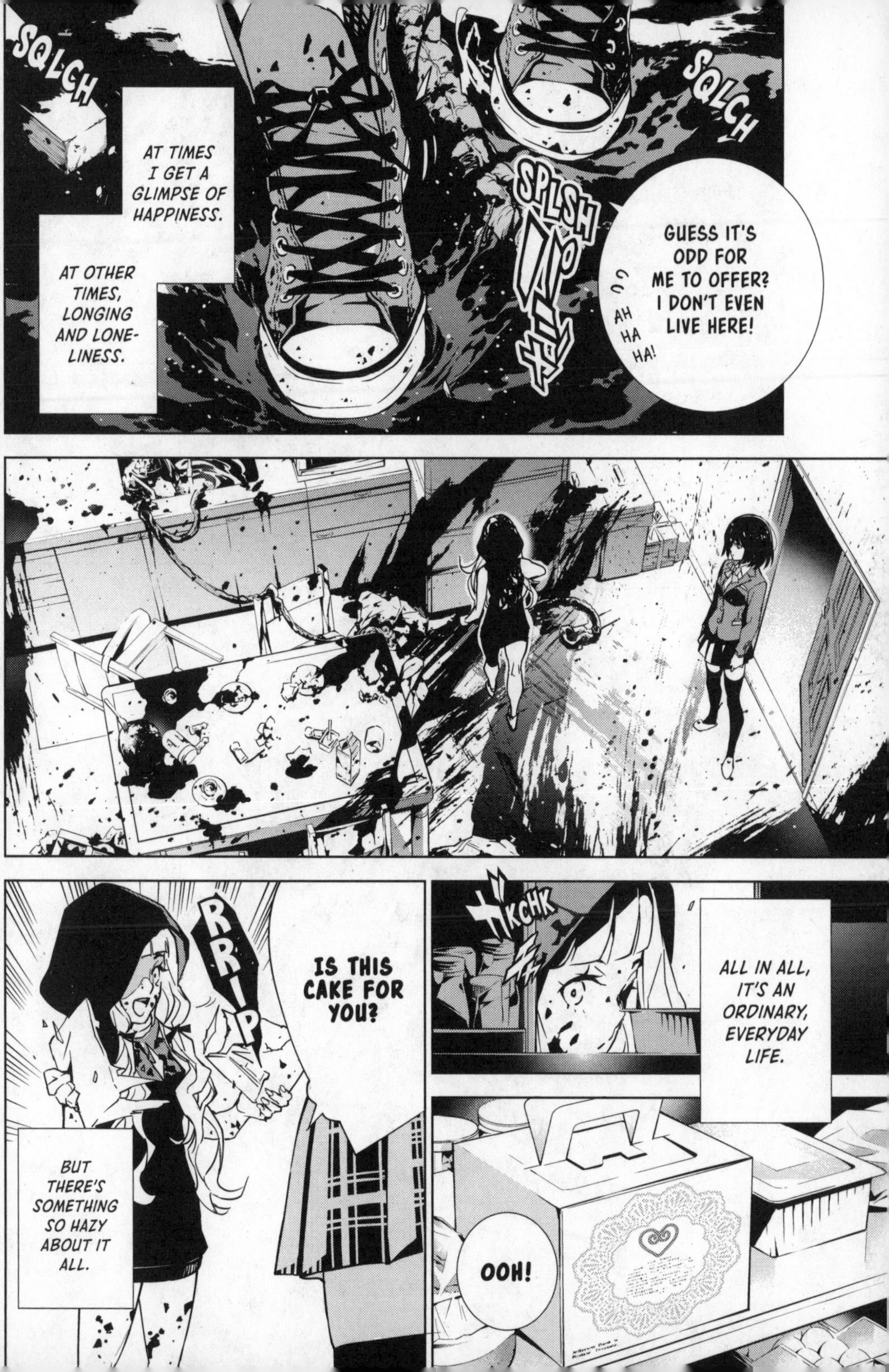
SQLCH
SPLSH
GUESS IT'S ODD FOR ME TO OFFER? I DON'T EVEN LIVE HERE!
AH HA HA!
SQLCH
AT TIMES I GET A GLIMPSE OF HAPPINESS.
AT OTHER TIMES, LONGING AND LONE-LINESS.
KCHK
ALL IN ALL, IT'S AN ORDINARY, EVERYDAY LIFE.
OOH!
RRIP
IS THIS CAKE FOR YOU?
BUT THERE'S SOMETHING SO HAZY ABOUT IT ALL.

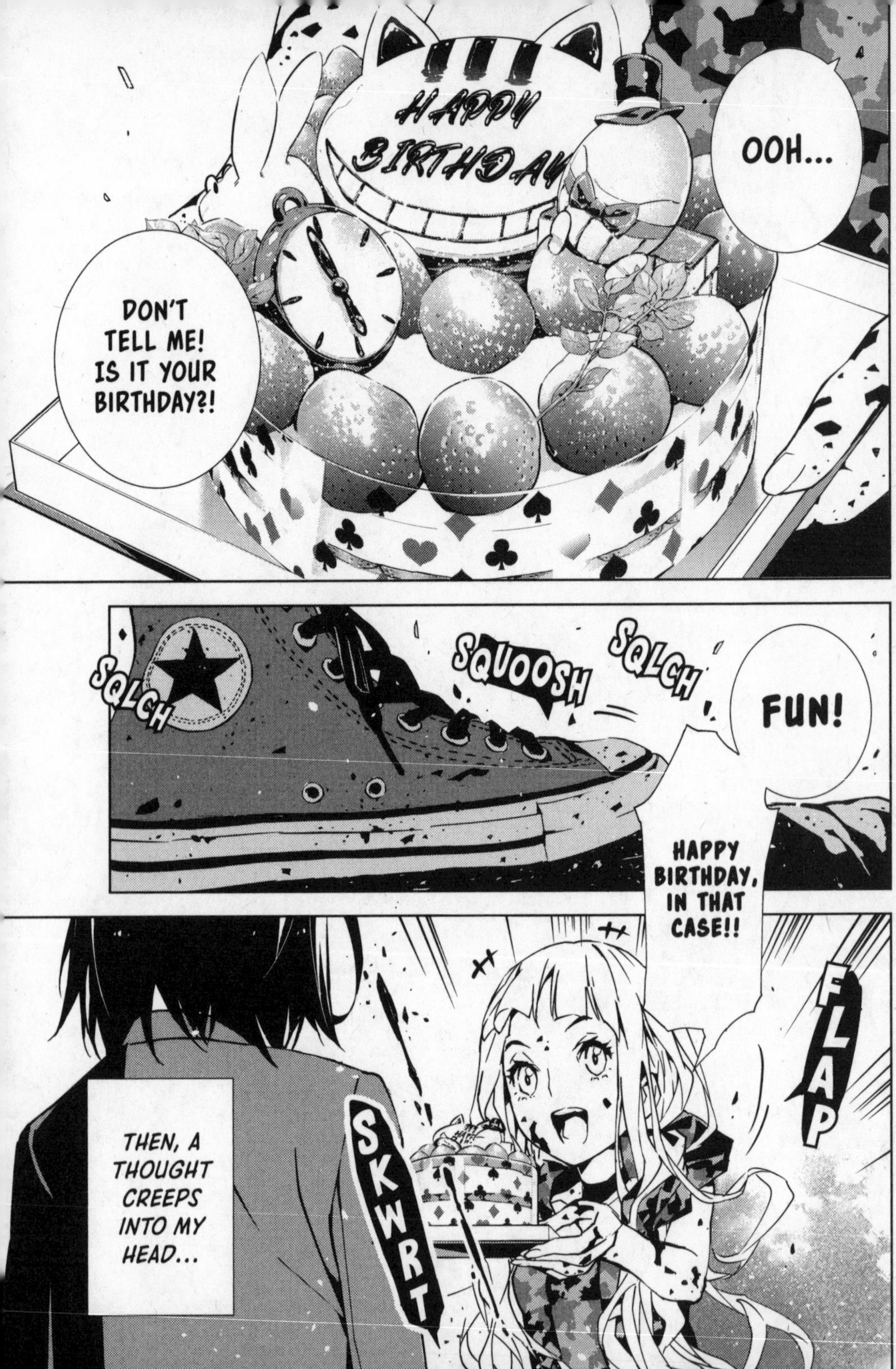
HAPPY BIRTHDAY
OOH...
DON'T TELL ME! IS IT YOUR BIRTHDAY?!
FUN!
SQLCH
SQUOOSH
SQLCH
HAPPY BIRTHDAY, IN THAT CASE!!
FLAP
SKWRT
THEN, A THOUGHT CREEPS INTO MY HEAD...

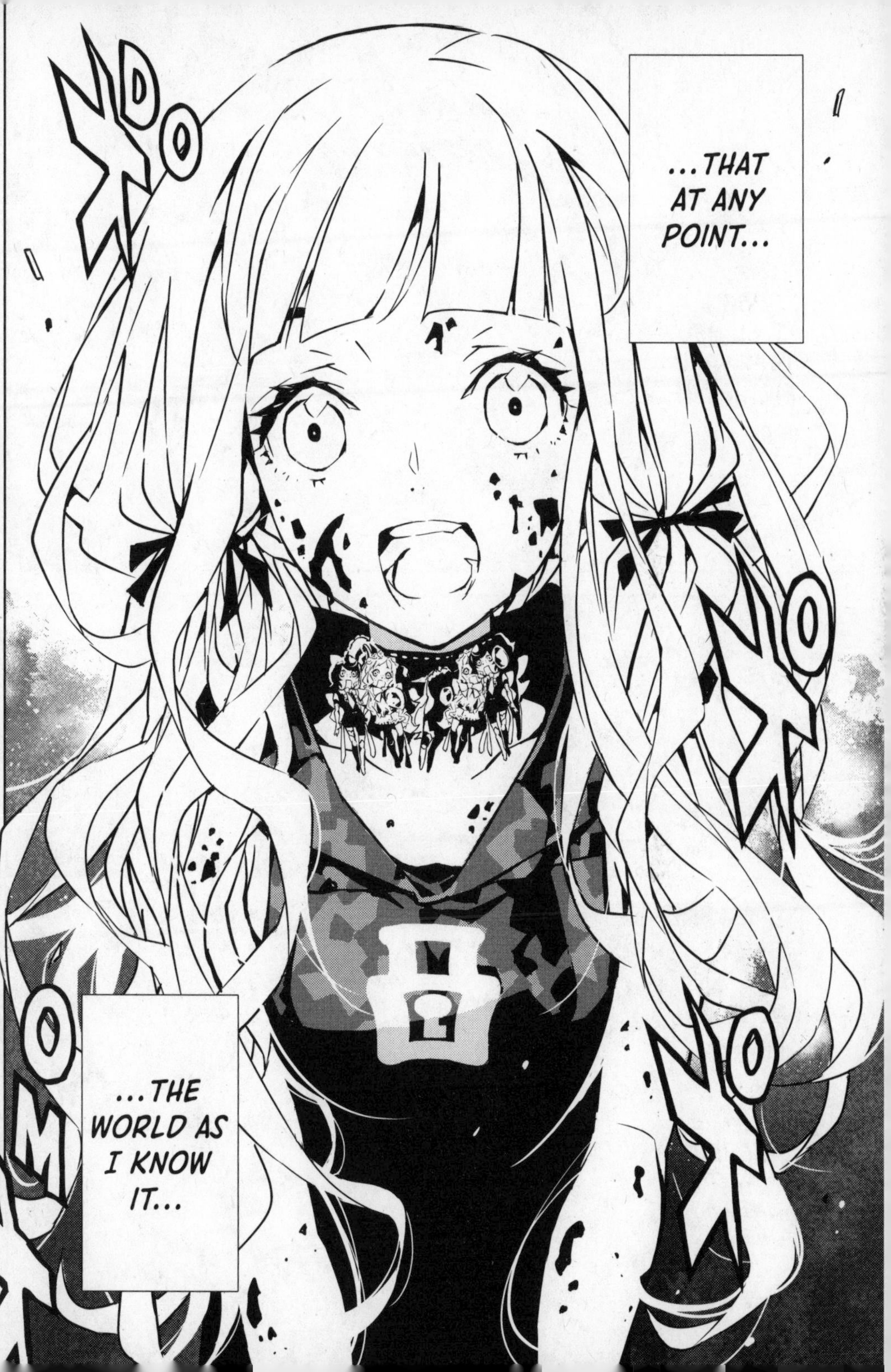
...THAT AT ANY POINT...
...THE WORLD AS I KNOW IT...

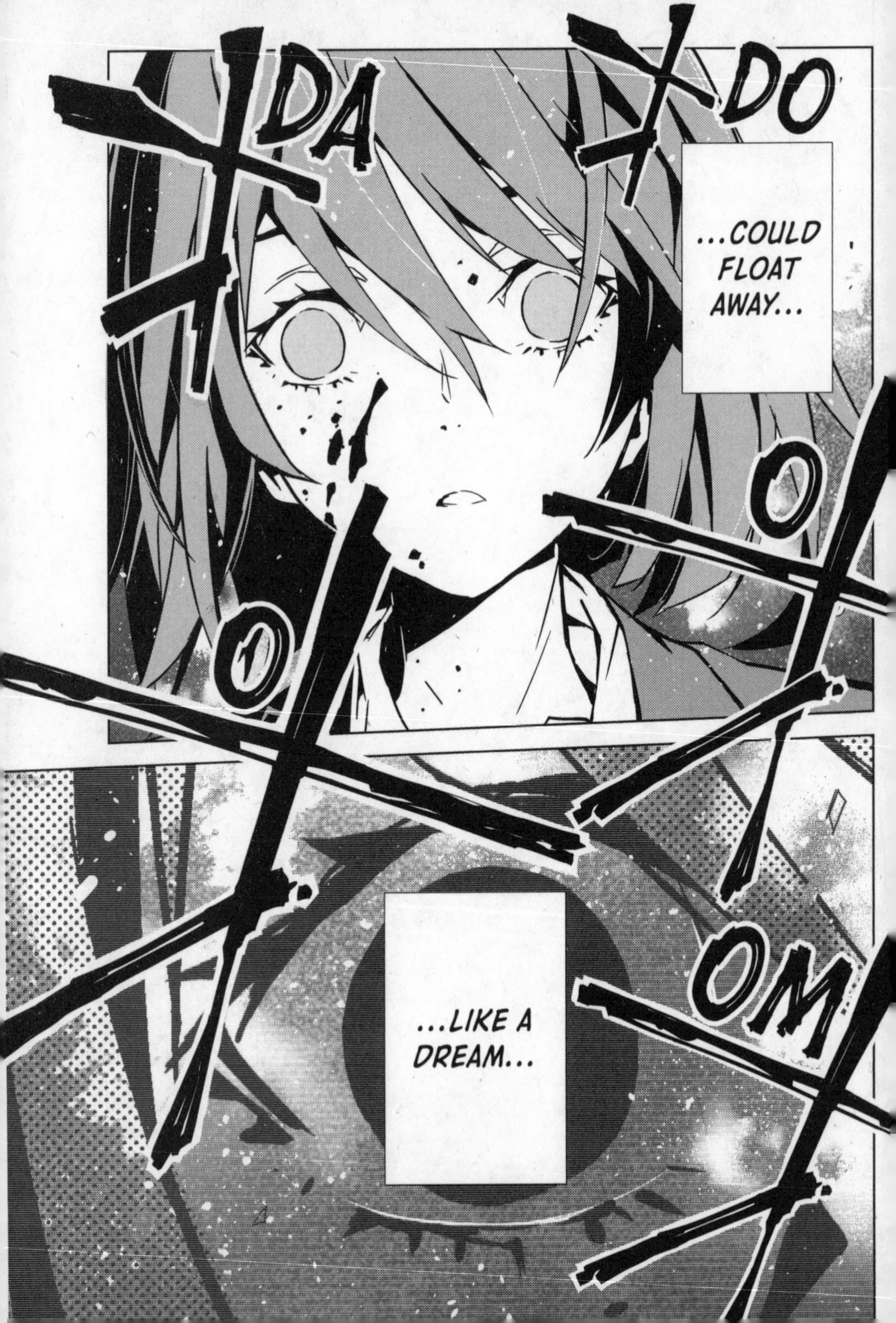
DA
DO
...COULD FLOAT AWAY...
O
O
OM
...LIKE A DREAM...

LICE®

Bondage Dream

SINo

Chapter 1:

SINoALICE®

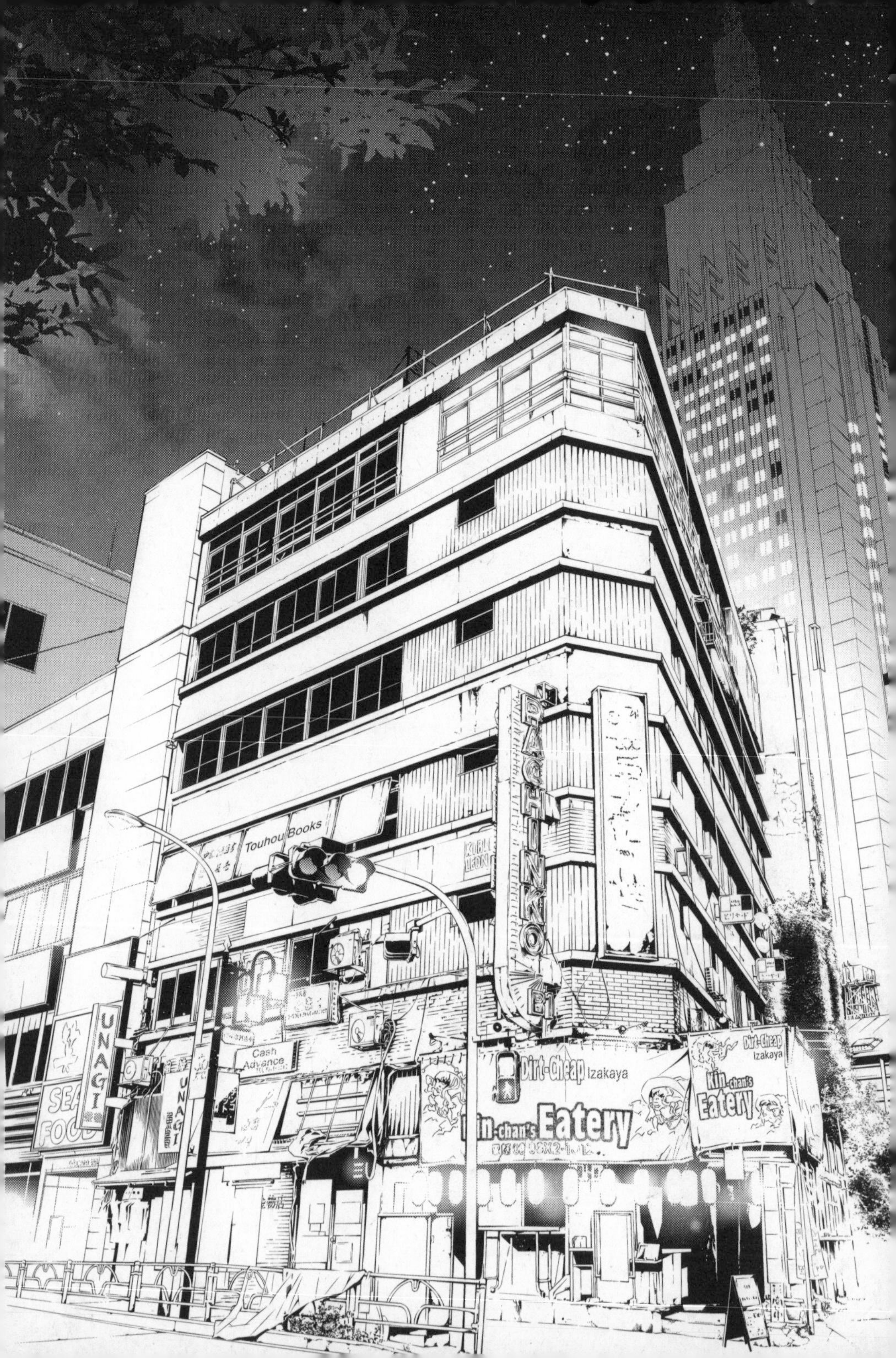
Touhou Books
PACHINKO
B1
UNAGI
UNAGI
Cash Advance
Dirt-Cheap Izakaya
Eatery
Dirt-Cheap Izakaya
Kin-chan's Eatery

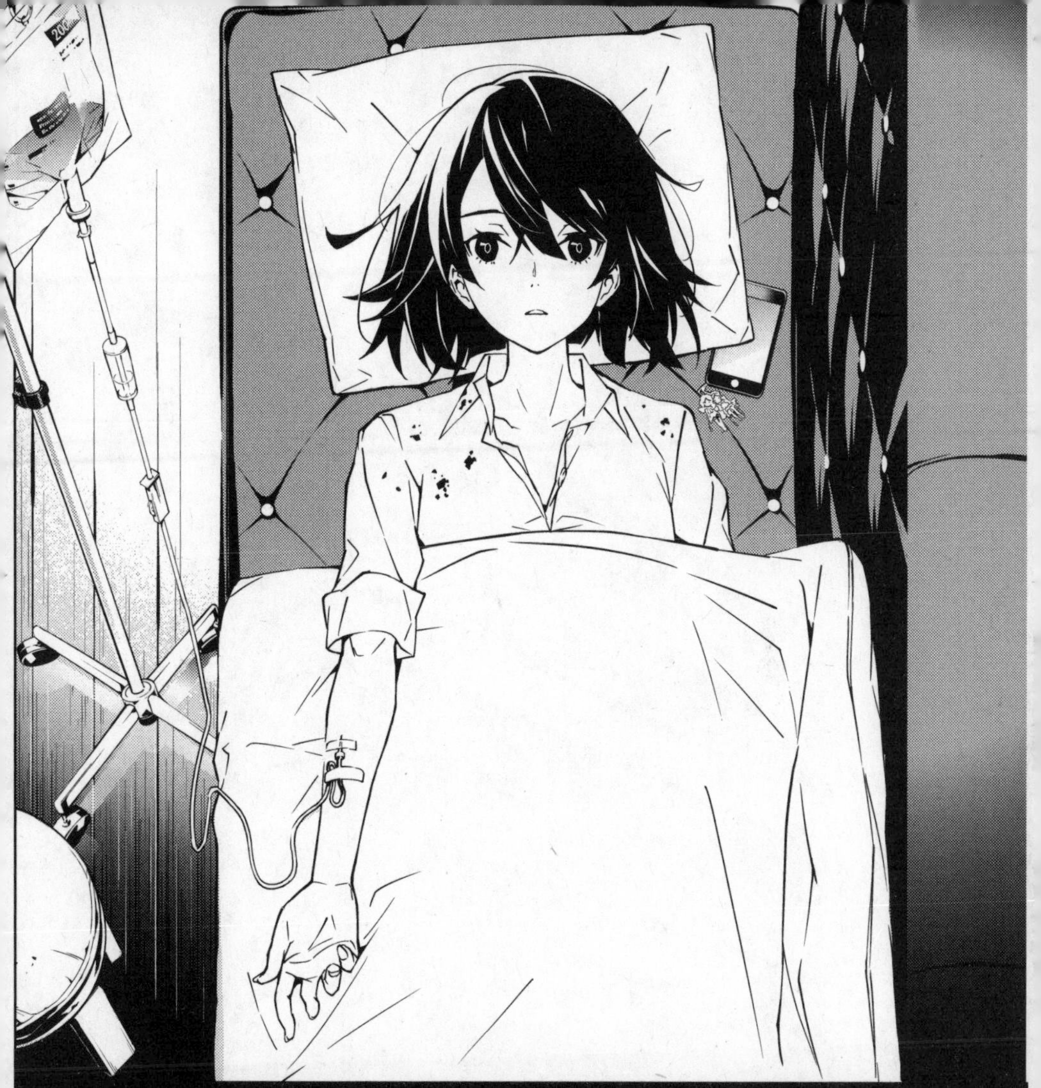

Chapter 2: Encounter Dream

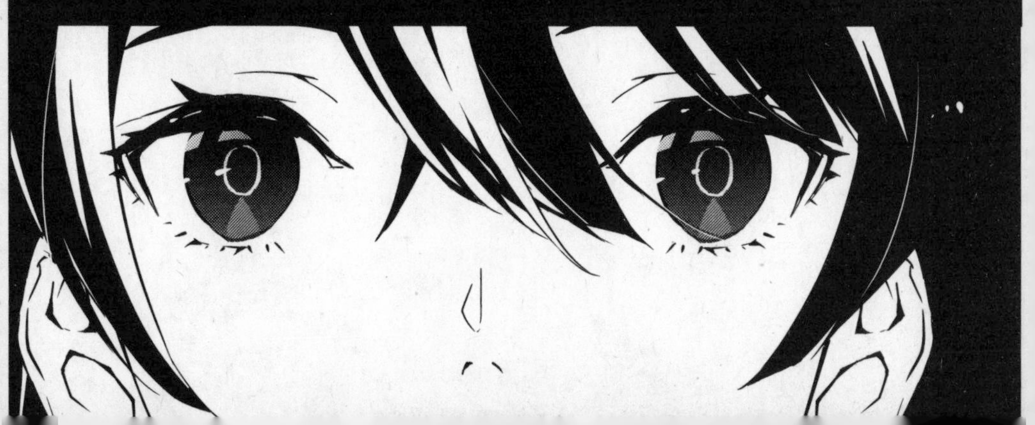

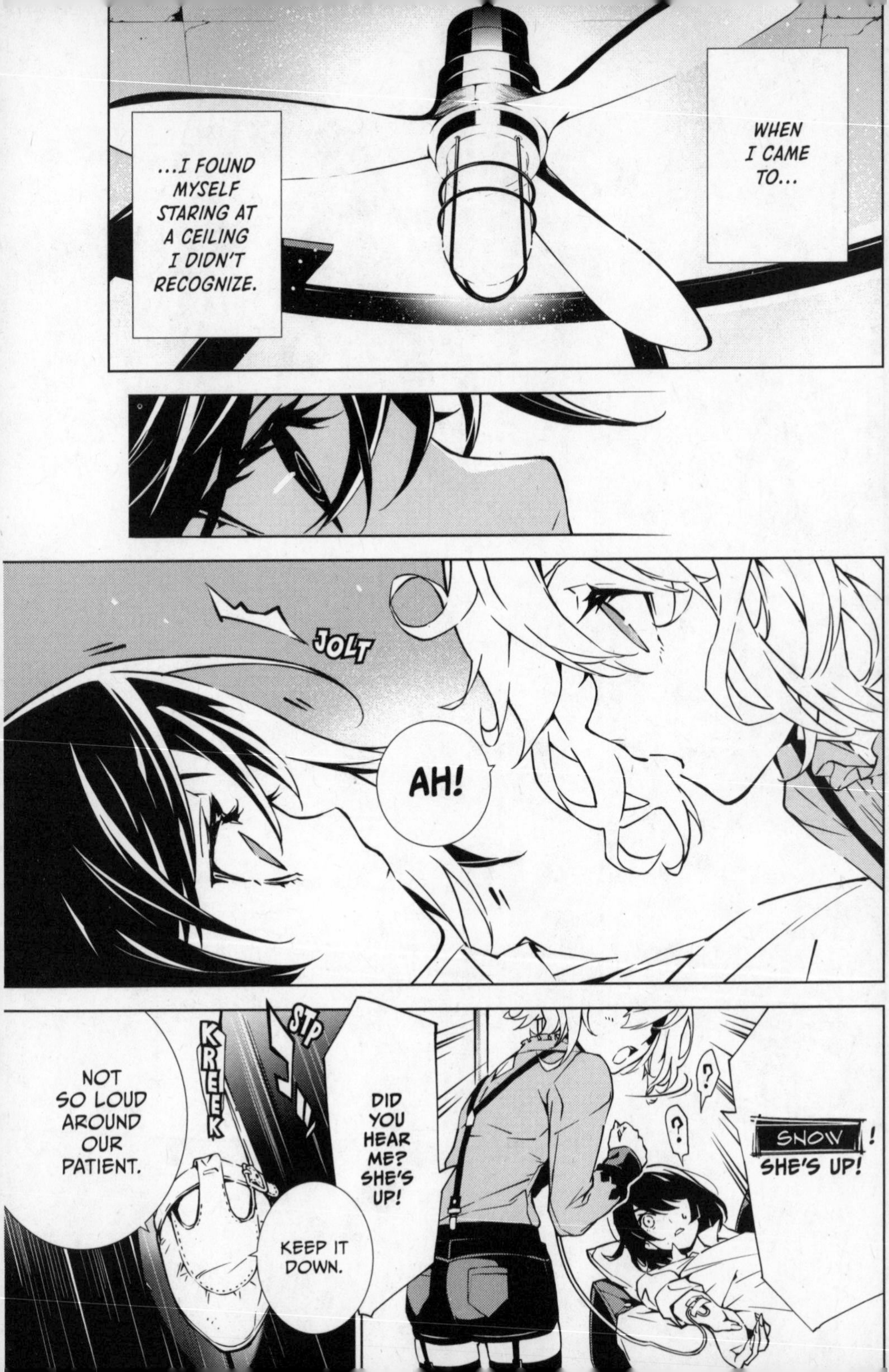
WHEN I CAME TO...
...I FOUND MYSELF STARING AT A CEILING I DIDN'T RECOGNIZE.
JOLT
AH!
SNOW! SHE'S UP!
DID YOU HEAR ME? SHE'S UP!
STP
KREEK
NOT SO LOUD AROUND OUR PATIENT.
KEEP IT DOWN.

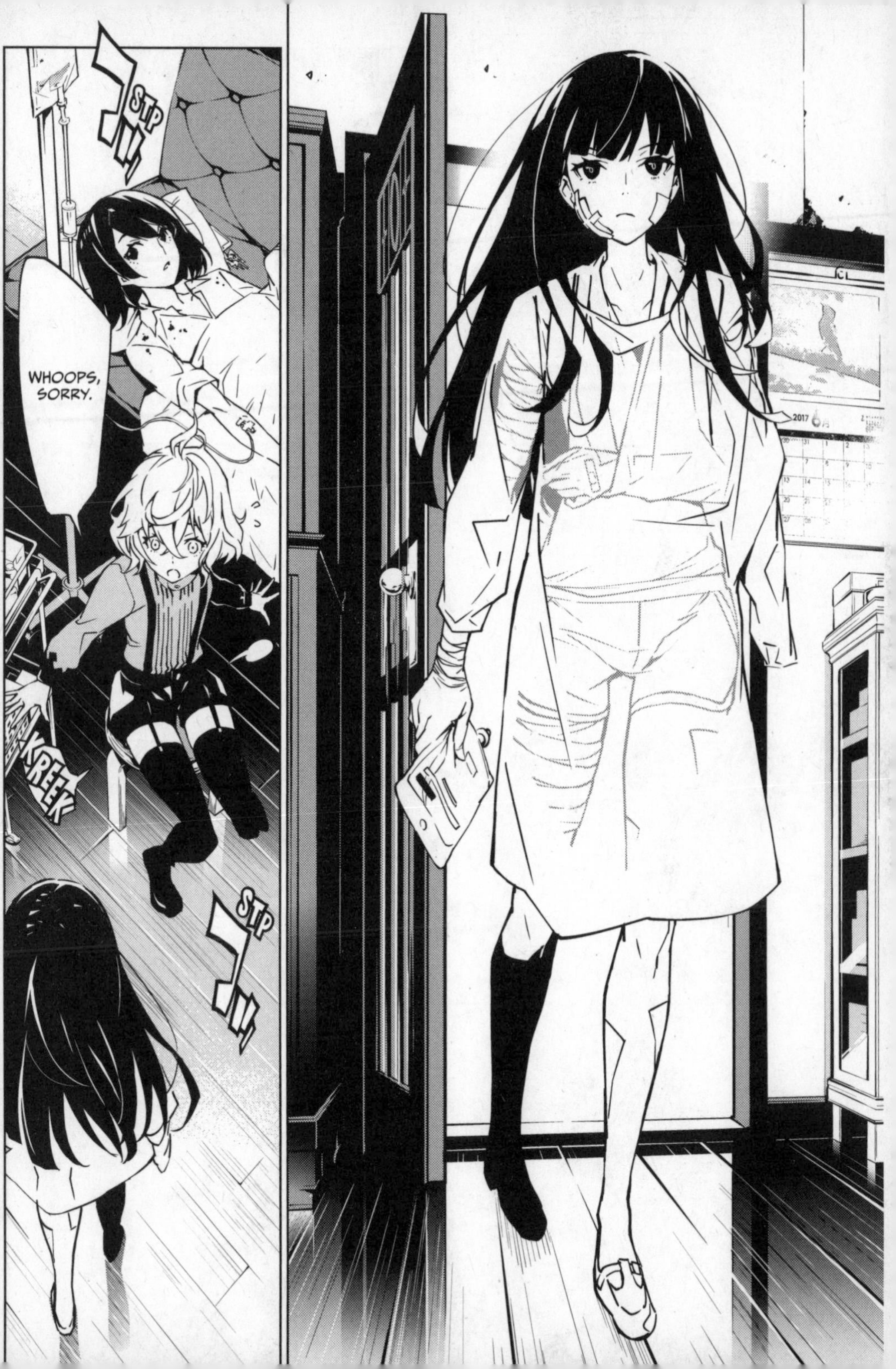
STIP
WHOOPS, SORRY.
KREEK
STIP

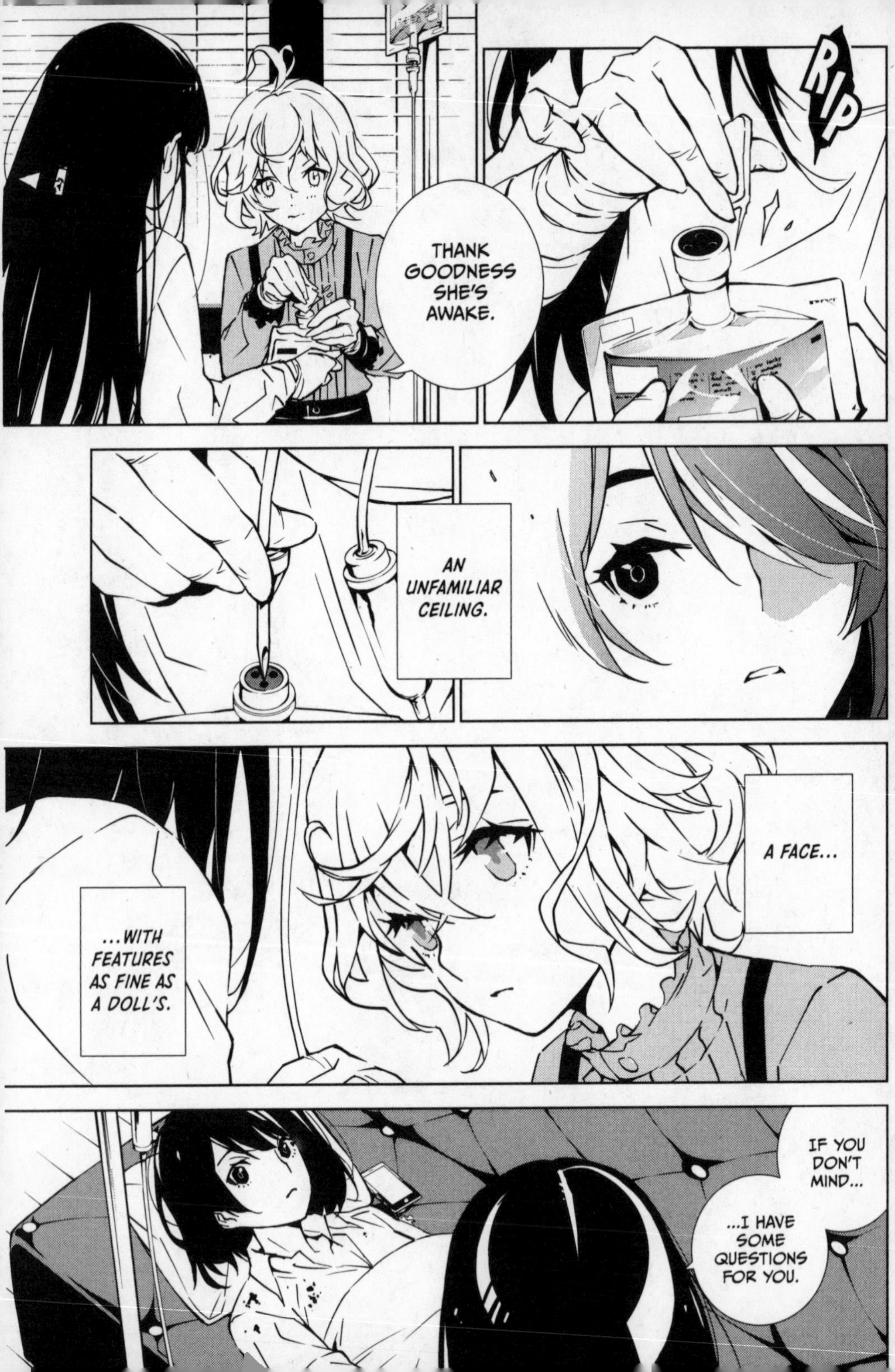
RIP
THANK GOODNESS SHE'S AWAKE.
AN UNFAMILIAR CEILING.
A FACE...
...WITH FEATURES AS FINE AS A DOLL'S.
IF YOU DON'T MIND...
...I HAVE SOME QUESTIONS FOR YOU.

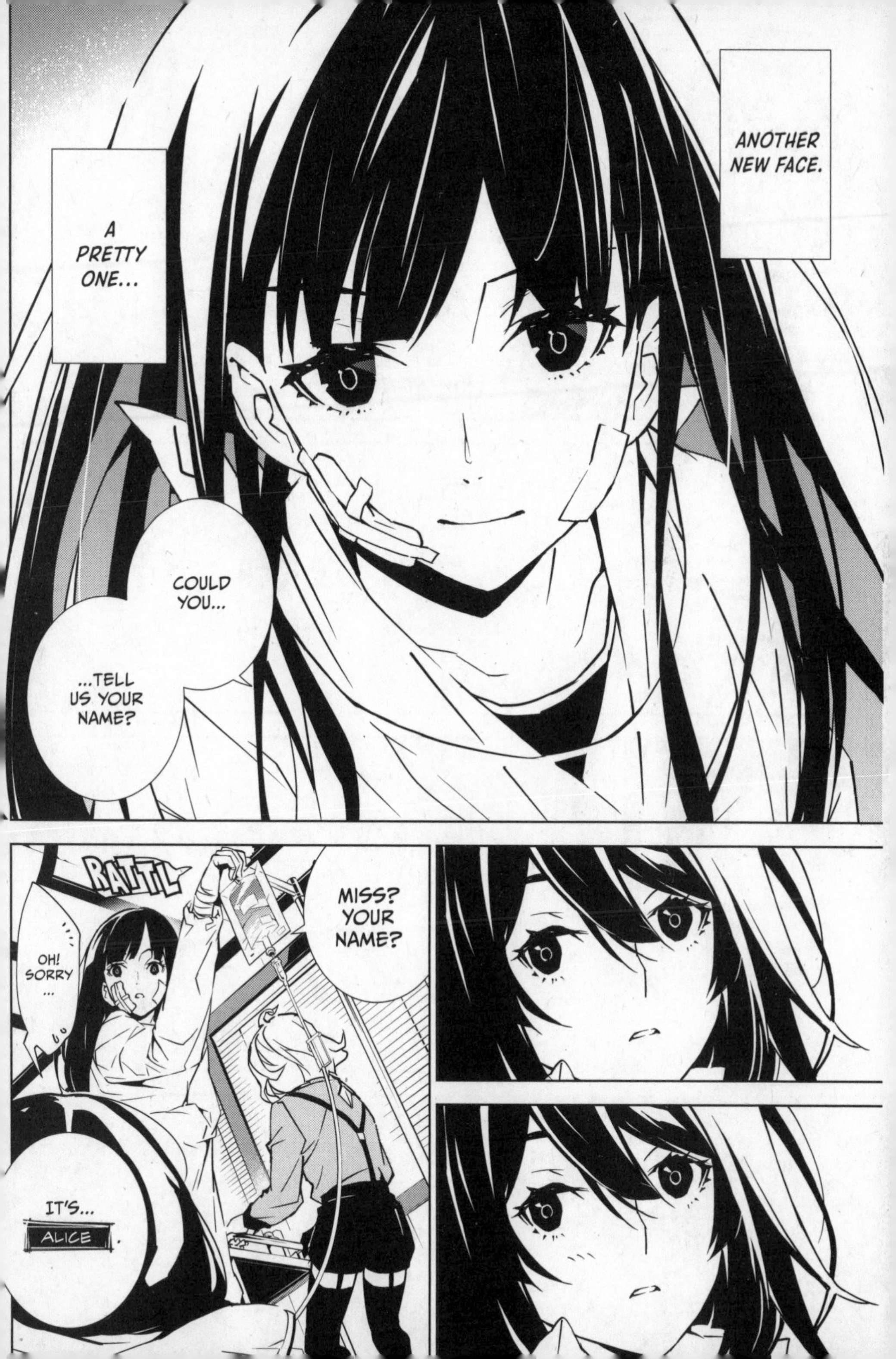
ANOTHER NEW FACE.
A PRETTY ONE...
COULD YOU...
...TELL US YOUR NAME?
MISS? YOUR NAME?
RATTL
OH! SORRY ...
IT'S...
ALICE.

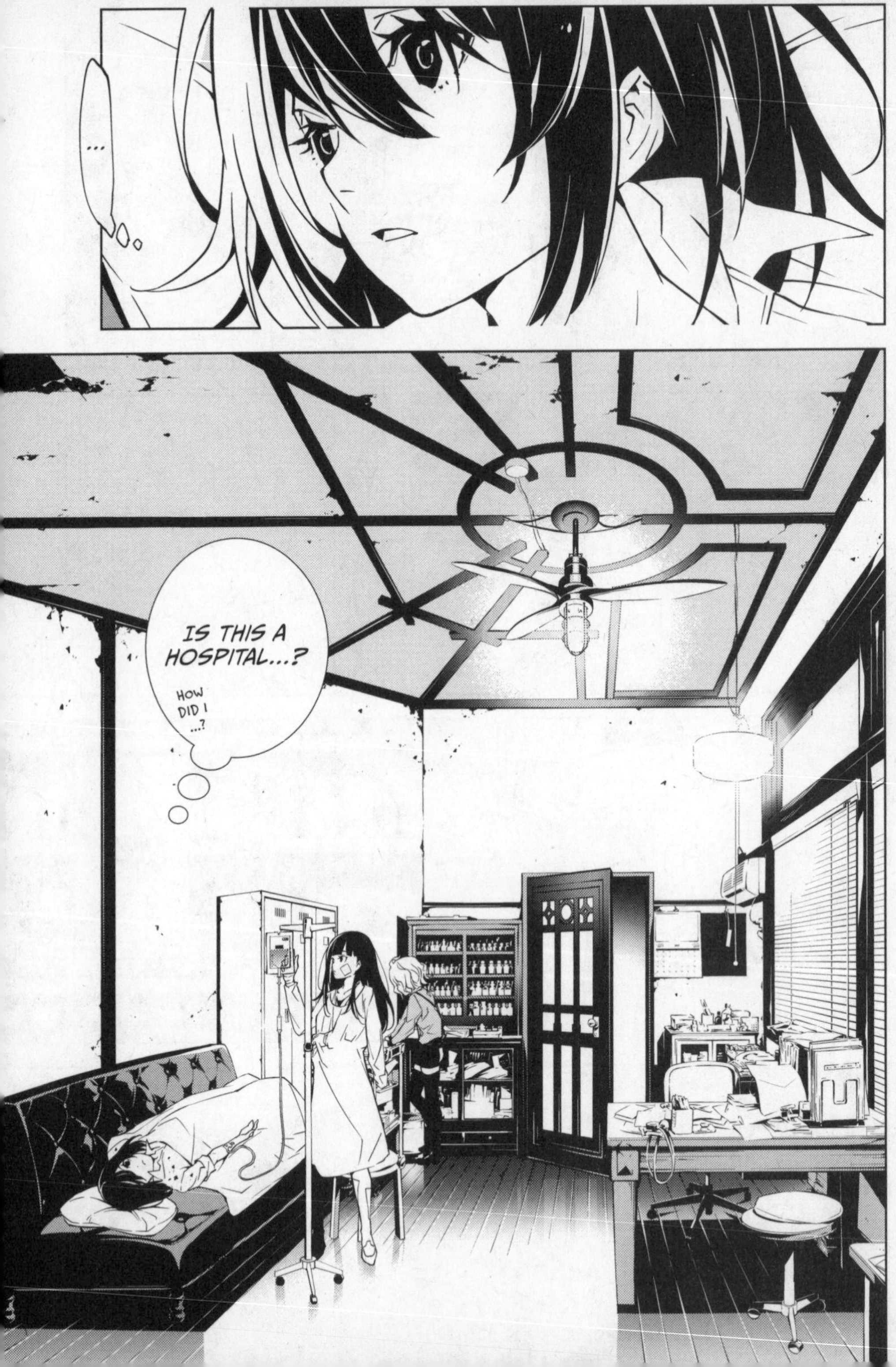
...
IS THIS A HOSPITAL...?
HOW DID I ...?

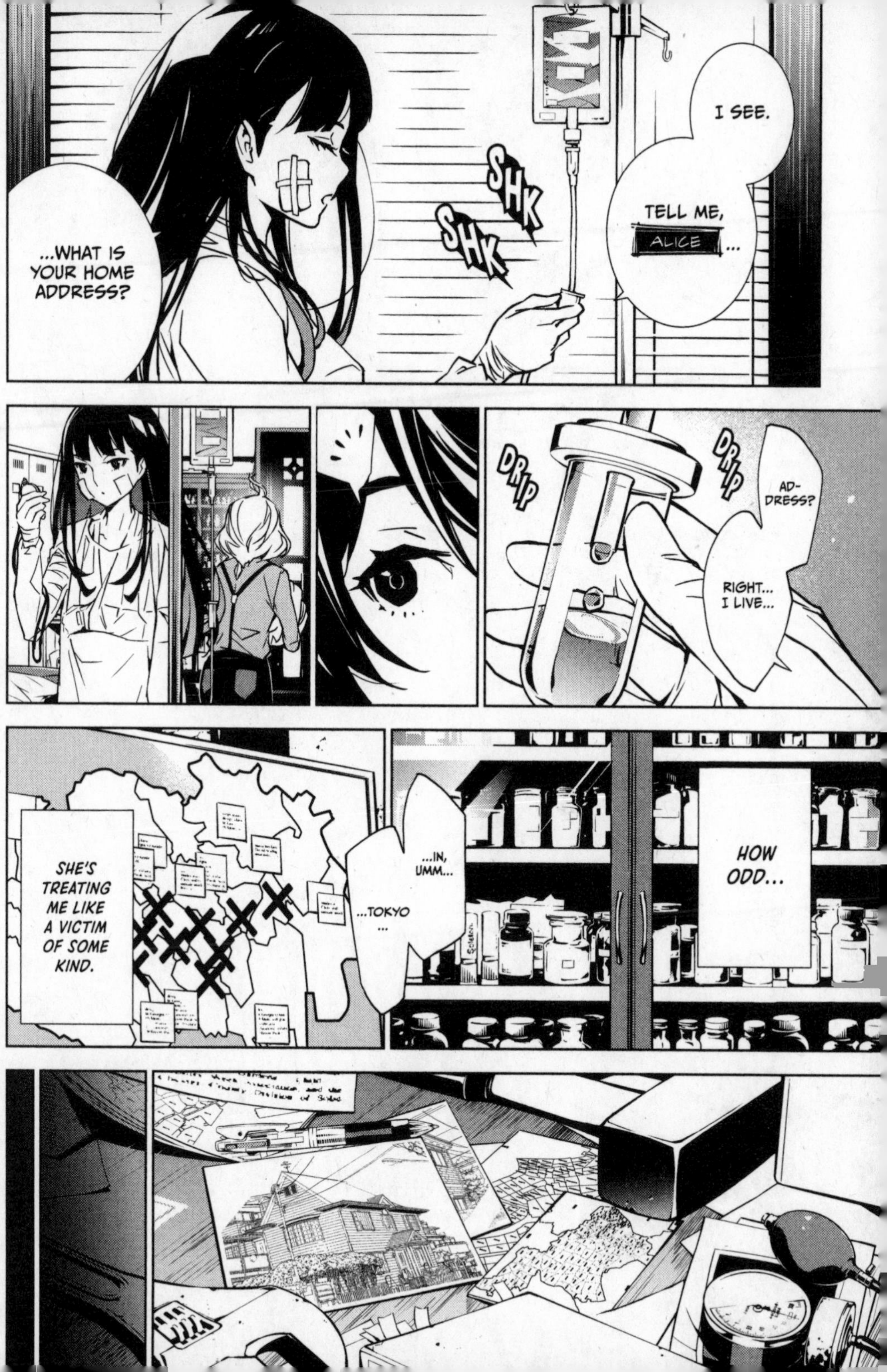
I SEE.
TELL ME, ALICE ...
SHK
SHK
...WHAT IS YOUR HOME ADDRESS?
DRIP
DRIP
AD-DRESS?
RIGHT... I LIVE...
HOW ODD...
...IN, UMM...
...TOKYO ...
SHE'S TREATING ME LIKE A VICTIM OF SOME KIND.

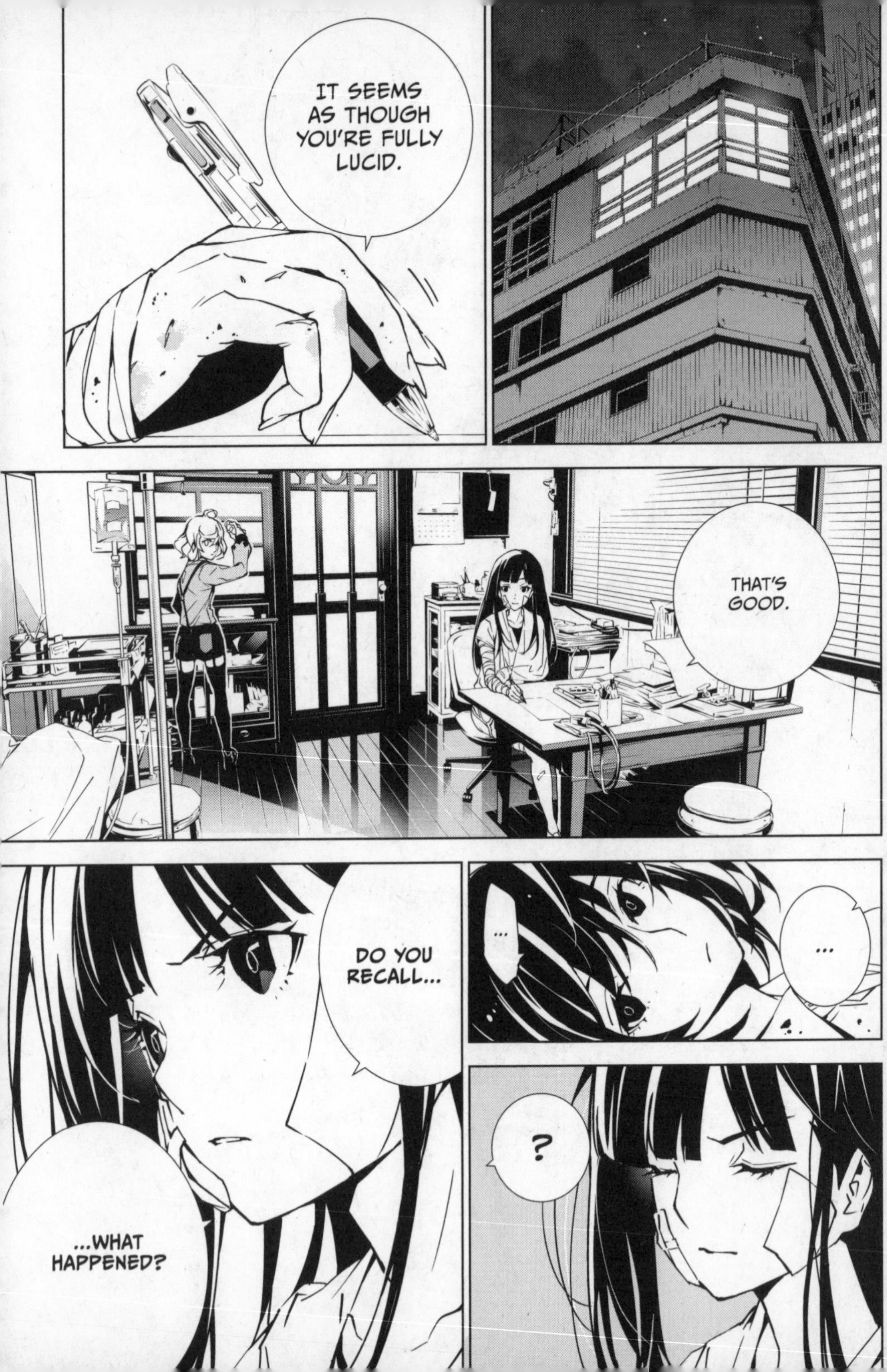
IT SEEMS AS THOUGH YOU'RE FULLY LUCID.
THAT'S GOOD.
...
...
?
DO YOU RECALL...
...WHAT HAPPENED?

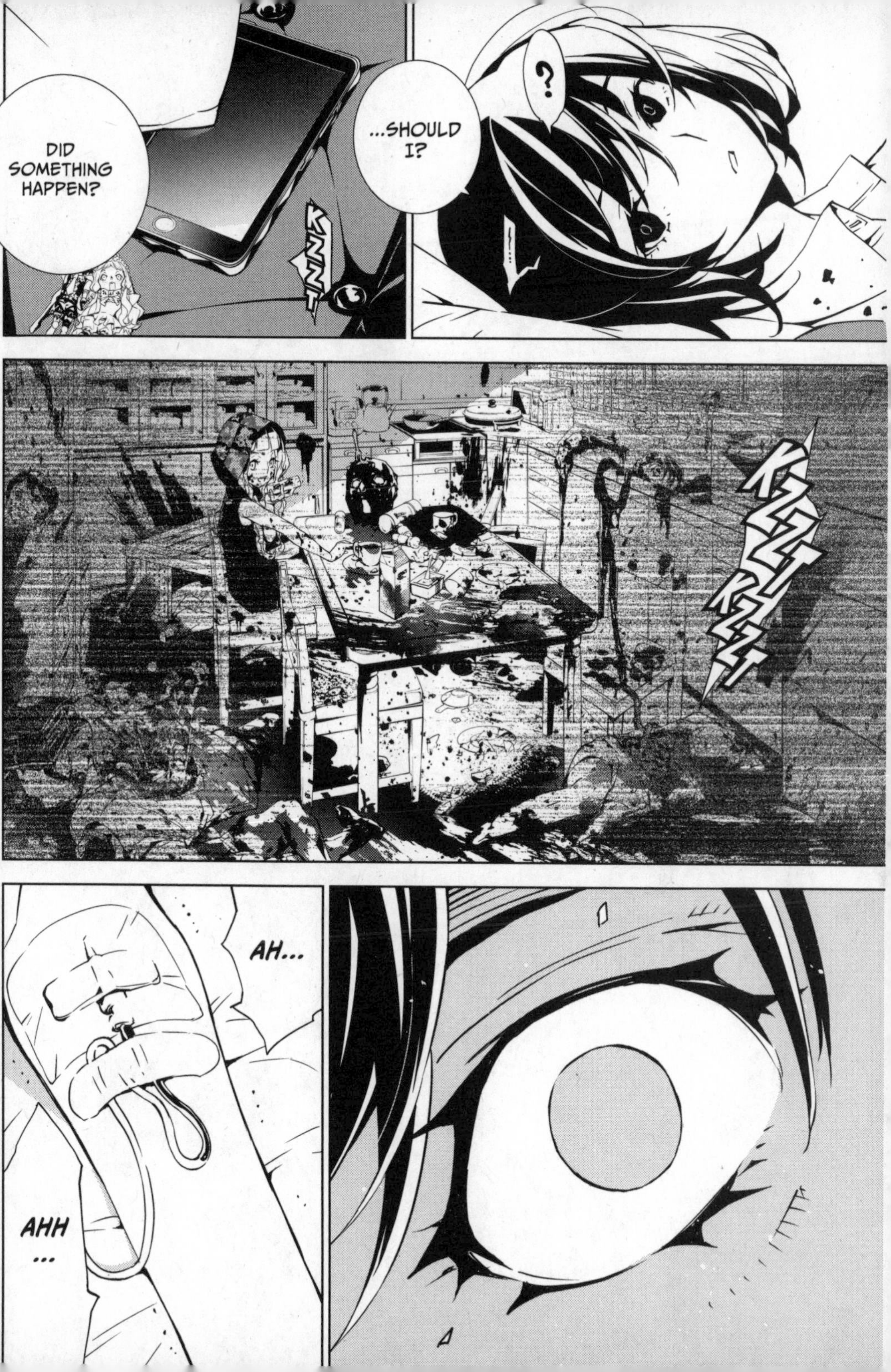
?
...SHOULD I?
DID SOMETHING HAPPEN?
KZZT
KZZT KZZT
AH...
AHH ...

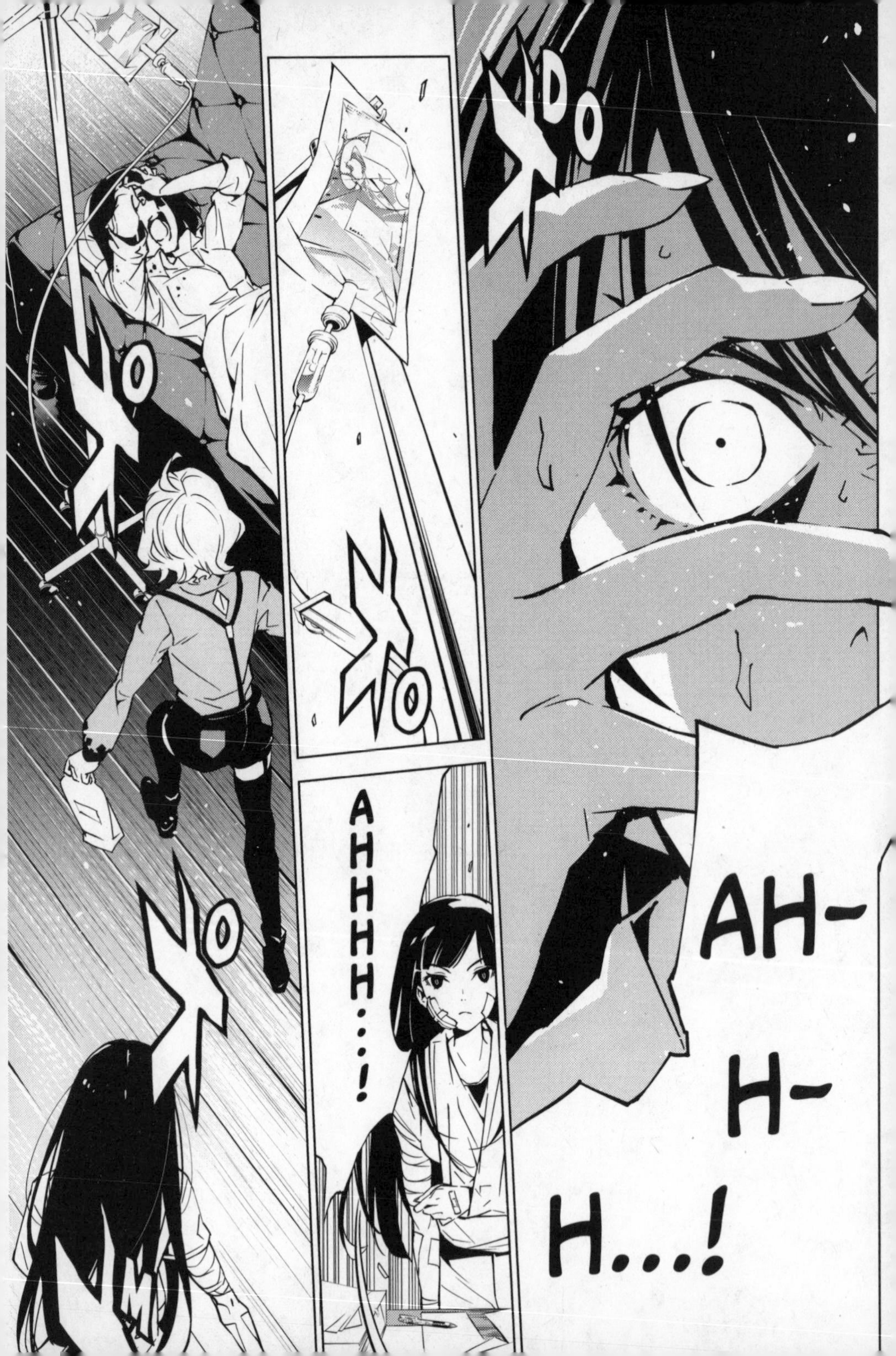
DO
AH-
H-
H...!
O
O
AHHHH...!
O
M

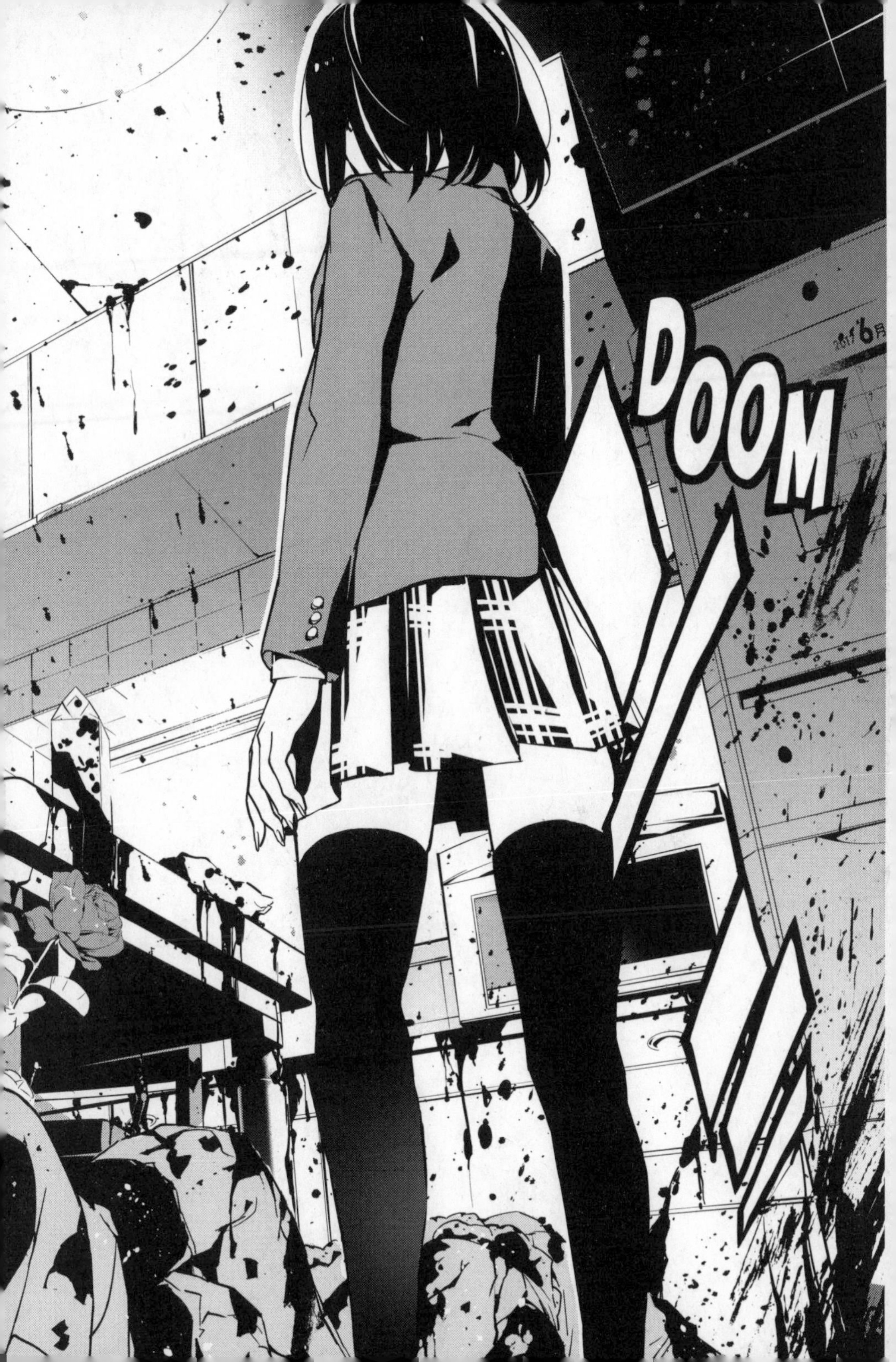
DOOM

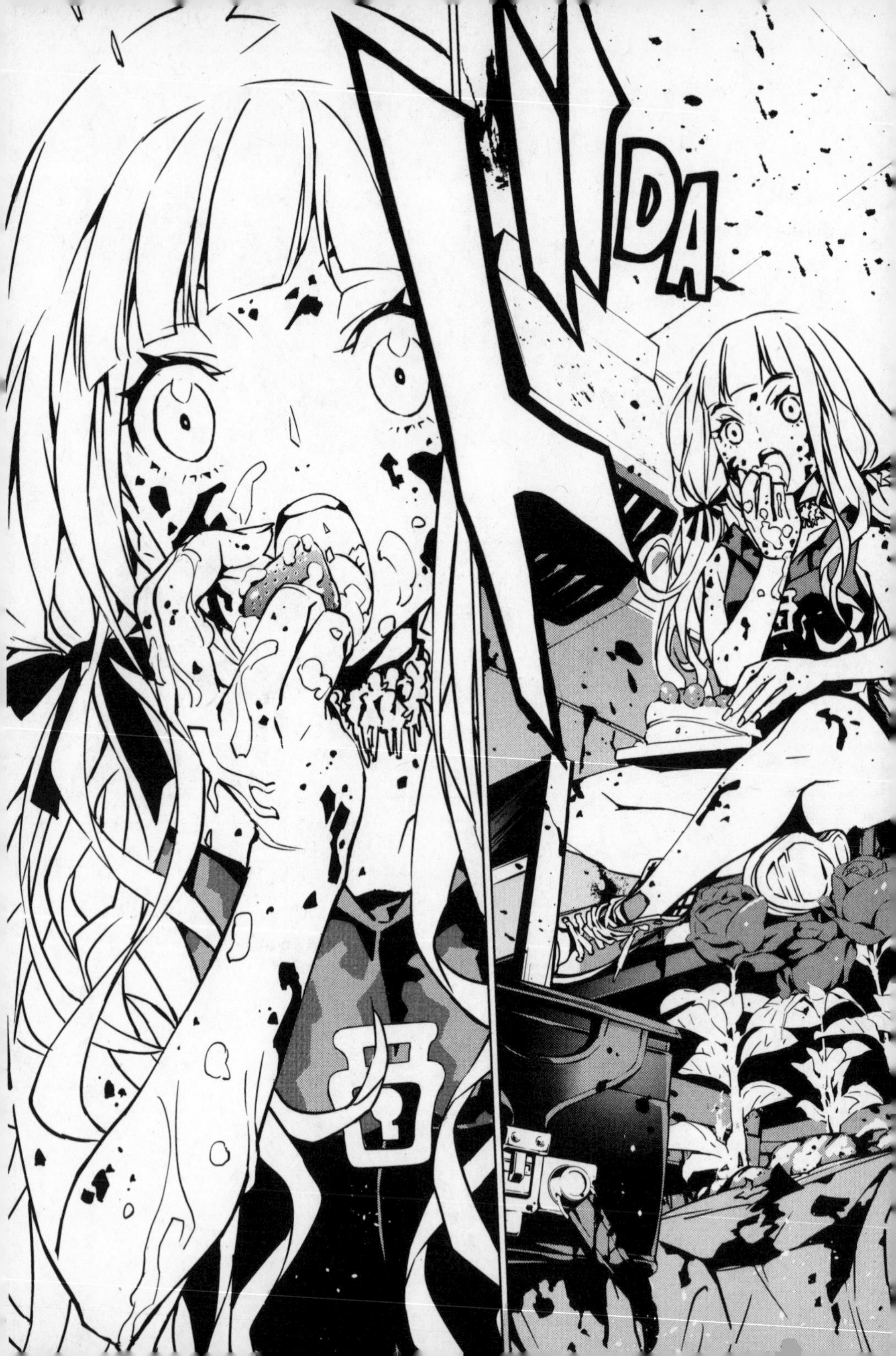
DA

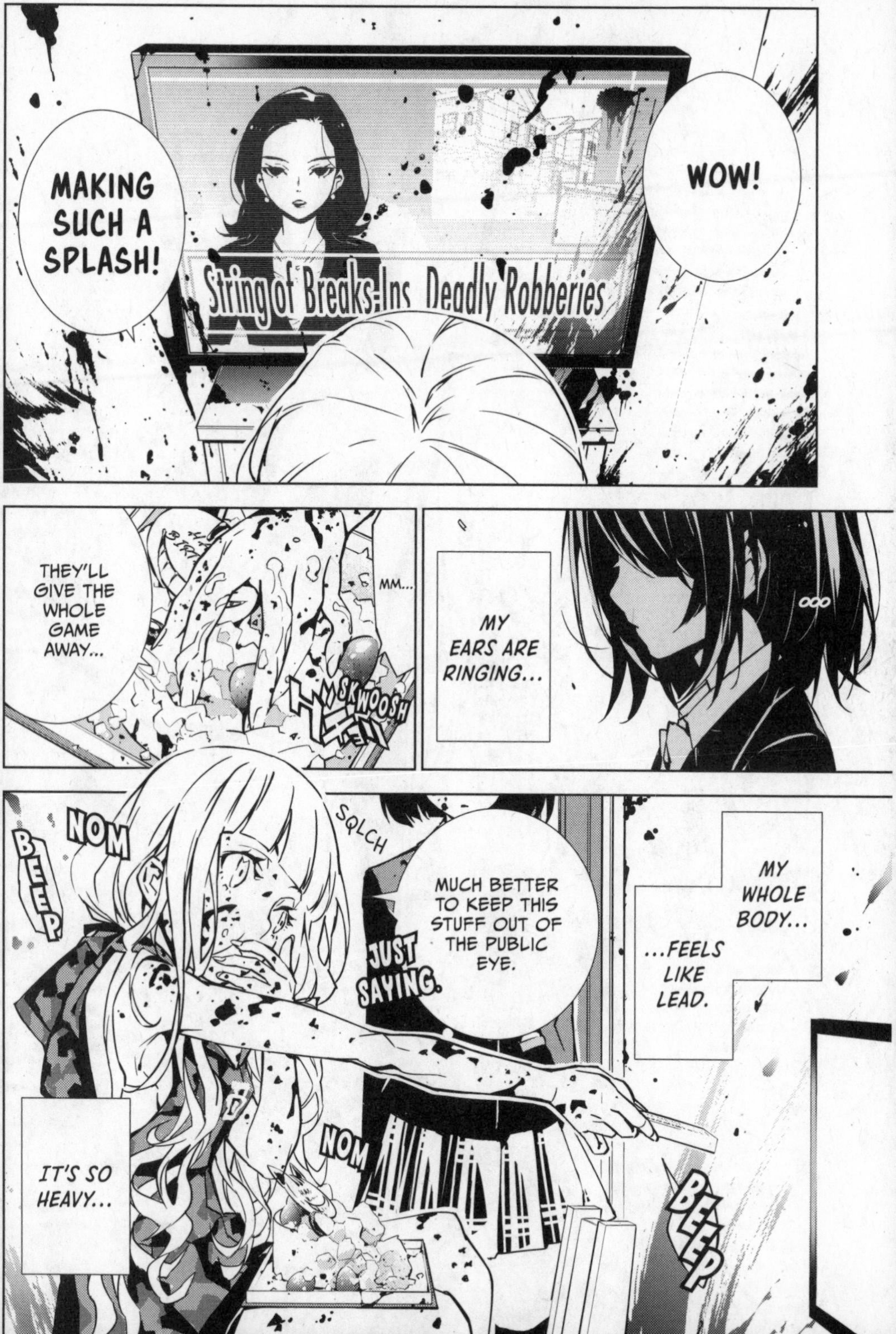
WOW!
MAKING SUCH A SPLASH!
String of Breaks-Ins Deadly Robberies
MY EARS ARE RINGING...
MM...
SKWOOSH
THEY'LL GIVE THE WHOLE GAME AWAY...
MY WHOLE BODY...
...FEELS LIKE LEAD.
MUCH BETTER TO KEEP THIS STUFF OUT OF THE PUBLIC EYE.
JUST SAYING.
SQLCH
NOM
BEEP
NOM
BEEP
IT'S SO HEAVY...

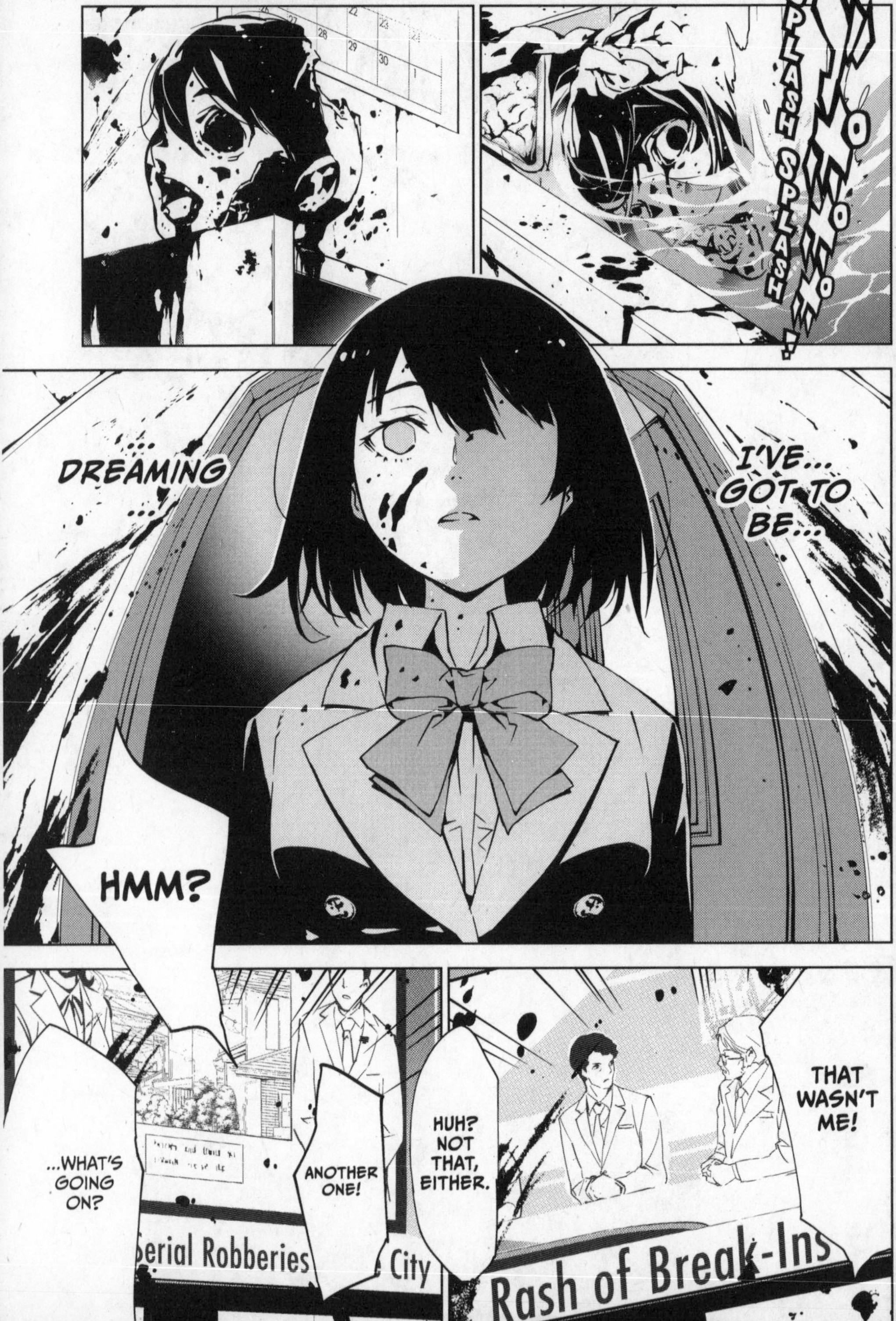
SPLASH SPLASH SPLASH
OOOOO...!
I'VE... GOT TO BE...
...DREAMING...
HMM?
THAT WASN'T ME!
HUH? NOT THAT, EITHER.
ANOTHER ONE!
...WHAT'S GOING ON?
Rash of Break-Ins
Serial Robberies
City

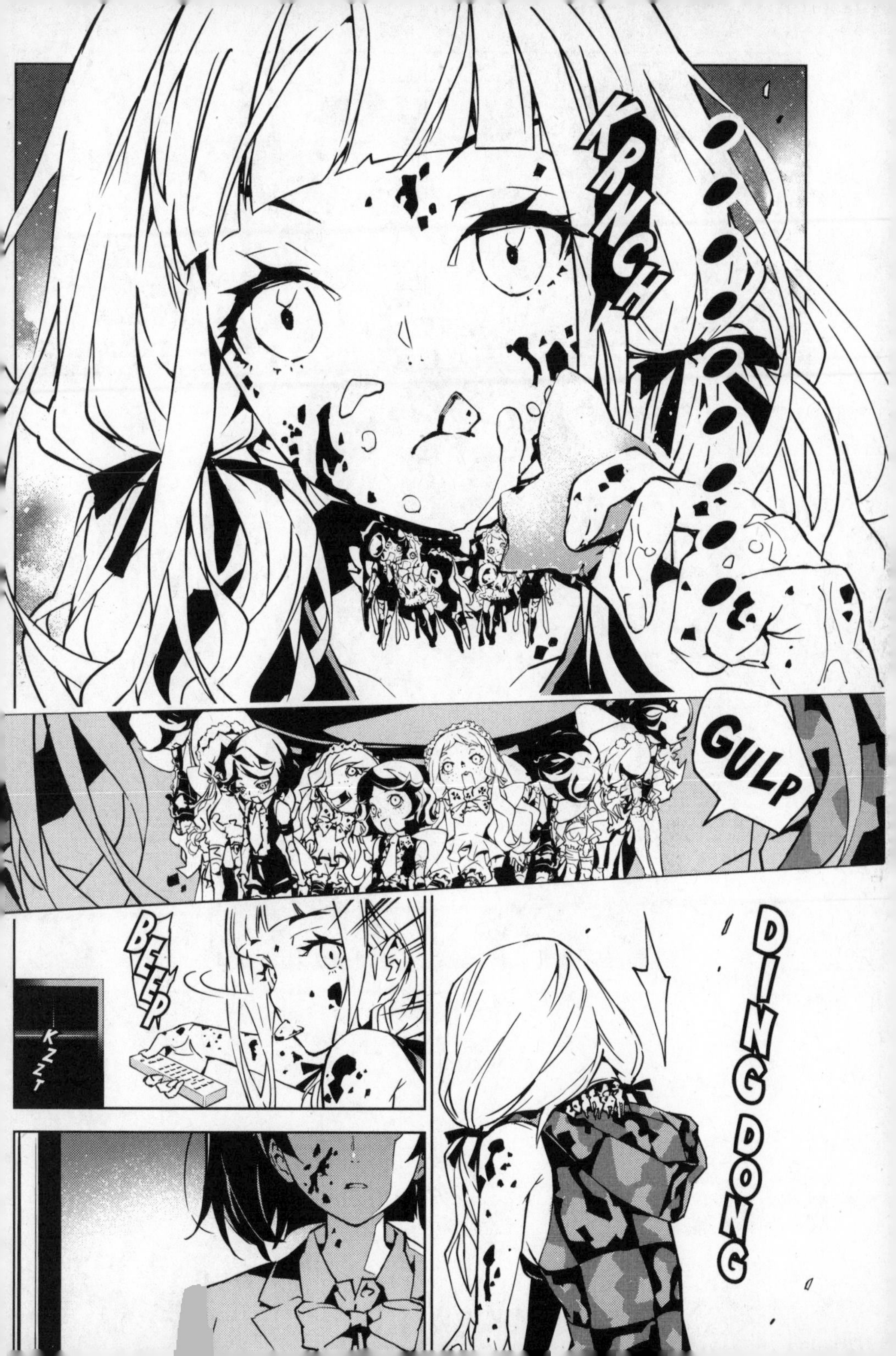
KRNCH
OOOOOOOOOOOO
GULP
DING DONG
BEEP
KZZT

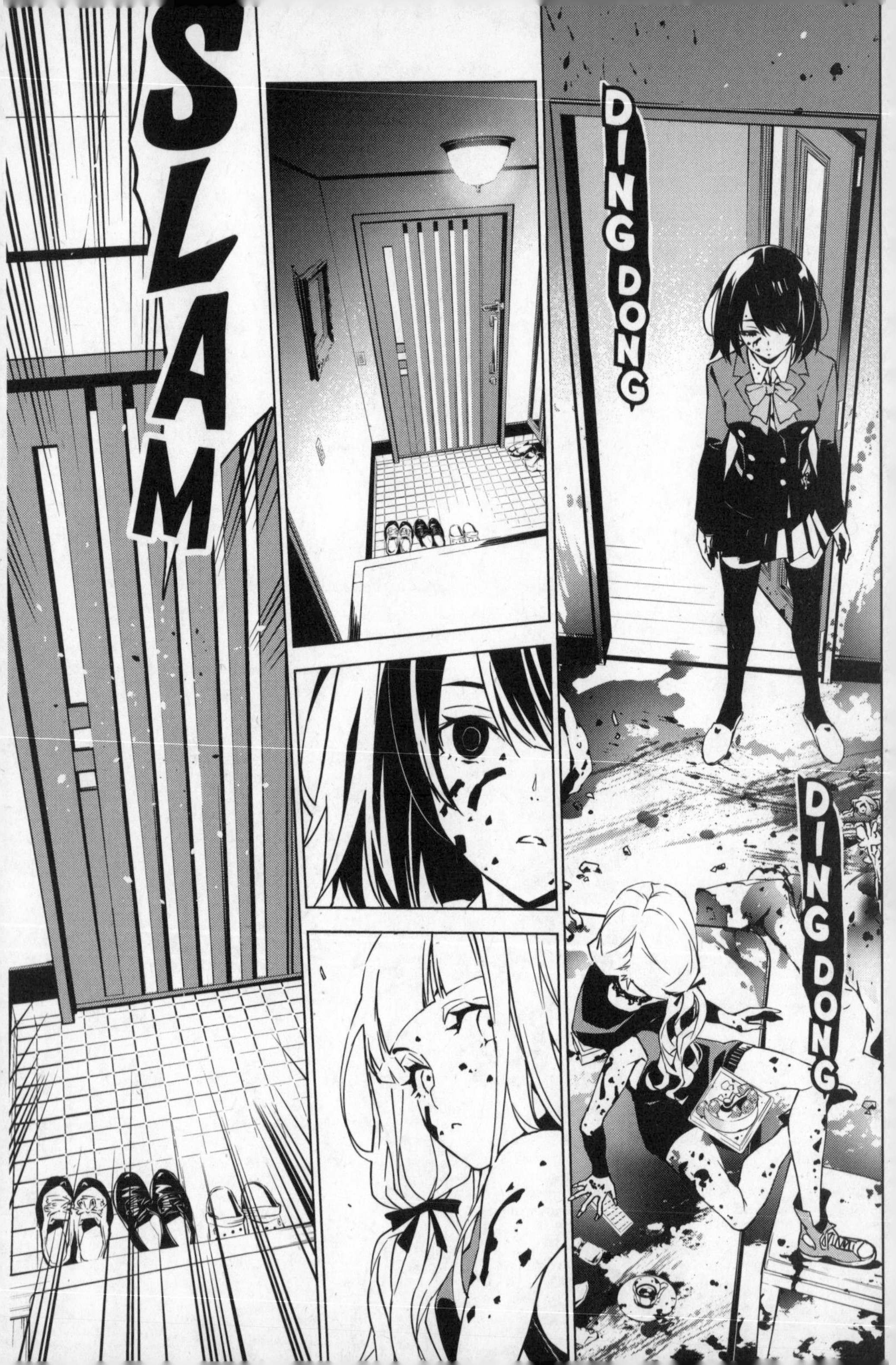
DING DONG
DING DONG
SLAM

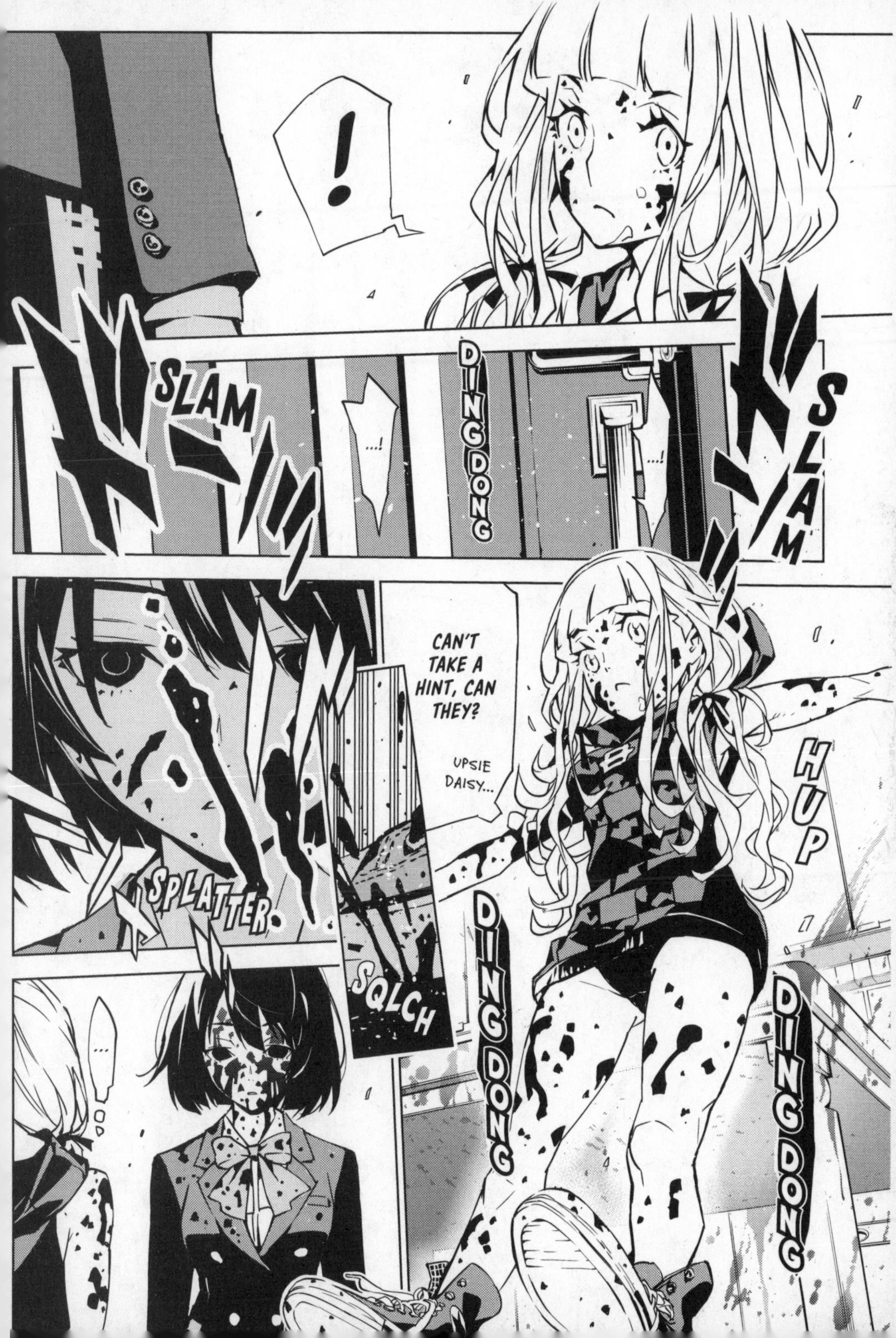
!
SLAM
...!
DING DONG
...!
SLAM
CAN'T TAKE A HINT, CAN THEY?
UPSIE DAISY...
HUP
SPLATTER
SQLCH
DING DONG
DING DONG
...!

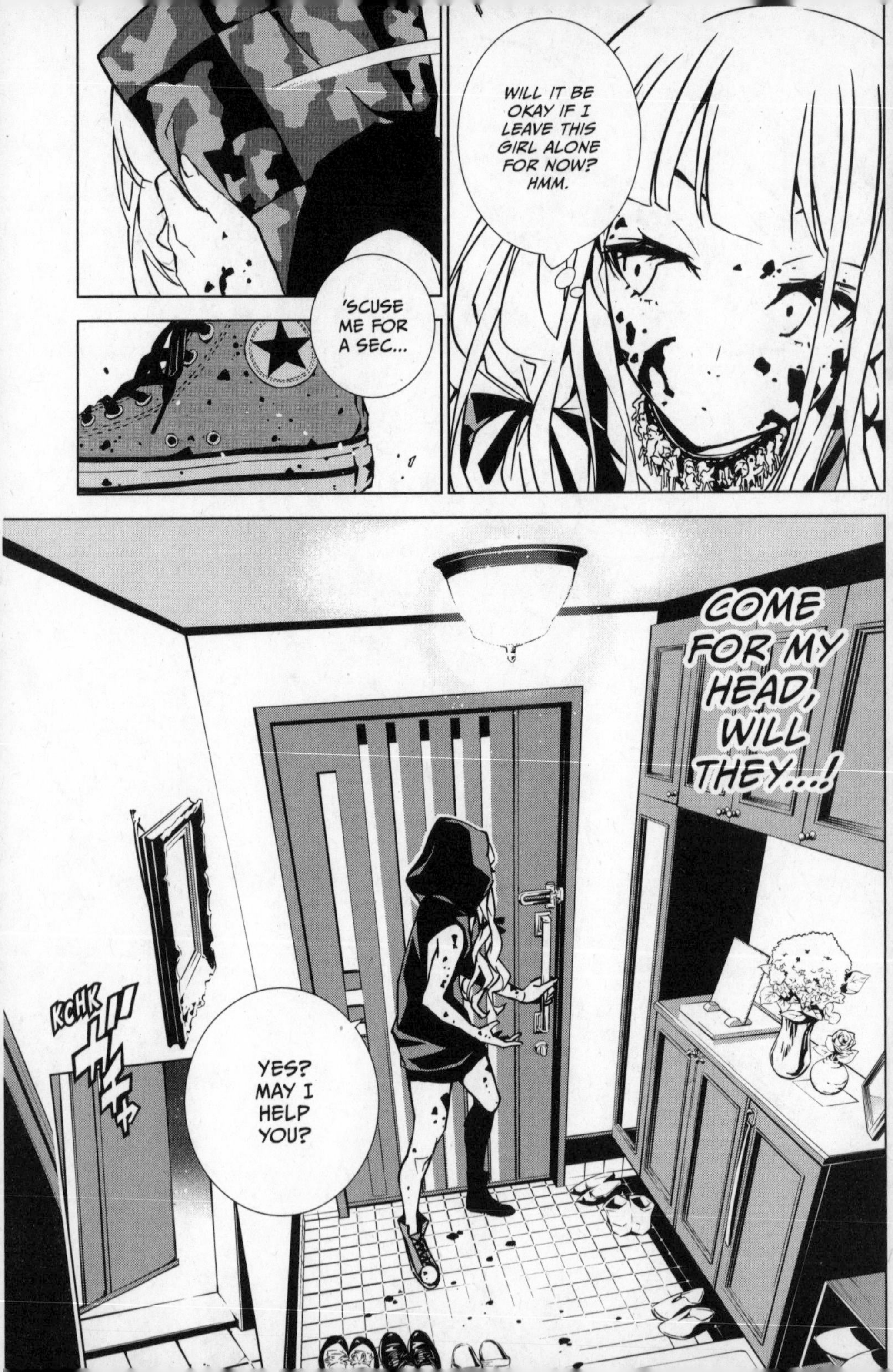
WILL IT BE OKAY IF I LEAVE THIS GIRL ALONE FOR NOW? HMM.
'SCUSE ME FOR A SEC...
COME FOR MY HEAD, WILL THEY...!
KCHK
YES? MAY I HELP YOU?

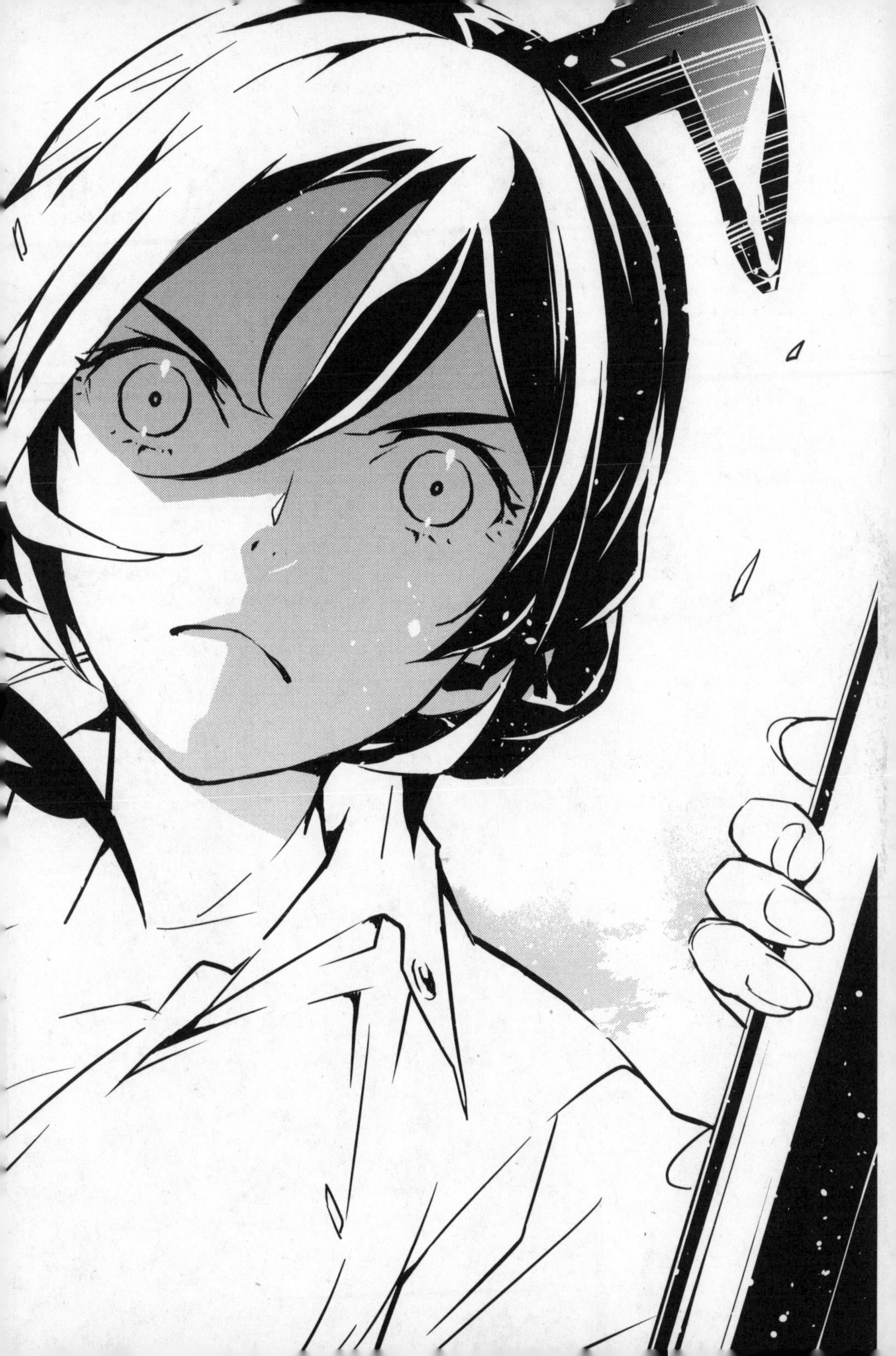

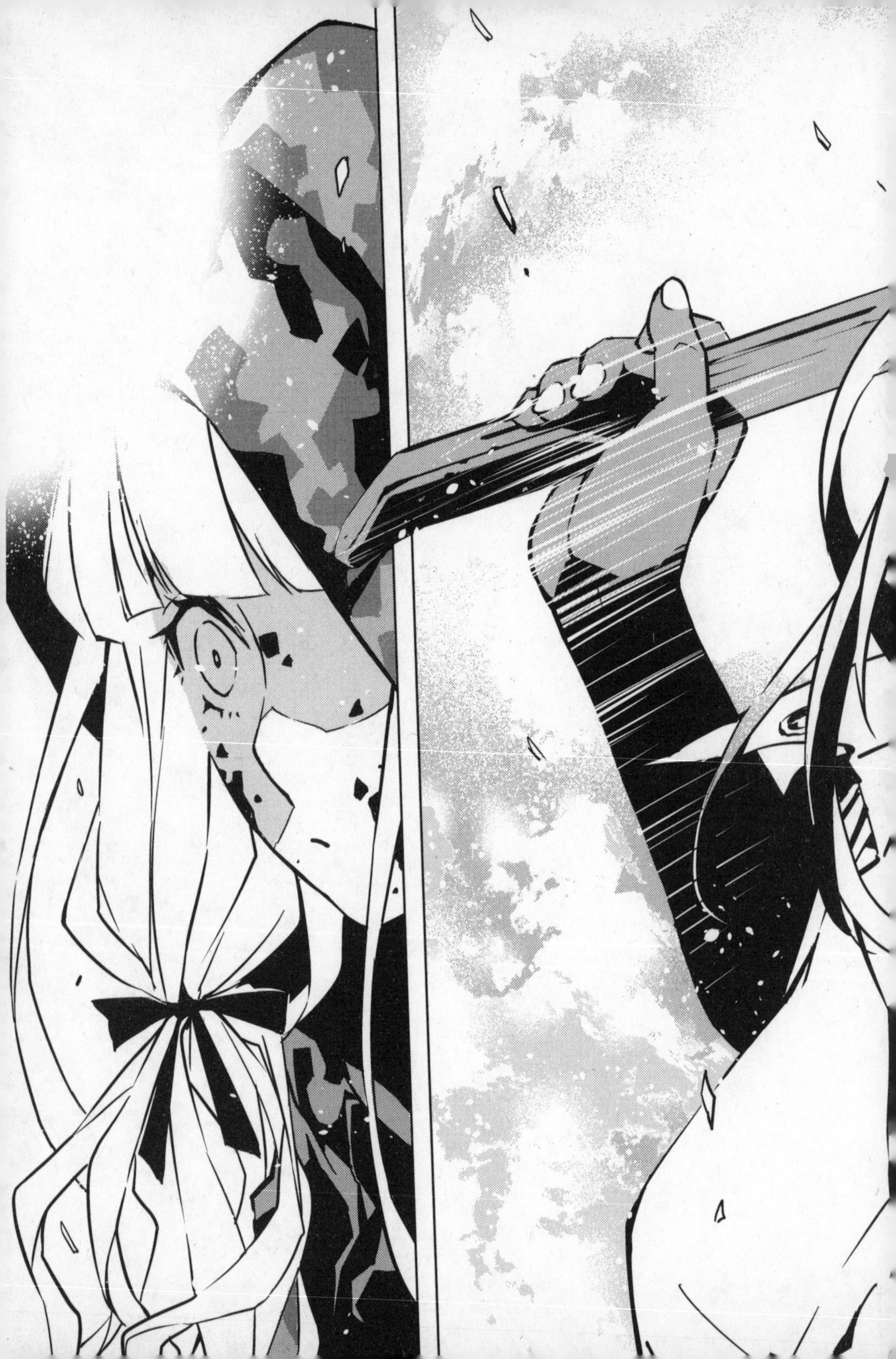

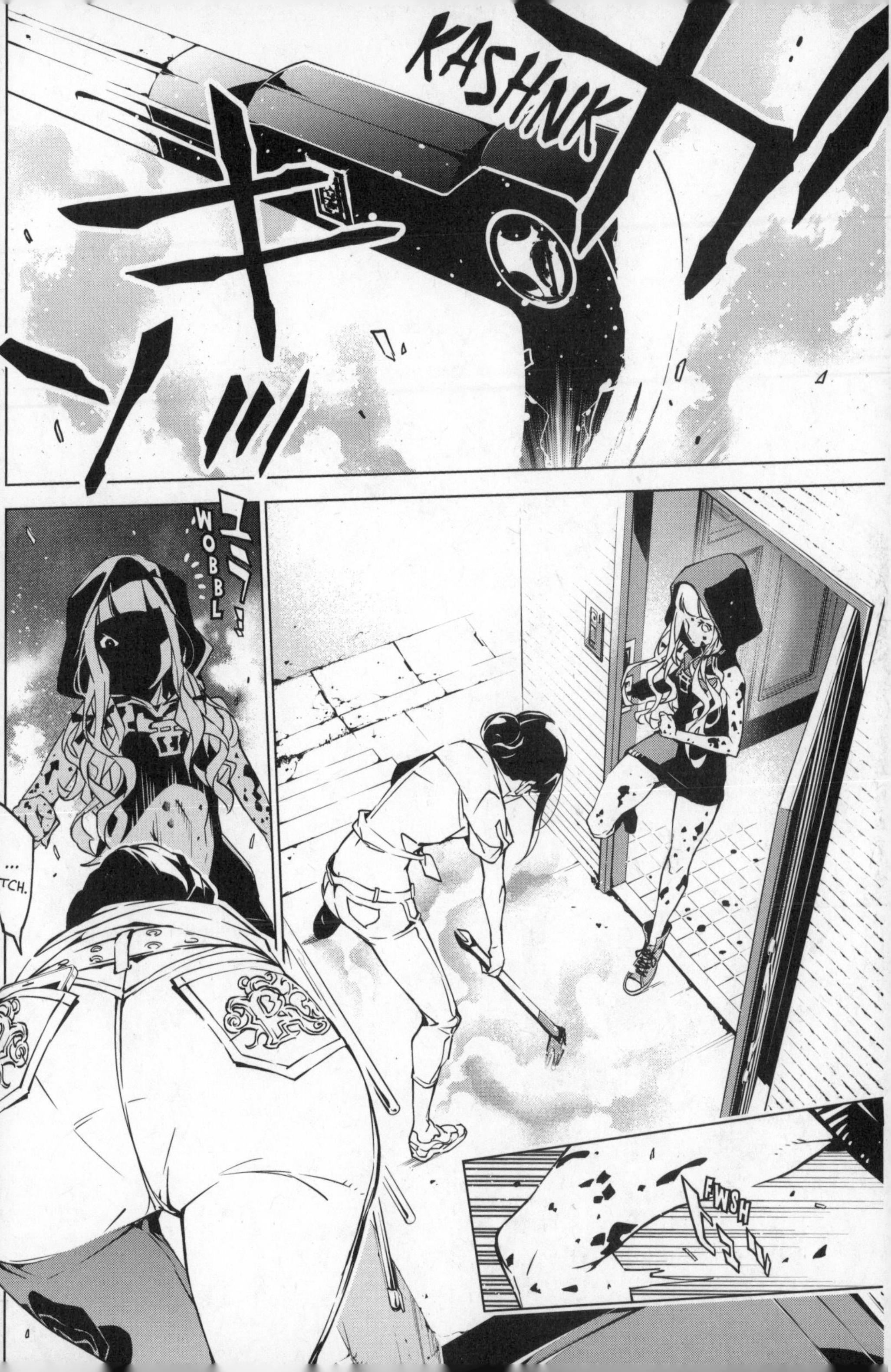
KASHNK
WOBBL
...TCH.
FWSH

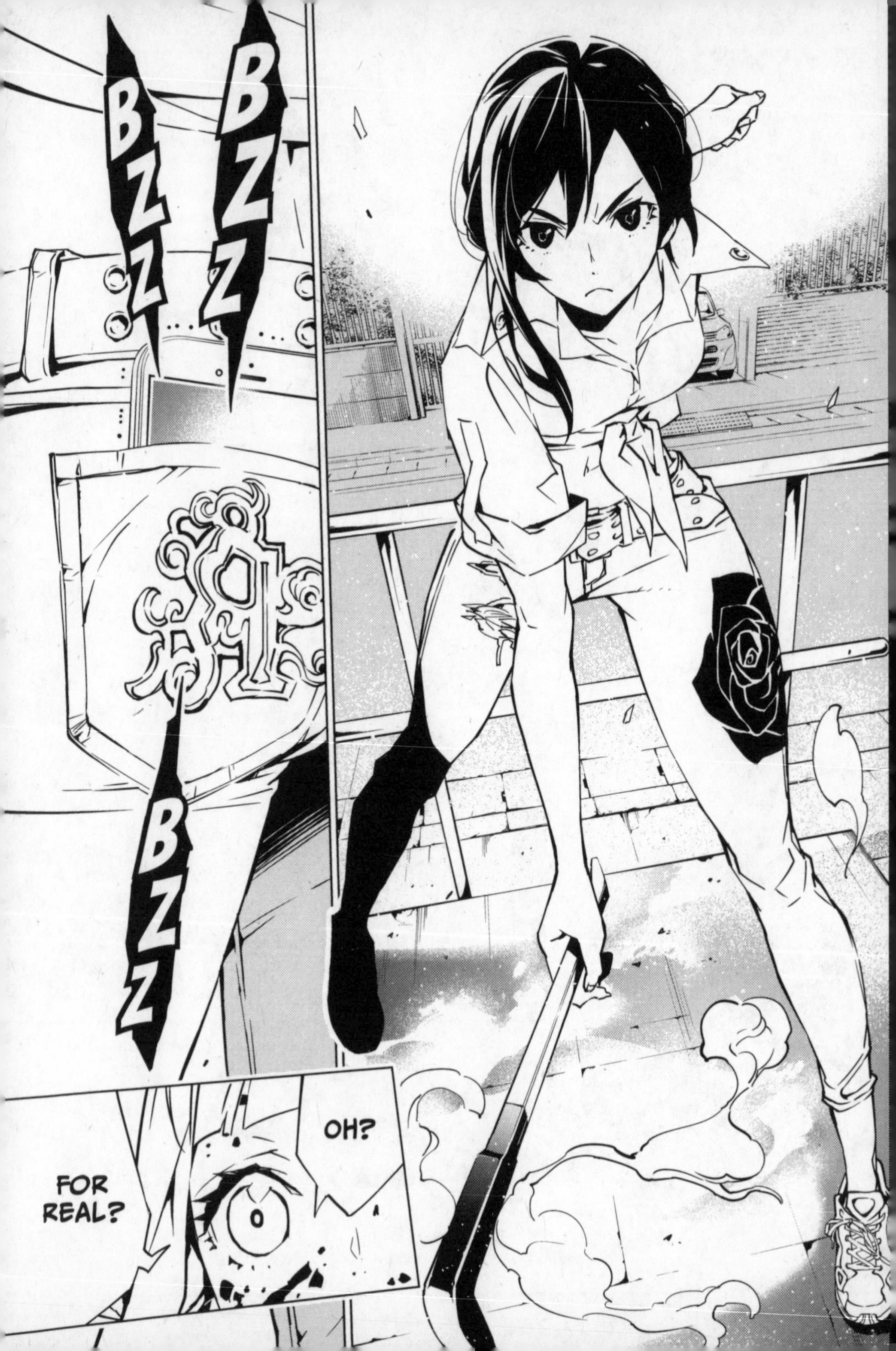
BZZ
BZZ
BZZ
OH?
FOR REAL?

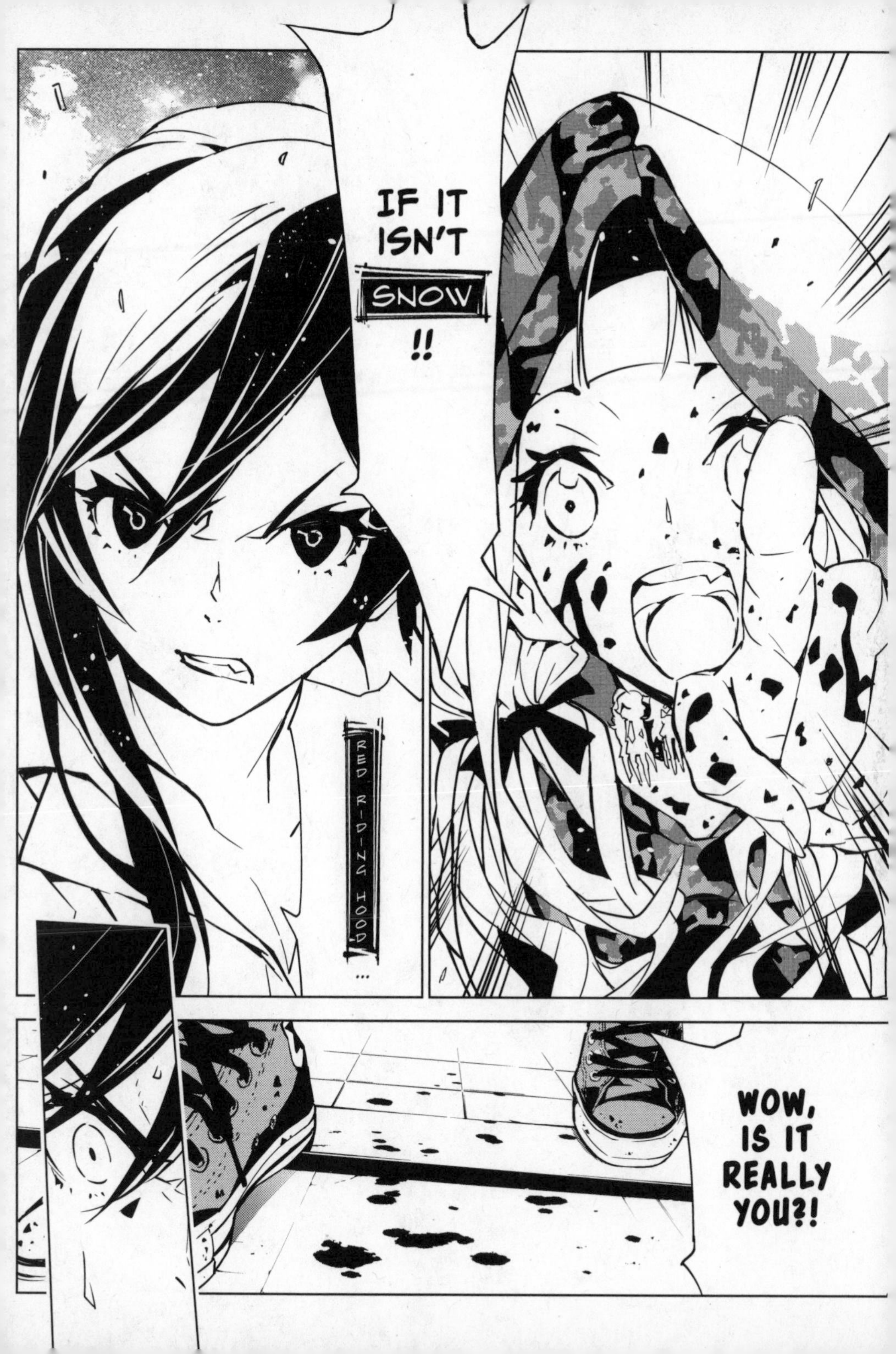
IF IT ISN'T SNOW!!
RED RIDING HOOD...
WOW, IS IT REALLY YOU?!

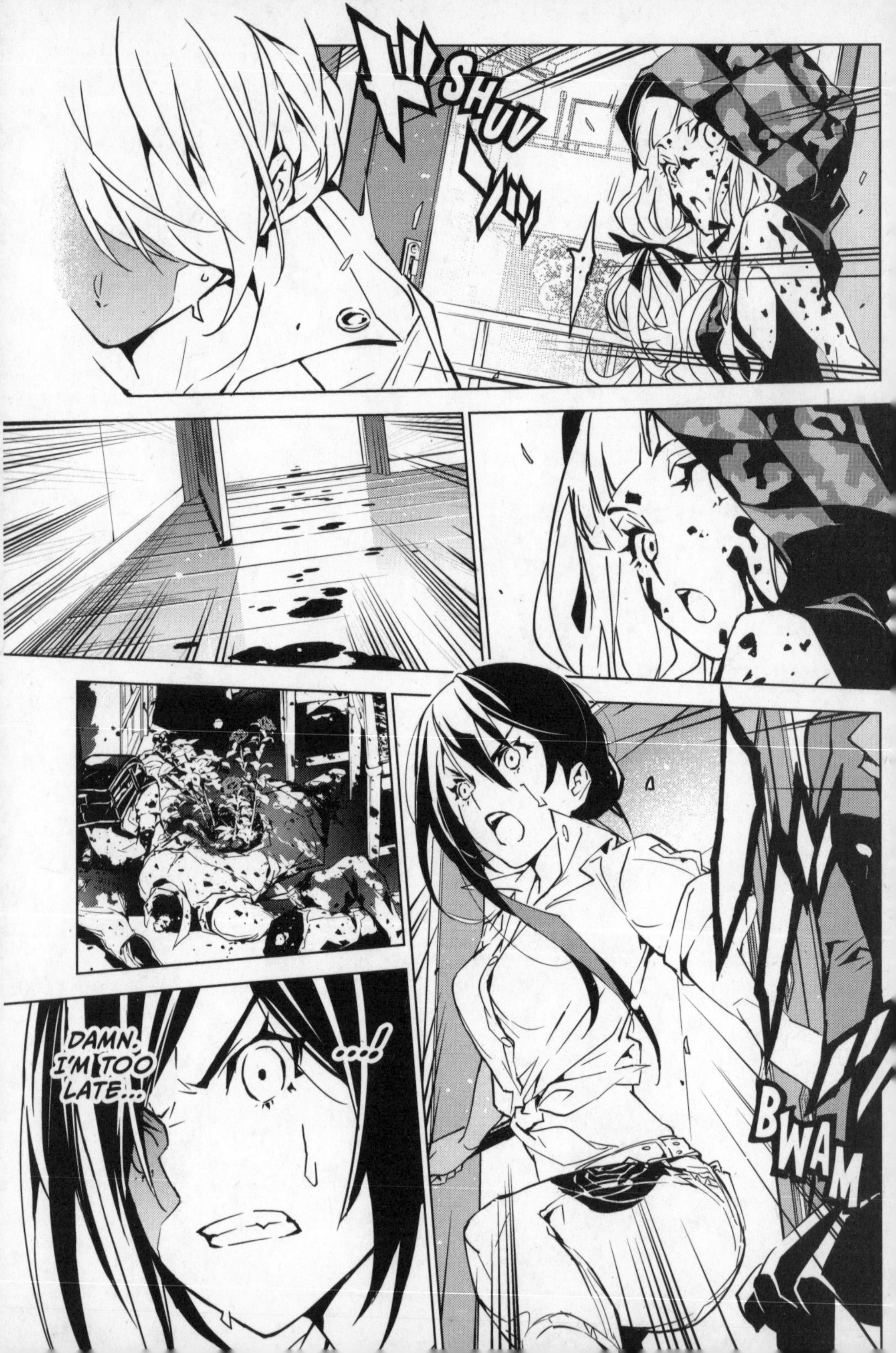
SHUV
...!
DAMN. I'M TOO LATE...
BWAM

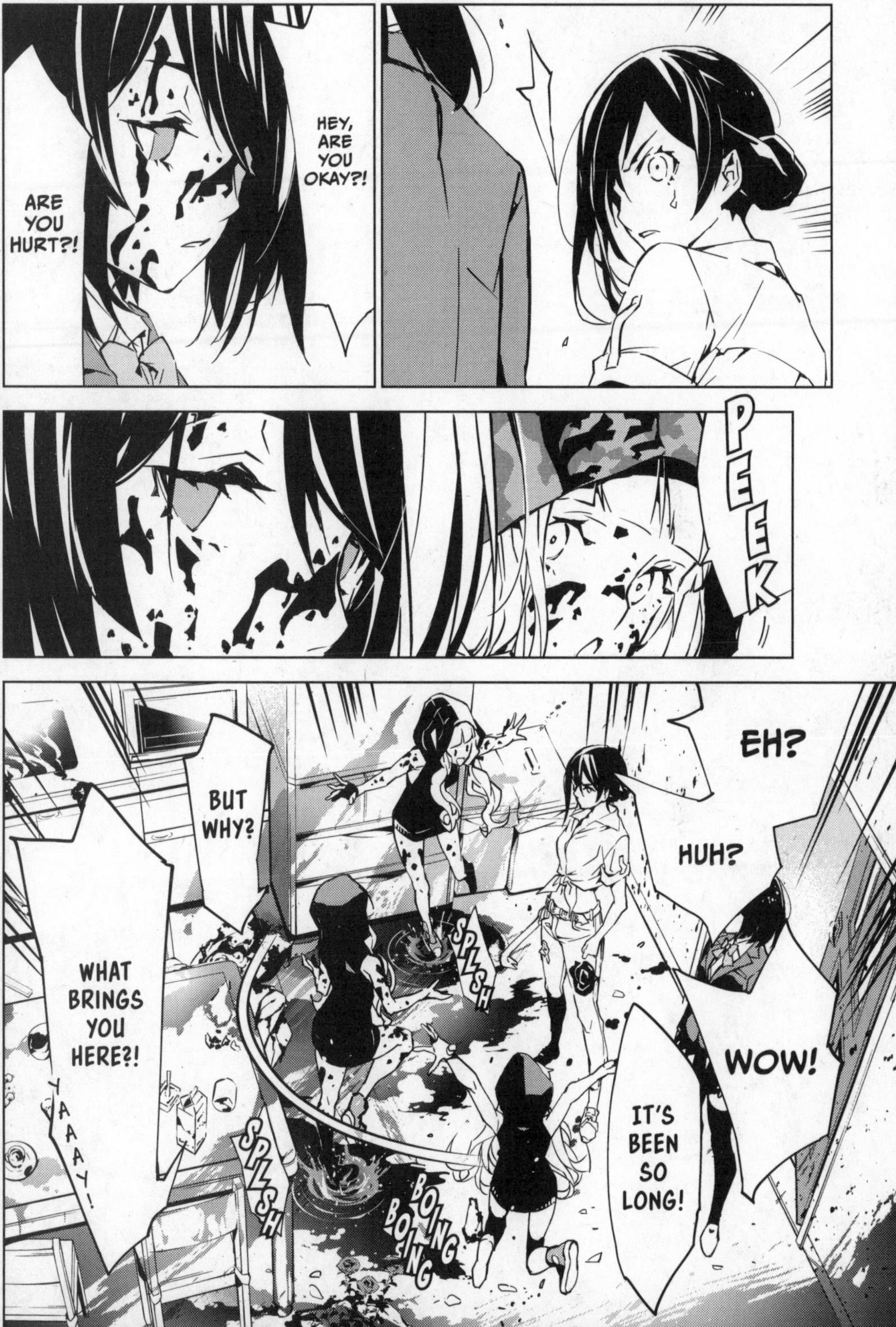
HEY, ARE YOU OKAY?!
ARE YOU HURT?!
PEEK
EH?
HUH?
BUT WHY?
WOW!
IT'S BEEN SO LONG!
WHAT BRINGS YOU HERE?!
SPLSH
YAAAAY!
SPLSH
BOING BOING

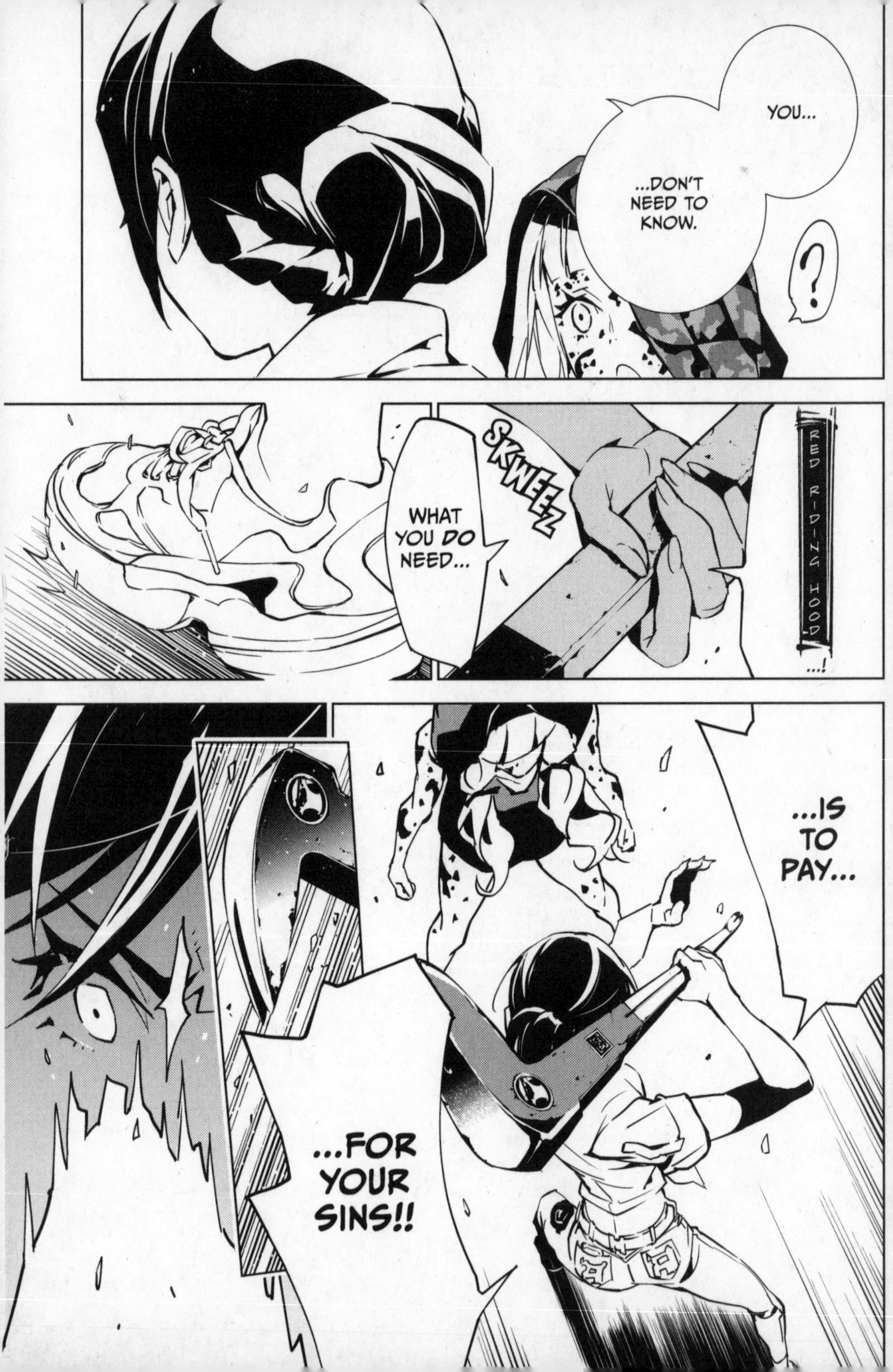
YOU...
...DON'T NEED TO KNOW.
?
RED RIDING HOOD
...!
SKWEEZ
WHAT YOU DO NEED...
...IS TO PAY...
...FOR YOUR SINS!!

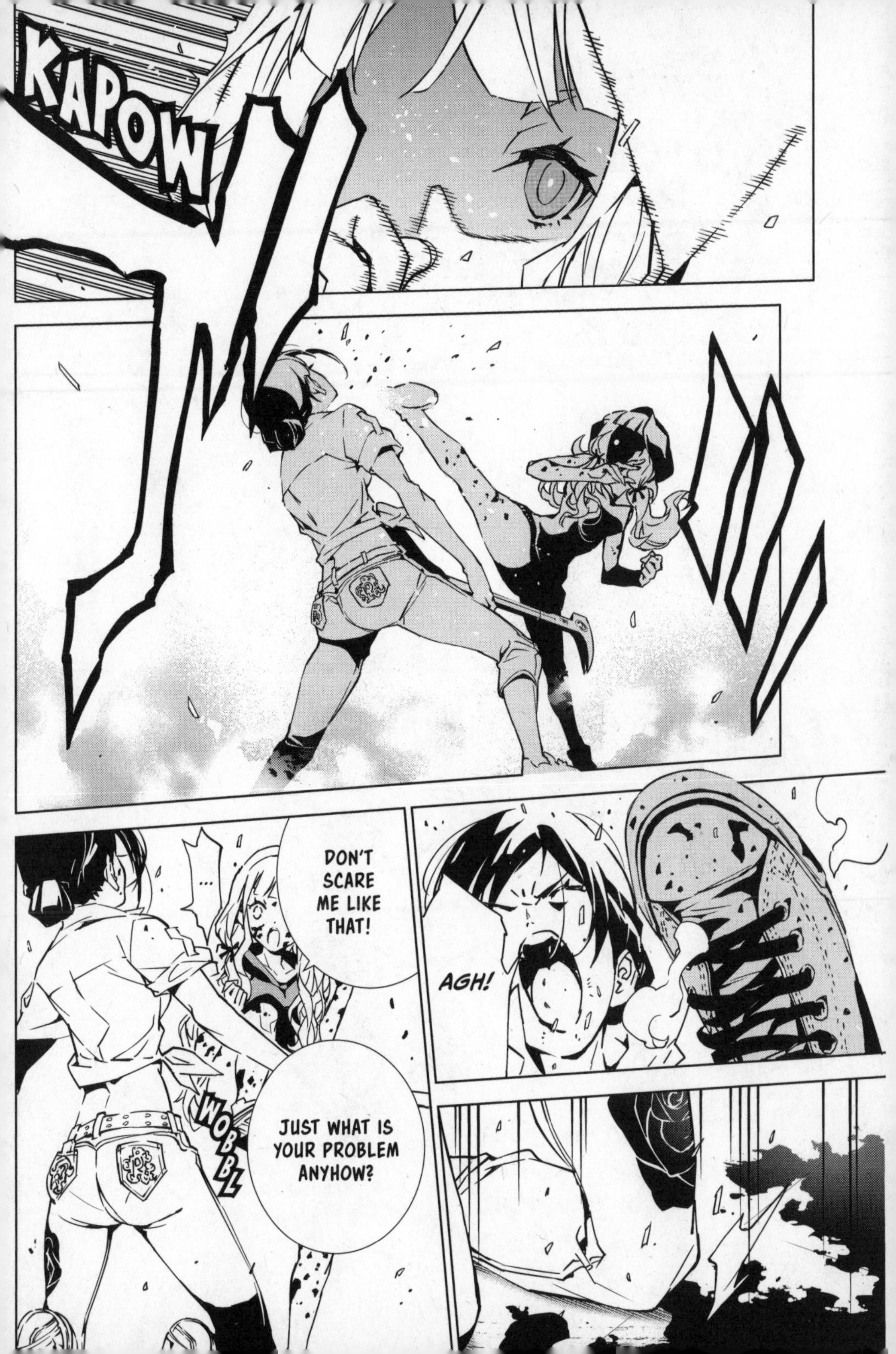
KAPOW
AGH!
DON'T SCARE ME LIKE THAT!
...
JUST WHAT IS YOUR PROBLEM ANYHOW?
WOBBL

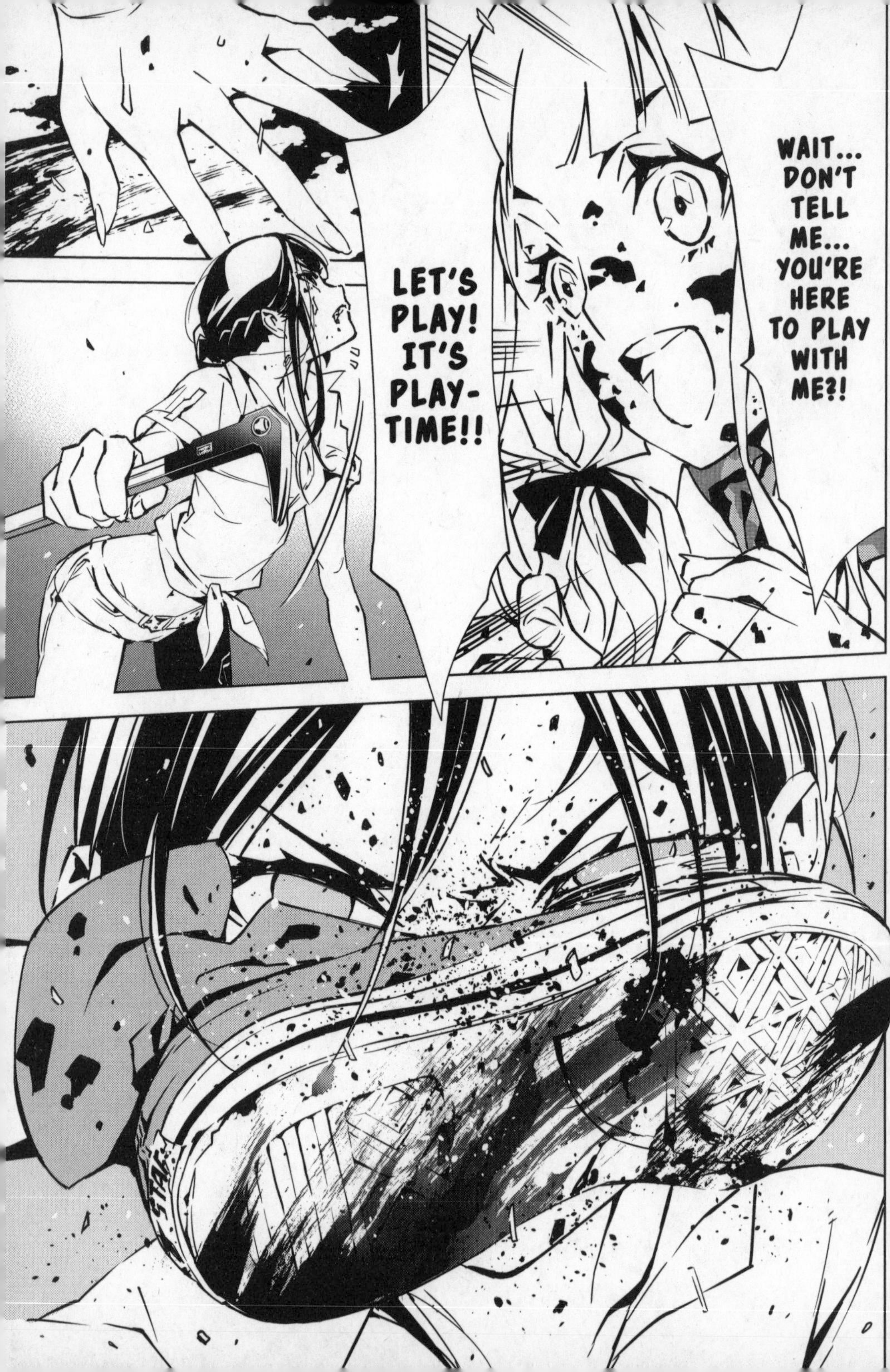
WAIT... DON'T TELL ME... YOU'RE HERE TO PLAY WITH ME?!
LET'S PLAY! IT'S PLAY-TIME!!

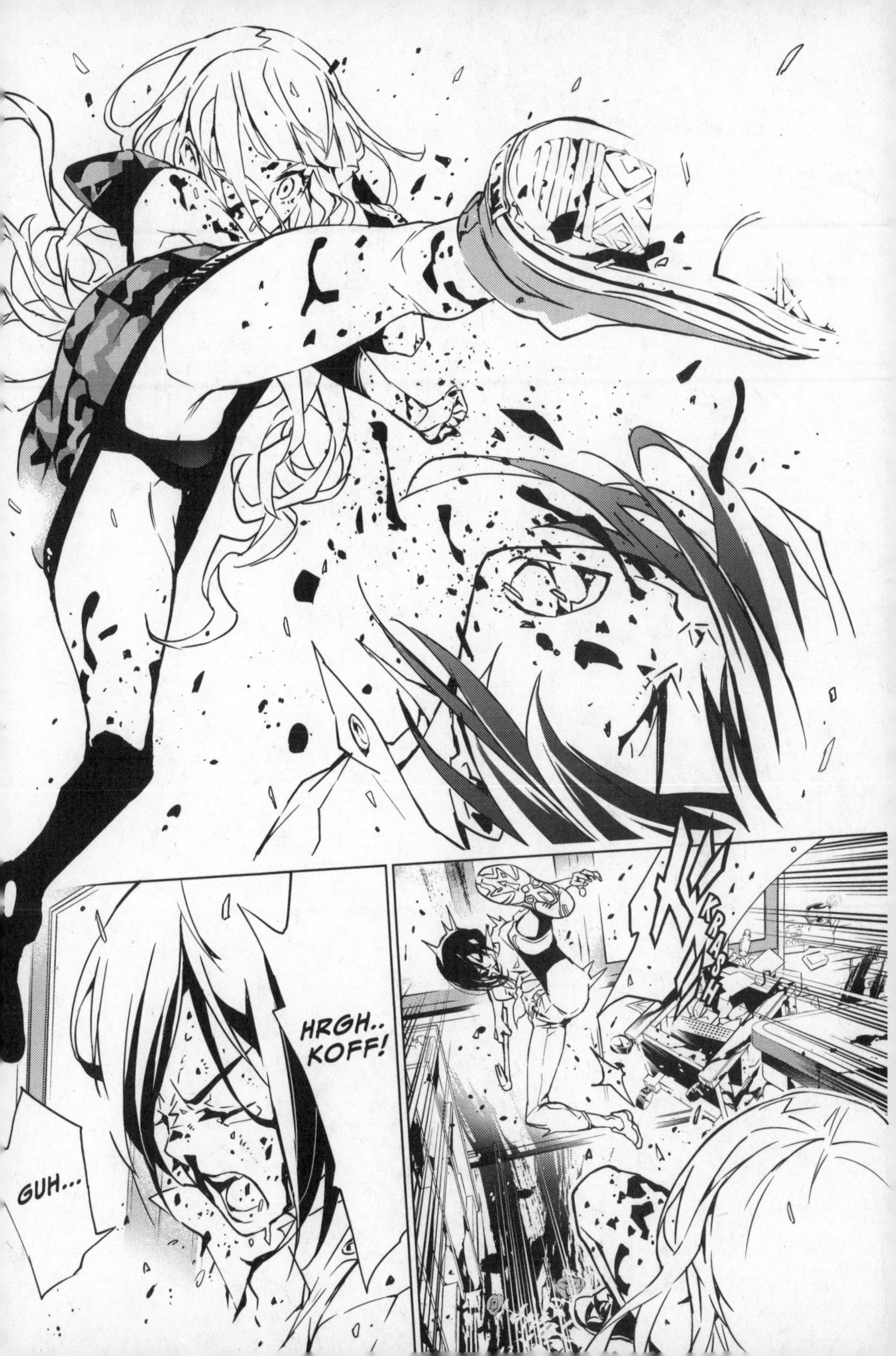
KRASH
HRGH..
KOFF!
GUH...

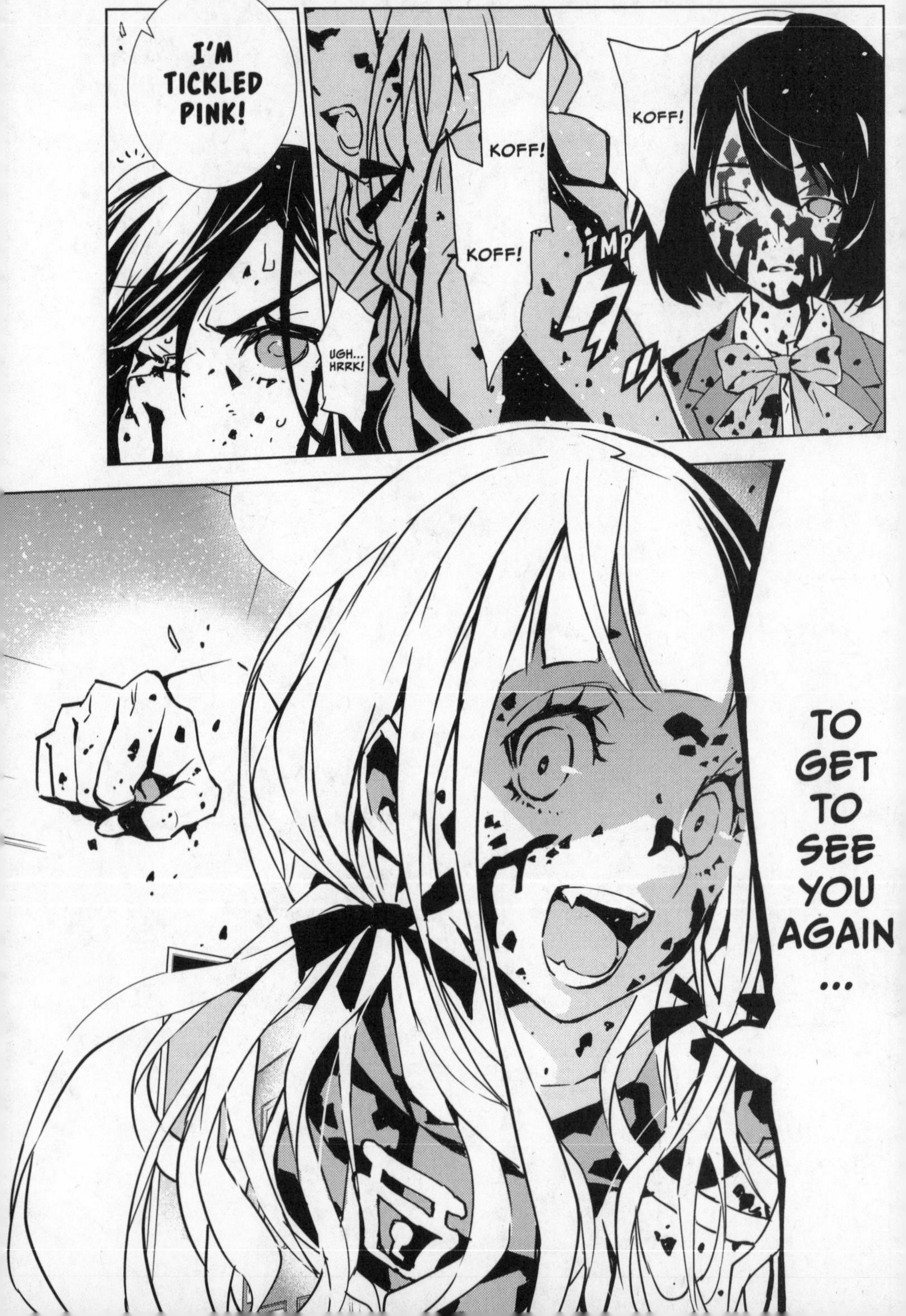
KOFF!
KOFF!
KOFF!
TMP
UGH... HRRK!
I'M TICKLED PINK!
TO GET TO SEE YOU AGAIN...

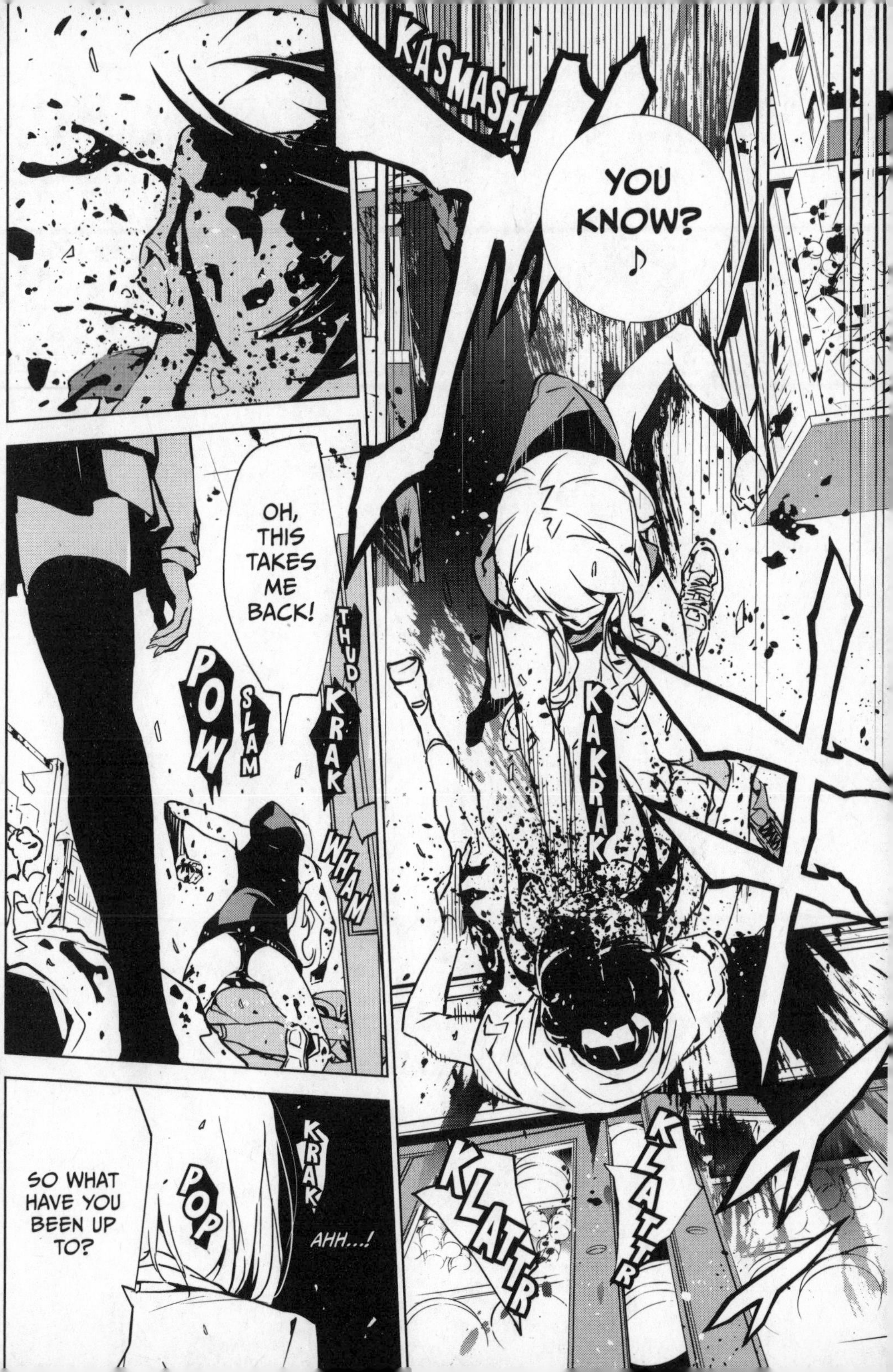
KASMASH
YOU KNOW? ♪
KAKRAK
KLATTR
KLATTR
OH, THIS TAKES ME BACK!
THUD
KRAK
SLAM
POW
WHAM
KRAK
POP
AHH...!
SO WHAT HAVE YOU BEEN UP TO?

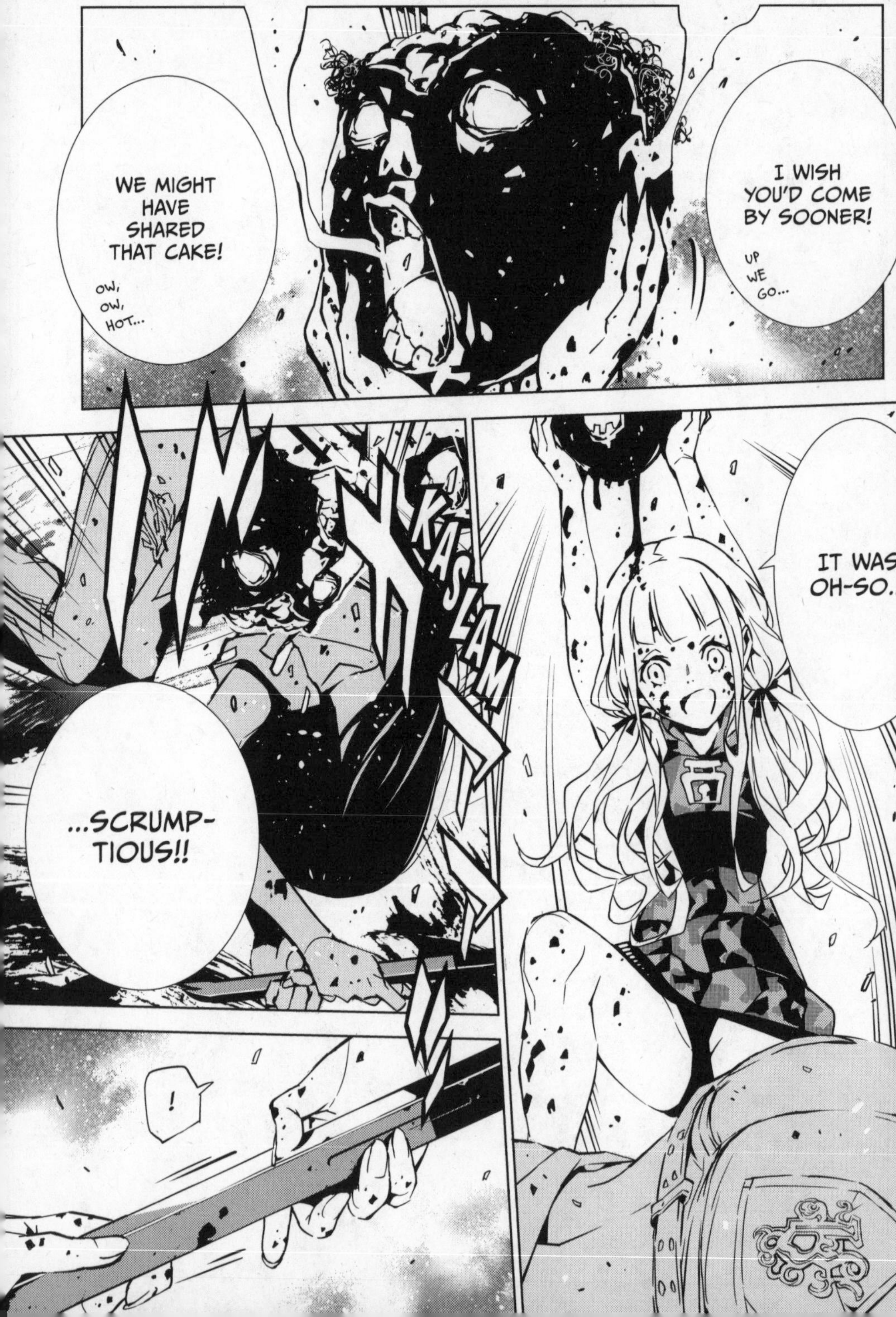
I WISH YOU'D COME BY SOONER!
UP WE GO...
WE MIGHT HAVE SHARED THAT CAKE!
OW, OW, HOT...
IT WAS OH-SO...
KASLAM
...SCRUMP-TIOUS!!
!

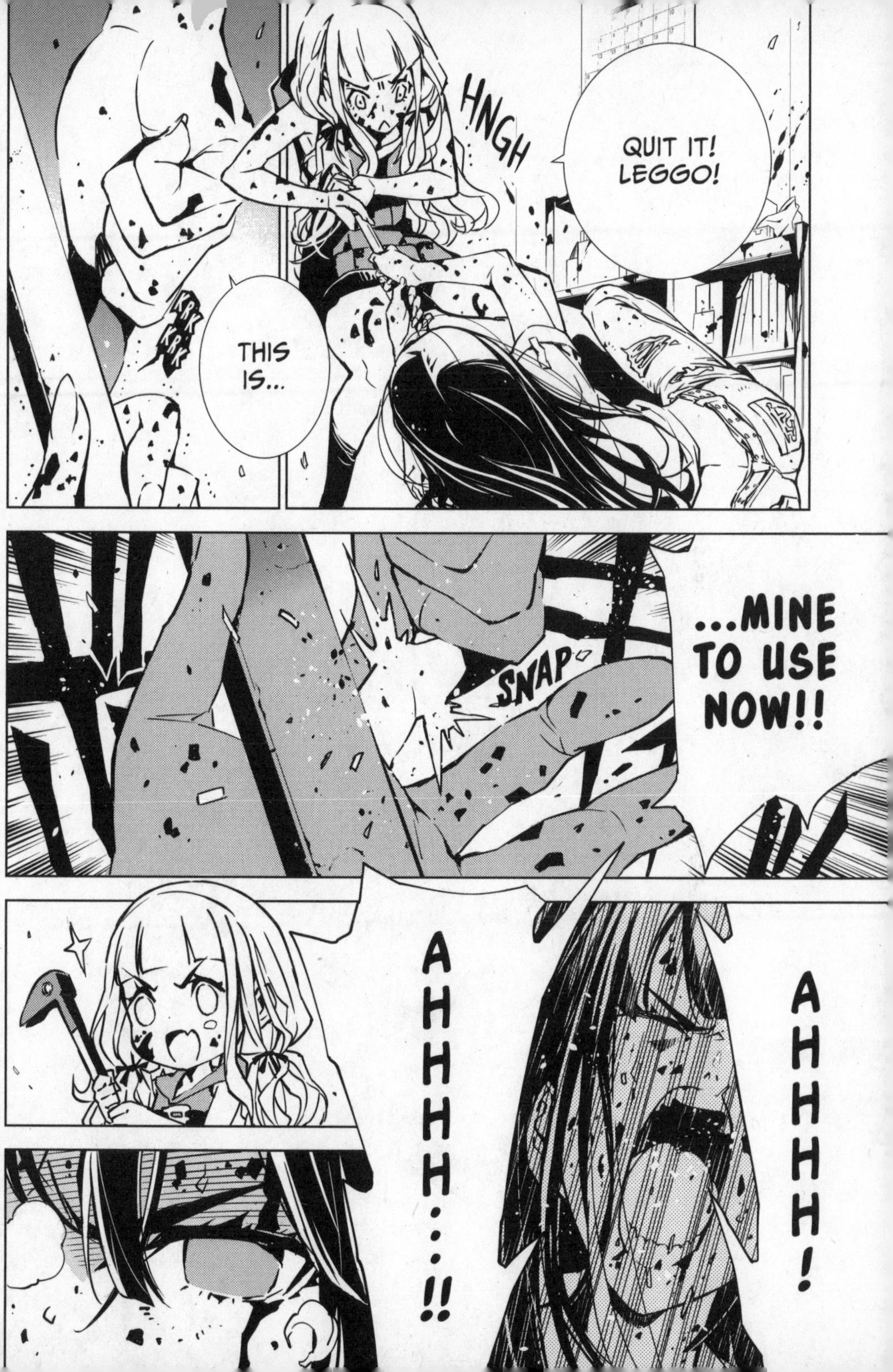
HNGH
QUIT IT! LEGGO!
KRK KRK
THIS IS...
SNAP
...MINE TO USE NOW!!
AHHHH!
AHHHH...!!

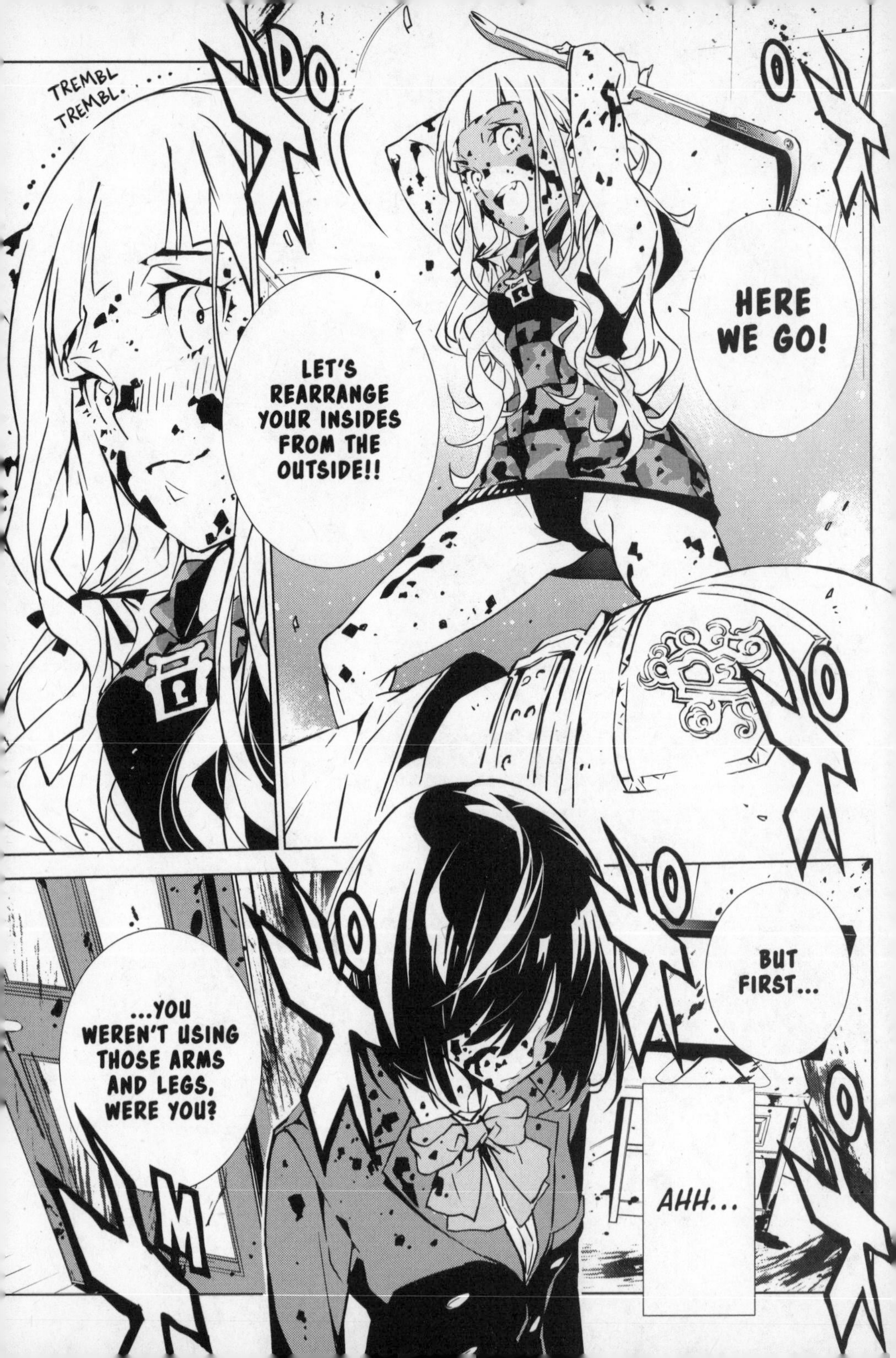
HERE WE GO!
LET'S REARRANGE YOUR INSIDES FROM THE OUTSIDE!!
TREMBL TREMBL
BUT FIRST...
AHH...
...YOU WEREN'T USING THOSE ARMS AND LEGS, WERE YOU?

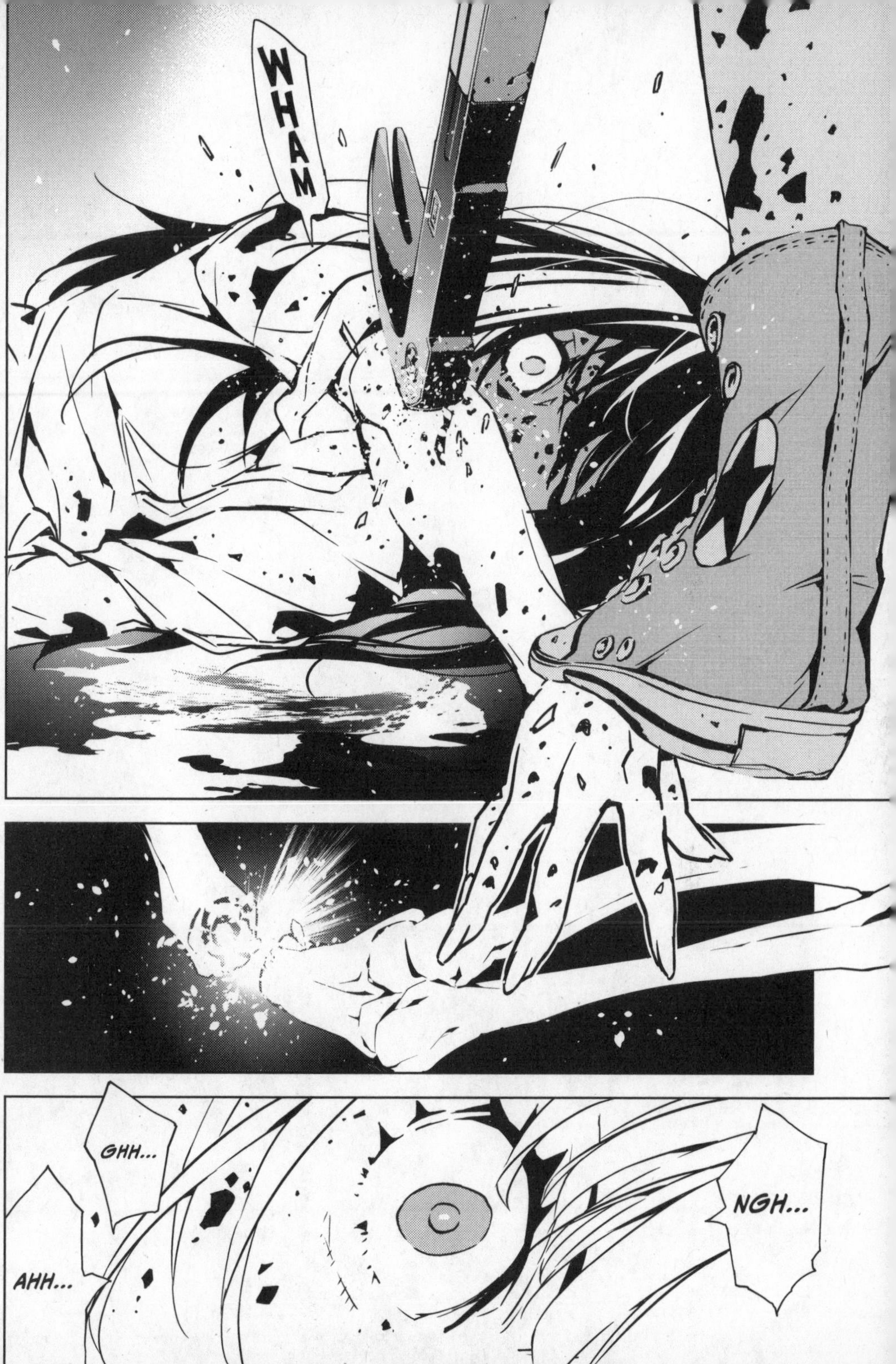
WHAM
NGH...
GHH...
AHH...

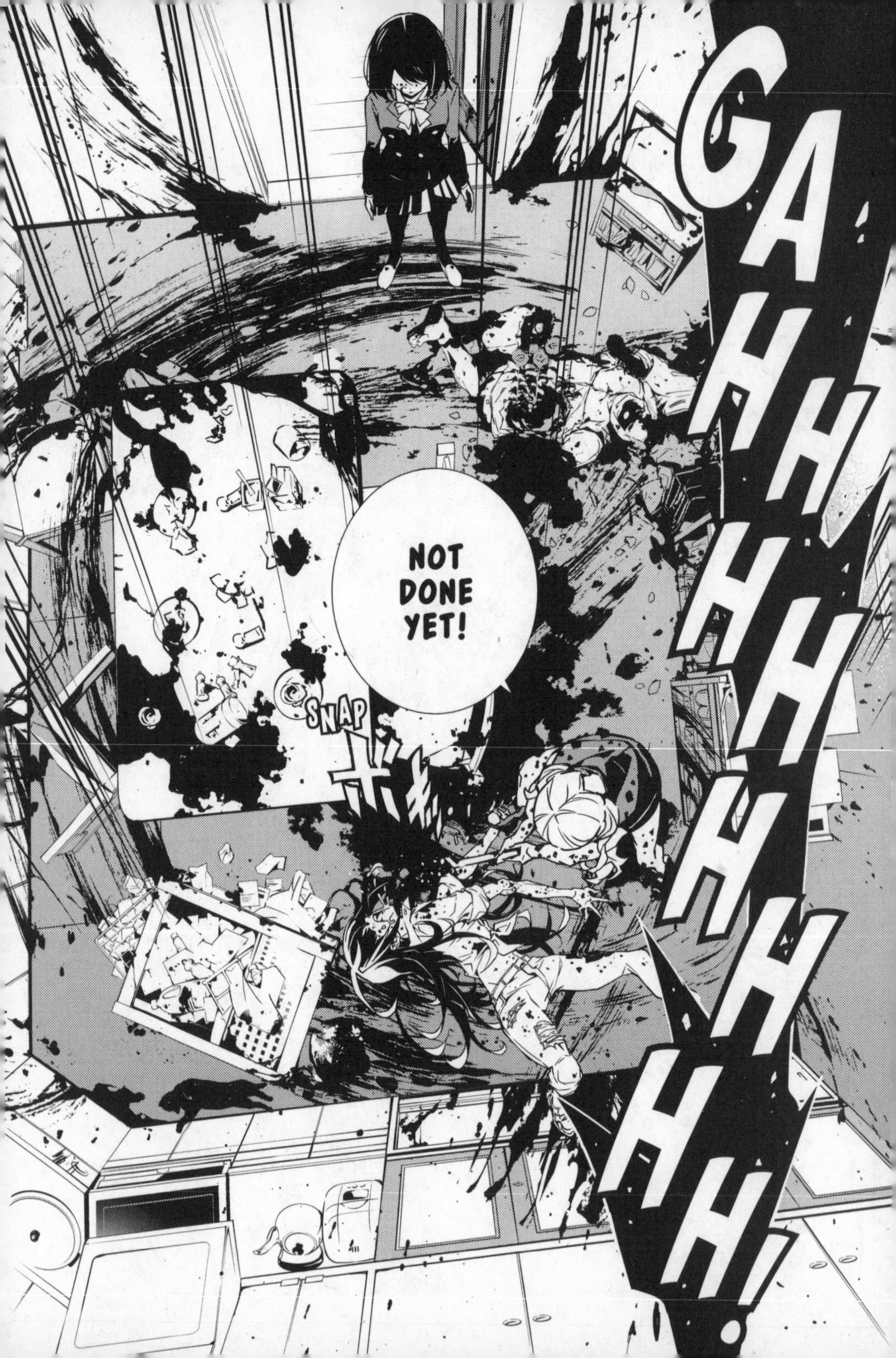
GAHHHHHHHHH!!
NOT DONE YET!
SNAP

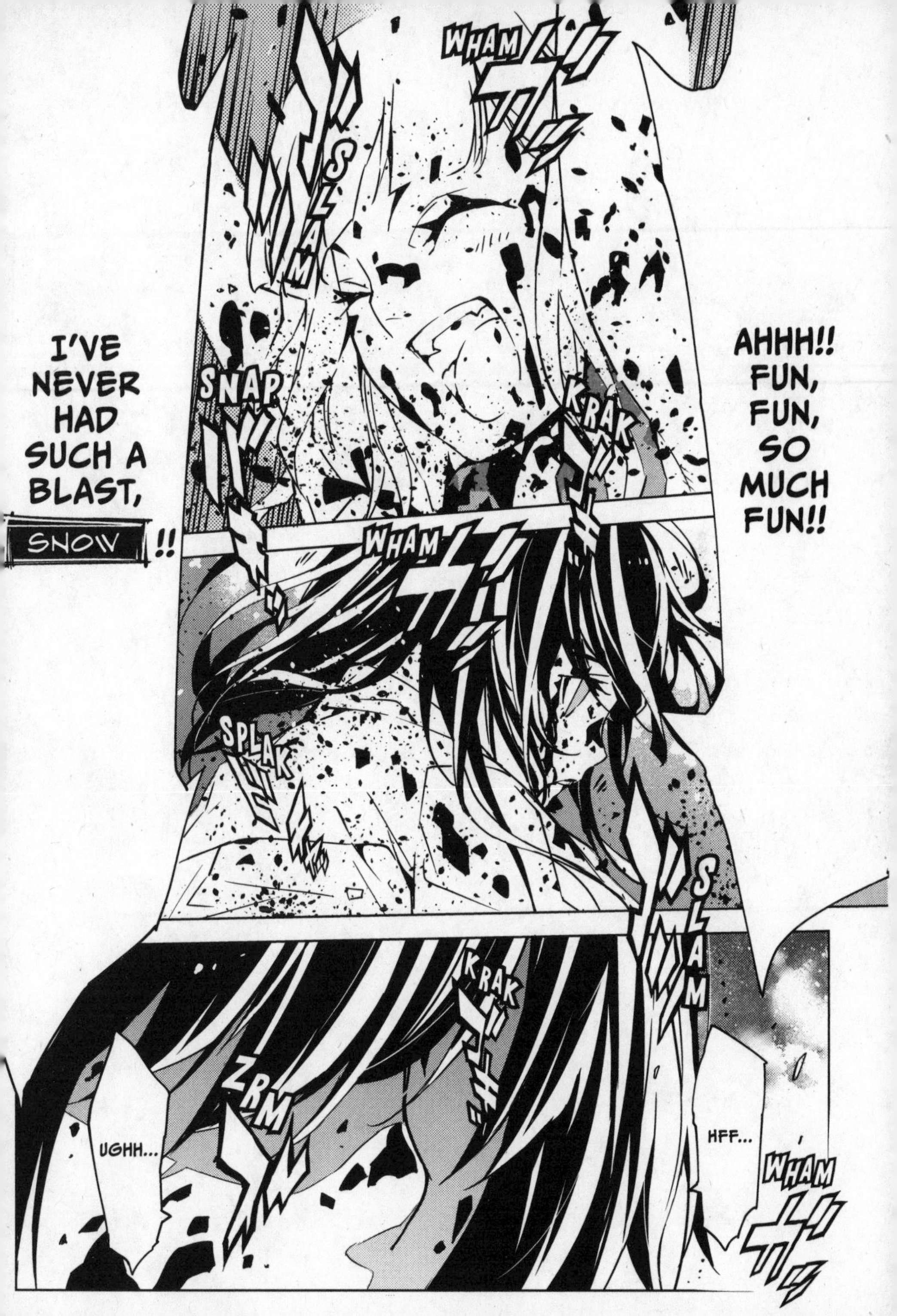
AHHH!! FUN, FUN, SO MUCH FUN!!
I'VE NEVER HAD SUCH A BLAST, SNOW!!
WHAM
SLAM
KRAK
SNAP
WHAM
SPLAK
SLAM
KRAK
ZRM
WHAM
HFF...
UGHH...

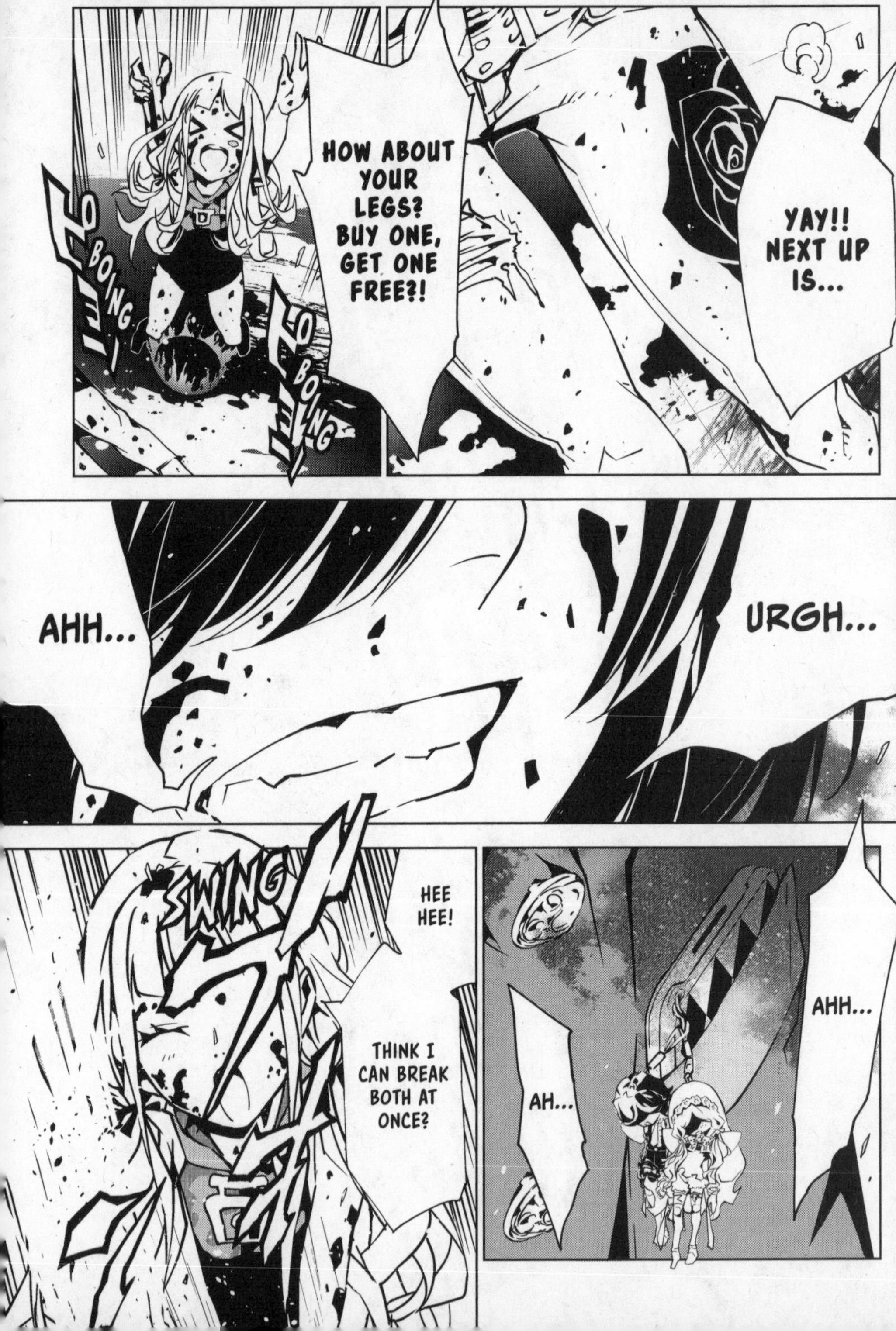
YAY!! NEXT UP IS...
HOW ABOUT YOUR LEGS? BUY ONE, GET ONE FREE?!
BOING
BOING
URGH...
AHH...
AHH...
AH...
HEE HEE!
THINK I CAN BREAK BOTH AT ONCE?
SWING

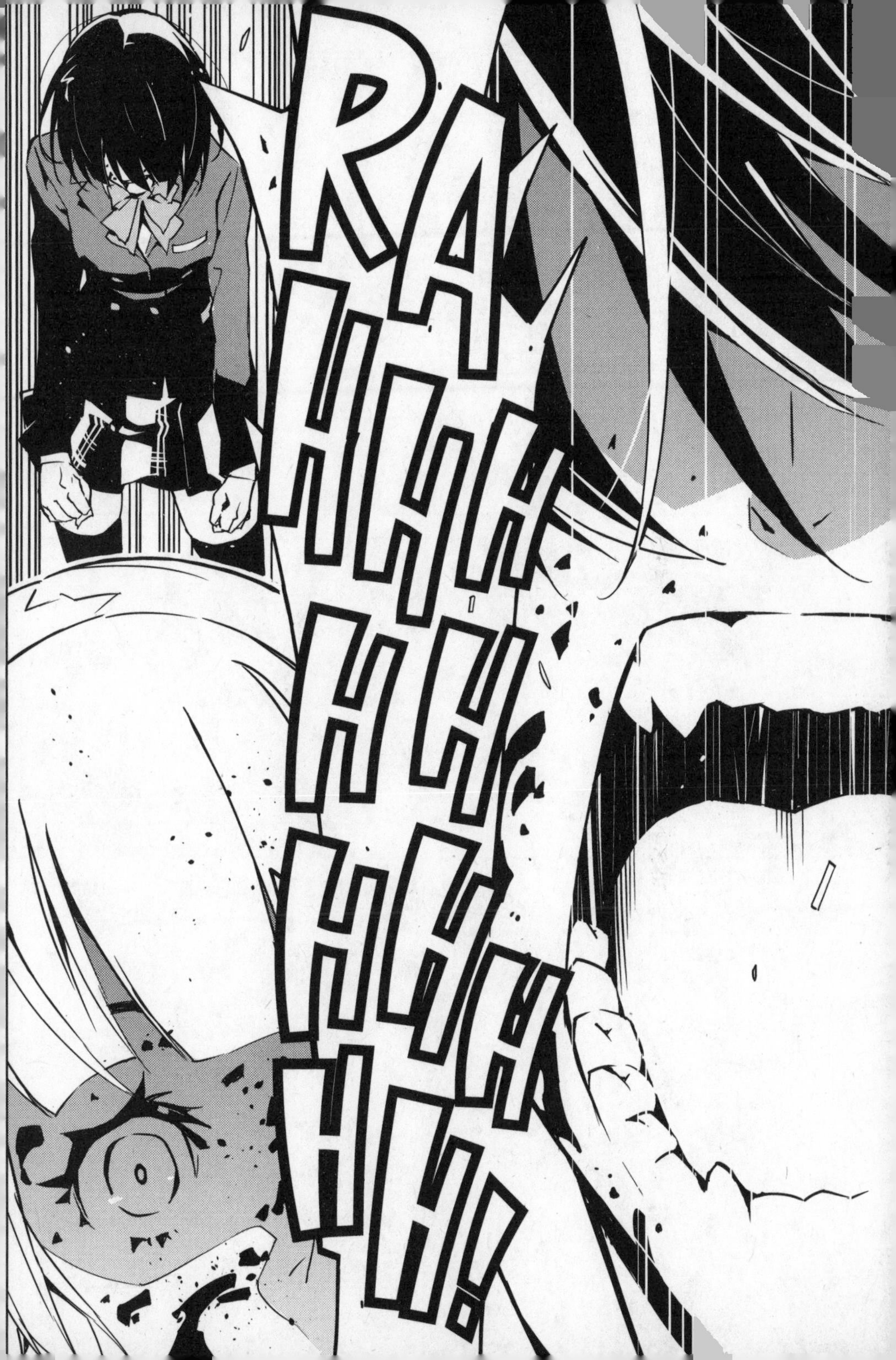
RAHHHHHHHHHHH!

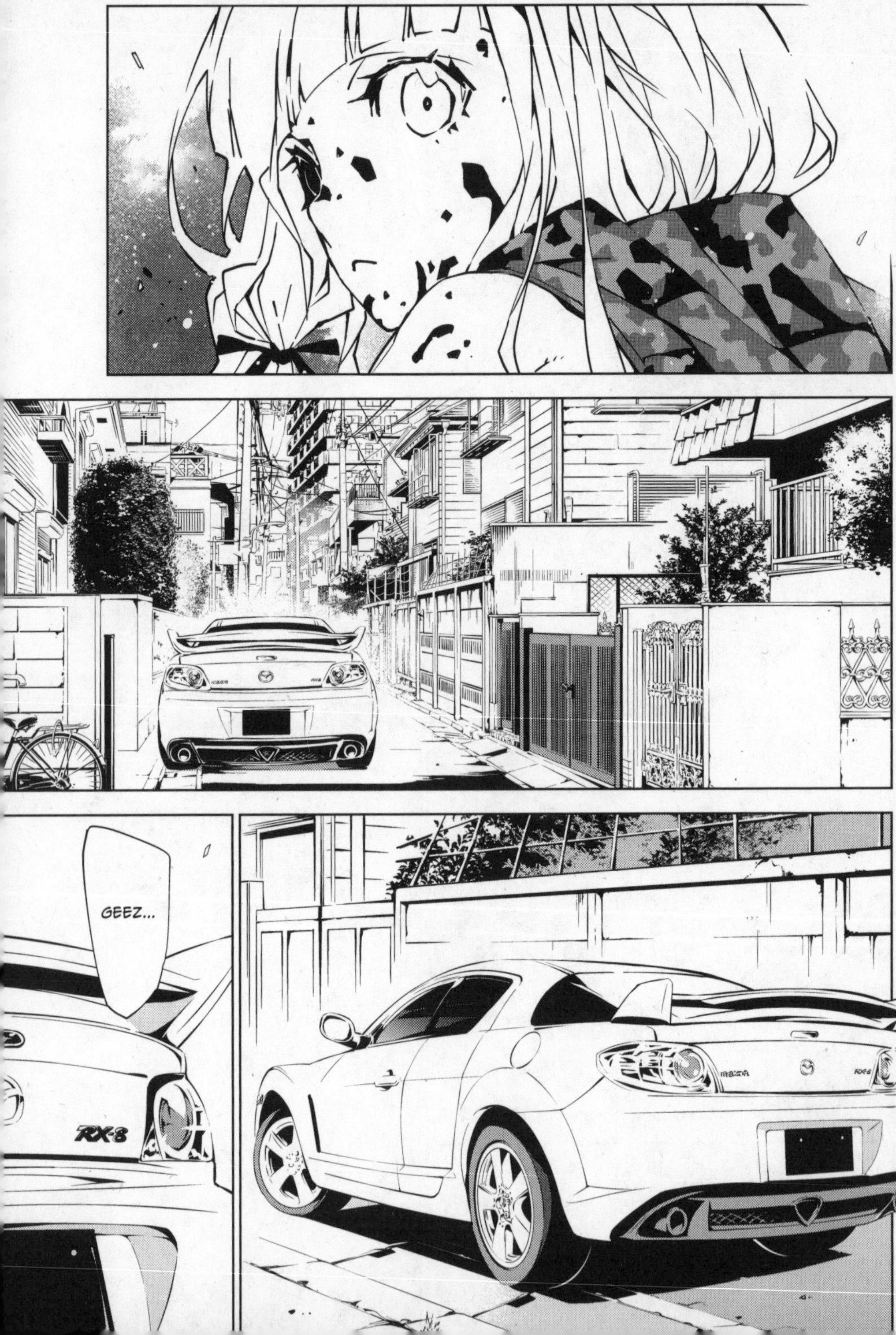
GEEZ...
RX-8

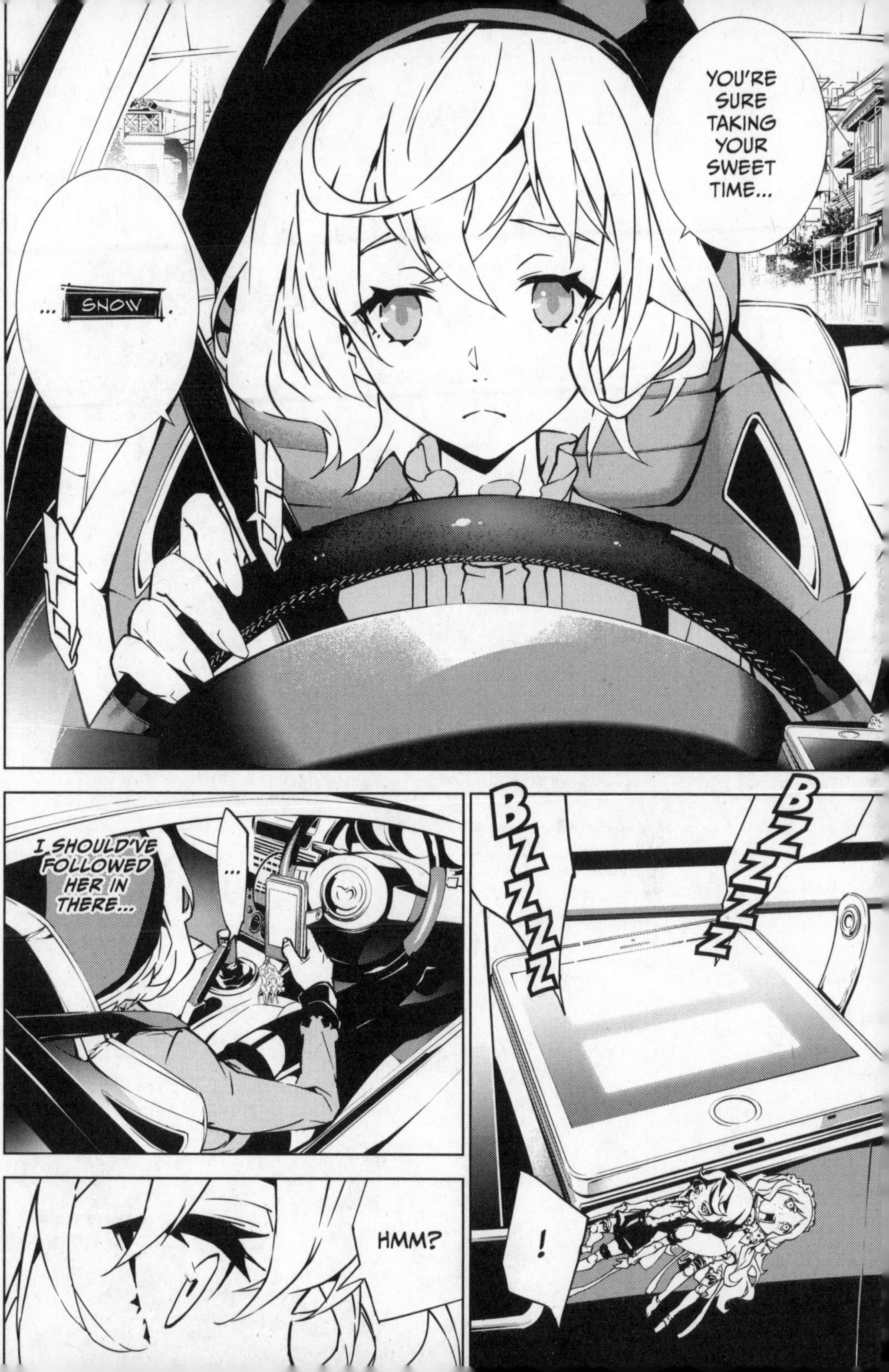
YOU'RE SURE TAKING YOUR SWEET TIME...
...SNOW.
BZZZZ
BZZZZZ
!
...
I SHOULD'VE FOLLOWED HER IN THERE...
HMM?

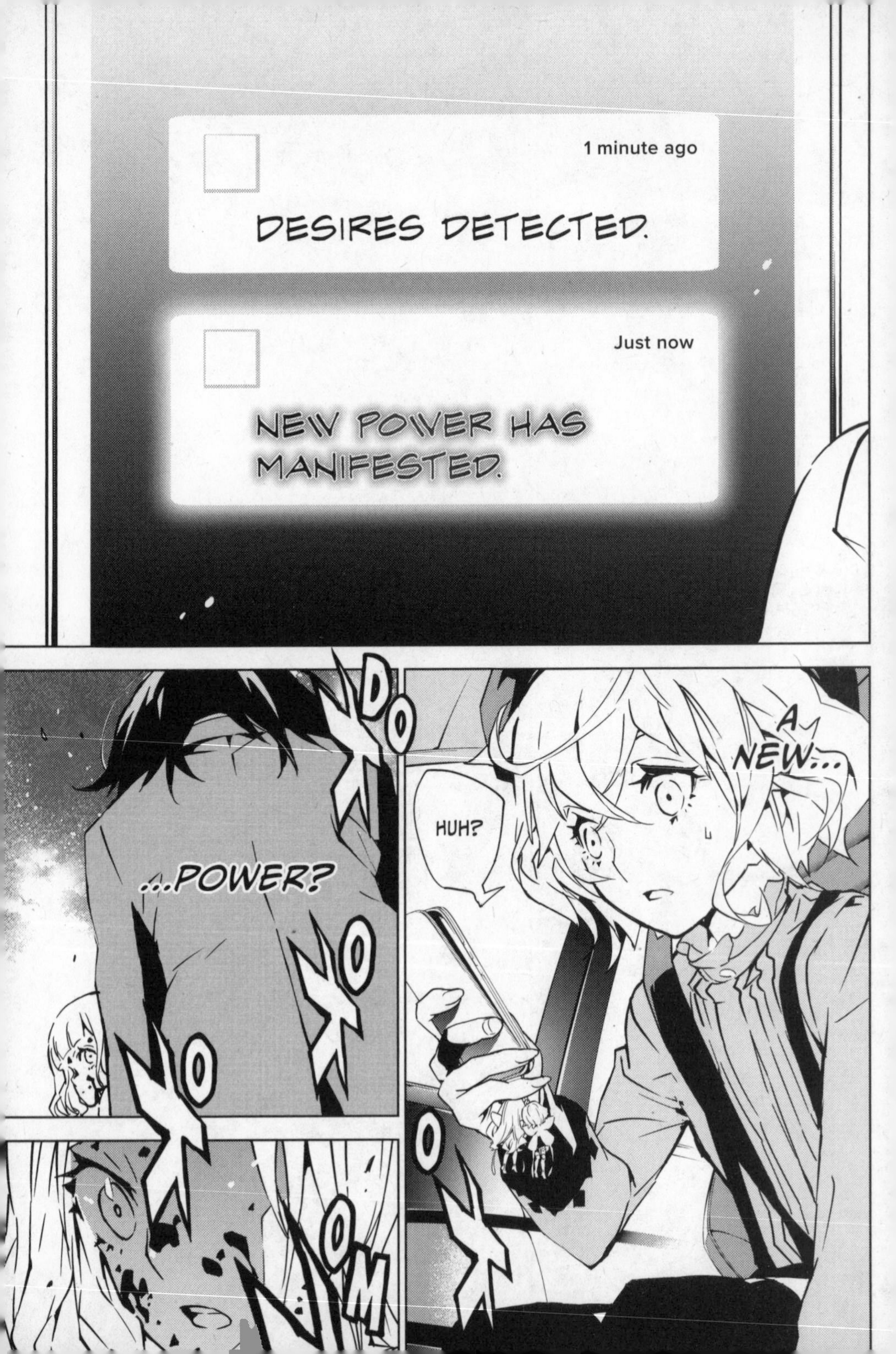
1 minute ago
DESIRES DETECTED.
Just now
NEW POWER HAS MANIFESTED.
A NEW...
HUH?
DO
...POWER?
O
O
O
O
O
M

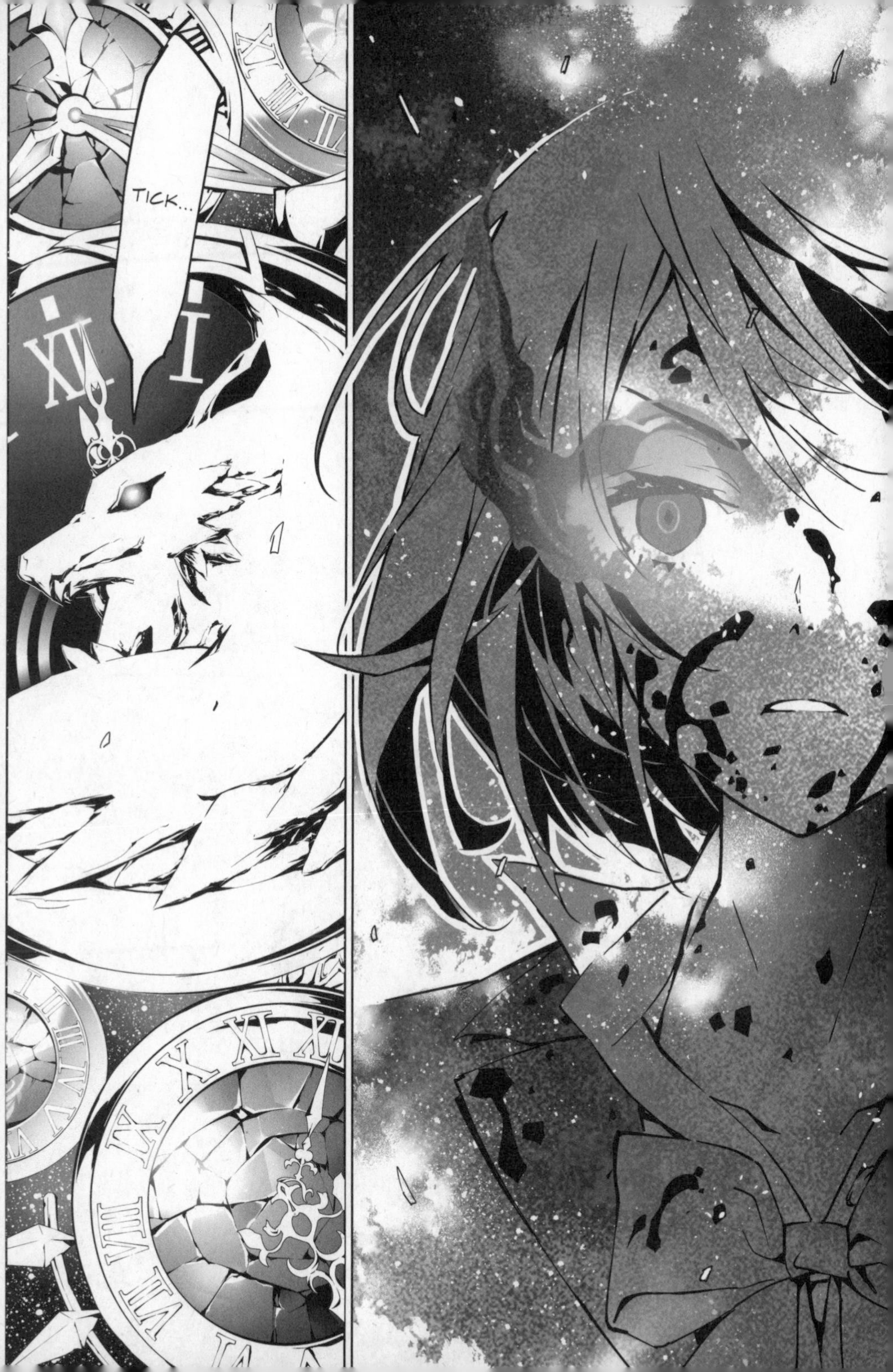
TICK...

SINoALICE

SINoALICE.

Chapter 3: Awakening Dream

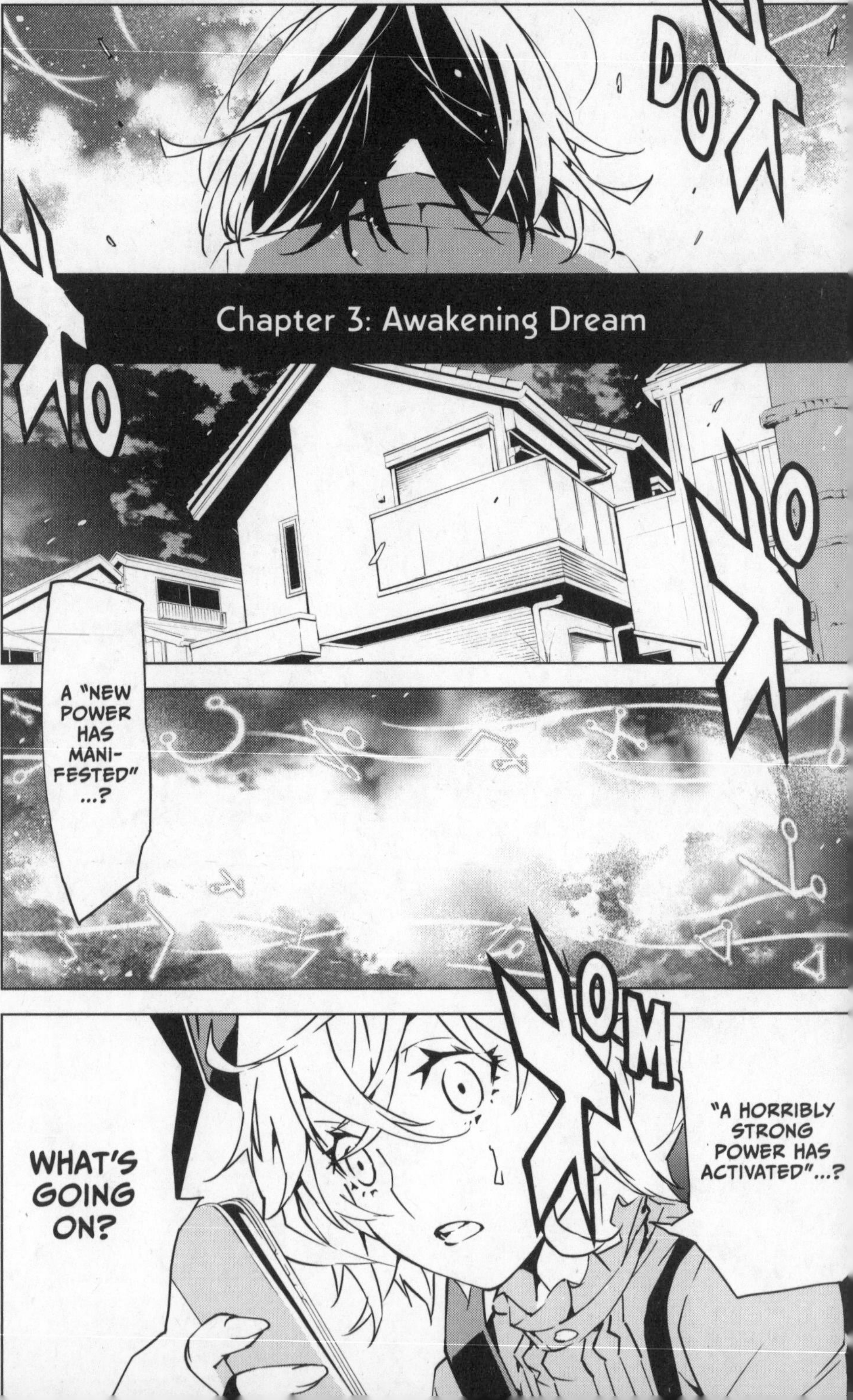
DO
O
O
A "NEW POWER HAS MANI-FESTED" ...?
OM
"A HORRIBLY STRONG POWER HAS ACTIVATED"...?
WHAT'S GOING ON?

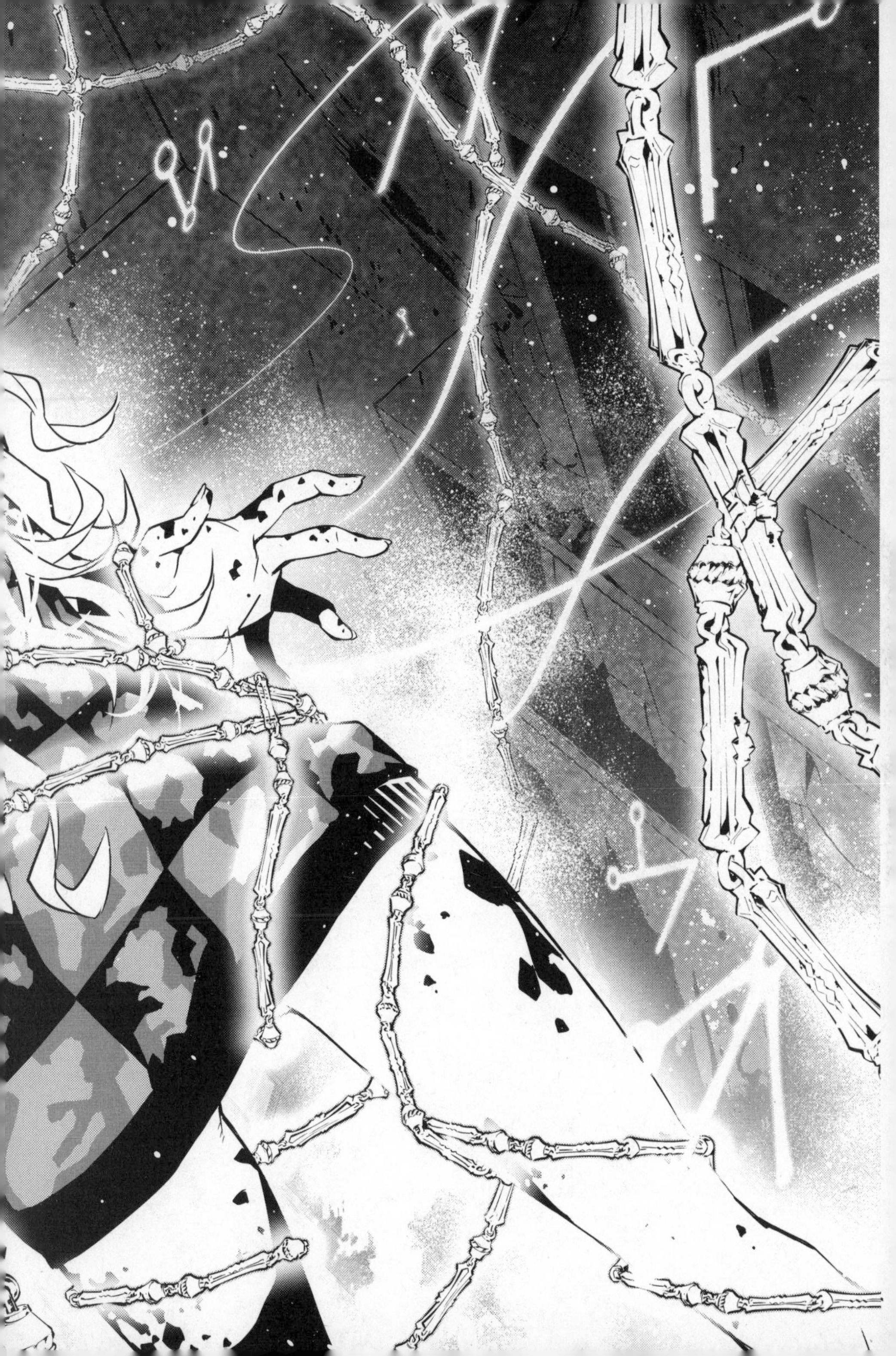

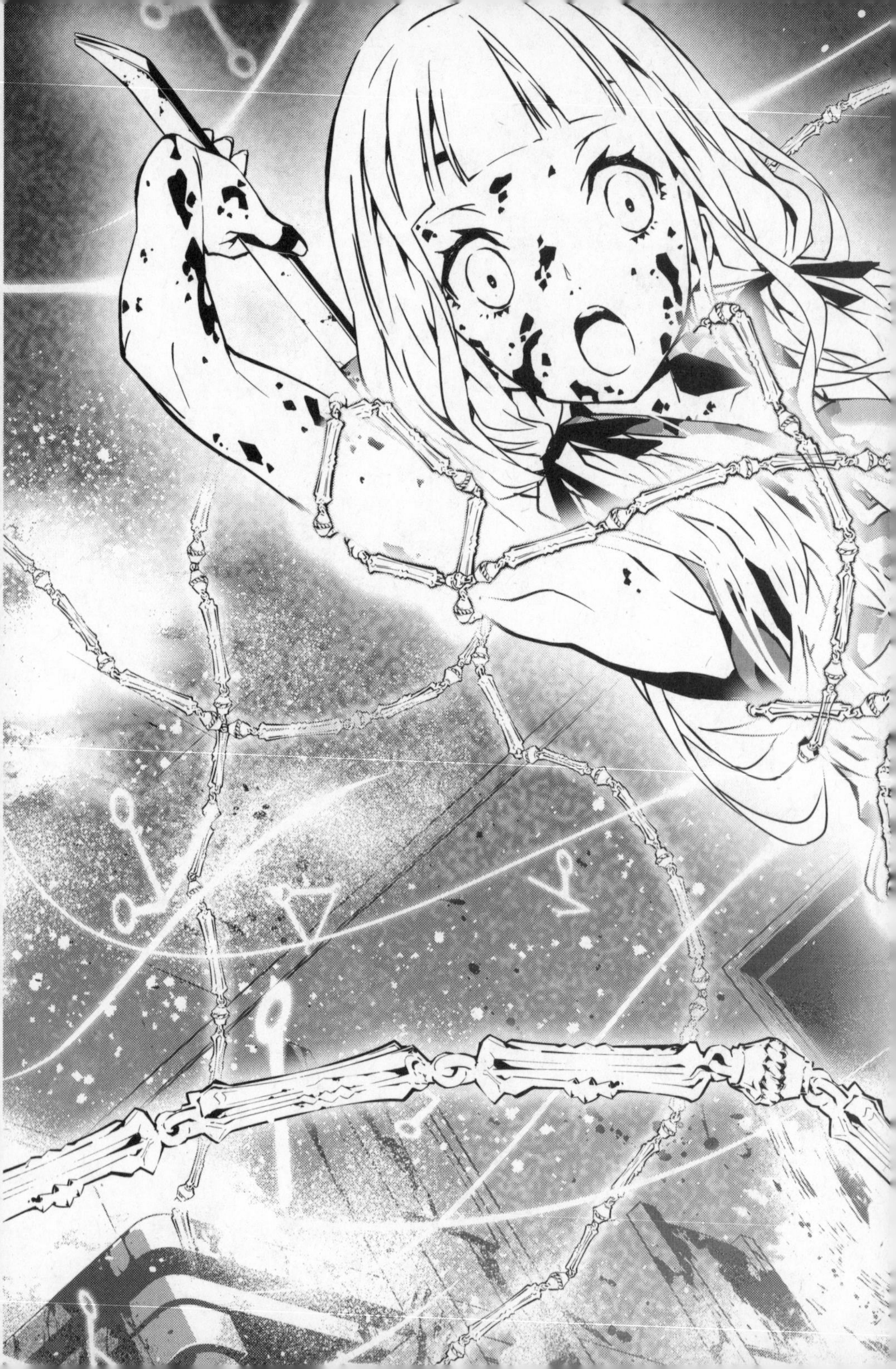

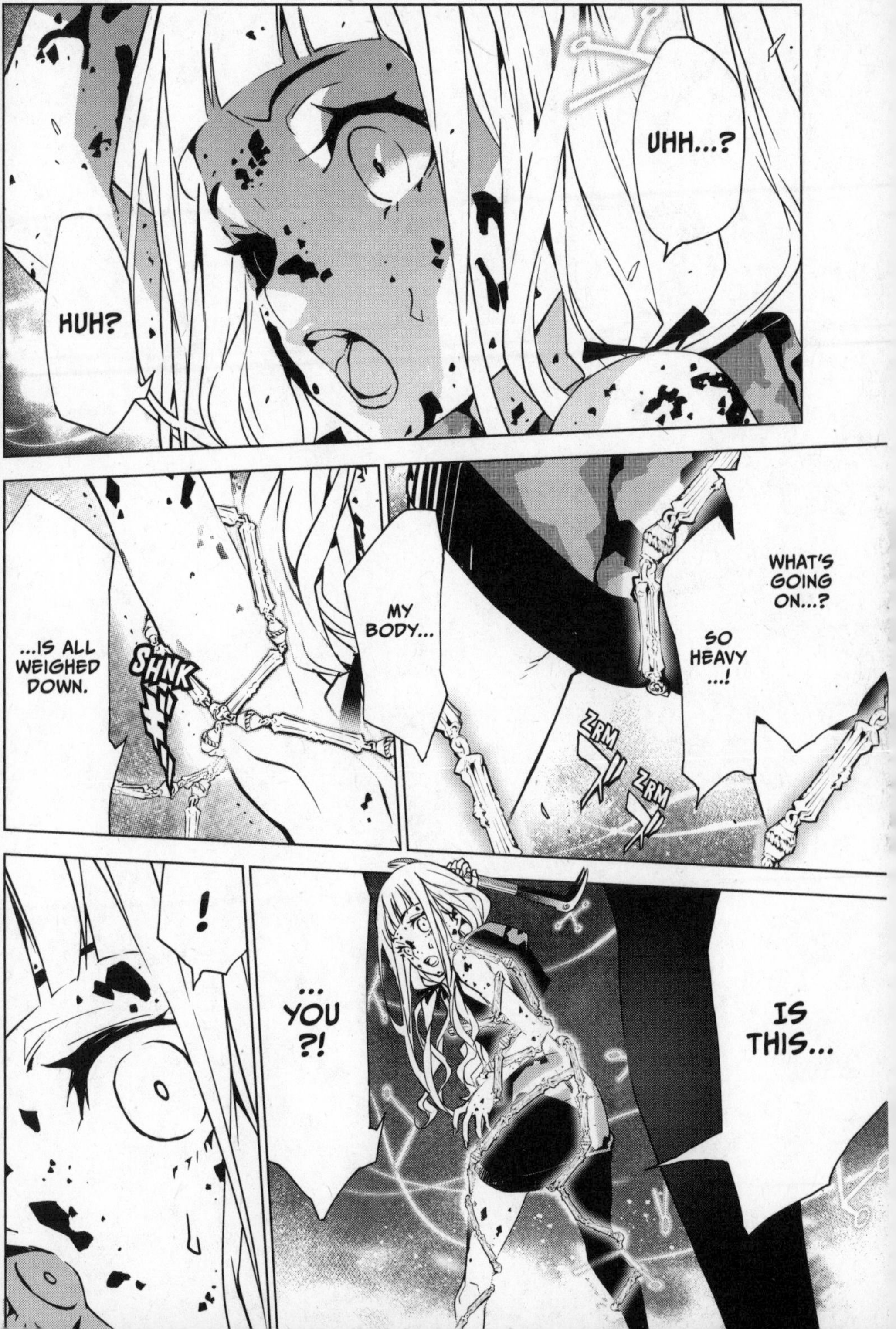
UHH...?
HUH?
WHAT'S GOING ON...?
SO HEAVY ...!
MY BODY...
ZRM
ZRM
...IS ALL WEIGHED DOWN.
SHNK
IS THIS...
...YOU ?!
!

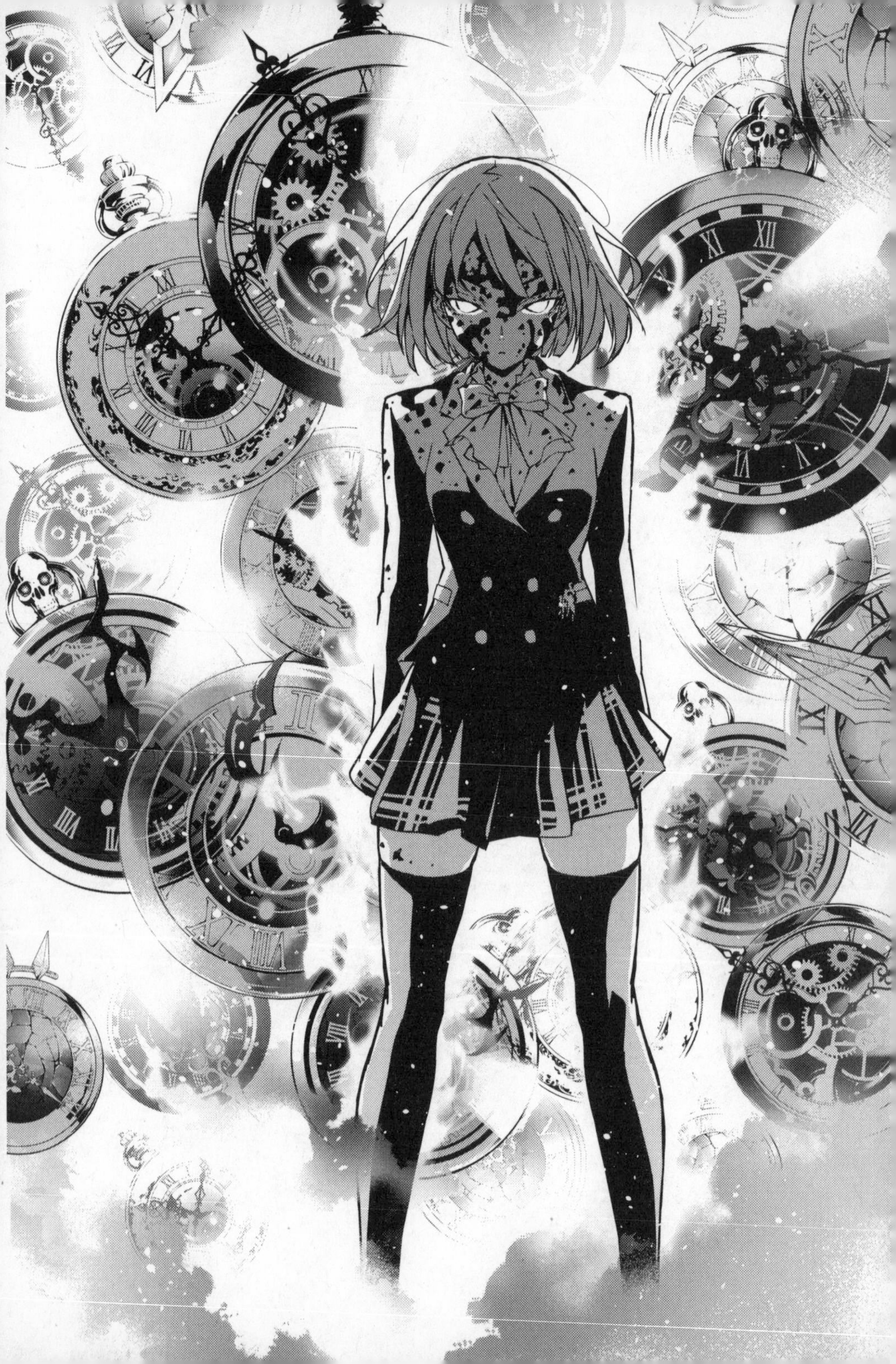

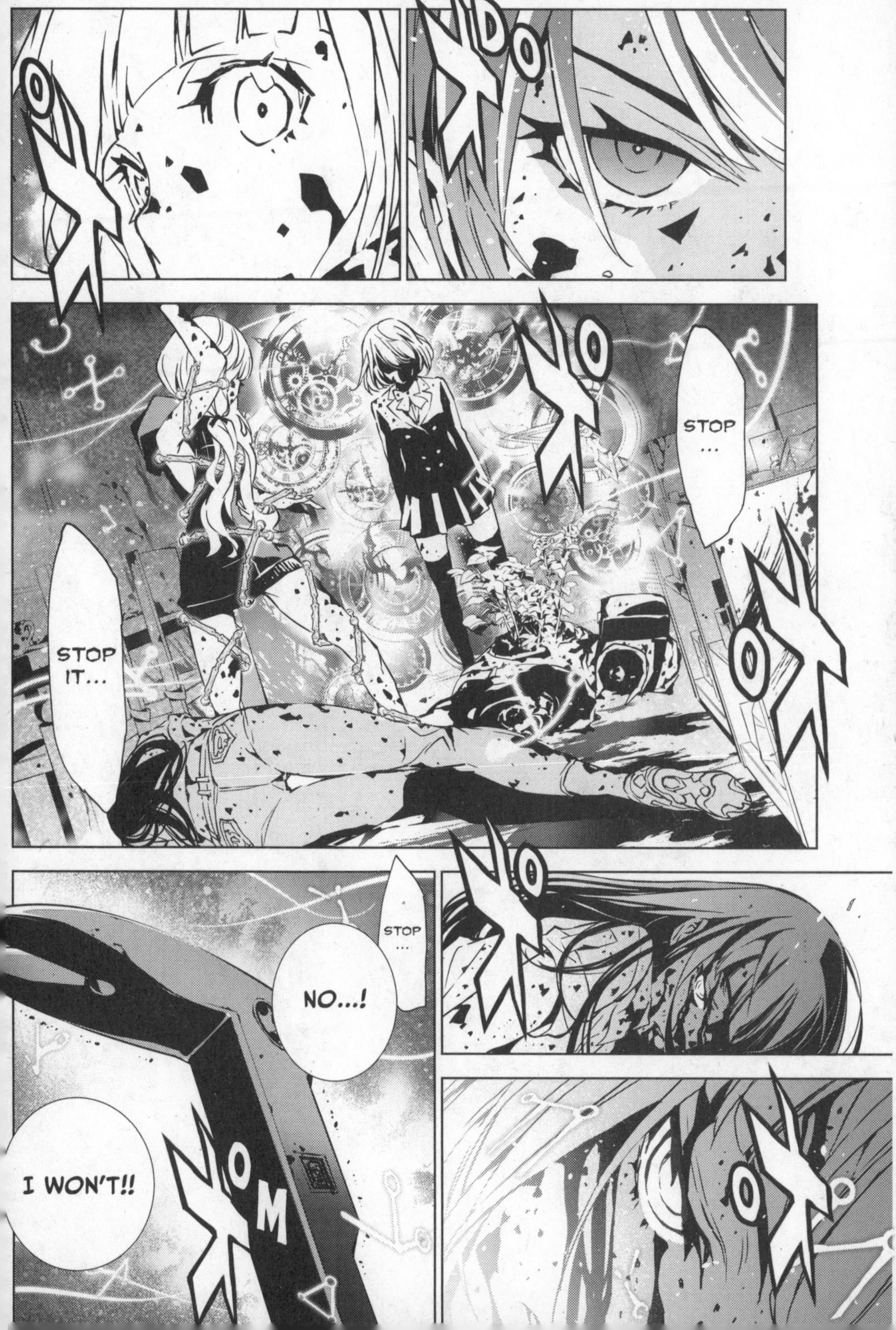
DO
O
O
STOP ...
O
STOP IT...
O
O
STOP ...
NO...!
I WON'T!!
OM

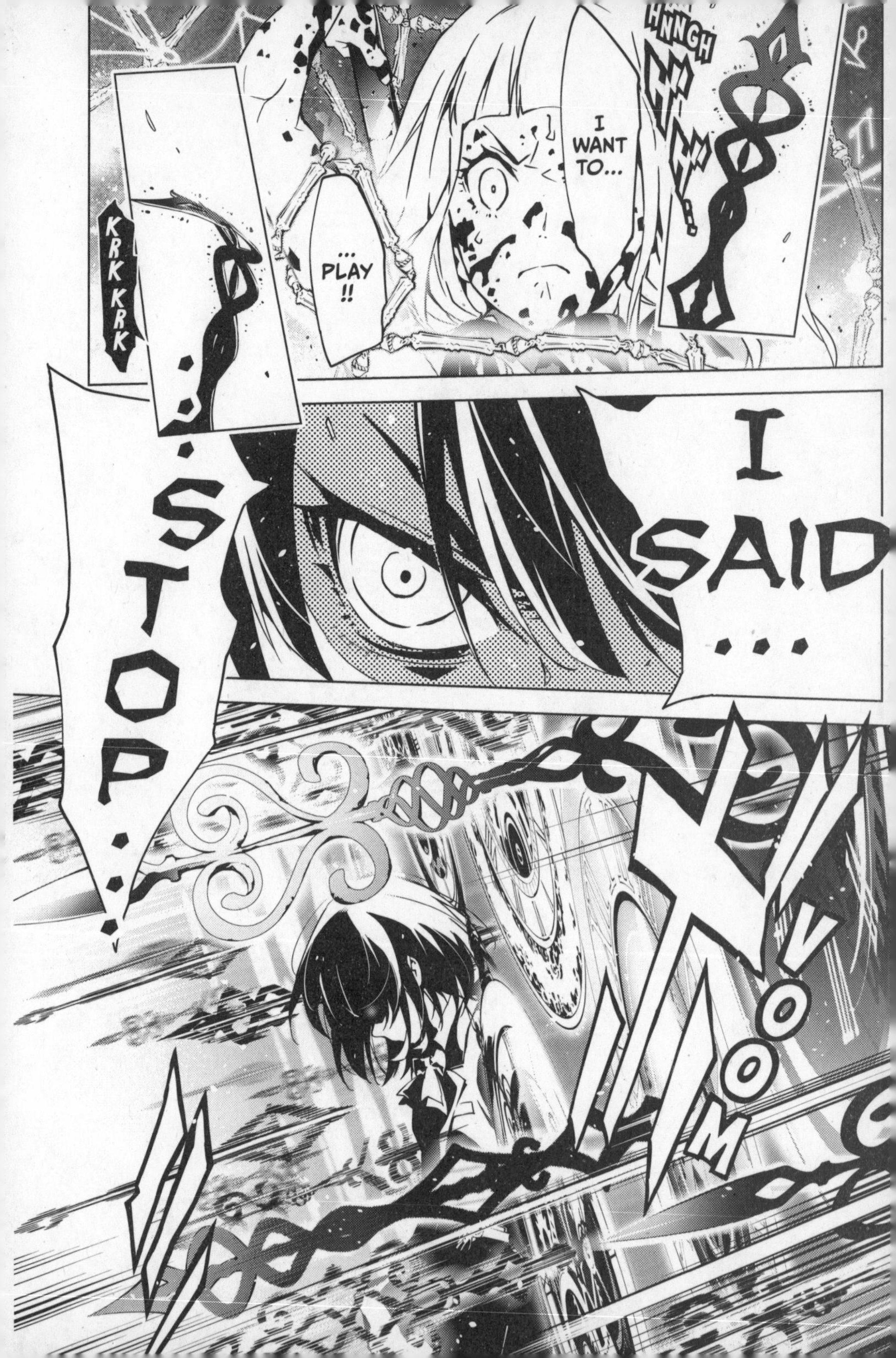
HNNGH
GP GP GP
I WANT TO...
... PLAY !!
KRK KRK KRK
I SAID...
STOP...!!
VOOOM

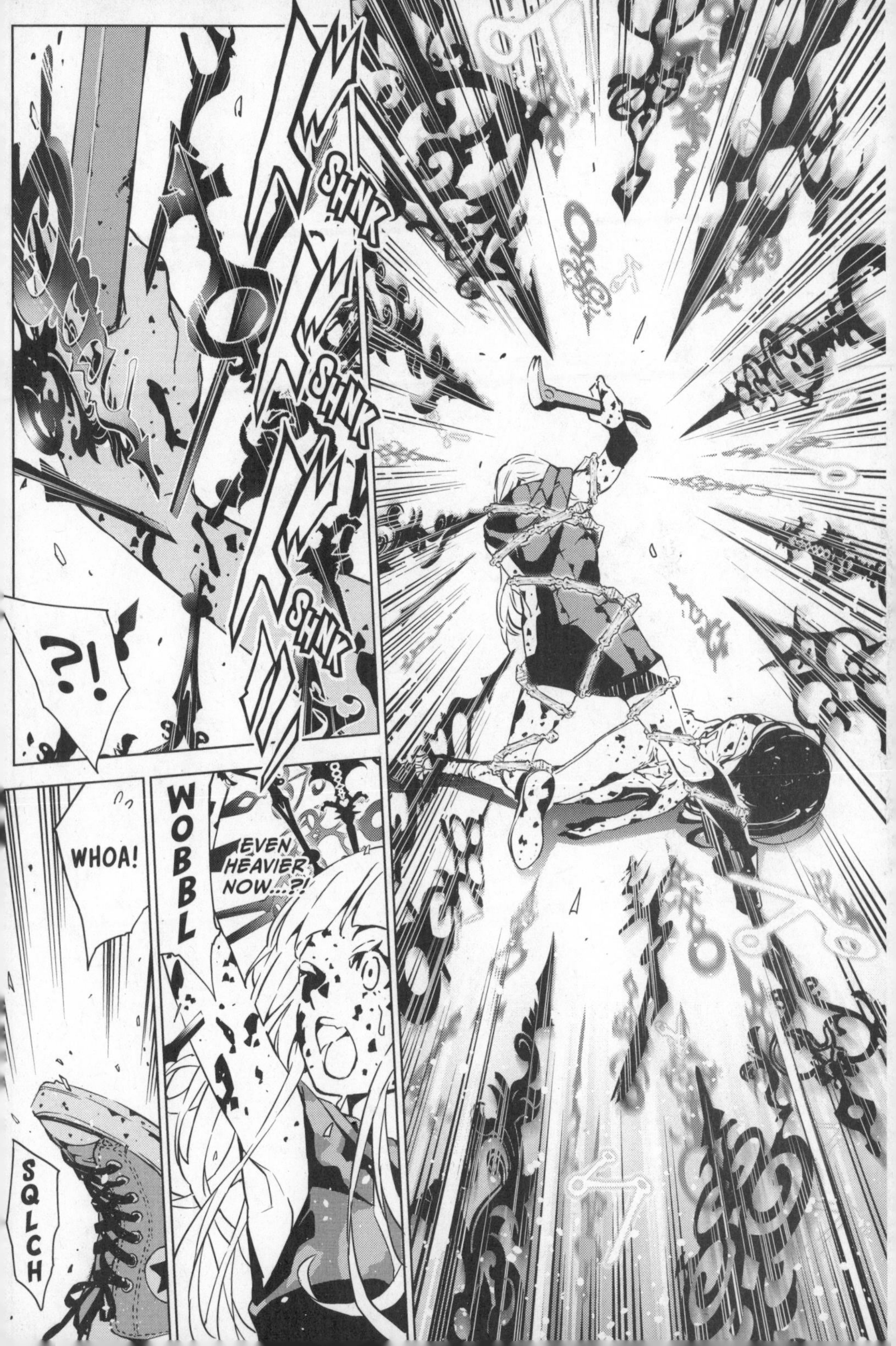
SHNK
SHNK
SHNK
?!
WOBBL
EVEN HEAVIER NOW...?!
WHOA!
SQLCH

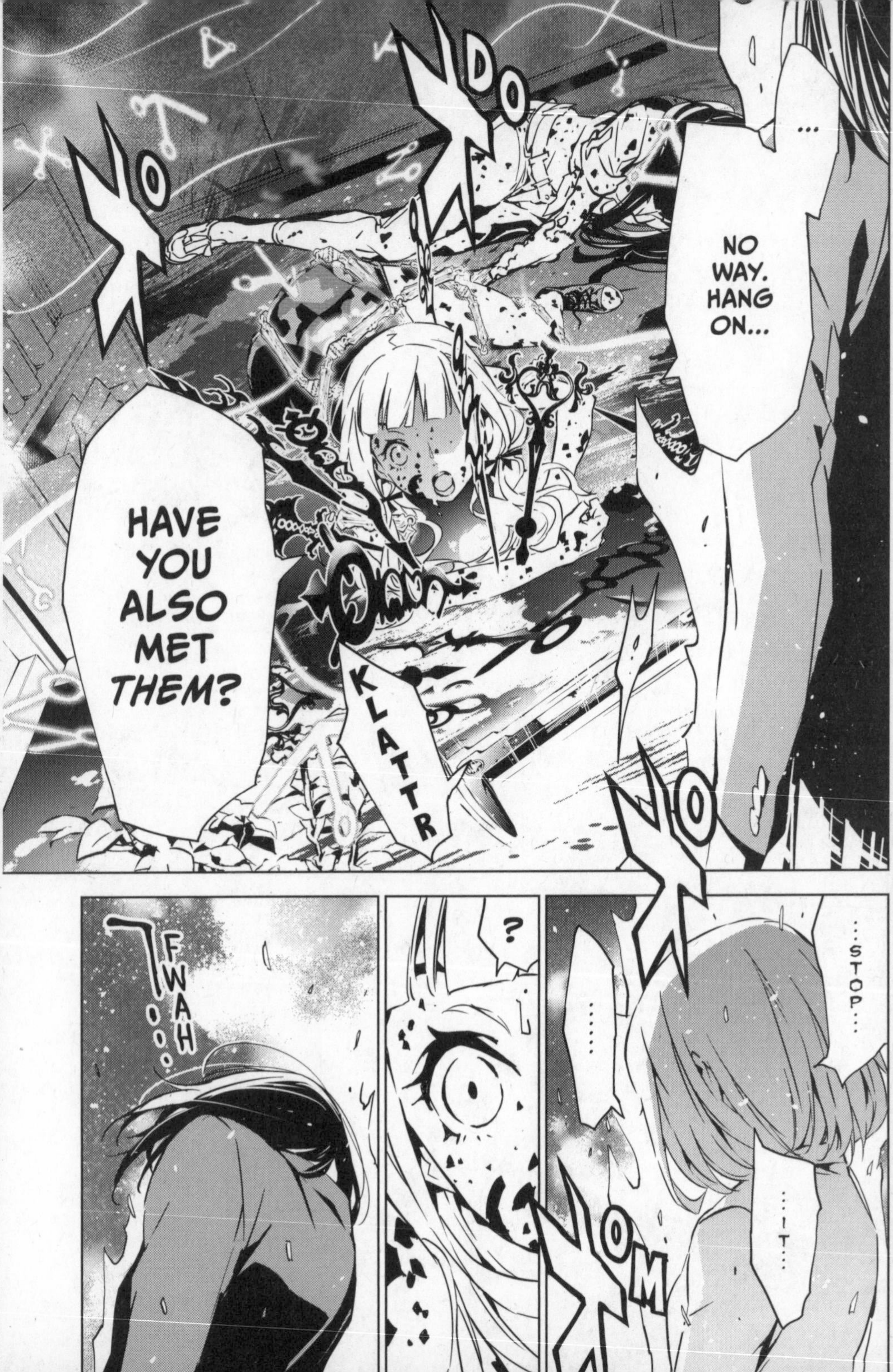
...
NO WAY. HANG ON...
DO
DO
KLATTR
HAVE YOU ALSO MET THEM?
DO
...STOP...
......
...IT...
OM
?
FWAH

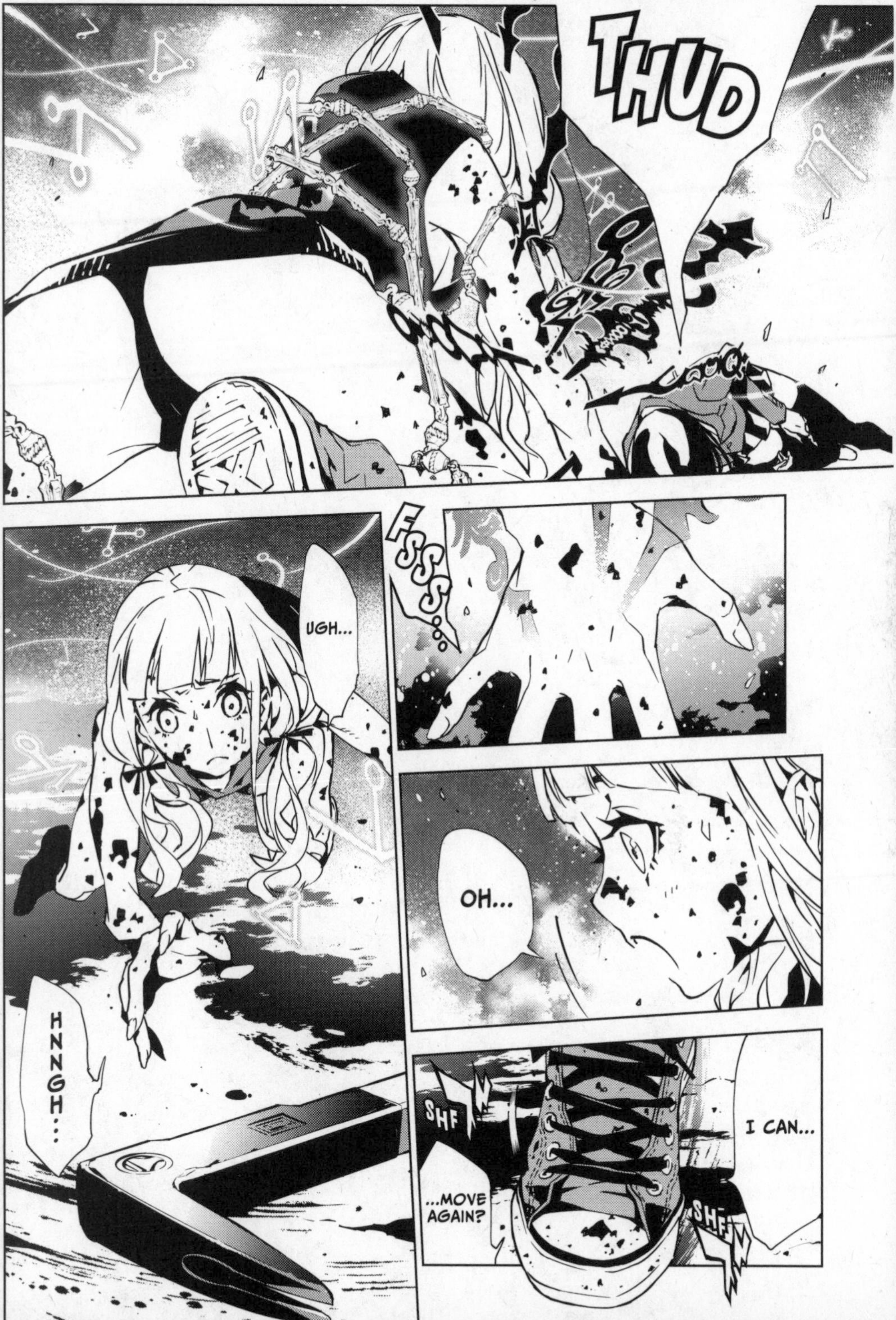
THUD
FSSS...
OH...
I CAN...
SHF
...MOVE AGAIN?
SHF
UGH...
HNNGH...

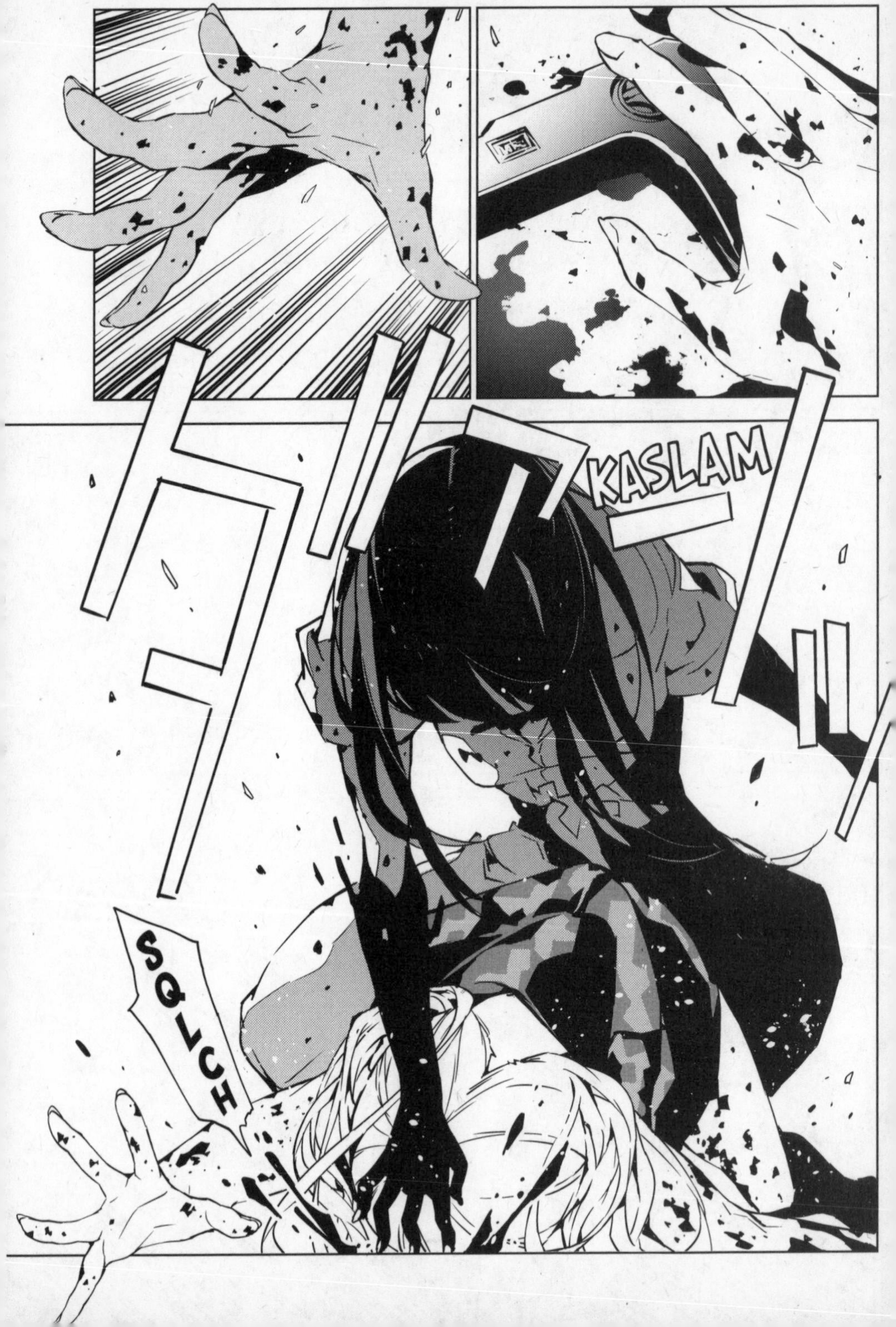
KASLAM
SQLCH

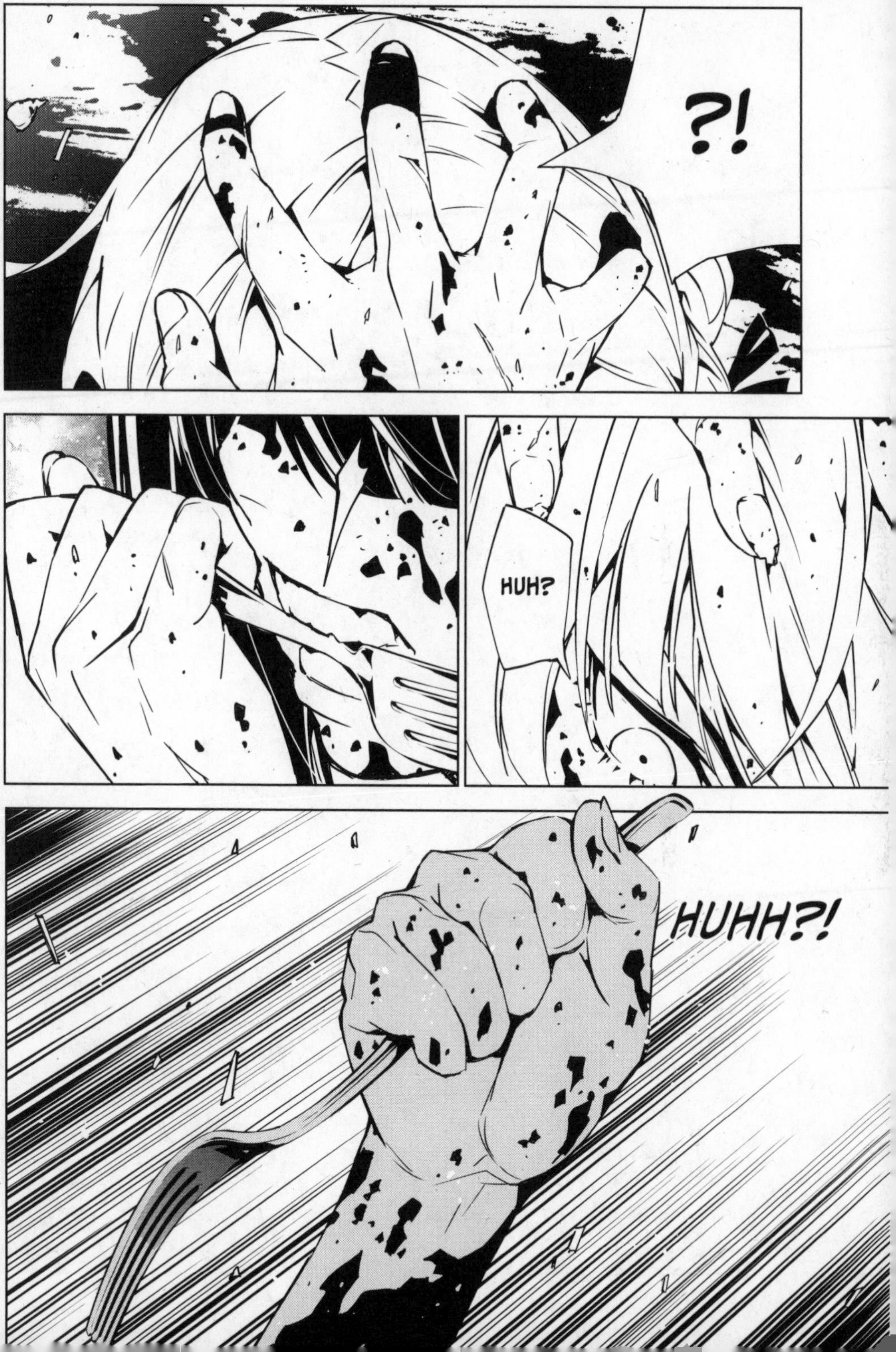
?!
HUH?
HUHH?!

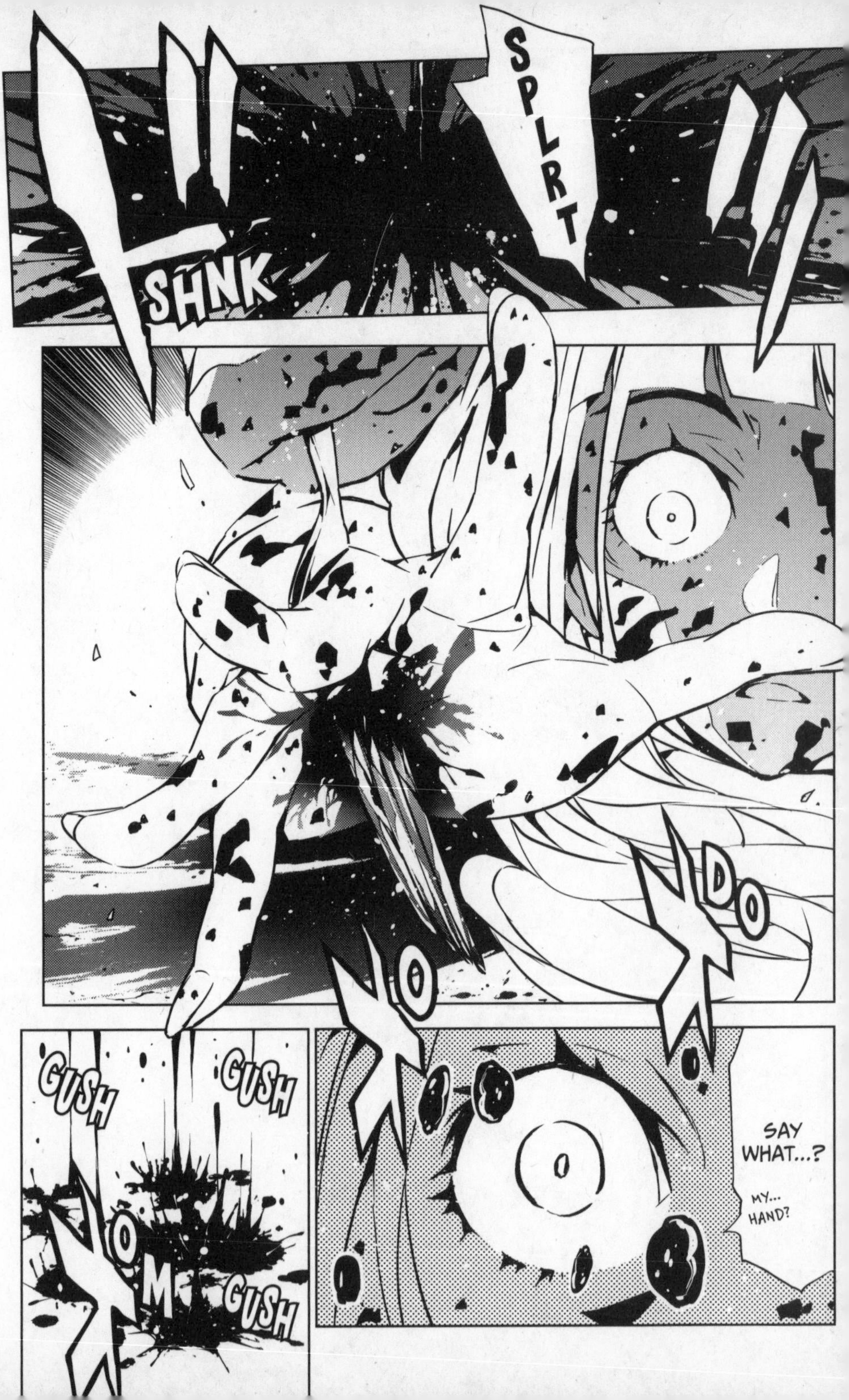
SPLRT
SHNK
DO
O
SAY WHAT...?
MY... HAND?
GUSH
GUSH
GUSH
OM

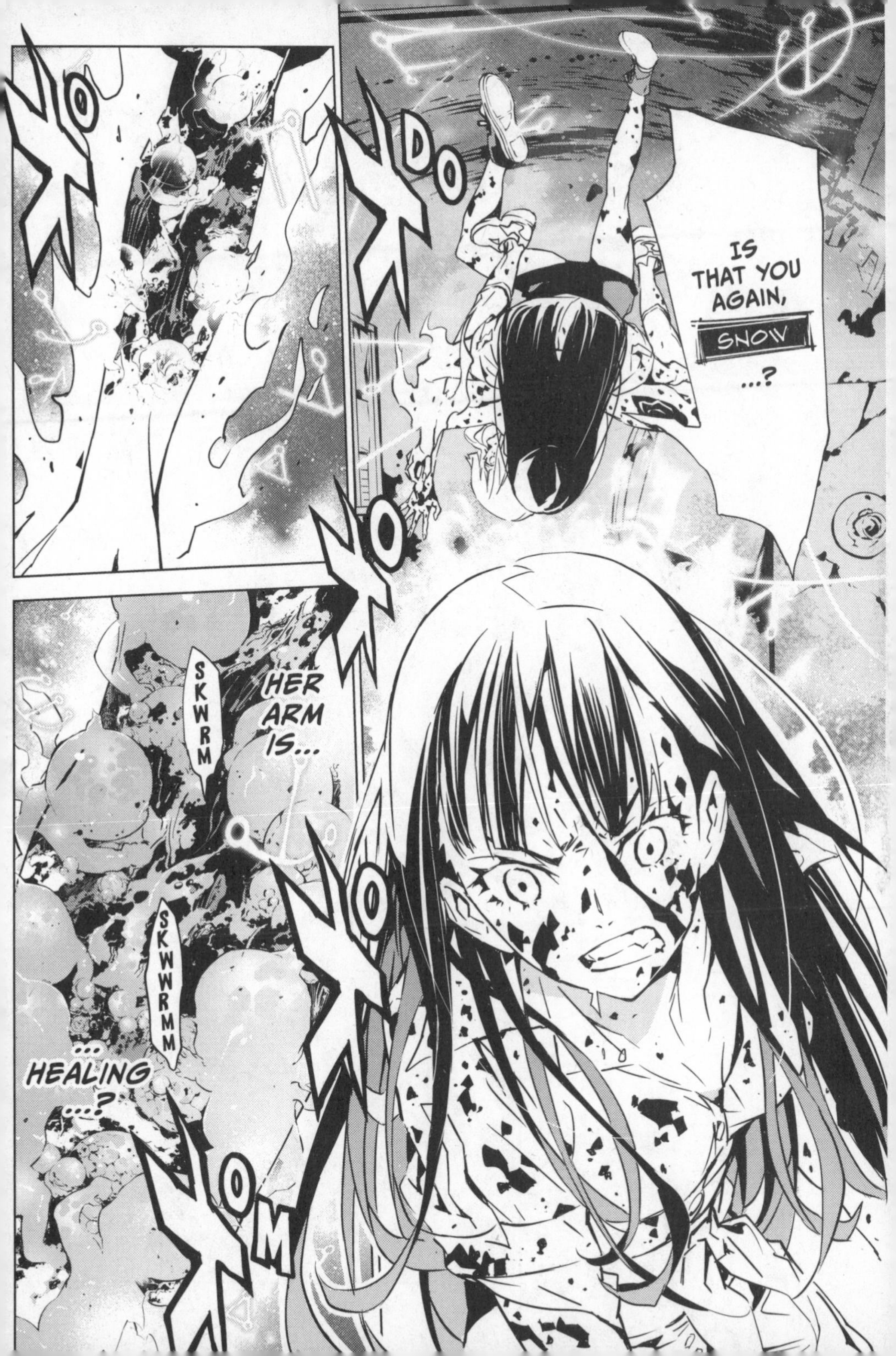

IS THAT YOU AGAIN, SNOW ...?
DO
O
O
HER ARM IS...
SKWRM
SKWWRMM
... HEALING ...?
O
O
M

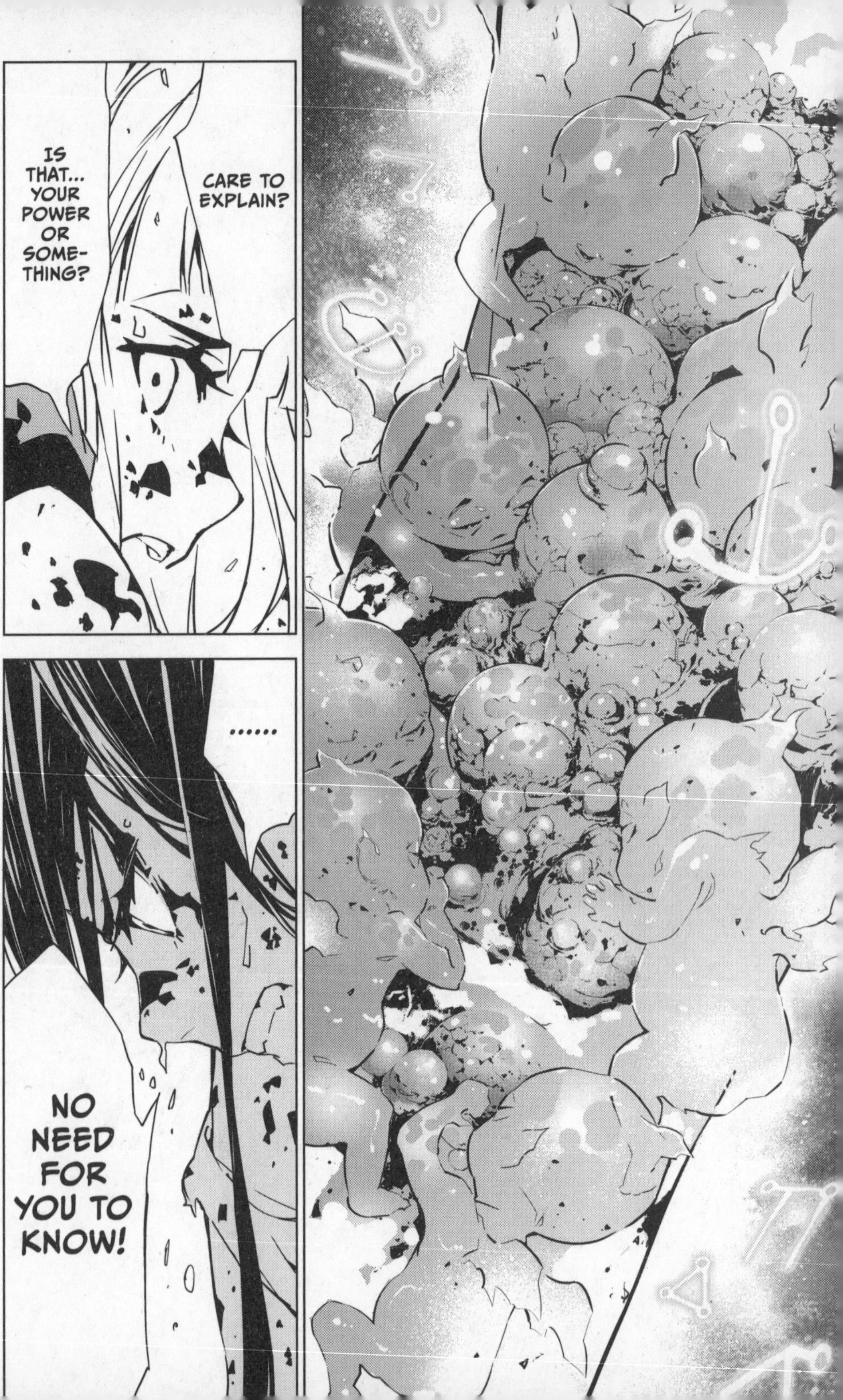
CARE TO EXPLAIN?
IS THAT... YOUR POWER OR SOME-THING?
......
NO NEED FOR YOU TO KNOW!

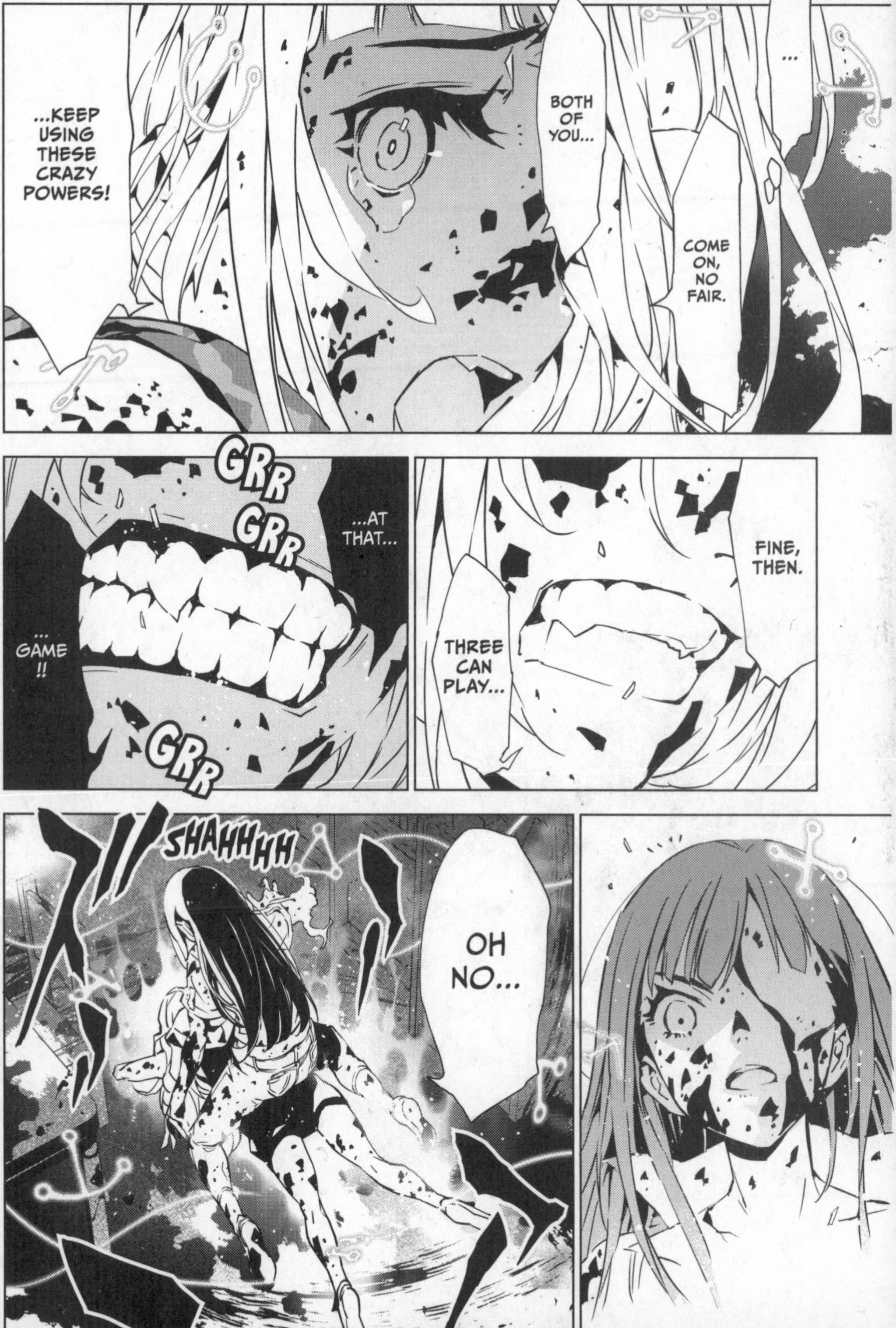
...
COME ON, NO FAIR.
BOTH OF YOU...
...KEEP USING THESE CRAZY POWERS!
FINE, THEN.
THREE CAN PLAY...
GRR
GRR
...AT THAT...
... GAME !!
GRR
OH NO...
SHAHHHH

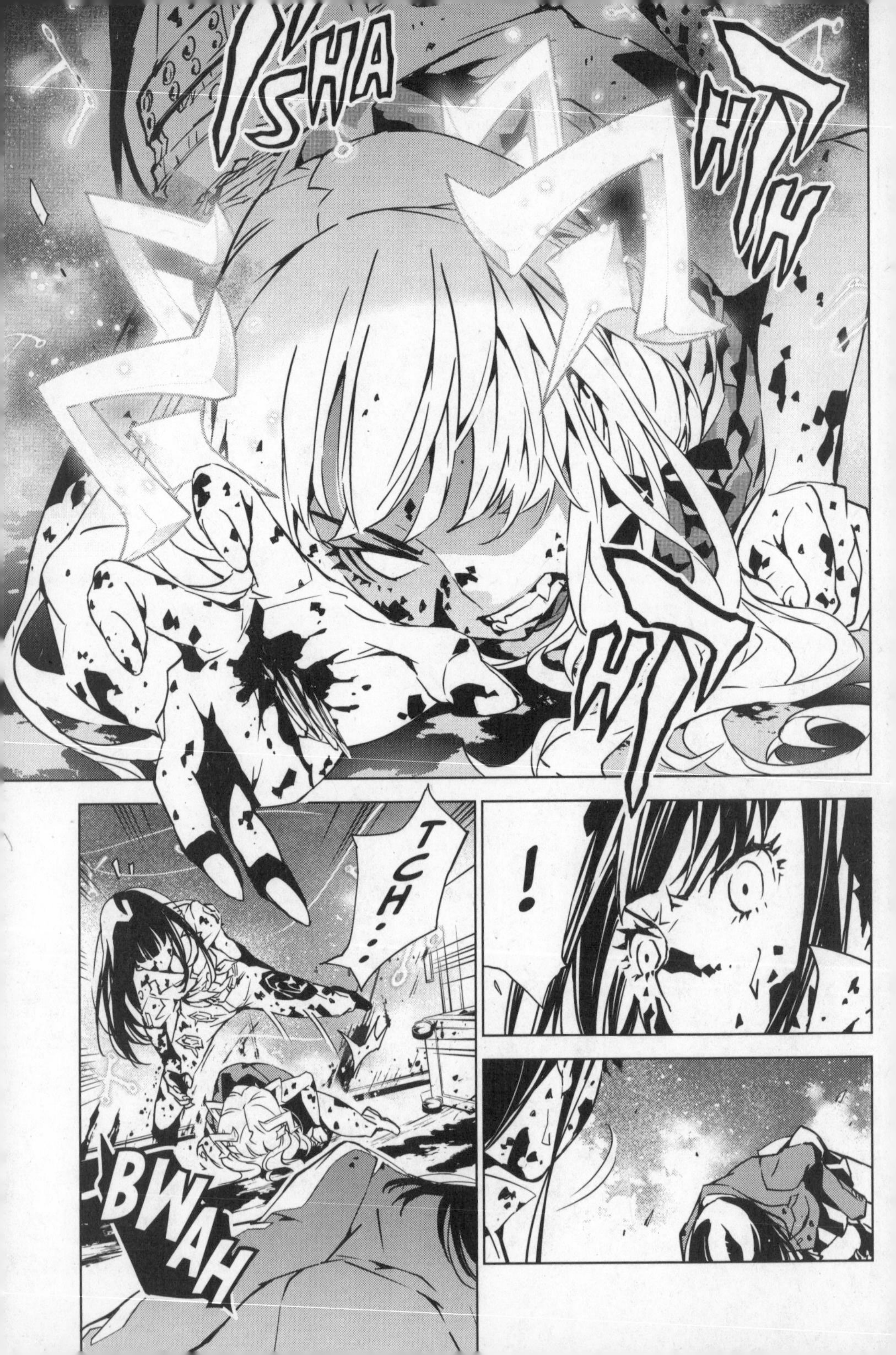

SHHH
VSHA
HH
!
TCH...
BWAH

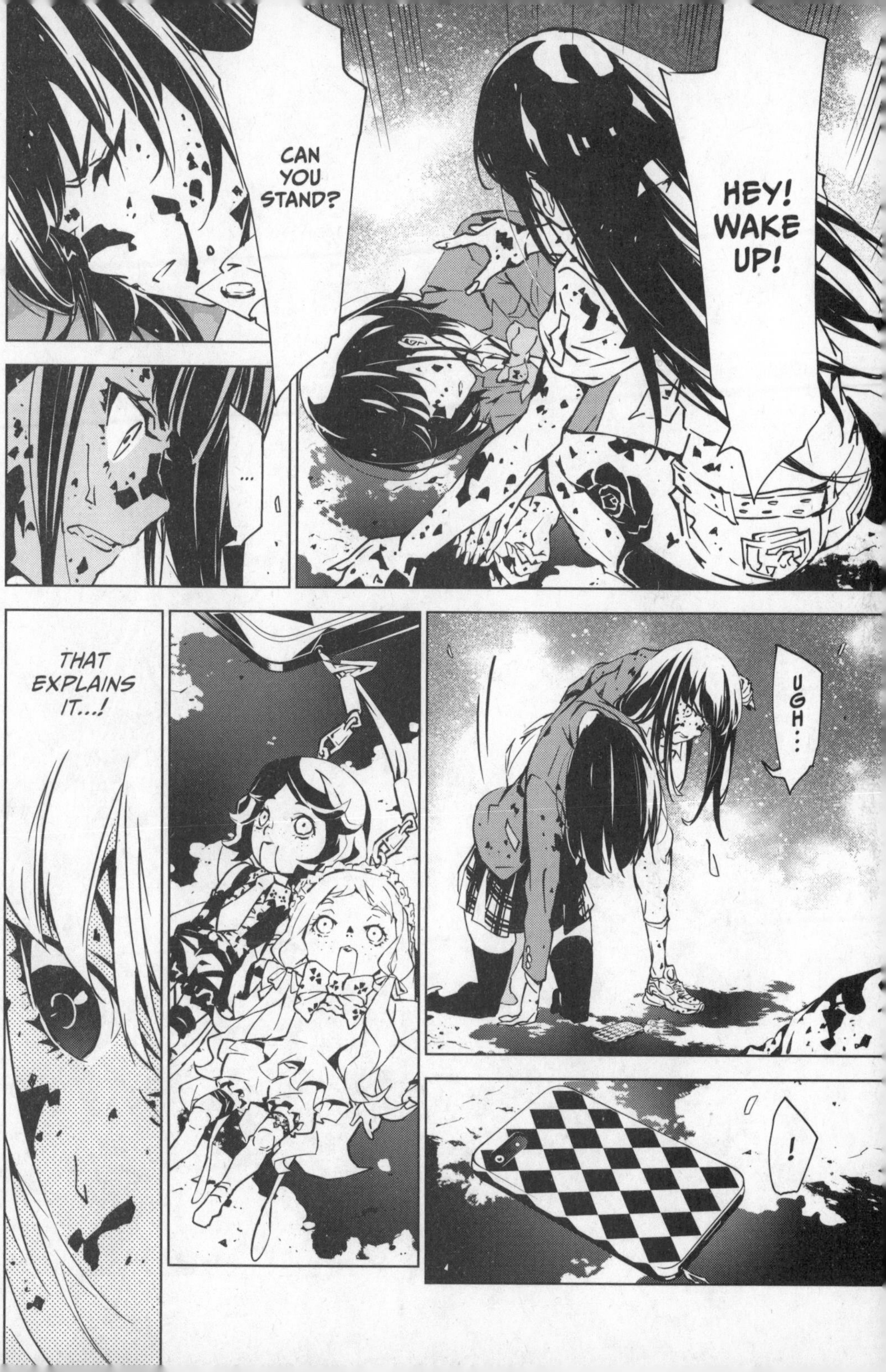
HEY! WAKE UP!
CAN YOU STAND?
...
UGH...
!
THAT EXPLAINS IT...!

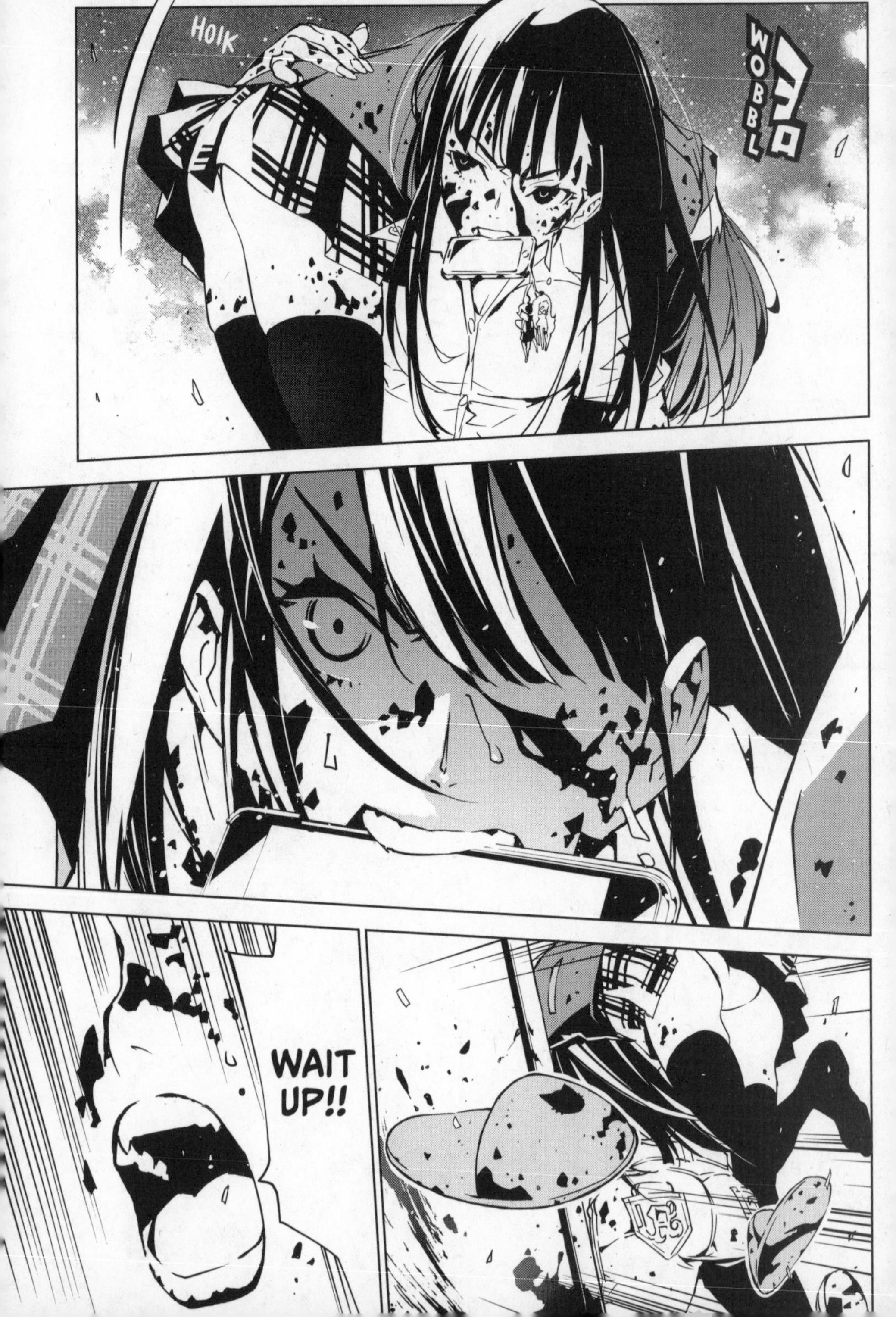
WOBBL
HOIK
WAIT UP!!

PLEASE... DON'T GO!
FSSS...
PLAY WITH ME!
LET'S PLAY SOME MORE!
DON'T...
...
HFF!
SPLAT
HFF...
DON'T...
HFF!
HFF...
... LEAVE ME...

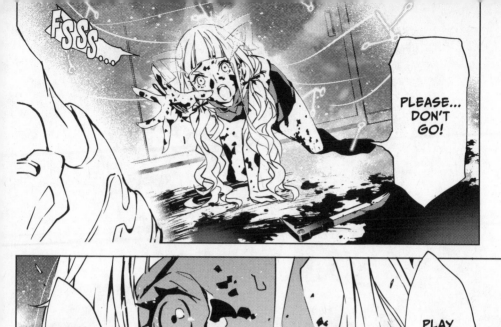

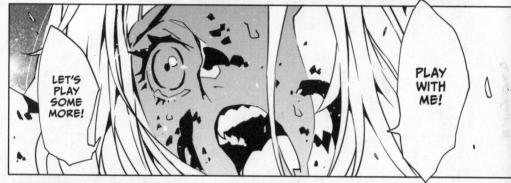

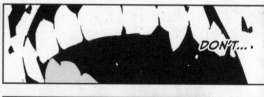

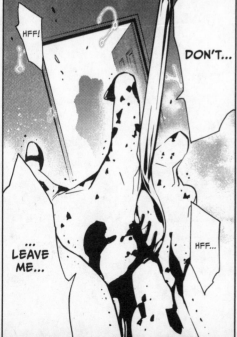

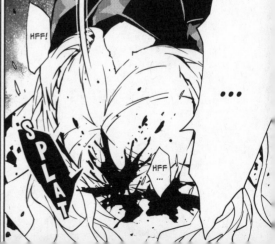

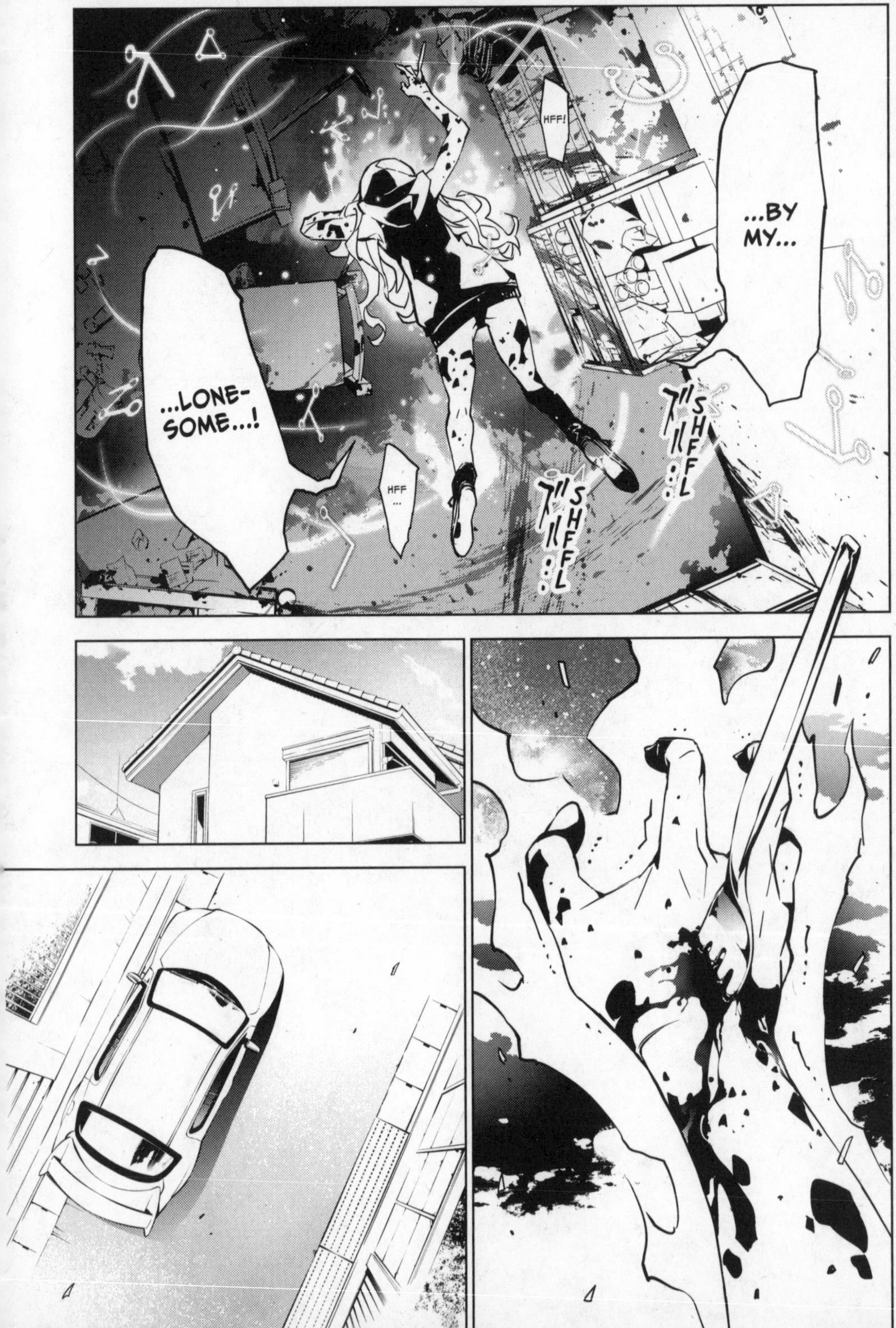
HFF!
...BY MY...
SHFFL
SHFFL
...LONE-SOME...!
HFF...

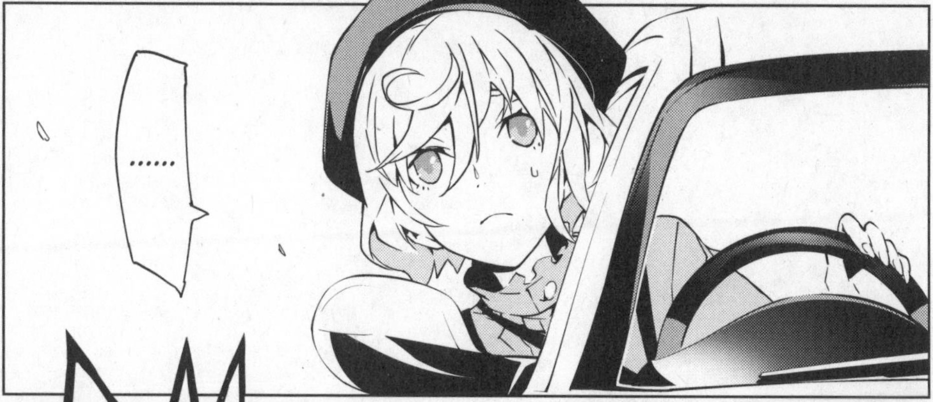
......
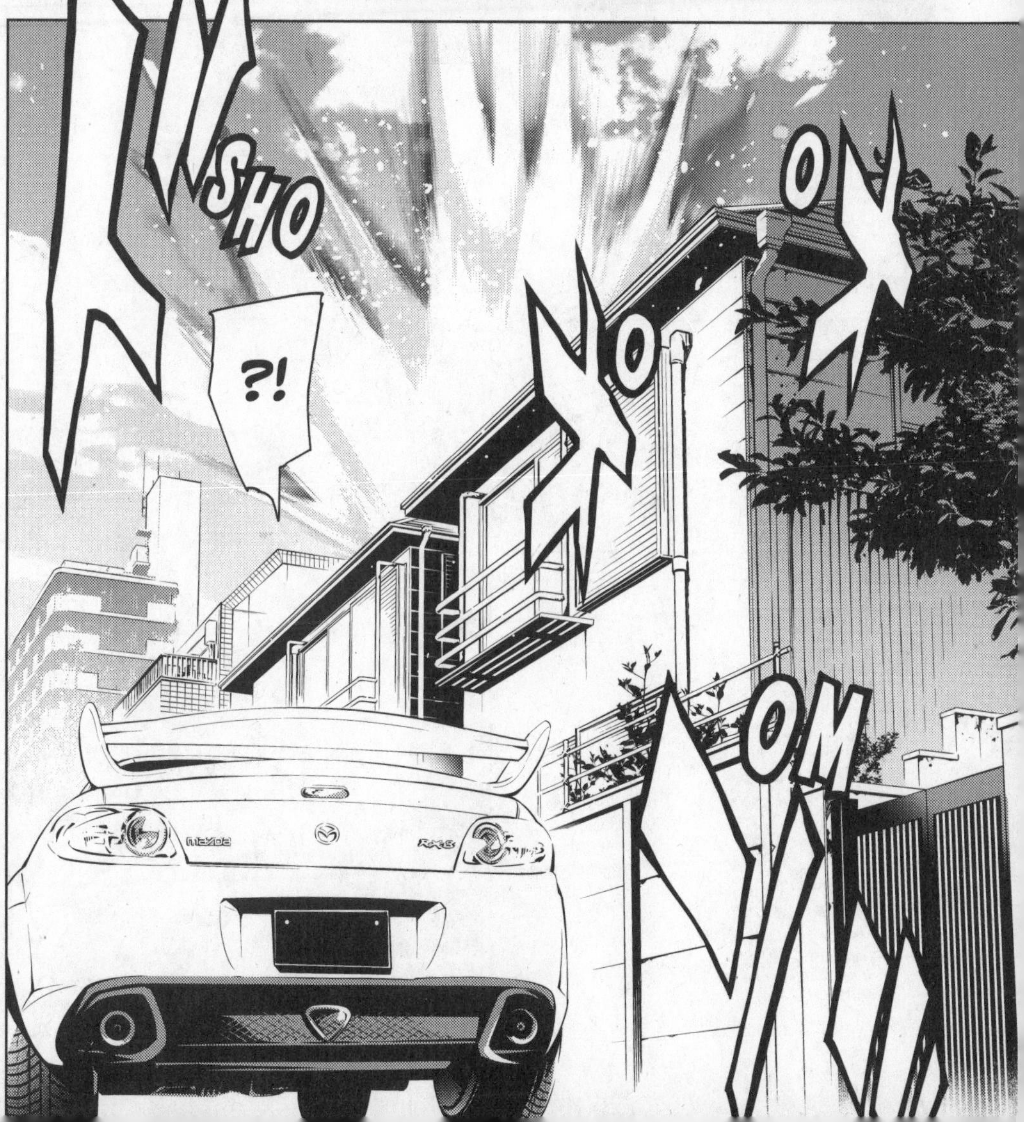
SHO
?!
O
O
OM

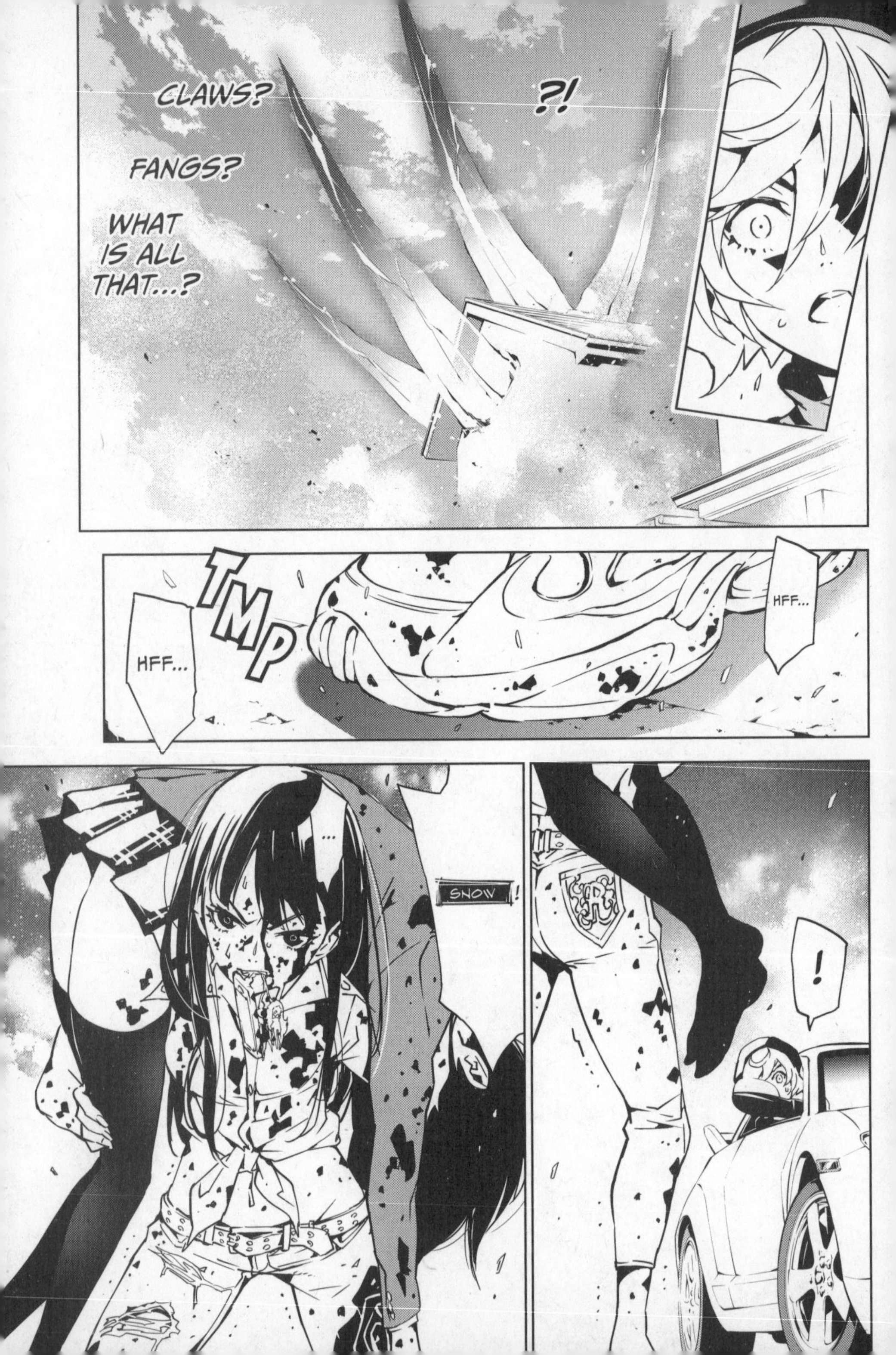
?!
CLAWS?
FANGS?
WHAT IS ALL THAT...?
HFF...
TMP
HFF...
!
...
SNOW !

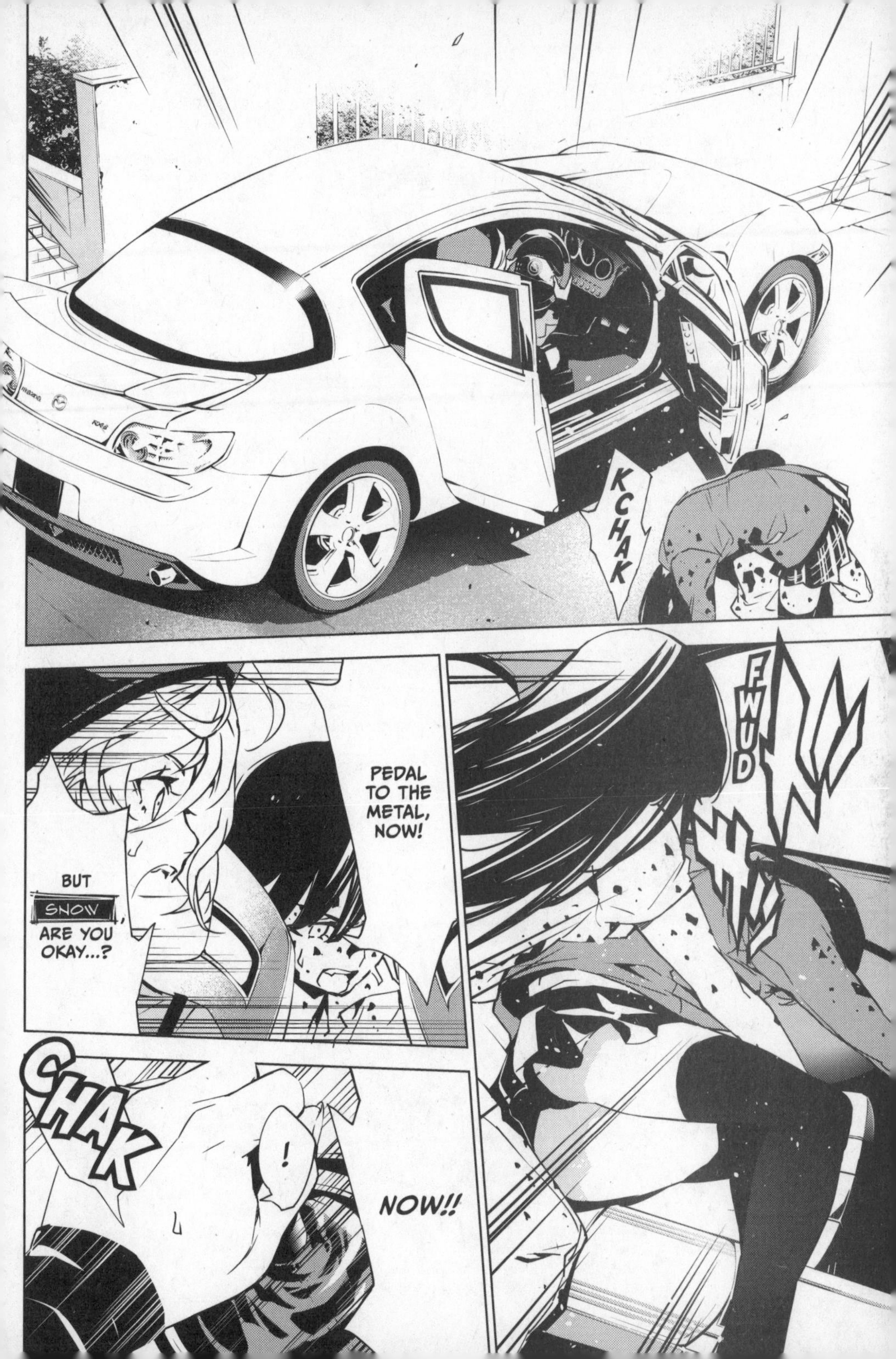
KCHAK
FWUD
PEDAL TO THE METAL, NOW!
BUT SNOW, ARE YOU OKAY...?
!
NOW!!
CHAK

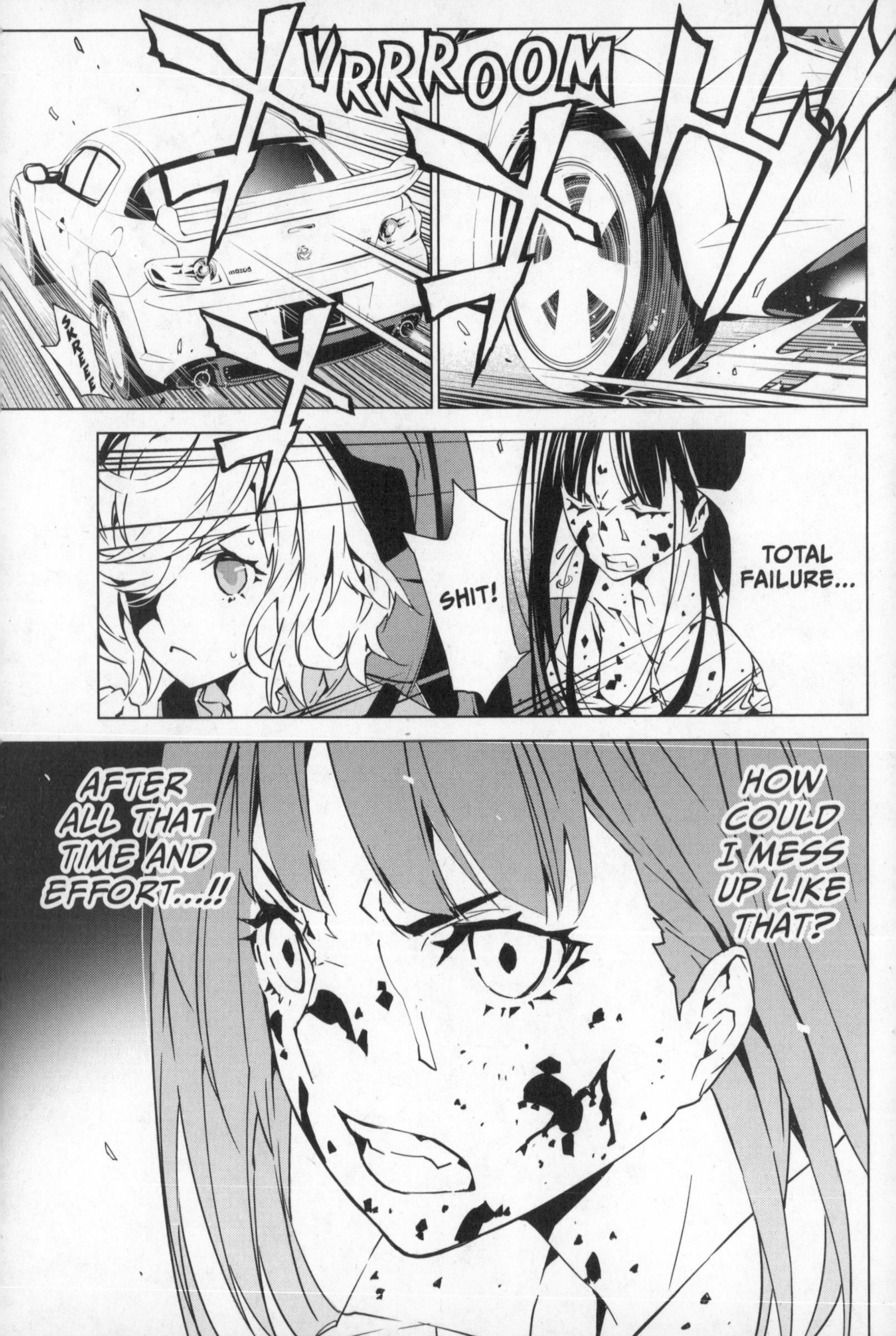
VRRROOM
SKREEEE
TOTAL FAILURE...
SHIT!
HOW COULD I MESS UP LIKE THAT?
AFTER ALL THAT TIME AND EFFORT...!!

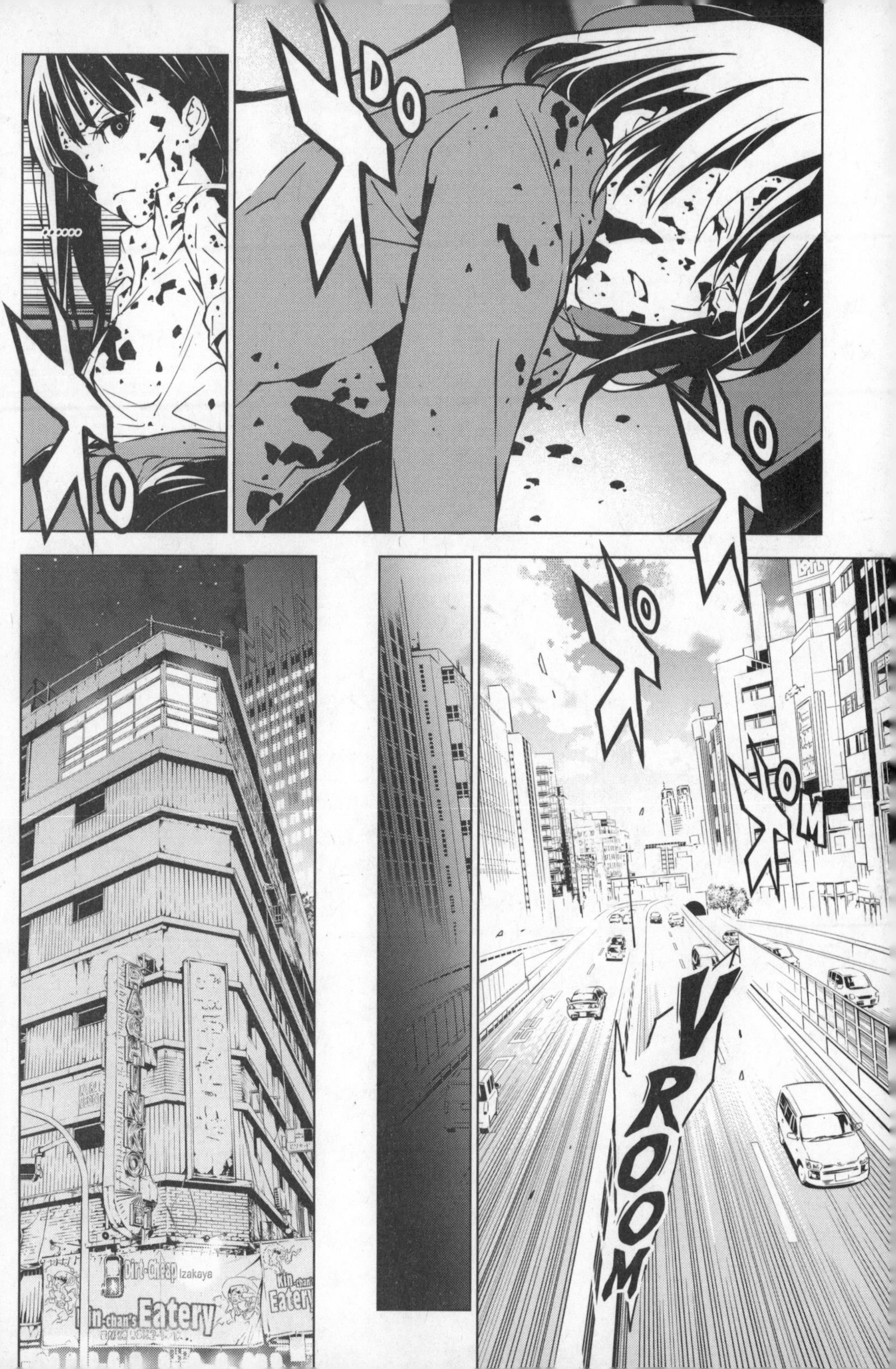
DO
O
......
O
O
OM
VROOM
PACHINKO
Dirt-Cheap Izakaya
in-chan's Eatery
Kin-chan's Eatery

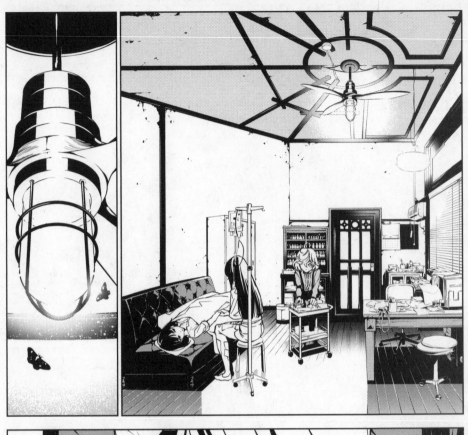

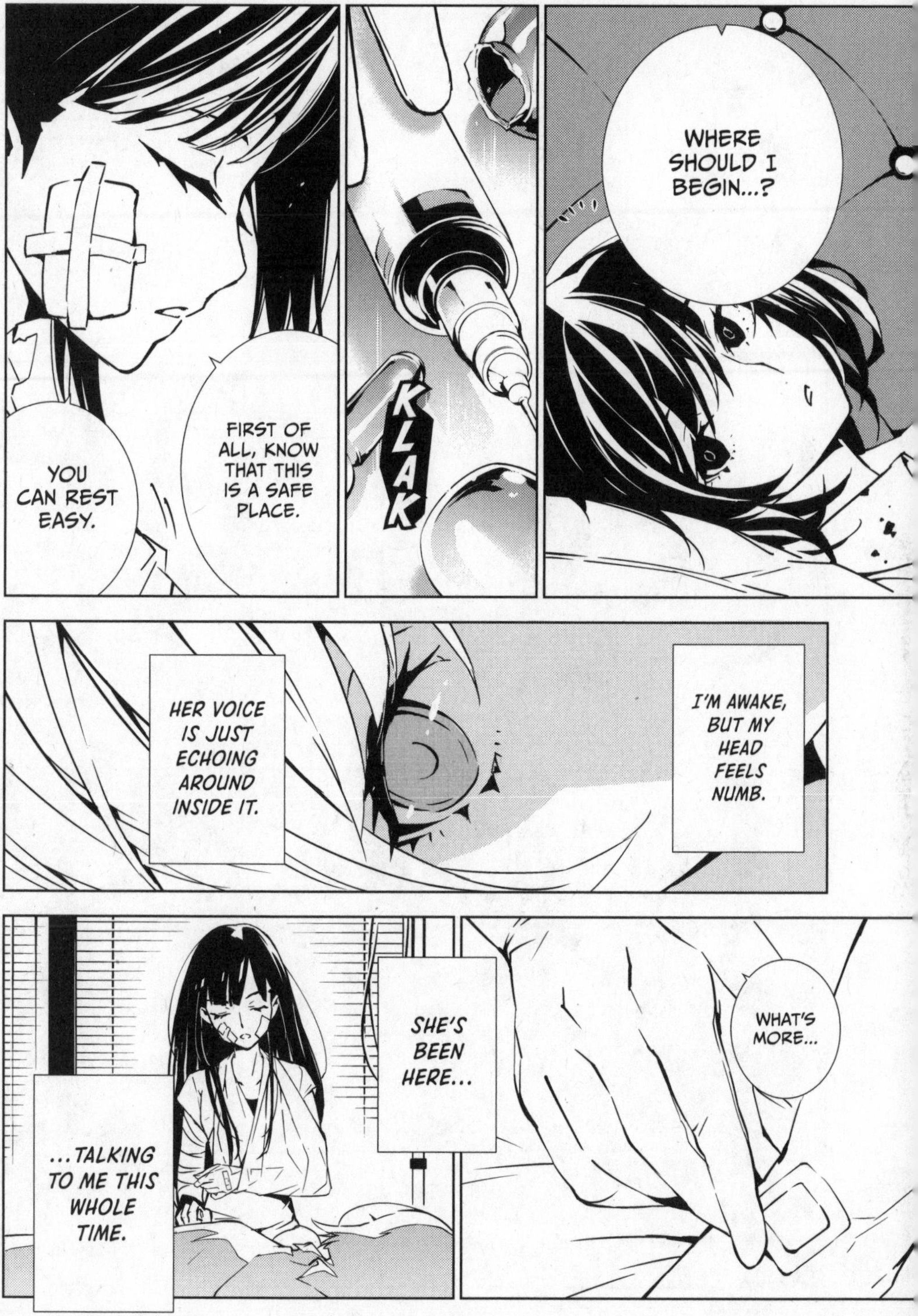
WHERE SHOULD I BEGIN...?
KLAK
FIRST OF ALL, KNOW THAT THIS IS A SAFE PLACE.
YOU CAN REST EASY.
I'M AWAKE, BUT MY HEAD FEELS NUMB.
HER VOICE IS JUST ECHOING AROUND INSIDE IT.
WHAT'S MORE...
SHE'S BEEN HERE...
...TALKING TO ME THIS WHOLE TIME.

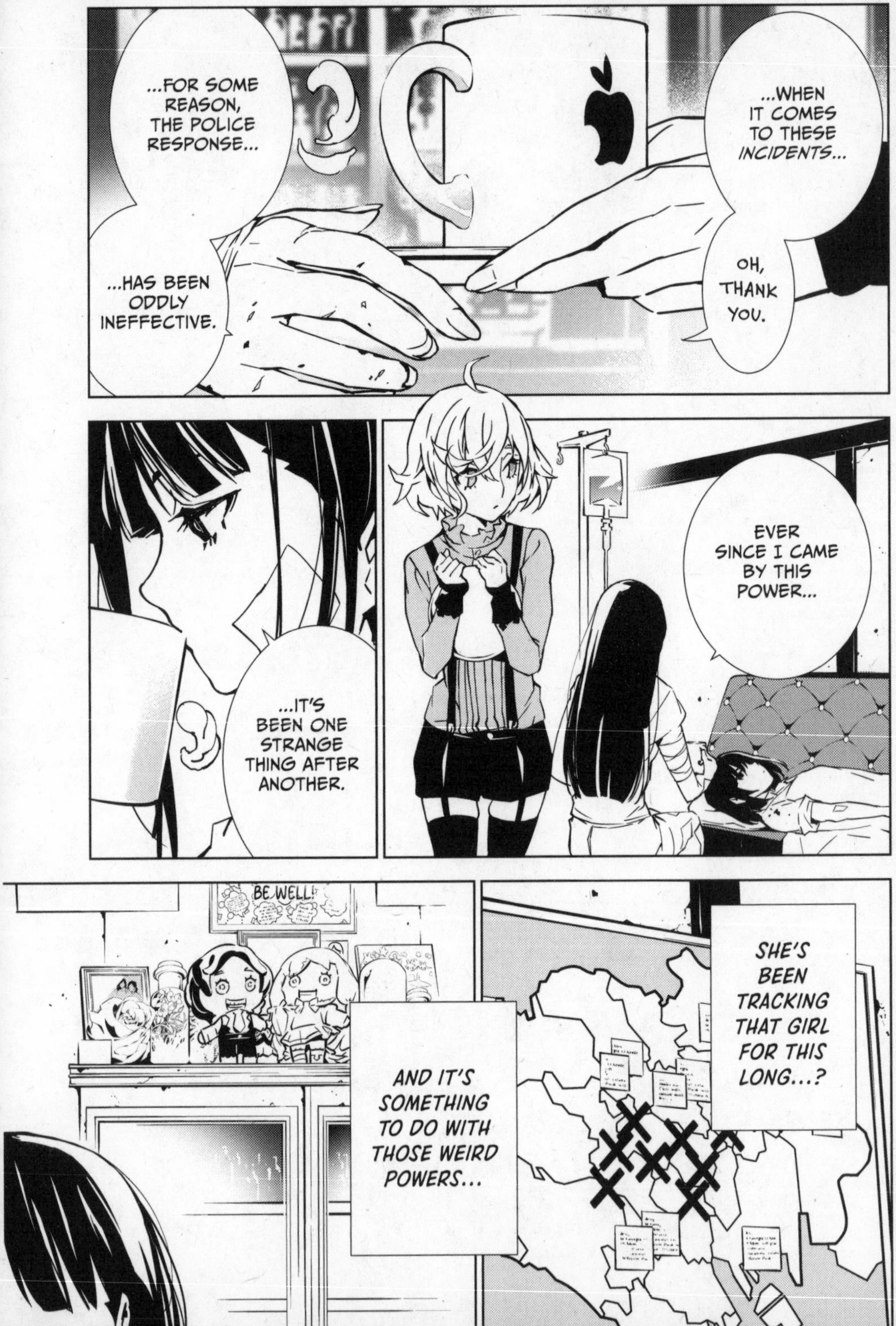
...WHEN IT COMES TO THESE INCIDENTS...
OH, THANK YOU.
...FOR SOME REASON, THE POLICE RESPONSE...
...HAS BEEN ODDLY INEFFECTIVE.
EVER SINCE I CAME BY THIS POWER...
...IT'S BEEN ONE STRANGE THING AFTER ANOTHER.
SHE'S BEEN TRACKING THAT GIRL FOR THIS LONG...?
BE WELL!
AND IT'S SOMETHING TO DO WITH THOSE WEIRD POWERS...

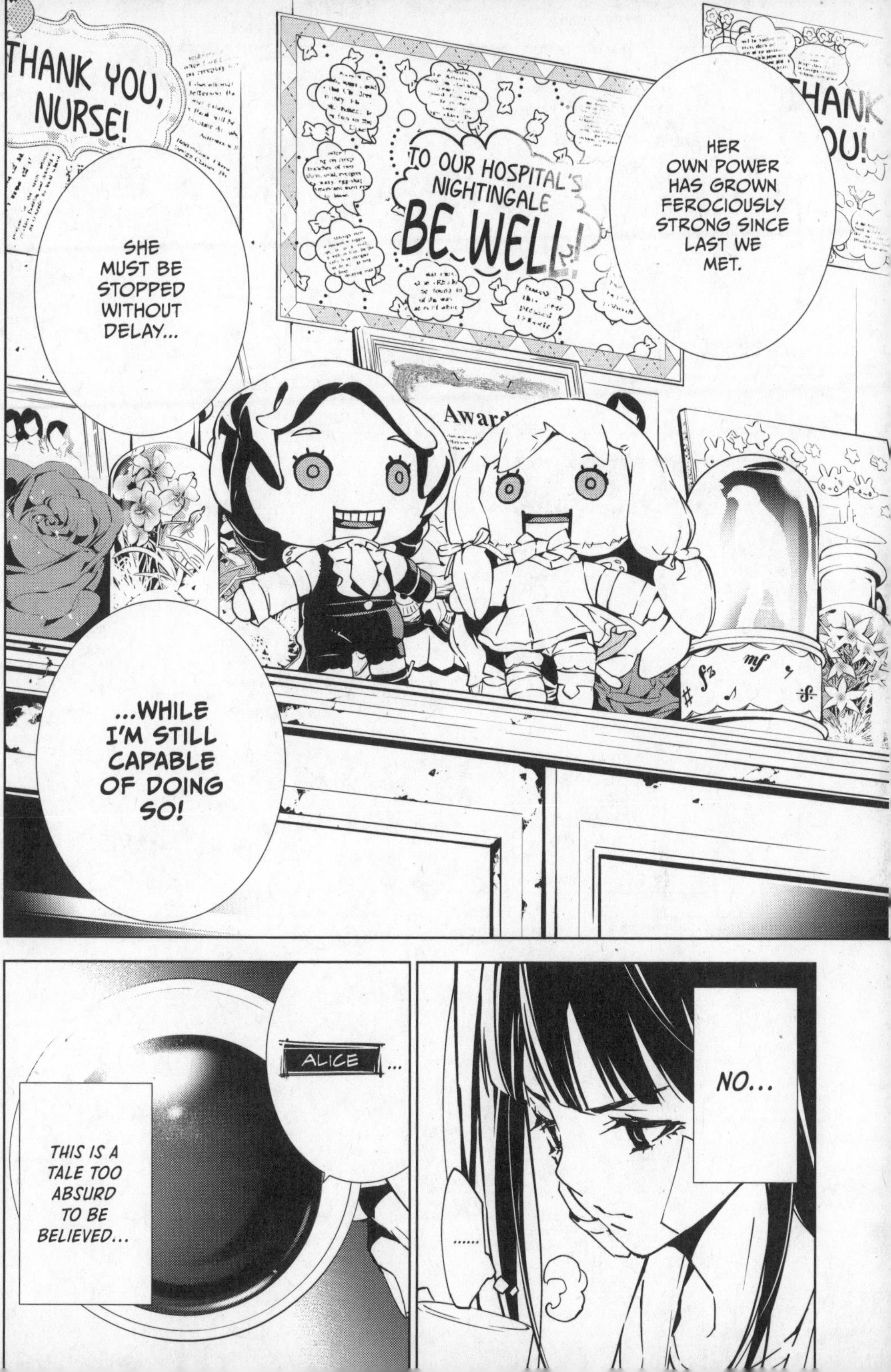

THANK YOU, NURSE!
TO OUR HOSPITAL'S NIGHTINGALE
BE WELL!
Award
HER OWN POWER HAS GROWN FEROCIOUSLY STRONG SINCE LAST WE MET.
SHE MUST BE STOPPED WITHOUT DELAY...
...WHILE I'M STILL CAPABLE OF DOING SO!
NO...
......
ALICE...
THIS IS A TALE TOO ABSURD TO BE BELIEVED...

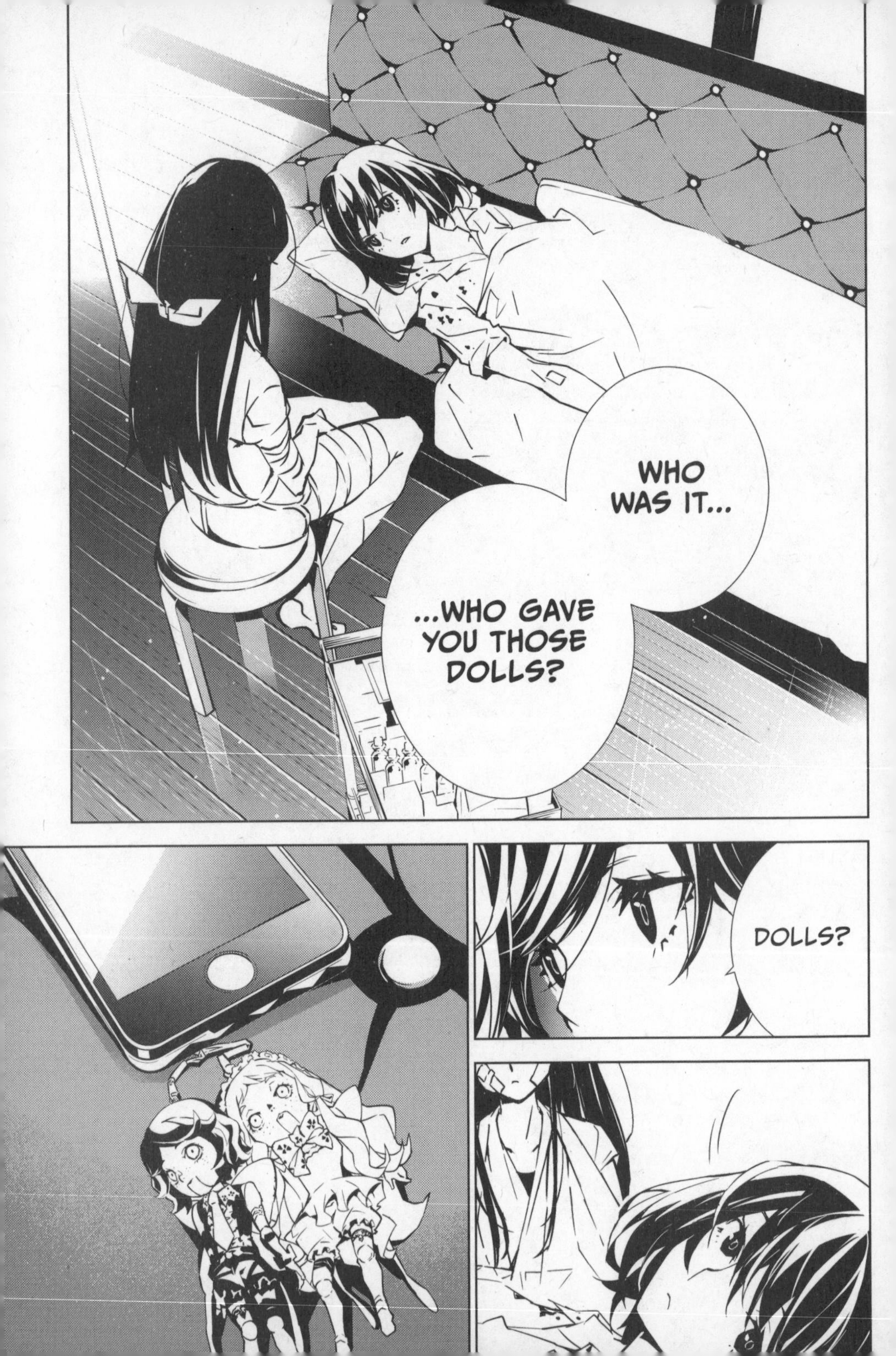
WHO WAS IT...
...WHO GAVE YOU THOSE DOLLS?
DOLLS?

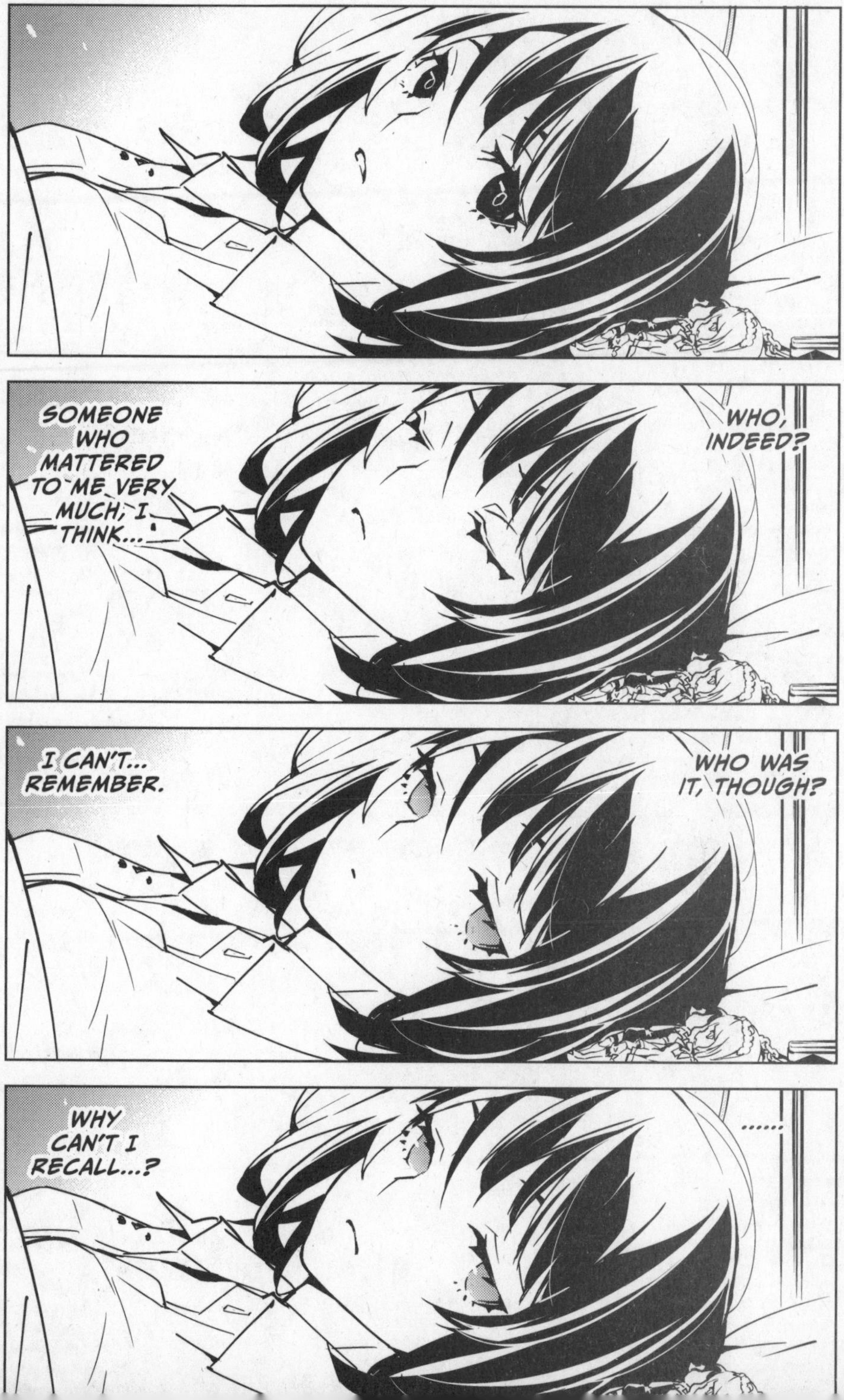
WHO, INDEED?
SOMEONE WHO MATTERED TO ME VERY MUCH, I THINK...
WHO WAS IT, THOUGH?
I CAN'T... REMEMBER.
......
WHY CAN'T I RECALL...?

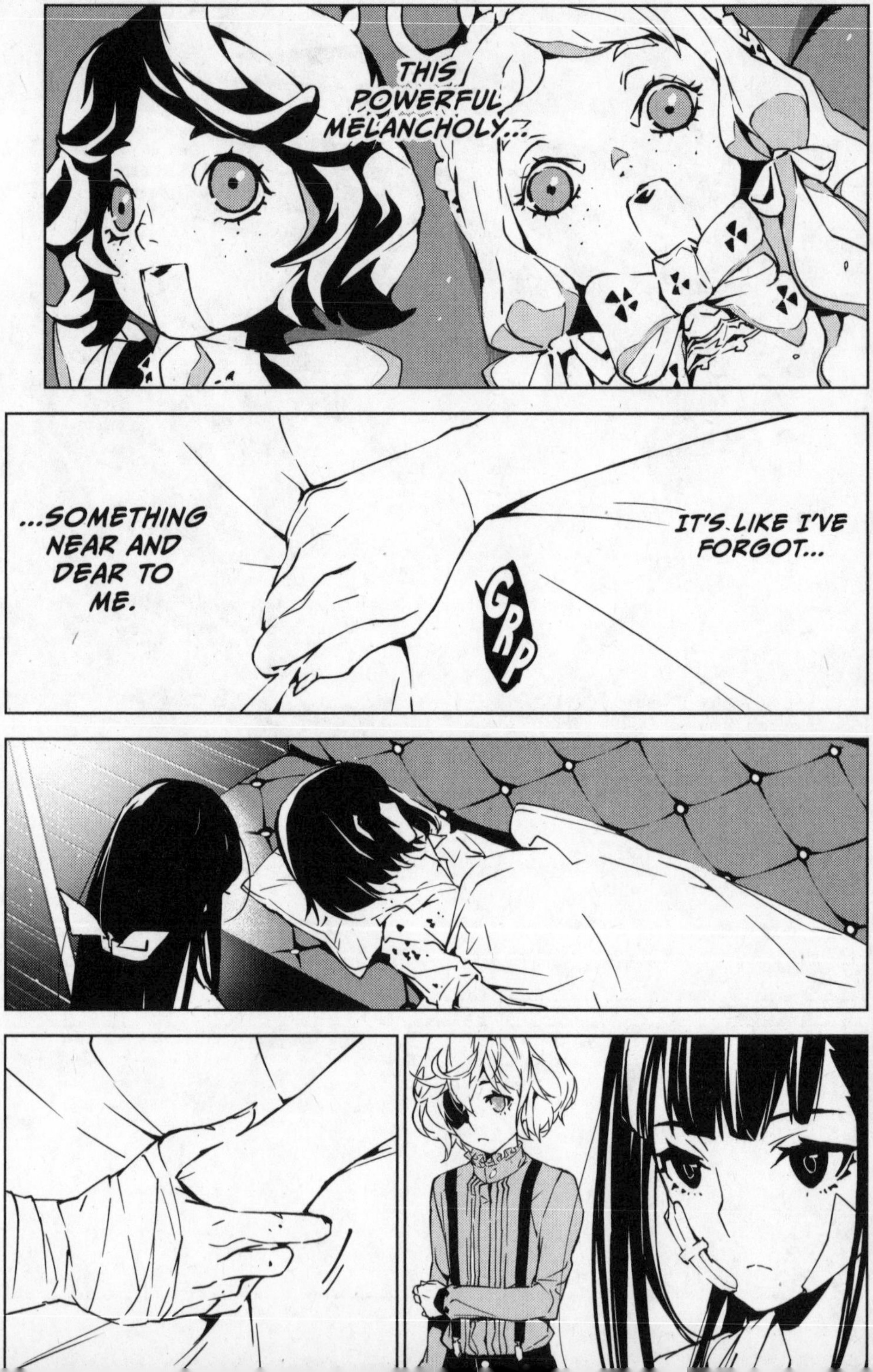
THIS POWERFUL MELANCHOLY...
IT'S LIKE I'VE FORGOT...
GRP
...SOMETHING NEAR AND DEAR TO ME.

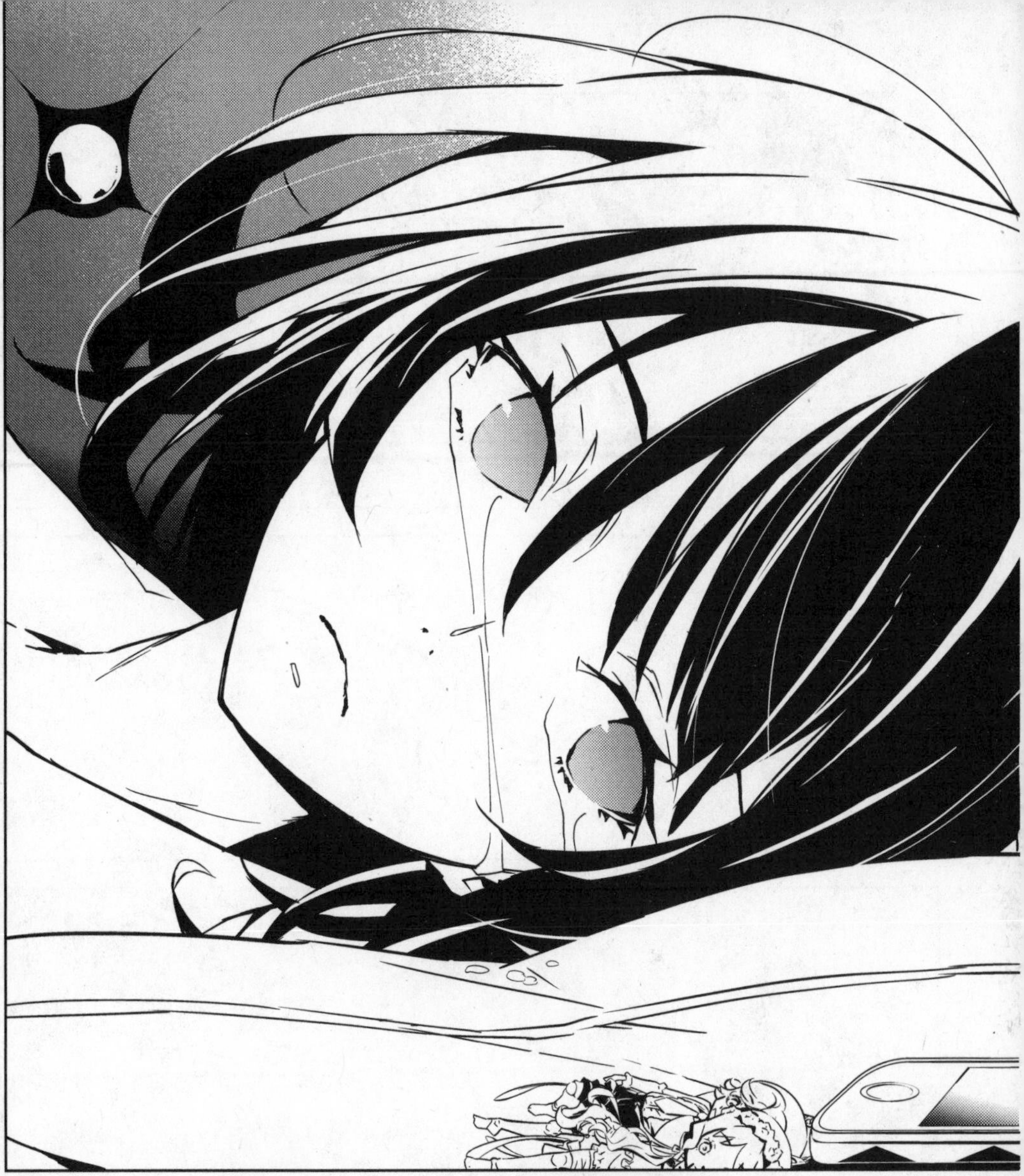
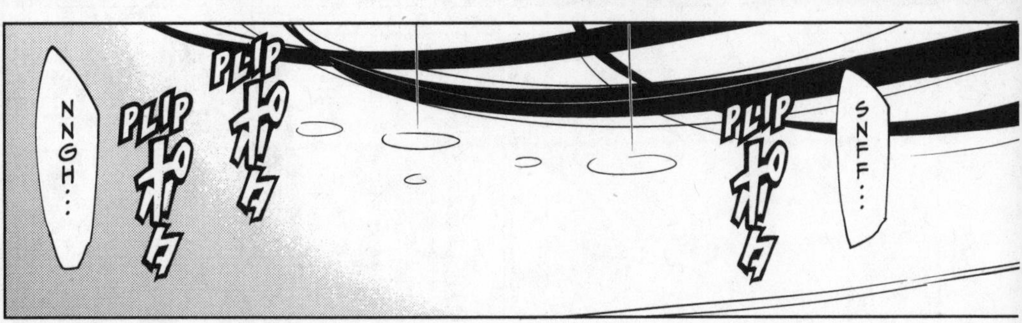
SNFF...
PLIP ポタ
PLIP ポタ
PLIP ポタ
NNGH...

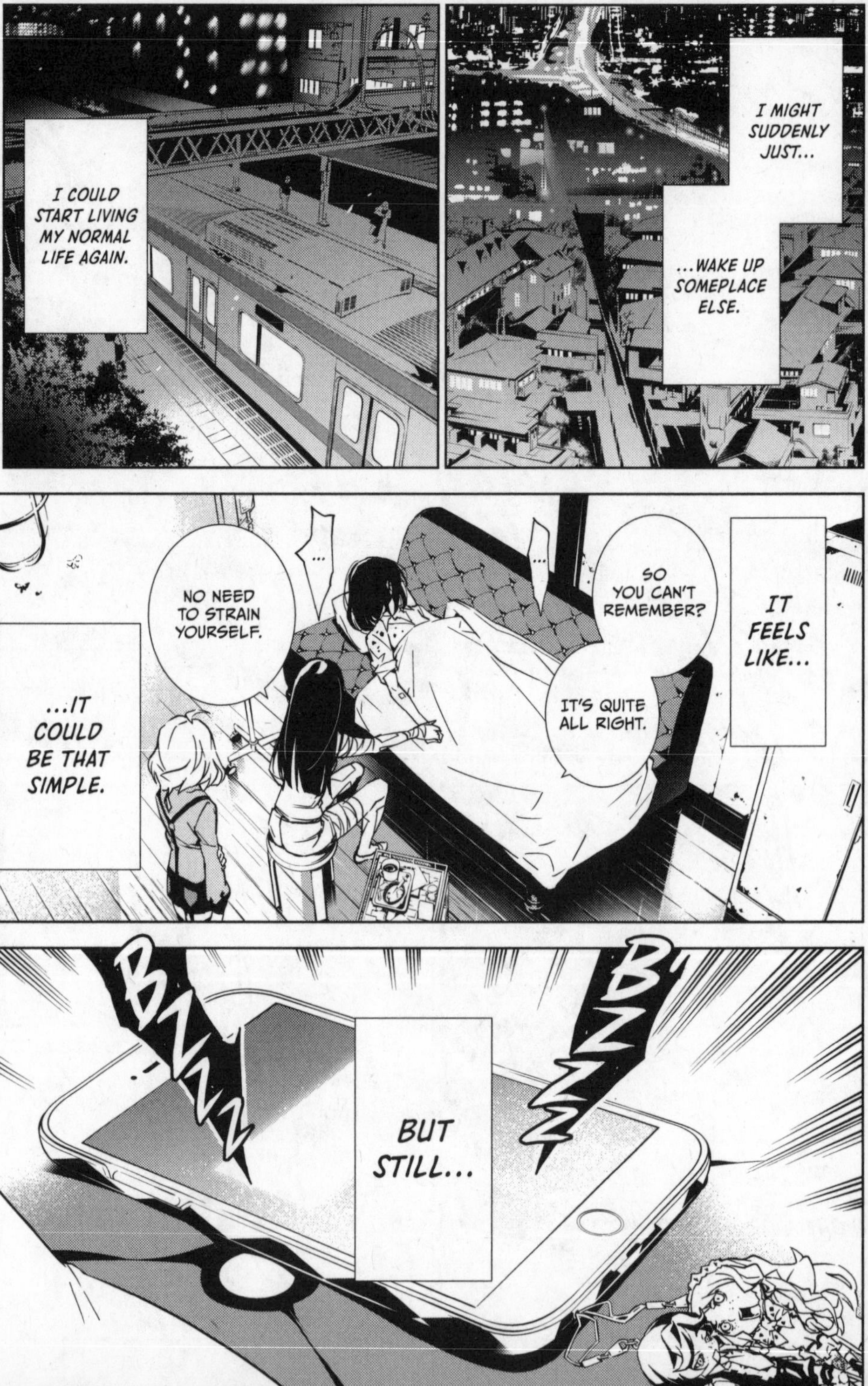
I MIGHT SUDDENLY JUST...
...WAKE UP SOMEPLACE ELSE.
I COULD START LIVING MY NORMAL LIFE AGAIN.
IT FEELS LIKE...
SO YOU CAN'T REMEMBER?
IT'S QUITE ALL RIGHT.
...
NO NEED TO STRAIN YOURSELF.
...
...IT COULD BE THAT SIMPLE.
BZZZ
BUT STILL...
BZZZ

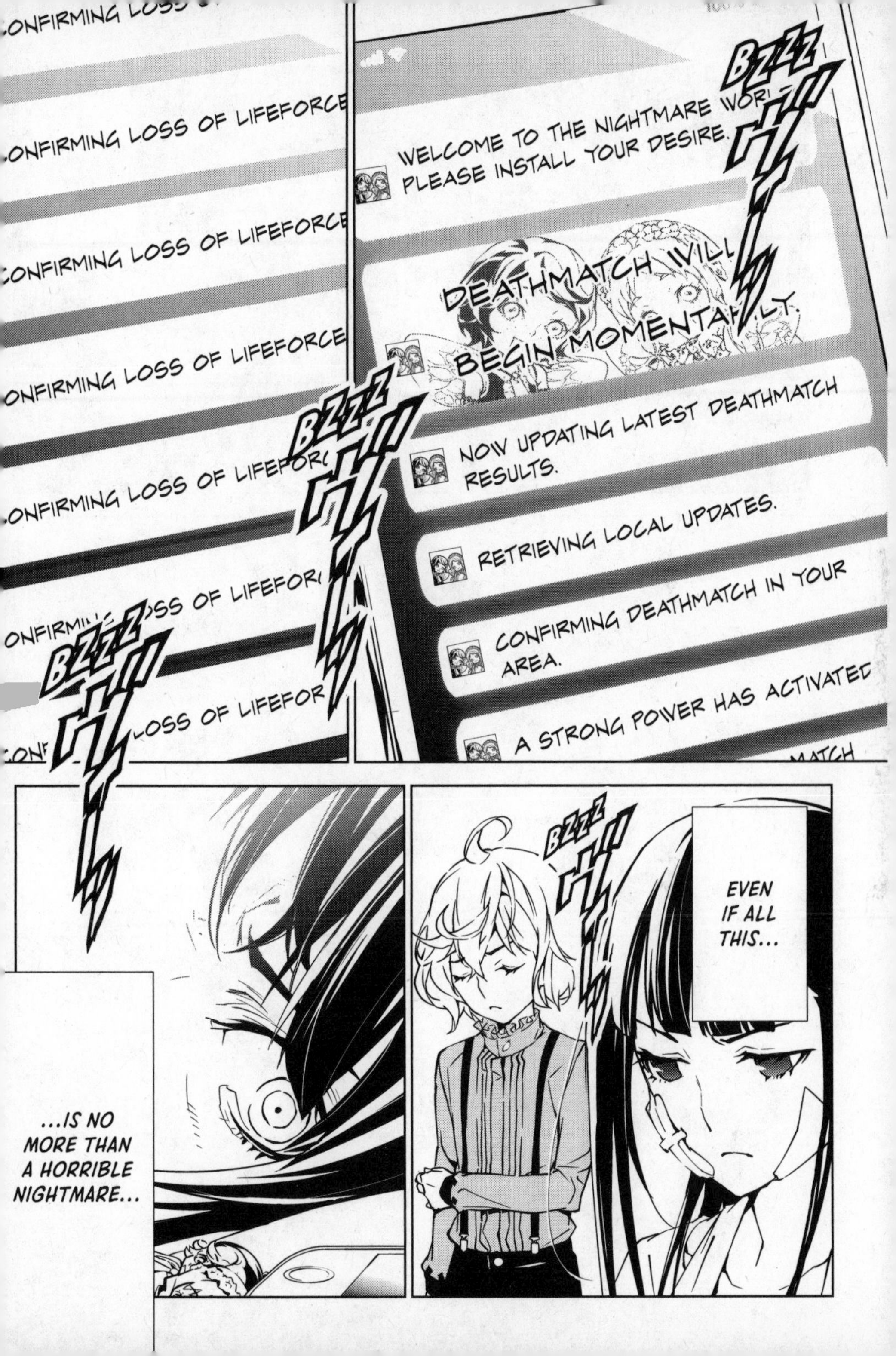
BZZZ
WELCOME TO THE NIGHTMARE WOR
PLEASE INSTALL YOUR DESIRE.
DEATHMATCH WILL BEGIN MOMENTARILY.
NOW UPDATING LATEST DEATHMATCH RESULTS.
RETRIEVING LOCAL UPDATES.
CONFIRMING DEATHMATCH IN YOUR AREA.
A STRONG POWER HAS ACTIVATED
CONFIRMING LOSS
CONFIRMING LOSS OF LIFEFORCE
CONFIRMING LOSS OF LIFEFORCE
CONFIRMING LOSS OF LIFEFORCE
CONFIRMING LOSS OF LIFEFOR
BZZZ
CONFIRMI OSS OF LIFEFOR
BZZZ
LOSS OF LIFEFOR
BZZZ
EVEN IF ALL THIS...
...IS NO MORE THAN A HORRIBLE NIGHTMARE...

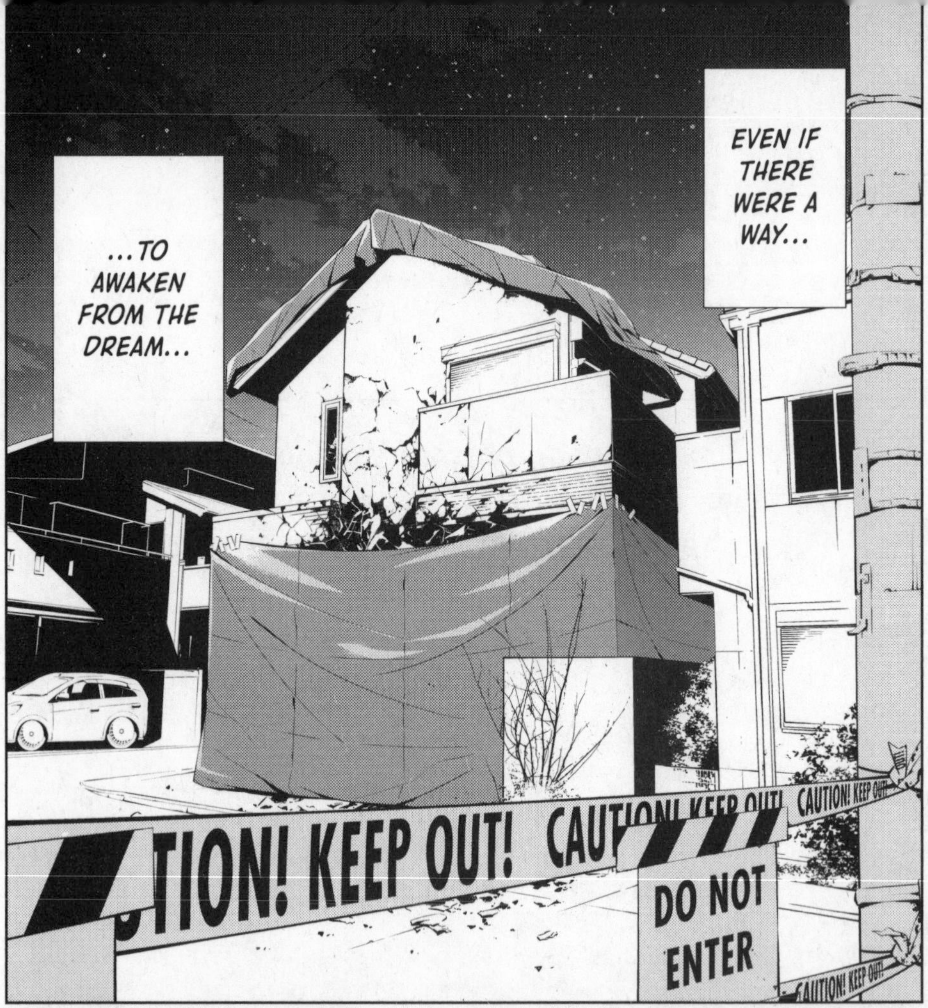
EVEN IF THERE WERE A WAY...
...TO AWAKEN FROM THE DREAM...
CAUTION! KEEP OUT!
TION! KEEP OUT!
DO NOT ENTER
CAUTION! KEEP OUT!

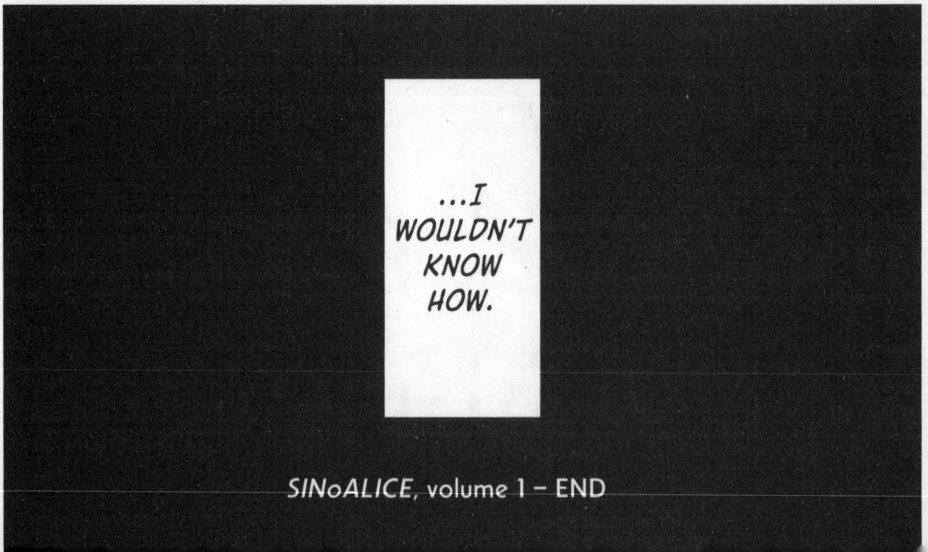
...I WOULDN'T KNOW HOW.
SINoALICE, volume 1 – END

To read a bonus short story exclusive to this
volume of *SINoALICE*, please turn to page 187,
where you'll find the text presented in
left-to-right reading order.

SINoALICE ®

choices. And that's enough for me.

I'm hurrying back now. Please let me come with you?

There. I expressed myself and told SNOW I wanted to join her on this. I knew she'd probably turn me down, but I had every intention of tagging along all the same. If I were willing to fight to keep anyone out of harm's way, it would be her.

Without even waiting for a reply, I jumped into the driver's seat, started the engine, and peeled out of the parking lot.

"Dazzling..." I muttered to myself. The rainy season may've been on the way, but at that moment, the clouds parted to reveal a perfect sliver of blue sky and sunlight.

THE END

Getting permission to drive was one thing, but what really stuck with me in a powerful way was the joy of voicing my own thoughts to someone and being treated with respect.

With the can of food still in hand, I stared at the refurbished car hood. My phone buzzed in my pocket.

Get the car back here on the double.

I've finally picked up RED *'s trail.*

Based on her pattern so far, she's going to break into another civilian home.

This time, I'll stop her before the damage is done.

Hurry. Give me an ETA for your return.

A series of messages from SNOW —a rapid-fire, one-sided barrage, which was nothing new. Not that I have anything against her decisive style of communication.

At the end of the day, I'm still a wimp who needs to be ordered around. Rome wasn't built in a day, and someone's personality can't change overnight.

But whatever! It's fine. However weak and wimpy I am, the fact is, I made it here, to this moment, by my own will, through my own

game, however, but a real-life battle royale.

I found myself staring out the window at the scenery rushing by, only half-listening to the ridiculous explanation. We'd already put my hometown far back in the rear-view mirror.

Cars, though! What a concept. A way to go anywhere your heart desires. Wherever, whenever... Alone, even.

Some powerful thoughts rose up in my head, and I couldn't help but hit SNOW with a series of quick questions.

"Erm, SNOW... So, this game... You have to travel around, find opponents, and, um...kill them? Those are the rules?"

"More or less."

"Well...let's say we were to work together. It's probably an advantage to have as many capable drivers as possible, right?"

SNOW gave me a slight smirk.

"What are you trying to ask me?"

I came right out with it and asked her to teach me to drive. She immediately turned down my request, citing my age and lack of a license. For the first time in my life, though, I pressed the issue. She relented in the end; how important are licenses and laws in a deadly deathmatch, after all? The argument earned me an exasperated sigh, followed by a wry grin.

stomach, and kicked her off with every ounce of my strength.

"Ahhhhh!!"

She collapsed backwards with remarkable force and plunged into the glass, and I used the momentum to push my own body up and over the railing. It was a straight drop, with the white sports car's hood waiting for me at the bottom. As my body impacted the machine, my mind and vision went blank.

~Post Contract~

"I never suspected you were a girl all along, GL," I said, staring at the crumpled hood from the passenger seat. Beside me, driving, was SNOW, the online acquaintance formerly known to me as GL.

"No one has ever accused me of being ladylike, I suppose," she said.

"But how did you know where to find me?"

"It's hard to explain, but let it suffice it to say that I used the game. It might look like an ordinary mobile game, but..."

Much of SNOW 's explanation left me more than a little lost, but according to her, the two puppets were hosting a "deathmatch game" in which I was now an unwitting participant. This was no video

driver's side window emerged the face of a young woman with intense, almost cold features.

"Is-is that...GL?!"

The woman leapt out of the car and shouted at me once more.

"Quickly! Jump down onto the hood!"

Mother's free hand shot out and wrapped around my throat. Pain. I was losing oxygen by the second. As my mind grew dim, I remembered GL's words.

No one else can make this decision for you.

But how could I decide? Me? My whole life had been a series of decisions made by someone else. It was just too much to ask at this point...

I was about to fade to black when Mother's words from the previous day echoed in my mind. *That's it! That's what I should've done all along! I've decided! It's settled!!*

The thought took over every synapse in my brain, and just like that, the dense fog lifted.

Yes, of course. It all made sense now... Mother had finally *decided.* For months she'd been practically bedridden, thinking it over. And over and over. Then, at last, she'd come to this decision.

Dear Mother had decided to kill me.

Heartbreaking as it was, that was the conclusion she'd reached.

"Time to make a decision of my own..."

I lifted both feet, planted them on Mother's

yapping about.

"Fine, fine... The rules can wait. Or just have your new friend tell you. No skin off our noses, not that we've got skin."

With that, they began floating up into the sky.

"Hang on!" I shouted. "I don't understand any of this! Tell me what's going on!"

Just before vanishing into the ether, the puppets turned for some parting words.

"Time's gonna get a move on again, bee-tee-dubs."

"So first, you might wanna think about solving your biggest problem. Y'know, the sharp, pointy one."

"Huh?"

Before I could work out what they meant, the world unfroze.

"Rahhhhhh!!"

Mother lunged at me with a blood-curdling shriek. I caught the arm holding the knife, but she was stronger than she looked, and the weapon steadily moved towards my head. The force pushed me against the railing of the balcony until I was bent backwards.

"Jump down!!" came a girl's voice from below, clear as day. With both of my hands gripping mother's arm, I twisted my neck around to discover the white car directly under our balcony. From the

They called themselves Parrah and Noya, and as I stood there stunned, they hit me with a volley of their machine-gun chatter.

"Let's jump right into the rules, shall we? Rule One is... Hmm?"

My phone was vibrating in my pocket with incoming messages.

"Excuse *you*."

"Ahem. Time is *supposed* to be stopped."

"...Must be another participant."

The puppets weren't pleased with the interruption, but I checked my phone anyway.

I'm nearby.

So just start screaming or something.

Let me know where you are somehow.

After glancing at the messages from GL, I looked to the street and spotted a lone white sports car zipping around the otherwise frozen world.

"Is that GL?" I wondered out loud. As if responding to my question, the car did a quick U-turn and started zooming toward our apartment building.

"Ah, must be you-know-you..."

"What'd you do to deserve such a prize of a partner, huhh?"

"Unlike you, that one's got desire to burn... Eee hee hee!"

I hadn't the slightest idea what the puppets were

"You're rotten, like all men!!"

I spun back around as she shrieked, just in time to find the tip of the knife coming towards my face.

~**Contract**~

"Wow, talk about a pulse-pounding cliff-hanger! How's this psycho thriller gonna end?"

"For real! Wait, do we even have pulses?"

An inexplicable sequence of events unfolded before my eyes. One moment, Mother was swinging the knife down with every intent of killing me. The next moment, she had frozen in place. Or rather, the entire world—including her—had come to a standstill. Then a creepy pair of ball-joined puppets seemed to materialize from within Mother's frozen form.

"Congrats are in order."

"Talk about a weak-ass signal, but we still managed to detect your *desire,* so you can thank us later."

"Ergo, we're here to sign you up for the big game."

"See, that sad and piddly little desire of yours has manifested an itty-bitty dinky *power.*"

"Eee hee hee hee!"

"Gya ha ha ha!"

threw open the door to my room. I scrambled to shove the phone in my pocket.

"Oh dear... Hiding something from Mother? What a naughty child you are."

A smooth, calm laugh as she drew closer.

"No, I understand. You're growing up, that's all. Of course you'd try to keep secrets from Mother."

Her mellow tone was at odds with her clenched right hand, which maintained a fierce grip on a kitchen knife.

"M-mother...?"

"Oh, I bet I know! You must be looking at *naughty* things on that phone of yours."

"N-no, I'm not. But Mother, we really have to talk," I said, inching away from the knife pointed straight at me.

"It's fine. To be expected, in fact. You're getting to be that age," she cooed. "Naked girls, right? They must make you feel all sorts of ways inside... You can't help it...as a man."

Her eyes were locked on me, without a trace of light in them. This was really it. Of course it was. I should've known.

"Mother, stop!"

"Boys will be boys!" she shouted, raising the knife. I spun around, ran out onto the veranda, and looked down from our third-floor apartment. A fall from this height wouldn't end well.

down, unwilling to think more on it.

~**Day of the Contract**~

"I'm baaack..."

"Welcome home."

"Huh?"

Normally, Mother wouldn't say a thing when I returned from a venture outside, so I was taken aback by her response this time.

She stood in the very center of the living room wearing a black dress, and it was clear she'd done her hair and makeup. The growing heaps of trash surrounded her. She flashed me a quiet smile.

"Oh, y-you're up? That's unusual. L-let me run and get changed. Then I'll make dinner? Sh-shouldn't take long!" The sight of Mother looking so different than normal sent me into a stammering fit before I ran into my room.

Instinctively, I knew. I knew Mother had come to some sort of decision, and, well, whatever came next was probably, likely, most definitely going to be horrible.

I whipped out my phone, loaded up the chat log with GL, and typed a single word.

Help.

No sooner had I sent the message than Mother

over the windows, eliminating my view to the outside world. When I went out on rare trips to do the grocery shopping, I would see signs of pranks and vandalism directed at our apartment.

~Days Until Contract: 1~

"That's it! That's what I should've done all along! I've decided! It's settled!!" came the shout from Mother's room late one night. Something about her tone sounded different than her usual eerie cries in the night. It was a voice full of joy, the sound of someone experiencing a eureka moment. I took note of that and crept up to her closed door.

"Mother? Is something wrong?" I asked through the door.

No response. Just a series of unsettling sounds, halfway between laughing and crying.

Instinctively, I knew that our days of living like this, together, were nearing their end. Something in her voice told me as much. I didn't know *how* it would all end, and I didn't want to know.

I decided to turn on the game again, and it showed me the chat log with GL, right where we'd left off.

No one else can make this decision for you.

The nausea returned, and I threw my phone

kept typing.

This would be for both your sakes.

Nothing good can come of inaction at this point.

You have to take charge.

No one else can make this decision for you.

The messages kept coming, and I couldn't find a rebuttal to his sound argument. As the messages went on, I started to feel nauseated.

"Gimme a break!" I thought. "I know in my head that you're right, but doing something about it is easier said than done!"

But I didn't have the courage to actually respond with that.

In fact, I stopped logging on to the game after that day.

~Days Until Contract: 29~

Mother's condition continued to deteriorate.

She would spend all day cooped up in her bedroom, only emerging far too infrequently for meals. Since she'd stopped bathing altogether, a stale, unpleasant odor pervaded the apartment. My own motivation dropped, so with no one bothering to clean anymore, dust, grime, and garbage piled up in our living space.

At Mother's request, I'd even tacked cardboard

Well, maybe he'd be someone like GL. As I stared at my gangly limbs with their lackluster muscles, I found myself wondering if I'd ever grow up to be a strong, decent man like him.

~Days Until Contract: 63~

This is about you two, isn't it?

My jaw dropped as I read the web article GL sent me. Mother and I had made the news, apparently, and it was hardly a piece written in good faith. Beneath a picture of us, the meat of the article was basically a laundry list of our so-called "eccentric behavior."

A recounting of Mother's outburst at the clinic, reports of strange voices at night... No one could deny any of that, but the rest? Neighborhood cats, massacred? Me being a kidnapping victim? None of that could be true.

Your mother presents a danger to herself and others. There's a chance she may really hurt you.

GL was ready and eager to provide me with a safe place to stay, so he asked for our home address. I couldn't bring myself to tell him, though. I knew that if he came for me, I'd never see Mother again, and she'd be all alone.

But GL ignored my feelings on the matter and

What came next is mostly a blur. For my whole life, my mind has had this fun habit of going hazy when it comes to painful memories.

Apparently, Mother's symptoms had been getting worse. I remember the doctor asking me about her dissociation, I think? And if the verbal abuse had intensified? Was she threatening me? That sort of thing. My memory of that office visit cuts off right at the point when she lunged at the doctor.

~Days Until Contract: 145~

Sounds like a case of codependence to me.

In recent days, the game had been doubling as a way to chat with my guild leader, who happened to be a former health-care professional.

Another message from GL appeared on my phone screen.

If she's giving you pushback about talking to someone at the child welfare center, you could always stay at my place in the meantime. I think removing yourself from the situation is a critical first step.

I immediately knew that GL was dead serious, since he wasn't one to hesitate or flip flop, and every message from him was fully formed and decisive. He could be brutally honest at times, but I knew it was for my own good. If I'd had a father...

oriented items.

"At least in games, no one else can see how you look for real, I guess."

I proceeded with the character creator, crafting a manly man whose vibes couldn't be more different than my own. I'd never gotten to pick out my own clothes before (tangible, virtual, or otherwise), so the wealth of options was almost stressful. A fun sort of stress, though.

~Days Until Contract: 152~

"Y-you're not seriously accusing me of abuse?!"

Mother sounded manic, and her roar echoed all the way from the examination room. Everyone in the waiting room shifted uncomfortably, and I picked up my phone, determined to hide the fact that I was all too familiar with that voice. I booted up the game that had become my latest obsession, and the loading screen sat there for what felt like an eternity.

"Ah, there you are! Would you join us in here, please?" said the doctor, peeking into the waiting room. The words hung in the air, louder than they'd needed to be. I didn't have to lift my gaze to know that every person there was now looking straight at me.

instead, which now betrayed a visible mark.

"Well done," she'd said, with acid in her voice. "Now you can't show your arms, just like you wanted." No more sleeveless dresses for the time being? Part of me was relieved. If I could throw a leg in the line of fire next time, then maybe miniskirts would be off the menu for a while. With that ridiculous scheme dancing in my head, I checked my phone.

"Huh? What is this?"

There was an unfamiliar icon on the home screen.

"A deathmatch...game?"

If Mother learned I'd been installing new apps without her permission, the belt would see some more use. As I shifted to delete the app, pain shot through my bruised arm.

"Oww... Wait, what?"

I'd meant to do a long press on the icon to delete it, but the phone registered it as a tap, and the app started up. It was a game I'd never seen or heard of before, with a pair of creepy, overly chatty puppets. For whatever reason, I was entranced by their rapid-fire speech.

"Oh, you get to make an avatar..."

The first available template was of a male character, so I decided to go for that default. The game then presented me with a lineup of male-

was the right look for me, but I knew how quickly Mother's mood could turn, so I kept any further thoughts to myself and accepted her style advice. A long wig and a hat completed the look for our outing, all to keep those in the neighborhood from learning that I wasn't, in fact, a girl.

We were plenty used to playing the parts of the perfect mother and daughter, not that I could tell you why. Since the time I was old enough to be aware of anything at all, the performance had seemed as natural as breathing.

But surely Mother had to realize that this couldn't last. Beyond the obvious changes to my body, my voice had started deepening recently. I loved Mother, of course, but I couldn't be her ideal daughter forever. Or at least that's what I believed.

~Days Until Contract: 196~

"Ouch..."

I flopped onto the bed, clutching the fresh bruise on my arm. My reward for telling Mother that I'd rather not wear sleeveless dresses anymore. She'd meant to deliver my punishment to a spot that would be hidden under my clothing—like she always did—but I had flinched away at the last moment, causing the belt buckle to land on my arm

that inconsistency, the memories would come flooding back. Memories of that day. The day I first met SNOW.

For most of my life, I had what you might call a *dependency* problem, but that day, I found it in myself to run away from home. Or perhaps it would be more accurate to say I *jumped* away.

PINOCCHIO'S Contract

~Days Until Contract: 282~

"Given the heat today, why don't you wear this?" asked Mother with a cheery smile.

The rays of the setting sun streamed into the dusty bedroom, where I stood stock-still in front of a mirror. Mother held a thin, chartreuse dress up to my body.

"Um... My shoulders would show," I said.

"They sure would," she said. "It's a good way to keep cool."

"My knees too. It's kind of short."

"Come on, you're young. Shorter is cuter."

With my growth spurt behind me, my just barely muscular shoulders and knees still managed to bulge out from the cutesy dress. I didn't think it

SINoALICE

The spring sky was overcast, hinting at the imminent rainy reason.

Stuffed to near bursting, my reusable shopping bag at last gave up and ejected a single food can, which tumbled to the ground and began rolling across the supermarket parking lot as if with a mind of its own.

"Darn it!"

Holding the straining bag tight against my chest, I shifted my balance and dashed after the rogue can, which decided to throw in the towel when it smacked up against the tire of a parked car. I crouched down awkwardly and snatched up the would-be escapee. As I stood back up, my eyes landed on the pure white sports car that SNOW had lent me for this errand. The pristine paint job was a perfect reflection of her as a person. However, a keen eye might've noticed that the luster of the car's hood didn't quite match the rest.

SNOW had told me that when the hood was being repainted, they couldn't match the original color exactly, and every time I spotted

SINoALICE
Concept Art 1

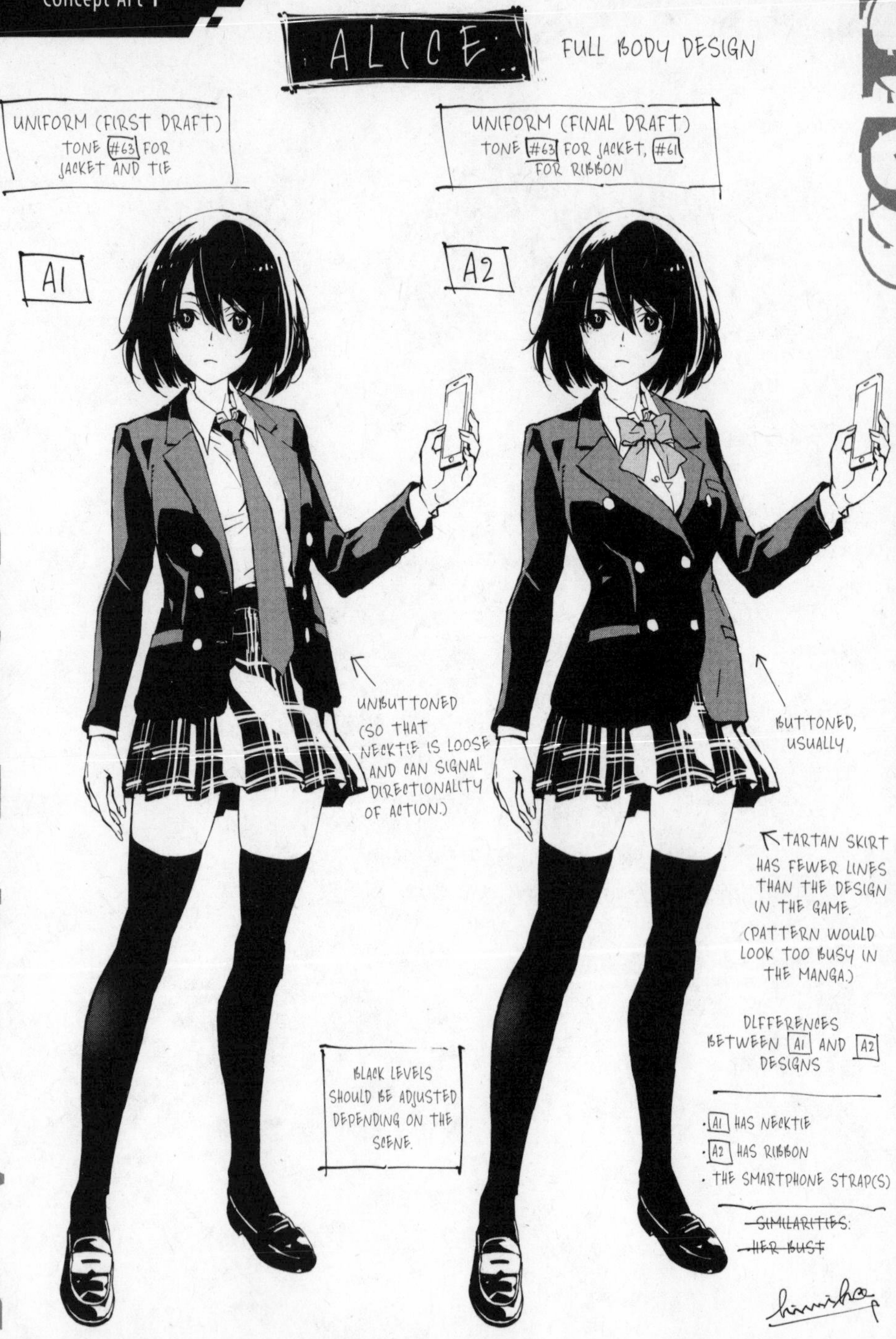
ALICE
FULL BODY DESIGN
UNIFORM (FIRST DRAFT)
TONE #63 FOR JACKET AND TIE
UNIFORM (FINAL DRAFT)
TONE #63 FOR JACKET, #61 FOR RIBBON
A1
A2
UNBUTTONED (SO THAT NECKTIE IS LOOSE AND CAN SIGNAL DIRECTIONALITY OF ACTION.)
BUTTONED, USUALLY
TARTAN SKIRT HAS FEWER LINES THAN THE DESIGN IN THE GAME. (PATTERN WOULD LOOK TOO BUSY IN THE MANGA.)
BLACK LEVELS SHOULD BE ADJUSTED DEPENDING ON THE SCENE.
DIFFERENCES BETWEEN A1 AND A2 DESIGNS
· A1 HAS NECKTIE
· A2 HAS RIBBON
· THE SMARTPHONE STRAP(S)
~~SIMILARITIES:~~
~~HER BUST~~

SINoALICE

Concept Art 2

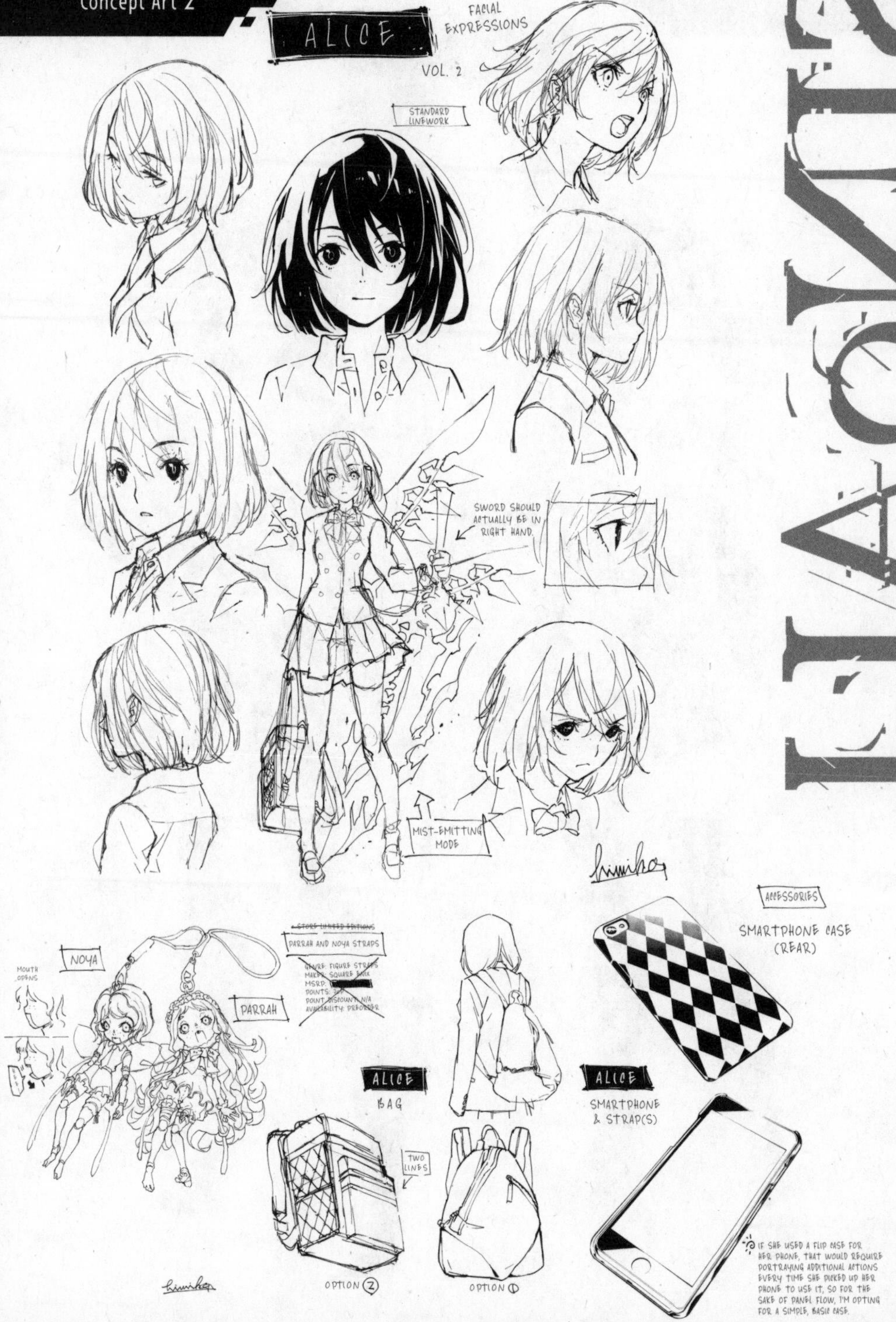
ALICE
FACIAL EXPRESSIONS
VOL. 2
STANDARD LINEWORK
SWORD SHOULD ACTUALLY BE IN RIGHT HAND.
MIST-EMITTING MODE
ACCESSORIES
SMARTPHONE CASE (REAR)
NOYA
MOUTH OPENS
PARRAH
STORE LIMITED EDITIONS
PARRAH AND NOYA STRAPS
GENRE: FIGURE STRAPS
MAKER: SQUARE ENIX
MSRP: [redacted]
POINTS:
POINT DISCOUNT: N/A
AVAILABILITY: PREORDER
ALICE
BAG
TWO LINES
OPTION ②
OPTION ①
ALICE
SMARTPHONE & STRAP(S)
IF SHE USED A FLIP CASE FOR HER PHONE, THAT WOULD REQUIRE PORTRAYING ADDITIONAL ACTIONS EVERY TIME SHE PICKED UP HER PHONE TO USE IT, SO FOR THE SAKE OF PANEL FLOW, I'M OPTING FOR A SIMPLE, BASIC CASE.

SINoALICE

Concept Art 3

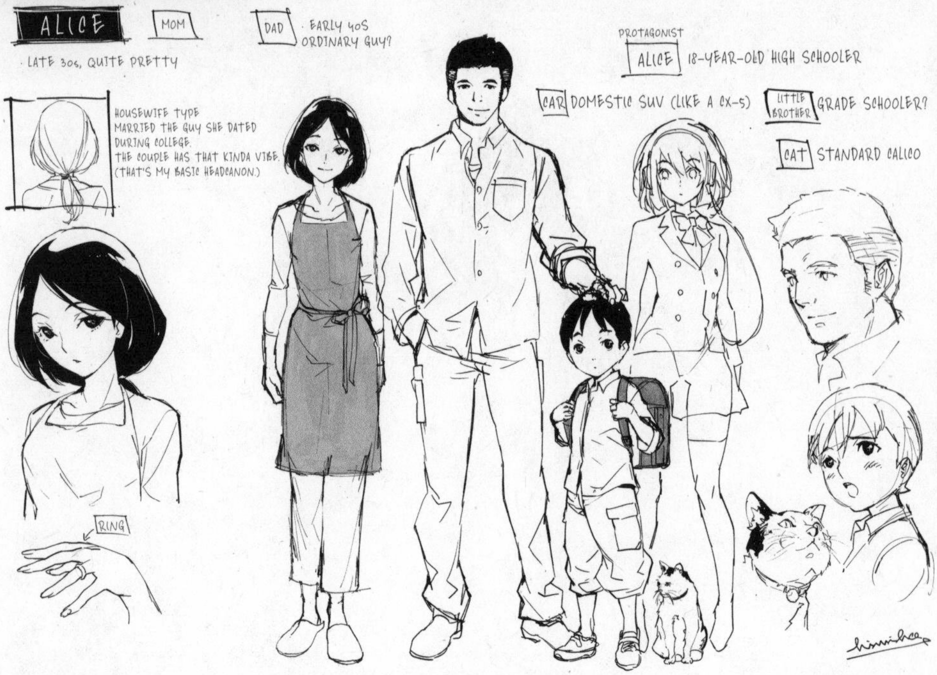
ALICE
MOM
DAD
EARLY 40S
ORDINARY GUY?
LATE 30s, QUITE PRETTY
HOUSEWIFE TYPE
MARRIED THE GUY SHE DATED
DURING COLLEGE.
THE COUPLE HAS THAT KINDA VIBE.
(THAT'S MY BASIC HEADCANON.)
RING
PROTAGONIST
ALICE 18-YEAR-OLD HIGH SCHOOLER
CAR DOMESTIC SUV (LIKE A CX-5)
LITTLE BROTHER GRADE SCHOOLER?
CAT STANDARD CALICO

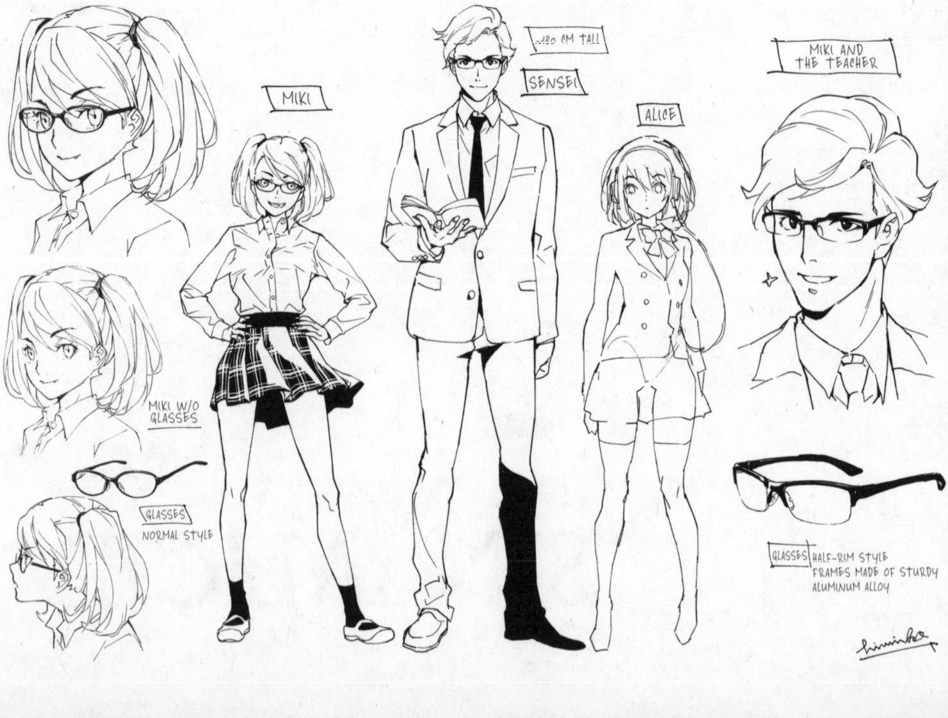
~180 CM TALL
SENSEI
MIKI
ALICE
MIKI AND THE TEACHER
MIKI W/O GLASSES
GLASSES
NORMAL STYLE
GLASSES HALF-RIM STYLE
FRAMES MADE OF STURDY
ALUMINUM ALLOY

SINoALICE®

Himiko

"Alice" may be just an ordinary name in English-speaking countries, but I've always loved it, personally. The word has this pleasant—one might say *wondrous*—quality to it.

Takuto Aoki

Writing the *SINoAlice* story is throwing the predictive text function on my computer out of whack. If I'm not careful, words that I use ordinarily will be altered in ways that make me sound like a middle school edgelord. For example, "power" and "lifeforce" get written in katakana, and when I go back to fix spelling errors, there's a high probability that the auto function will change whole words into katakana as well, since that's done so frequently in this script.

[Ed. Note: Katakana is a syllabic script in the Japanese writing system used for loanwords and emphasis, among other things. In this case, using katakana to write these words in Japanese would have a similar effect to using all caps or leetspeak in English.]

Yoko Taro

Lewis Carroll, author of *Alice in Wonderland*, was known for taking nude pictures of young girls. Some scholars say, "He just admired their pure and innocent nature," while others claim, "No, he was a pedophile." In any case, I hope you enjoy the world of *SINoAlice*, which definitely has nothing to do with *that* Lewis Carroll.

SINoALICE ®

Volume 1

Original Concept: Yoko Taro
Story: Takuto Aoki
Art: himiko
Character Design: Jino

Translation: Caleb D. Cook
Lettering: Phil Christie
Cover Design: Phil Balsman
Editor: Leyla Aker

SINoALICE Volume 1
© 2020 himiko, Takuto Aoki/SQUARE ENIX CO., LTD.
© 2020 Yoko Taro
© 2017–2022 SQUARE ENIX CO., LTD. All rights reserved.
First published in Japan in 2020 by SQUARE ENIX CO., LTD.
English translation rights arranged with SQUARE ENIX CO., LTD. and SQUARE ENIX INC.
English translation © 2022 by SQUARE ENIX CO., LTD.

All rights reserved. Published in the United States by Square Enix Manga, an
imprint of the Book Publishing Division of SQUARE ENIX, INC.

ISBN: 978-1-64609-150-8

Library of Congress Cataloging-in-Publication data is on file with the publisher.

Printed in the U.S.A.
First printing, July 2022
10 9 8 7 6 5 4 3 2 1

SQUARE ENIX
MANGA & BOOKS
www.square-enix-books.com